Understanding
the Korean War

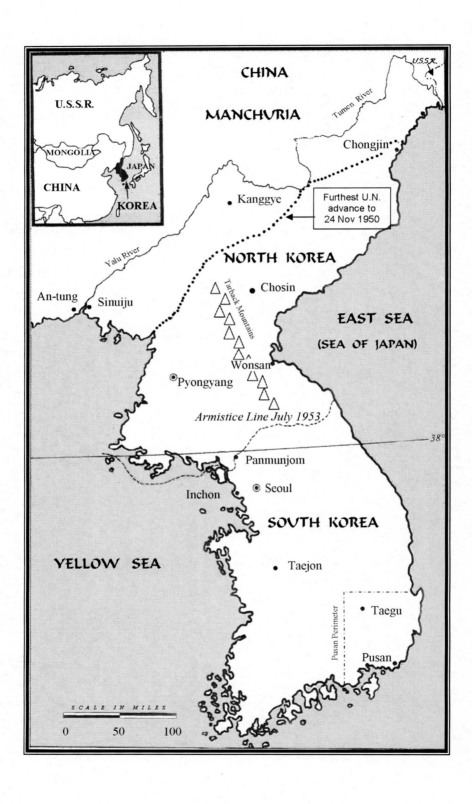

Understanding the Korean War

The Participants, the Tactics and the Course of Conflict

ARTHUR H. MITCHELL

McFarland & Company, Inc., Publishers
Jefferson, North Carolina, and London

FRONTISPIECE: Map of Korea. Courtesy of Billy C. Mossman, *Ebb and Flow: November 1950–July 1951*, p. 6, with additions by Frances Fleming Chavous.

LIBRARY OF CONGRESS CATALOGUING-IN-PUBLICATION DATA

Mitchell, Arthur H., 1936–
    Understanding the Korean War : the participants, the tactics and the course of conflict / Arthur H. Mitchell.
        p.   cm.
    Includes bibliographical references and index.

    ISBN 978-0-7864-6857-7
    softcover : acid free paper ∞

    1. Korean War, 1950–1953. I. Title.
DS918.M56 2013
951.904'2—dc23   2013020993

BRITISH LIBRARY CATALOGUING DATA ARE AVAILABLE

Front cover: With her brother on her back, a Korean girl trudges by a stalled M-26 tank at Haengju, Korea (photograph by Major R.V. Spencer, Department of the Navy, Naval Photographic Center, 1951, from selected images from the "War and Conflict" collection, National Archives and Records Administration, USA)

Manufactured in the United States of America

McFarland & Company, Inc., Publishers
    Box 611, Jefferson, North Carolina 28640
    www.mcfarlandpub.com

To combat veterans

Contents

Preface: The Evolution of a Reluctant Soldier

I seem like an unlikely person to be writing military history. As a teenager my strong interest in history centered around big, dramatic events and colorful, powerful personalities. The Korean War came along when I was in junior high school, and I recall following events of the conflict (with a map on the wall of my room), but it left me with no powerful imprint. I don't recall any of my friends and classmates having any particular interest in what was happening there. Not only had I not heard of anyone who was killed in Korea, I knew no one who had even been there. Given the looming reality of the draft, I did not look forward to being in the army.

Like just about everybody of my generation, my boyhood perception of war was entirely conditioned by World War II. Five of my uncles had served in that one. I saw the exciting post–V-E Day parade in Boston, signifying complete victory over Germany. In the following total defeat of Japan I never heard anyone question the use of atomic bombs, at the time or much later. Our neighborhood hero was Charlie Sweeney, who was a pilot on the attacks on both Hiroshima and Nagasaki.

One indication of my awareness of the Korean War came to mind recently when my senior sister told me that she and her husband were on hand to see Douglas MacArthur come along in a motorcade driving out of Boston to adjoining Quincy (as part of his nationwide exposure in late 1951). I did not attend, surely due to (the rest of) my family's strong Democratic allegiance. The whole family saw Harry Truman speak at an early morning short appearance before a huge crowd in Quincy Square in 1948, and he did give the other party hell! On the other hand, my diary in 1952 shows I was initially enthusiastic about Ike, but I know the powerful appeal of the Democratic Party soon overrode that.

1

One thing that was clear in my mind at that time was a very negative feeling about eventual military service — the rough, hard regimentation of it all, even without, with the end of the Korean War, any immediate threat of being plunged into the violence of warfare. In due course, however, by the late 1950s I found myself in the army, but after what I saw as the demanding experience of basic training, I was shuffled off to personnel training. While many other recruits went on to advanced infantry, armor, or artillery to train in manly martial skills, I was learning to type. From there I migrated into intelligence, which suited me fine — no roughing it in the field (and with a Top Secret clearance). Although I was just a lowly enlisted man, I observed a lot about the craft of tactical intelligence as well as learning about the effective army system of organization and administration (to do things, there is a right way and a wrong way, and then there is the army way; and it works). Later, in the reserves, I had some further infantry training, so I did have some short exposure to both ends of the reality of army life. At the time, I was just glad to get my military obligation over with. When I look back at that time, however, I find it sobering to contemplate my luck of the draw — too young for Korea and too old for Vietnam.

In graduate studies at Trinity College, Dublin, I was able to pursue my strong interest in the achievement of a free Irish state and society, doing a dissertation on the labor movement. I followed that up with a study of the political aspects of the Irish independence movement, seeking to put the physical force side of the movement in its proper perspective (time was to show that the violent part kept getting out of the bottle). As academics, Alan Greenberg, Judson Lyon and I became involved in research in comparative liberation movements, a complicated study we did not complete. Running parallel to this preoccupation with early twentieth century Ireland was my abiding interest in the role of Irish people in urban American politics and government, specifically what happened in my native Boston, and I intend to return to that study (right after Korea).

When I became a college professor, my teaching duties focused on western Europe and on Britain in particular, but over a period of time I became increasingly drawn to the German experience and, beyond that, to a broader perspective of world development, turning to Russia and China. I gained satisfaction and confidence in historical understanding by going to both of them twice. I now found myself returning to a focus on Germany and to Hitler and the Nazis in particular. Anyone with a strong interest in the mid–twentieth century has to confront the ability of Hitler to forge the most powerful political and military force of that era and then oversee its dissipation. Traveling in Germany with my colleague Joe Siren, whose specialty is Germany, I concluded that an aspect of Hitler that had not been given adequate attention was Hitler's self-assumed identification with Berchtesgaden and the Obersalzberg ("The Fuhrer in the Mountains," etc.), which led to my book *Hitler's Mountain: The Fuhrer,*

Obersalzberg and the American Occupation of Berchtesgaden, published in 2007. As part of that work, I followed the involvement of the U.S. Third Infantry Division from its arrival in Morocco in late 1942 until it occupied Berchtesgaden at the end of the European war. In following the activities of that division, I found myself often recalling similar experiences I had had in the army, barring, of course, the all-important matter of combat and all related to that. In any case, I had no further interest in digging up fresh perspectives on that war. There were loads of historians at work on that.

Surely, I was overestimating my slight military experience in this matter, but nevertheless I found myself being drawn into the reality of military culture and war. At that time I was writing about and editing (with David Doyle) a collection called *Irish Soldiers, American Wars*, which covered the period from the Mexican War to the post–Civil War battles with American Indians. I saw that study, however, as part of my overall interest in the Irish in American life and beyond. It made me alarmed and sad to recognize the truth of Martin Van Creveld's assertion that war is the most confused and exciting of human activities. Yet, Homer in *The Iliad* long ago spelled out the tragedy in pain, agony and death of that recurrent enterprise.

Then the Korean War came back into my view. Beginning in the 1970s the deepening American involvement in Vietnam had got so much historical attention and had generated such controversy that I chose not to do more than draw parallels between the Vietnamese situation and what Ireland had gone through to achieve political independence. But before Vietnam there had been a violent confrontation in Asia between capitalist democracy and totalitarian socialism. A factor that had been lingering in the back of my mind about the Korean conflict was how the Chinese Communist forces in late November 1950 had been able to rout the American military into precipitate, headlong retreat. Out of my initial examination of that episode I came to an awareness of the prevailing American attitudes about Asians and their perspectives, which surely was a major part in the ensuing debacle. Reading Sun Tzu (*The Art of War*) and the related writings of Mao Zedong was most revealing about military tactics, psychology and culture. I was appalled to learn — at its cost — that the American military knew nothing about or chose to overlook these Chinese strictures.

A little more than four years ago, I decided to look at the Korean War and to approach the subject not with just another chronology of events (already a well-trodden path) but by examining a variety of specific aspects of the conflict, with the clear purpose of unveiling the reality of war from the ground up — the experiences of combat soldiers, how they lived and survived, and how they related to the Korean people and, more ominously, to Chinese soldiers. There would be a deliberative effort to limit, except when necessary, descriptions of the doings of the high command (important messages from General Jones to Colonel Smith, self-serving reports to the Pentagon, the posturing of the likes of Douglas MacArthur). I sought to omit abstractions like "casualties" when referring to those killed or wounded.

I was a bold fellow to think I could write a book of value about what happened in that peninsula between 1950 and 1953. I had never taken a course in Asian history and initially knew little about it; moreover, there were heaps of books by serious historians about what went on in Korea and northern Asia in that period. But I went ahead anyway, with some interviews with veterans and reading a wide variety of works, including documents and memoirs, with a particular focus of the Chinese/Formosa matter leading to Chinese Communist intervention in Korea at the end of 1950. Despite some important recent revelations from Russian and Chinese sources, I found that many of the studies of the war itself followed the same basic chronology with a fresh insight thrown in from time to time, while some of the books looked only at a narrow aspect of the subject. There I saw an opening for the approach I fancied — examining a wide variety of important aspects of the conflict while tying it all together with a basic overview.

As I got into the subject, I found that I was impressed by the resilience, energy and contentiousness of this small but clearly defined nationality lodged between great powers. It is not by chance that the national dish of Korea is *kimchi*— a fiery mixture of fermented cabbage, garlic, spices and more.

I was amused to find that the Koreans sometimes had been termed, with good reason, the Irish of the Orient. I have been (justly) accused of finding an Irish angle in just about everything, so I was stimulated to see that Simon Winchester, in his mid–1980s travel book *Korea: A Walk Through the Land of Miracles*, was struck by the characteristics shared by the Irish and Korean people, and, moreover, how parts of Korea strongly reminded him of the west of Ireland (with one of his chapters being titled, "The Irish Island"). On the other hand, I found that every time Winchester encountered American soldiers in his treks across the country he described them as vulgar, brash, dirty and violent. I am aware that there is a certain kind of Englishman who, one way or another, resents having the Yanks displace Britain as the superstar on the world stage, but what I found problematic in Winchester's descriptions is that all of the Americans he encountered (this time; he had been there before) had negative, nasty attitudes towards Koreans, and Korean people resented this.

Studying war-torn Korea of the early 1950s, I found mixed views by American G.I.s about their experiences with Koreans. But with the U.S. military presence reduced to about 30,000 and the massive economic development of the country by the 1980s, I found it surprising that claims of this situation persisted. Although Korean–American relations since 1953 are outside the scope of my study, I wanted to find out more about this.

Thinking about the near-term Korean experience, I have come to realize that the long-held disturbing mentality of the North Korean Communist regime is more than just a hangover from the Korean War; it is part of a deeply embedded dichotomy growing out of the end of Asian war in 1945 which encompassed the two dominant worldviews. It appears to me that the irascible, not to say threatening, antics of the North Korean regime are reflective of some qualities of many Korean people. There is a refusal on its part to recognize that its long effort to forge a successful experiment in totalitarian socialism, combined with a bizarre family dynasty, had resulted in poverty and isolation, while the other part of Korea, despite a bumpy path, has emerged into a prosperous, developed and democratic society. Faced with the shambles of an economy, with no alternative besides criminal efforts to destabilize the southern state, the Korean Communists have turned to the modern-day version of saber rattling, of the missiles and nuclear weapons sort. The Russian and Chinese governments, not to mention the Americans and Japanese, for some time have been faced with the business of dealing with this rogue regime. There are, of course, more nasty events to come, but most probably there will be at the least a difficult if not violent end to that story.

To at least partially overcome my lack of graduate studies and publication on the subject at hand, I concluded that, at a minimum, I should go to see the place where these events took place. Previously, it had been a source of satisfaction and assurance to me that I had spent a lot of time in the places I had written about. So, I went on a short visit to the Republic of Korea in July 2009. Not only did I find the people in Seoul and environs friendly, lively and organized, but when I saw the rows of steep hills I immediately thought of the experiences of G.I.s when they encountered that land and its topography.

In a manner of speaking, what I was doing in the book was to string together slight military experience with an equally slight direct knowledge about the place I was writing about, which, to some historians, might seem a recipe, if not for disaster, then for the production of a shallow and overconfident critique of the subject. I hope potential critics will see that this is not what I have produced. From a professional point of view, it is not advisable to jump from one country or specialty to another (you become something of an intruder), and most historians wisely do not attempt this. However, with my mounting absorption in the whole subject, it is too late to turn back. As was the case with my previous books, I like what I have written so far, so that is a good sign.

One of the pleasures of life is the many people you encounter, either in person or on the printed page. A constant source of stimulation for writing this book has been my friend, colleague and traveling companion Joseph B. Siren, who has contributed a short overview of Korean development to 1900 for this study. Old friends Tom Bingay, Jack Downey, Mike Gerry, Tom Greland and Jim Watson, as on other occasions, gave me comments (mostly constructive) about the various drafts of the work. *Mile Buiochas* to another cadre of companions, these in Ireland — Charlie Callan, Frank Darcy, Rayner Lysaght,

Aidan O'Hara, Padraig O Snodaigh and Chris Woods. To get at the written record I had most enjoyable access to the National Archives in Washington, D.C., as well as a shorter visit to the Imperial War Museum in London. The interlibrary loan services of the Salkehatchie Campus Library and of the University of South Carolina provided me with a ton of material of all sorts, and I am grateful to Dan Johnson, Ed Merwin and all the library staffs for their continuing and amendable help. An indomitable group of computer gurus— Milton Harden, Brian Martinez, Ric Douglas, Kristin Smokes and Leroy Still — kept my heap of text within manageable bounds. I also acknowledge with sincere thanks the small research grants provided by my campus and university. In writing about a country there is nothing like seeing, feeling and touching the place, and my visit to Korea gave me that experience. *Man-se!* (Long Life!)

Introduction

The Korean War of 1950–1953 was not a big war, but a relatively short one in a limited area of conflict. After a year of intense combat the struggle ground to a stalemate, and the war could have ended at that point except for the principled stand by the United States, led by Harry S. Truman, on the issue of repatriation, that no prisoner of war should be forced to return to his country of origin. The Communist side rejected this assertion for two years as it would have provided clear evidence that many of its combatants did not want to live under Communism. The horrific effect of this lengthy standoff was the prolonged detention of American, Korean and other allied POWs in dire circumstances.

From an American perspective the Korean episode came in the wake of the "Big One," so-called World War II. At least the second time around the title was closer to the reality. "World War I" certainly was not a world war, but by employing that term historians and politicians of the countries involved endeavored to spread the blame around. It was a European war, caused by European rivalries, fought in Europe, with the United States, as an adjunct to Europe, being dragged in. The second general war was much like the first in terms of causation, location and alignments, but with an Asian component as Japan sought to emulate the major European nations. Total victory for the Allied side left the United States at the pinnacle of power. While basking in that great achievement, just half a decade later the United States received the rude challenge of Korea.

There was a background to this state of things. In looking at organized violence in the modern world it is necessary to confront the reality that the United States emerged out of the European conquest of the Western Hemisphere. Following up on the spectacular Spanish seizure of most of a great swath of land from Mexico to Tierra del Fuego (with the Portuguese completing the Iberian achievement in Brazil), the English began the construction, on a much slower and modest scale and with the hearty influx of a mass of Irish and German immigrants, of what evolved into the most dynamic society of the modern world. The new American nation had the advantages of a mass of territory rich in resources with only a small indigenous population with which to contend. Equally important was the English heritage of an emerging civic society — that is, a community where nonviolent politics prevailed.

Given these foundations, the new United States proceeded to largely dominate all of its neighbors, both militarily and economically, reaching beyond these to cultural and political ascendancy. The aggressive, ambitious force thus created found its fulfillment in the American people's sweep to the West Coast, followed by a reaching out into the Pacific Ocean by 1900. In doing this, the United States encountered its western European kith and kin doing the same thing.

By the opening of the twentieth century several European states- big and small — had fought their way into Africa and Asia. Repeatedly as European imperialists worked to consolidate their control in various places, the natives resisted; thus there was a series of "limited wars." No matter how this European encroachment is presented by some of its historians, it was generally viewed by Asians as invasion and subjection. At the first good opportunity most Asians struggled to throw off the European yoke. For its own purposes, the Japanese created the opportunity. The wildly ambitious aspirations of Japanese expansion came crashing down when overwhelmed by American industrial and scientific might.

Looking at Asia in a broader view in the twentieth century, it occurs to me that Japanese expansion in its last and most ambitious phase was indeed the forerunner of Asian liberation from the control of Europeans and their kin. Although not in the way that Japanese imperialism envisaged it, a form of the Greater East Asia Co-Prosperity Sphere has come to pass. America's successful war in the Pacific overlaid and partially concealed the process, but the powerful force continued to grow. At the inauguration of the Communist government of China in October 1949 when Mao declared, "China has stood up," his assertion could have been applied to Asia as a whole.

In the course of American expansion into Asia during the past century the Korean conflict was part of America's economic and military penetration of the region. In turn, the United States has come into violent contention with people of the Philippines, Japan, Korea, China and Vietnam. The justification for such ventures could not be provided solely by the need to prevent the spread of Communism, as that ideology as an organized force did not exist at the time of the earlier involvements. The "Open Door" policy the United States advocated in the 1890s effectively meant that everybody, including the likes of drug dealer Warren Delano, could try to exploit the great lure of the China market. In the later engagements the United States has conducted essentially defensive actions to halt the widening influence of a powerful and resurgent

China. The political standing and economic achievement of China has been increasingly apparent since the guns went silent in Korea in July 1953.

In 1945 the United States stood as the new dominant power in Asia. It was now faced with the rapidly rising tide of Asian nationalism. This force was linked to communism, with its social and economic appeal. This combination found its most important manifestation in China. The Communist victory in China found its driving force in a deep-felt Chinese desire to end a century of European (and then Japanese) domination and humiliation. A collision between these powerful forces shortly resulted, with Korea being its setting, and the Korean people being its progenitors— and victims.

The Korean War of 1950–1953 was a contained conflict divided into two episodes. At the beginning the United States intervened in a civil conflict to prevent a client state from being conquered by its northern rival and then, having achieved that, went beyond its initial objective to attempt the conquest of North Korea. Communist China took action, determined to stop the Americans from taking over its bordering neighbor south of the Yalu. It also achieved its initial objective and also then went beyond that to try to drive the U.S. forces out of the south. Neither achieved these expanded ambitions, and the conflict ended where it began. Notwithstanding the glorious American total victory of 1945, there is much historical evidence that a limited episode of violence with an inconclusive outcome is a good way to end a violent conflict for all involved. The most important benefit that the United States derived from the Korean conflict was the abundant evidence that it provided for the idea, already developing, that a very substantially expanded military capacity was required to sustain the United States and its western European allies in the continuing contest with international communism. From that point of view, Korea was a hard lesson, but that seems to be the only kind that counts.

CHAPTER ONE

Prelude to War

While in Beijing in 2006 I had a short conversation with a Chinese engineer about the clash of our countrymen in Korea in the early 1950s. In departing, he asked, half-jokingly, "Who won that war?" In the spirit of our brief discussion, I replied, "Nobody."

By any standard, the war that broke out in Korea in 1950 was a strange affair for the United States, its military and its South Korean ally. With its topsy-turvy course of events in its opening round, it must be unique in the annals of warfare. In its first six months there were wild gyrations: the U.S. Army having plunged into to it ill-prepared at the end of that June, first gaining what seemed to be a toehold at the end of the peninsula, then swinging to a complete turn-about with the effective seaborne incursion at Inchon, which resulted in the decimation of the North Korean Army. From there followed the rapid movement into North Korea, the capture of its capital of Pyongyang, and the approach to the northern border of the Yalu River; victory was in sight. Then, another sweeping turnabout with the massive Chinese intervention, which drove the invaders deep into the south, a drive which, to many, appeared to be unstoppable. But, at great cost it was halted, contained and then driven back to the 38th parallel, where the war began.

After these dramatic events, the next two and a half years were anticlimactic, an extended period of bloody stalemate. During the war's three years hundreds of thousands of soldiers on both sides were killed, not to mention the many who suffered crippling wounds. Americans were once again fighting Asians, as in the Pacific war against the Japanese, which had ended but five years before the Korean episode exploded. Like Vietnam later (where Americans again fought Asians), it became a source of bitter partisan controversy at home, but unlike the Vietnam issue this internal dispute seemed to soon fade as Korea merged into the wider matter of the Cold War. Indeed, to many Americans Korea came to represent a harsh but successful effort to stem the spread of communism. A closer examination of the conflict reveals episodes of poor judgment on the part of the military leaders. This situation seems understandable in the context of the overwhelming victory achieved by the United States at the end of the recently completed Second World War. A further price paid was the death and mutilation of tens of thousands of young American men. An estimated total of two million people were killed or wounded, with the great majority of these being Korean civilians and soldiers. As well, there was massive damage in most of the country of buildings, roads and just about anything that could be bombed or blown up. A common recollection of some U.S. soldiers about Korea is that it was a land of one hill after another, followed by mountains.

This study is not another chronology of events in that conflict. It does provide a minimal account of the different phases of the war, but the focus is on the various factors that are the necessary foundations of actual violent encounters. Without supplies, weapons, logistics and all the other basic ingredients to mount a military campaign, a war would quickly break down to an ineffective, confusing fiasco, with the elements of disorganization, conflicting orders, troop and supply bottlenecks far surpassing the condition that exists at the initiation of almost all military ventures. As Martin Van Creveld has noted, war is the most exciting and confusing of human activities. More important, for the purpose of this study is Napoleon's assertion: an army travels on its stomach.

There are many general chronologies of the Korean War — some of which are worthy of specific mention due to the quality of their analysis and comprehension, among them being those by Roy Appleman, Max Hastings and Stanley Weintraub — as well as a host of studies of specific aspects, usually military operations. The general studies only occasionally and briefly deal with non-combat matters, then directly return to battle for page after page. Studies of specific aspects lack a general sense of what the conflict was all about. My purpose is to encompass all the major non-combat factors in the conflict. The object is to look at warfare, in this case, from the bottom up. This book can act as a complement to the "big battle" approach to military history.

It is appropriate to begin with a brief appreciation of the extraordinarily defined and resilient history of a people caught between the two giants of northern Asia — China and Japan. This is provided by Professor Joseph Bibb Siren, who lived in Japan as a young man and who has traveled with this writer to Japan, Korea, China and Russia.

The Korean Past (by Joseph B. Siren)

The Koreans have sometimes been termed "the Irish of the Far East" due to, among other things, their resolute and fiery spirit.[1] With a population of

30 million in 1950 (20 million in the south and 10 million in the north), their country — of eighty thousand square miles — has clear geographic definition: a peninsula with the Yalu and Tumen rivers defining the north. With a length of six hundred miles and a width of about 180 miles across a mid-point waist, it has a 500-mile border with Manchuria reaching over to the east to a small frontier with Russia.

This northern Asia country has a mountainous spine tapering off only at the southern tip. Its mountains have shaped Korean history, often isolating Koreans from one another as well as from outsiders. Even today with a modern communications and transportation infrastructure, Koreans have many entrenched regional customs and habits.

Two compelling themes dominate Korean history, with historically powerful China to the west and an expansive Japan to the east. Korea has been described as a shrimp between two whales, with its past often dwarfed by its mighty neighbors. Korea has also been viewed as a conduit between its neighbors, usually serving as the route by which Chinese culture diffused to Japan.

Korea has a rich and unique legacy of its own, dating back to the third millennium B.C. Legend holds that Dan'gun (an offspring of a god and a bear) constituted a Korean state in 2333 B.C. with its capital Pyongyang. This era is known as Old Chosan, the translation of which is "Land of the Morning Calm." For centuries thereafter Korea consolidated its unique indigenous traditions with institutions liberally imported from China.

Han Dynasty China acquired direct control over Korea a century before Christ, and while it exercised political mastery for only a few generations its cultural impact remained for centuries. In time, Confucian philosophy became more entrenched in Korea than in China itself. During the fourth century three native kingdoms arose — Koguryo in the north, Silla in the southeast and Paekoke in the southwest. This era of "the three kingdoms" was eventually dominated by Silla and then Koguryo (with the name of the latter evolving to Koryo, the source for the English word *Korea*).

Like most of East Asia, Korea experienced several generations of Mongol influence before ushering in the lengthy and prosperous Joseon Dynasty in 1392. The Joseons adopted Confucianism, moved the capital to its present location at Seoul, fostered Korea's *hangul* alphabet superseding Chinese-like ideographs, and under its fabled military hero Admiral Yi-Sun-Sin warded off two Japanese invasions. Ultimately Korea recognized the suzerainty of the Quing (Manchu) Dynasty in the seventeenth century, adopting its xenophobic exclusion of foreign trade until the late nineteenth century.

Christianity arrived in Korea under the impetus of French missionaries in the early 1800s, which resulted in a violent reaction in which converts and missionaries alike were massacred. Despite a variety of obstacles, Christianity, roughly split between Catholic and Protestant denominations, grew to include about a quarter of the population, marking the highest percentage in an Asian country barring the Philippines. In the wake of the American penetration of Japan by Admiral Peary, Korea was confronted with the arrival of a British-owned but American-crewed vessel, which met with violent opposition and a near-war by an aggressive United States, the upshot of which was the establishment of pro forma diplomatic ties in 1852.

The floundering authority of the Manchus coupled with the ambitions of both Japan and Russia made Korea a much desired objective in the 1890s. Korea sought assistance from Russia, but that abruptly ended when a recently modernized Japan imposed a protectorate before asserting a much disputed annexation in 1910.

Japan pursued a highly exploitive policy in Korea but was responsible for the construction of a substantial infrastructure. A notable achievement was the development of a huge hydroelectric system, including the Chosin reservoir (which in time was to become ingrained in American military history) and similar facilities along the Yalu River. These became the principal sources of electrical power in Manchuria, which also came to be controlled by Japan, directly after 1931.[2]

During the course of the Japanese occupation, its control in Korea became increasingly harsh, including the banning of the Korean language, the pillage of artifacts, persecution of Christians and mandated worship at Shinto shrines. The eradication of Korean history and culture from school curricula was balanced by the introduction of modern science and technology. A particularly heinous Japanese action was the widespread abduction of young Korean females to serve as "comfort women" in Japanese military brothels in several countries. The U.S. Air Force did some bombing of industrial and military sites in Korea, but the damage was not major.[3] As a result of the long Japanese occupation, the educated Korean elite spoke and read the language of Nippon, but the heritage of the Japanese presence made anything Japanese anathema to the great majority of people in the newly freed country. A total of 700,000 Japanese civilians, as well as 270,000 military personnel, were withdrawn after the war, taking with them the core of Korea's administrative and technical expertise. Before leaving, some Japanese officials warned the United States of the powerful Communist movement forming in the north.

A large number of Koreans served in the Japanese imperial forces during that war, which was partially offset by small numbers of Koreans who used the mountainous terrain to obstruct Japanese control. Some of these rebels were forced to shift to Manchuria and China proper, where they formed the basis of the Korean communist party. This involvement enabled the post-war North Korean leadership to base their authority on their record of opposing Japanese control of their country, while drawing attention to those elements in the south who collaborated with the Japanese. In addition, as warned by the Chinese nationalist government in 1942, there were two divisions of

Koreans in the Soviet army which could be shifted to Korea — with ominous political consequences.[4]

In virtually sole occupation of Japan since 1945, by 1949 the U.S. regime there was coming to a close, although it was assumed that the United States would continue to have bases there. The large armed forces it maintained in Japan, despite inadequate funding, were considered to be necessary to provide a bulwark against Russian penetration from the north. As well, the United States had been intimately involved since the late 1940s in the Chinese civil war, having provided huge amounts of military aid to the anti–Communist side, with much of it falling into the hands of the victorious Communists. The U.S. military maintained large army and air force contingents in China after 1945 for the primary purpose of facilitating the withdrawal of Japanese troops but also to "provide logistic support to the Chinese government," that is, to the disintegrating regime of Chiang Kai-shek. It even produced a Shanghai edition of the *Stars and Stripes* for a few years. The last U.S. forces were withdrawn in early 1949, just before Chiang's government collapsed. The defeat of the client nationalist regime in 1949 was a severe setback for the United States. Communist control of the world's most populous country marked a major geopolitical development. The general response in the United States to this momentous development was one of denial of its implications, which joined in the developing domestic controversy about who lost China. An important function of a military organization is to anticipate possible future opponents. The Army War College could not be any help as it was closed during World War II and did not reopen until 1950.[5]

It was as a result of the spread of Asian communism that the United States reentered the affairs of the northern Asian mainland. Beginning in late June 1950 the American government directly intervened in internal conflicts in two adjoining Asian countries — Korea and China. These actions were matched by the Soviet Union in fostering and supplying the North Korean attack on the South in June 1950 and the Chinese Communists with their armed entrance into the conflict the following November. Although the circumstances of U.S. intervention were different in both places, they were related. In Korea the United States intervened almost immediately after North Korea launched a crushing invasion of South Korea. Without prompt American action the Communist forces from the north would have achieved their anticipated quick total occupation of the south.[6]

In the case of China, the United States intruded on the tail end of the Chinese civil war, in which by the end of 1949 the Communist armies had gained control of all of mainland China and were preparing to invade the island refuges of their Nationalist opponents on Hainan (in the South China Sea) and Formosa (Taiwan in Chinese) islands. In April 1950 Hainan was captured without serious opposition and, after taking over several small islands, the Communist army made rapid preparations to seize the final objective of

Formosa. According to some intelligence sources, this campaign was anticipated to begin in the summer of 1950; the U.S. State Department and the Central Intelligence Agency concluded the Communist effort would be successful.[7]

The United States had been deeply involved in both countries in the wake of World War II. With the Soviet Union occupying the northern half of Korea (with the 38th parallel being the line of division) the American army moved into the southern half. Two rival governments soon emerged, with a Communist regime in the north and a non–Communist one in the south. The withdrawal of Soviet occupation units in 1948 forced a similar measure by the Americans the next year, leaving behind two competing Korean governments and military forces taking shape.

The U.S. Army occupation of South Korea initially was seen as a temporary arrangement, with the possibility of a United Nations–supervised unification of the two entities to follow. Communist obstruction of such a development resulted in the United States taking a different view of its position in South Korea. It began providing economic aid to that part of Korea and helped to organize local security personnel. This does not indicate any strong interest in a further position there. In September 1947 the Combined Chiefs of Staff, Dwight Eisenhower chairman, declared, "From the standpoint of military security, the United States has little strategic interest in maintaining the present troops and bases in Korea." In the event of conflict with the Soviet Union, they said, "our present forces in Korea would be a military liability."

The following year the National Security Council concluded, "The U.S. should not become so irrevocably involved in the Korea situation that any action taken by any faction in Korea or by any other power in Korea could be considered a *casus belli* for the U.S." It did, however, support the further development of a constabulary force to provide "effective protection for the security of South Korea against any but an overt act of aggression by North Korean or other forces."[8] Although as Far East commander, he did not have security responsibility for South Korea, Douglas MacArthur had the same view. In January 1949 he told the Joint Chiefs that South Korea could not defeat a North Korean invasion, the United States should not commit combat troops if there was such an invasion, and that the remaining U.S. military should be promptly withdrawn.[9] The next year the National Security Council declared that it supported the formation of a South Korean army but, concerned about such a force being used in an attack against the north, one without heavy weapons— artillery, tanks and fighter aircraft. A further limiting actor was that there were insufficient funds for this equipment left in the mutual support legislation. A small advisory body of 500 U.S. military was given the responsibility of training the new force, but Gerald Henderson is not the only one to say that it would have been prudent to have retained a combat regiment.[10] In an important statement in January 1950 Secretary of State Dean Acheson, while declaring a hands-off position regarding China and Taiwan, did not include South Korea in the U.S. defense perimeter in the Pacific. At about the same time, when asked in a closed hearing before the Senate Foreign Relations Committee if the United States would go to the defense of South Korea if it was attack by the North, he stated, "I do not believe that we would undertake to resist it by military force."[11] So, in effect, the position of South Korea was left up in the air.

A general perception about the great wars of the United States would run in importance from World War II to the Civil War, World War I, the Revolution and Vietnam. With the exception of Vietnam, all were fought to victorious conclusions. What about Korea? In any way, can this conflict be seen as an epic, or was it merely a disagreeable interruption of the post-war glow of achievement? From a positive perspective, the conflict in this Asian peninsula in the early 1950s built up into a true epic, drawing in several countries, principally the United States and communist China, while the stage for the struggle was Korea and its people, about two million of whom died in its course. As in other epics, it was filled with mayhem, atrocity, heroism, despair and all the rest that go into this kind of saga.

From an American point of view this war is often characterized as unnecessary, ugly and useless, revealing a lack of understanding of Asian culture, political mismanagement, raging controversies about communism and personalities, military lack of preparedness, and operational ineptitude. Several American historians have called the war a forgotten one, a wrong one and more. In this author's perspective, this is a mistaken assessment. In more ways than one, it was a necessary one, carried out with all the limitations and abilities of the American people. It forcefully brought to the fore the whole matter of addressing communism, Asia and Third World development.

Hanging over the conflict was the American recollection, hardened into popular culture, of the glorious total victories of the U.S. military both in Europe and the Pacific in the conflict that had ended in 1945, and which was followed by a tidal wave of self-congratulatory movies, television series and books galore. That created a most unseemly and misleading precedent about the nature of armed conflict. Most wars do not end with totality either in victory or defeat. The limited achievement of the American involvement in Korea punctured the complacent assumptions of many Americans about the greatness and domination of their country, which caused a reaction that rejected this involvement as unworthy and profitless, while from other quarters came demands that total war be employed, using atomic bombs to erase this stain, something like the response of the Athenians in a similar situation in the Peloponnesian war. In that episode, at least some of the Greeks came to a recognition of the consequences of hubris. In more ways than one, the Korean episode was a maturing experience for many Americans about the limitations of violent conflict, increasing their awareness of Asia and its people and the American responses to these matters. Yet for many the cry of "No more Koreas" became a blind and unthinking response — Vietnam. If, as has been argued, the Korean commitment had very little utility, then that in Vietnam turned out to be a national humiliation.

Another comment often heard about the Korean affair was that it was fought in a deeply unattractive place, which calls to mind the assumption that this kind of event somehow should take place in a much more inviting setting. What was so attractive about the mountains of Italy, the jungles of New Guinea, the hedgerows of Normandy, the bitter winter campaign in Belgium in the "Big One"? Since war is essentially a criminal activity, it is well that the venue so often is decidedly uninviting.

The destruction and carnage that resulted from the Korean conflict for many seemed to present a picture, if not of a hopeless future for the Korean people, then of one that was dim and negative. The overriding eventuality, however, turned out to be the impressive unfolding of a renewed, prosperous and confident people, yet with an nasty appendix (North Korea) that found its root in the social revolution that swept much of Asia, but eventually degenerated into criminal activity, nuclear posturing, even famine and a cruel and obscene personality cult. But all that lay ahead.

Two Koreas

The U.S. military occupation of the southern zone was led by General John Hodge, a tough, gruff artillery officer without political experience. Civil Affairs officers did not appear until October 1945. He greeted one group of them by stating that the three things troops in Japan feared were gonorrhea, diarrhea and Korea, "and you've got the third." Due to a variety of difficulties, A. Wigfall Green declared, "Morale among military government officers and enlisted men was at rock bottom during the first year of the occupation."[12] Repeated political turmoil was bewildering to Hodge, who was glad to be asked to leave by the new Southern Korean government in 1948. In that year two Korean republics were formed. In the south in an election supervised by a United Nations commission, Syngman Rhee, having returned from many years of exile in the United States, won election as South Korea's first president and was to remain in that position until 1960. In a tumultuous political environment, Rhee succeeded in maintaining effective control, but his supporters, later formed into the Liberal Party, consisted of a conservative, propertied, financially secure, educated segment of the population, which had no roots in the peasant masses.

While political arguments raged with similar opponents, little was done to address the massive social and economic problems despite limited U.S. economic aid. According to Gerald Henderson, with little independent political experience, South Korean society was riddled by factions of all sorts, which, with U.S. aid pouring in, escalated beginning with the war: "Factionalism battened on war and corruption. War magnified the mistakes of inexperienced officers, and corruption added to the constant need for the factional leader's protective cloak."[13]

With this situation so widespread, it is a wonder that so many South Koreans were willing to oppose the northern invasion when it came. With little industry, South Korea was a land of peasant farmers, but land transfers to tenant farmers were slow in coming and limited in scope. Rhee's government focused on defeating Communist advocates and just about anyone else opposing it.[14] Despite a variety of restrictions and outright repression, there was a huge growth in the number and distribution of newspapers, expressing a wide range of political views.[15] General Hodge came to believe that Koreans were the "most politically-minded people I have ever met" and declared that it was not for nothing they were called "the Irish of the Orient," a phrase that was to be repeated by several other observers.[16] In that period there was a proliferation of political activity, with a noted propensity for oratory (another Irish characteristic). This situation was combined with a massive increase of students in higher education and a subsequent increase of unemployed university graduates — another element of volatility.[17]

The purpose of the U.S. Army advisory group was to train a Korean army, one without tanks, combat planes or heavy weapons. Journalist Keyes Beech, while in Korea at this time, saw the army personnel there as "a dumping ground for every misfit, gold brick and incompetent west of Hawaii." He noted, as well, that the Korean operation was last in line for materials of all kinds: "What got through to Korea was what the army in Japan didn't want." American occupation troops had a harshly negative view of Korea compared to the allure of Japan and, among other things, had to contend with massive theft of their supplies.[18] Donald Portway, no friendly observer, declares that some South Koreans believed that "the American Military government had as its basic purpose the provision of banquets, gifts and feminine company." Bong-young Choy cites one eyewitness who held that the occupation army "was courteous on the surface" but the conduct of American officials and Syngman Rhee supporters "was shocking."[19] Not only were there public executions of opponents but already spy networks were operating "at all levels which even reached into individual families." A common complaint of many Koreans of northern origin was that its leaders were only southerners; this "perpetuated an ancient political and social feud between northern and southern Koreans."[20]

Meanwhile in the north, the Russian occupation of North Korea beginning in 1945 resulted in the construction of a model communist state, with a reputed guerrilla fighter, using the name Kim Il Sung, put forward as its leader. His birth name was Kim Song-ju; to many it was clear that this was a "phony Kim Il Sung," as the original Korean patriot would have been a very old man by that time. In fact, this Kim had long served as an officer in the Soviet Army, as did many other Korean exiles. He was to remain as the "great leader" of the North until his death in 1994, to be succeeded by his apparently unstable son, who remained leader to 2011 and designated one of his sons to follow him.[21] An early Central Intelligence Agency assessment — that of December 1947 — observed, "The USSR appears to be making preparations to accord full recognition to the North Korean puppet regime."[22]

The Communists carried out massive land reform, although most of the large landowners were in the south and most of those in the north fled when the Russians arrived. North Korea had a considerable industrial base as well as a huge hydroelectrical system, both developed by the Japanese, and all large industrial facilities were nationalized. The Communist government also stimulated the promotion of national culture and education. According to Andrei Lankov, "To many contemporaries [the Communist regime] seemed to be (and at that stage probably actually was) somewhat more efficient and remarkably less corrupt than its rival in the South." Its land reforms and a variety of other programs received popular support, which "made many Koreans believe that the new people in power in Pyongyang were indeed striving to improve the life of the majority."[23] On the other hand, this was a one-party dictatorship in which all opposition was rooted out by police action. Dominating the regime was the Soviet-trained group led by Kim Il Sung, with the Kim leadership eventually developed into a full-blown personality cult (which has continued to the present), the magnitude of which would have embarrassed even Comrade Stalin. With Russian assistance, the Communist government began a large-scale military buildup including a substantial tank force. A test of its military effectiveness was soon to come. To demonstrate its hostility to the American-sponsored government in the south, in 1949 the new northern regime cut off electrical power being sent there from the Japanese-built power plants. The U.S. Corps of Engineers responded by installing two huge generators, one at Seoul and the other at Pusan.[24]

The Soviet withdrawal from the north in December 1948 pressured a similar action by the United States the next year, which was completed by June. The U.S. State Department opposed withdrawal at least at that time, while the Pentagon insisted on it. Left behind were about 500 members of the Korean Military Augmentation Group, which had the heavy task of continuing the development of an army for the new state.[25] While the U.S. Army was preparing to leave the south Syngman Rhee, on one hand, urged the United States not to pull out all of its troops, while on the other hand, in April 1949, he expressed confidence in the capacity of his fledgling government, declaring that South Korea's military was "rapidly approaching the point at which our security can be assured, provided the Republic of Korea is not called upon to face attack from a foreign source." It never arrived at that point before it was put to the test. Rhee sought a commitment, a "guarantee" that the United States would defend his new government, but this was refused.[26]

After direct withdrawal from the north the Soviet government began to forge an effective military force there. At the end of 1948 a Russian military mission arrived at Pyongyang, with four of its generals being armor specialists. According to Peter Faber, "The Korean People's Army was indeed to be built around an armored core." Among the Soviet instructors, "tank specialists from Mongolia were required to have five years" of armor experience, a secondary education, fluency in Russian and, of course, political reliability. About ten Soviet advisors, who were required to wear North Korean Army uniforms, were attached to each North Korean division. The following year the Soviet government granted forty million dollars in credit to buy Soviet arms, with the result that the Communist force was well equipped, albeit with older weapons, for the coming attack.

As the time drew near for action, almost all of the 7,000 Soviet advisors were withdrawn; Stalin ordered that none should be captured, and none were, although there were some near misses.[27] As the North Korean military closed in on the Pusan peninsula, the lack of professional military advice prevented the northern army from achieving completion of its campaign.[28] After the Chinese intervention of November 1950 the Soviets returned still under cover but in substantial numbers. An estimated 72,000 (26,000 of whom were there at one time — in 1952) Soviet air personnel were in North Korea and Manchuria during the war, usually in civilian clothes. As a POW in Pyongyang in October 1951, Richard Bassett saw two small groups of uniformed Russian soldiers.[29]

A major factor in the Korean Communist desire for war was the large-scale influx of soldiers who had served in the Chinese Communist Army and, following the end of the Chinese civil war in late 1949, upon Kim Il Sung's request, began returning to Korea.[30] A secret treaty between Communist China and North Korea of mutual defense which provided Chinese military support was reportedly agreed to in March 1949.[31] This support was substantial, resulting in the augmentation of the northern army with experienced soldiers in organized units, estimated at between 50,000 and 70,000, bringing with them 12,000 rifles, 620 machine guns and 240 artillery pieces. It provided the backbone (about one-third) of the personnel for that force.[32]

Despite the Soviet-provided military buildup and frequent northern-inspired border incursions designed to destabilize the southern regime, throughout most of 1949 Joseph Stalin, rejecting Kim Il Sung's advocacy of invasion of the south, was concerned about violent incidents along the border between the two Koreas, this concern extending to the possibility of South Korea attacking the north, which would have created international effects he did not want at that time.[33] Contradicting Kim's argument that with many people in the south prepared to revolt against the Rhee regime, the time for invasion had arisen, in September 1949 the Soviet Politburo concluded that the Communist regime was neither militarily nor politically prepared for war.[34]

Confronted with Kim's insistence, on January 30, 1950, Stalin agreed "in principle" to support this military venture.[35] His change of position seemed to be due to the added security given to the Soviet Union by its possession of the atomic bomb, the victory of the Communists in China, the controversy in western Europe about the formation of the North Atlantic alliance, and an apparent lessening of American involvement in Asia. Stalin proceeded to put in place detailed plans for the operation but required Kim to consult with Mao and the other Chinese leaders, who gave their consent or at least did not oppose the venture. Given that the Chinese government had transferred large numbers of soldiers and their equipment to North Korea, its position was not surprising.[36]

In the immediate post–Pacific war period Korea was of slight importance to the American military high command while the Russians in the north vigorously developed Communist control. Various U.S. policy decisions amounted to an open invitation for Korean Communists to take over the rest of the peninsula. One of these was reached as early as September 1947, when a group of policy planners concluded that the United States should leave South Korea to its own fate.[37] In June 1949 the Joint Chiefs of Staff concluded that Korea was of little strategic value and "commitment by the U.S. of U.S. military forces in Korea would be ill-advised and impractical"; this assessment was shared by Douglas MacArthur.[38] Secretary of State Dean Acheson was much more concerned to bolster the French effort in Vietnam, which was already confronted with a Communist-led insurrection.[39]

An ambiguous position continued. With no commitment to back up South Korea in a military crisis, the U.S. government demonstrated its continuing connection to South Korea by means of economic and military aid and the creation of a military advisory unit, while declaring that the withdrawal of American troops did not lessen United States interest in the Republic of Korea. As late as March 1950 the most Secretary of State Acheson could declare was that there was good reason to hope that South Korea could survive a northern assault. Two months later he again declared that his department continued to stress the importance of South Korea.[40] In January 1949 Douglas MacArthur, commander of the Far East Command, declared his opposition to U.S. military support for an endangered South Korea.[41] Diplomat and strategist George Kennan was informed by "a very high Air Force officer" that if there was a military crisis in Korea the air force could deal with the matter.[42]

As time was to show, MacArthur, based on his World War II experience, also had an inflated estimate about what the air force could do in Korea. The war in Korea was fought over a land mass of hills and mountains, not through attacks on isolated Japanese bases and vulnerable naval forces. When President Truman asked MacArthur in October 1950 about the effect of a Chinese intervention in Korea, MacArthur said it would result in "the greatest slaughter," which only could be effected by massive air attacks. Time was to show that there was a great slaughter,[43] but not in the way MacArthur envisaged it; rather, it was like the prophecy offered to King Croesus.

Although MacArthur had not been asked to have some sort of a plan for a military response to a Communist invasion of the south, some consideration was given to this clear possibility. As American troops were being withdrawn, a plan to evacuate American civilians in that event, insultingly called "Operation Chow Chow," was prepared.[44] The high command of the army had not completely ignored the possibility of war in Korea. In 1948 the logistics branch of the army General Staff had prepared a plan to anticipate U.S. intervention in such an event, but this proposal did not seem to register or result in further planning in the Far Eastern Command.[45] In his memoirs, John Singlaub asserts that MacArthur's command did have a plan to come to the aid of a threatened South Korea, but such a plan did not anticipate confronting a "massive, coordinated surprise assault."[46] The existence of such a plan must have been buried in army archives because the response to the attack was piecemeal, slap-dash and chaotic.

MacArthur's outlook concerning Korea in the time immediately leading up to the outbreak of the war is reflective of a strange mentality that some critics have said was characteristic of the man. The only time he was there at that time was to make one of his grand statements at the inauguration of the Republic of Korea in 1948. Having become identified with that institution, was he really prepared to stand by and see it swept away? Neither then nor later did he spend more than a few hours at a time there (and never a night). Olympian detachment has its drawbacks. For advice on what was occurring in Korea his principal source of information was the seriously flawed analysis of Charles Willoughby, his intelligence chief, who became notorious for telling MacArthur what he wanted to hear.[47] John Gunther, the popular historian who was in Japan when the war broke out, observed that although MacArthur had no direct political or military responsibility for Korea, "as commander in chief of the Far East Command, he might well have given developments in Korea a more penetrating scrutiny than he did."[48]

MacArthur's immediate reaction to the beginning of the North Korean attack, of course, was that it was just another border incursion. Gunther relates that about noon of that fateful day of June 25, 1950, State Department representative John Foster Dulles, about to board his departing plane, asked MacArthur if the situation was serious enough that he should stay in Japan. MacArthur told him "not to bother to stay behind to cover it."[49] Dulles was so concerned about MacArthur's response to the situation that when he returned to Washington he reportedly told one of his aides that MacArthur should be "hauled back to the United States immediately." In the days leading up to the Chinese onslaught of November 1950, MacArthur declared that there were no more than 30,000 Chinese military in north and his "final offensive" would destroy the remaining North Korean opposition. He hailed the disposition of the X Corps in the eastern sector as "a brilliant tactical movement," which was quickly followed by the crumbling and flight of the corps.[50]

Following the U.S. withdrawal, the northern Communist regime attempted to stir up insurrection in the south, claiming, in September 1949, that 77,000 opponents of the Rhee government were involved in 1,184 clashes with that regime. Among other places, there was serious anti-government opposition in the southwestern corner of the republic, which was crushed by the South Korean military, with many executions to follow.[51] Within months of the declaration of the Republic of Korea (ROK) and the election of Syngman Rhee as its president in 1948, the National Security Law was passed by its new National Assembly which resulted in a large-scale suppression of leftist support, principally the Korean Workers' Party.[52] According to Carter Eckert et al., "Rhee embarked on a campaign of anticommunist witch hunts that eventually affected tens of thousands of people," many of whom had no connection with the Communist groups. "All major organizations, including the military, the press and educational institutions, were subjected to scrutiny and purge."[53] When in early 1949 an invigorated National Assembly passed a broad-based land reform measure to which the conservative Rhee objected, he responded with the arrest and jailing of sixteen assembly members, which effectively stifled further legislative assertion and land reform. By the spring of 1950 60,000 people were in prison on political grounds.[54]

The strong arm of repression was the Korean National Police, taken over from the Japanese occupation. In the words of Donald Portway, during the Pacific war the Japanese/Korean military police were "universally hated"; indeed, "no more sadistic body of men could be imagined and the Korean policemen were even worse that the Japanese." In their occupation zone, the Russians got rid of this force, while the Americans kept it. "As a result," Portway declares, "the national police remained an abomination to all decent people." Going further, he states, "By nurturing a police state many moderates were driven into the Communist camp."[55]

Louise Yim had the same general impression. A lifelong supporter of Korean independence and a cabinet member, Yim estimated that despite government efforts, communist and related movements were growing in strength. Government sweeps against opponents, she noted, also were directed at political moderates, including journalists and literary people, who were accused of being in cahoots with communist revolutionaries. She recalled that period: "The West Gate Prison yard in Seoul resounded to firing squads. The prisons throughout the country were bursting with Communists and leftist sympathizers. At a single moment, we were purging ourselves of a fifth column, preaching democracy, and also curbing it where we felt it was dangerous. It was confusion. It was dangerous and yet we knew it not."[56] The national police force gained a reputation for brutality and when Rhee in 1960 was driven out of office this organization was purged of those who were holdovers from the

Japanese period.[57] In the middle of the Korean War — in February 1951— one horrific incident occurred when an ROK contingent, led by a colonel who later became head of the national police, rounded up and massacred a reported 719 villagers in one place who were suspected as protecting Communist guerrillas.[58] During 1951–52 the South Korean government claimed its forces had killed 20,000 armed opponents in the south, which is evidence that anti-government activity remained strong.[59]

The May 30 election for the South Korea National Assembly, which took place shortly before the invasion and from which the Communist-aligned parties were excluded, showed wide support for candidates who were not part of the Rhee political organization.[60] Not only did Communist partisans try to disrupt the election, but North Korea attempted to upstage the event by proposing the formation of an all–Korea legislature. Despite huge voter participation in the elections, the poor showing of the Rhee forces could only be seen by communist North Korea as evidence of weak political cohesion in the south.[61]

The Communist underground in the south, led by Pak Hon-yong, was so confident of its strength that it assured the North Korean leadership that an invasion would set off a widespread rising in other parts of the country following the capture of Seoul, effectively ending the Rhee regime. This view was also held by some North Korean generals.[62] But no general rising took place, one factor being the determined repression of a major rebellion which took place at the southern tip of the peninsula at Yosu and Sunchon in October 1948 conducted by the South Korean Constabulary; in the central region large numbers of houses had been burned in the areas of guerrilla support.[63] As well, Kevin Mahoney attributes the lack of an uprising to the fact that the need for secrecy about the invasion plan prevented southern supporters from being informed, "hence no preparations had been made to support it."[64] But according to Stanley Weintraub, substantial North Korean guerrilla units began filtering south in early June and surely must have some effect in carrying out their mission of disrupting transportation and communications when the fighting began.[65] In any case, some in the ranks of the northern army must have surmised that something beyond a reputed large scale exercise was about to take place when Russian military advisers were withdrawn from North Korean regiments.

An invasion did take place — on a Sunday, a time often employed by attackers at other times and places, a relaxed time for defenders when a third of its soldiers were on leave, sent home to work in the rice harvest.[66] It began early that morning — the same time of day and the same day of the week, of course, as did the Japanese assault on Pearl Harbor. (Sunday on an American army post is a day when even the birds remain silent.) Among the information about a northern attack was one provided by an informant about the formation of a large tank unit (in late May).[67] Louise Yim, for one, convinced that such an action was imminent, on her own initiative dispatched a few agents into the north who reported all the hallmarks of pending military action. They reported: "We saw tanks. We saw infantry. We saw planes. We saw whole villages, near the 38th Parallel, which have been emptied to make room for the soldiers." When she told President Rhee of her findings, he replied that his "Army Intelligence has not reported anything like this.... Anyway, I am sure that if we attack, the Northern soldiers would come over to us and their army would be defeated in a week or ten days."[68]

As the North Korean attack begun on June 25, 1950, was to show, in addition to Chinese support, the Russians had equipped the northern forces with tanks, fighter planes and heavy artillery, while the Americans gave none of these weapons to the southern army. This lack was due to two primary factors. There was the concern that if the southern army had heavy weapons it might attack the north to bring about Korean unification. A second consideration — in the vital matter of tanks — was the position voiced by General William Roberts, the U.S. general in charge of training the southern army since 1945, and his staff: the topography of the country, with its many rivers and mountains as well as its poor road capacity, made the terrain unsuitable to tank warfare. Moreover, the formation of a South Korean tank unit would require extensive training and the tank threat effectively could be countered by mine fields and anti-tank guns.[69]

There had been an attempt at defection by two South Korean battalions the previous year when some of their commanders led their troops across the border, but most of the ordinary soldiers quickly found their way back to the south.[70] Roberts joined with other members of his training staff when, at the beginning of 1950, he told William Sebald, U.S. diplomatic representative to Japan, that the South Korean (ROK) army "was excellent," only needing some more anti-aircraft guns, a few fast naval vessels and a dozen old P-51 fighter planes. Roberts also claimed that he could "hold the Commies" if they attacked. In March, however, he expressed private doubts about the matter. On the eve of the war, on June 15, the Korean Military Advisory Group (KMAG), of which Roberts was head, was emphatic in stating that, due to poor equipment and bare supplies, the South Korean Army would only be able to effectively defend for fifteen days.[71] At the same time the South Korean minister of defense privately confided to Sebald, "Much work remained to be done before the ROKs could match the North Koreans."[72]

In October 1949 U.S. Ambassador to Korea John Muccio was told of the clear advantages held by the northern army. A matter that had to have some impact was that all of the top leaders of this force had served in the Japanese Imperial Army, while the leaders in the North Korean force were hardened veterans of the Red Chinese and Russian armies.[73] Publicly at least, Roberts remained strong in his assessment of his "best shooting" little army. Departing for the United States just when the North Korean invasion began, Roberts reaffirmed his confidence that the army he had trained would defeat northern interlopers.[74]

This assessment was also given to presidential envoy John Foster Dulles during his Korean visit shortly before the war began.[75] According to William Stueck, to justify the withdrawal of U.S. troops there, "Army representatives deliberately overestimated South Korea's strength in comparison to North Korea." When Secretary of Defense Louis Johnson and Chairman of the Joint Chiefs of Staff Omar Bradley visited Korea and Tokyo a few days before the attack took place, MacArthur's staff informed them that the South Korean military could "maintain itself, unless the Soviets openly support[ed] North Korea in an armed invasion."[76] While they granted that the South Korean Army was lacking in tanks, artillery and more, U.S. Army advisors in Korea stressed the readiness and spirit of the Korean infantry. An officer in the South Korean Army, however, recalled that American advisors "rated one-third of our battalions combat-ready in 1950, and that was a generous assessment."[77]

As has been noted by several historians, events quickly demonstrated how wrong General Roberts' public professions were. Communist tanks— estimated at four hundred in number — not deterred by river crossings, had a devastating impact on South Korean troops. (Was he unaware of the long history of combat engineers installing pontoon and other temporary bridges?) The rapid defeat of the ROK Army revealed the grave deficiencies of the American training program. Although a promised rising of Communist supporters in the south did not materialize, the "People's Army" appeared well on its way to achieving the conquest of the south within the time frame of, at most, its six-weeks plan.[78] Stanley Sandler estimates that "many, perhaps most" South Korean troops changed sides.[79] Yet the South Korean Army did not entirely collapse and imposed heavy casualties on its opponent, a factor which became important in the extended conflict that resulted from U.S. intervention.[80] The fact that the U.S. military had to use American flesh and blood in the event is a depressing commentary on the failure of the U.S. Army training group in its creation of an army for the Republic of Korea.

According to Marguerite Higgins, there were more than 400 North Korean tanks, as opposed to the Tokyo command's estimate of 65, while James Minnich says there were 500 T-34 tanks. The number appears to have been 150 T-34s. In addition, the North Korea army had about a hundred fighter planes of varying quality.[81]

An Army at Rest

Then there was the U.S. military establishment in Japan. It had four combat divisions, second only to the forces in the continental United States, where there were five. There was only one in Germany. There was the general assumption that if there was to be another war it would be a major conflict with the Soviet Union in which nuclear bombs would be the primary weapon; thus, the primacy of the U.S. Air Force.[82] By all accounts, the army units were poorly equipped and under strength, with 43 percent of the enlisted ranks from the lowest category of education and having related attributes.[83] In volatile northern Asia, with the continuing rivalry with the Soviet Union as well as the emergence of a new and dynamic China and with increasing border clashes in Korea, the occupation troops seemed to be preoccupied with various recreational activities, which is the usual condition of peacetime occupation troops.

Some officers complained about the low standards of discipline, which they blamed on the recommendations of the post-war Doolittle Commission, sometimes called the "GI Gripe Board." Headed by air force hero General Jimmy Doolittle, popular with the enlisted ranks, the purpose of the commission was to examine a deluge of complaints by soldiers about the highly superior status assumed by many in the officer caste in that conflict.[84] If the largely vacationing enlisted men in Japan failed to adhere to the spit-and-polish standards of yesteryear, the Doolittle proposals apparently changed very little in the relationship between the commissioned and "other ranks" (British terminology here). A couple of practices signaling subordination persisted: the salute protocol (enlisted man initiates salute and holds it until officer ends it), the address of sir (sire?) to your betters, and other forms of medieval claptrap. Army recruit query: Why salute at all, why, sir? Answer: you are not saluting the man, but the uniform, which indicates authority.

With no new equipment forthcoming, one useful enterprise undertaken by the occupation army, Operation Roll-Up, was the recovery and repair of army vehicles and weapons in Japanese factories left over around the Pacific from World War II, but many of them were outdated and deficient. Recovered radio equipment often proved to be defective; explosives failed to explode; rust was merely painted over.[85] Retired Major General Julian Thompson paints a dismal picture of the situation in terms of both weapons and vehicles: the Eighth Army was supposed to have 225 recoilless rifles, but only had 21; "of the 18,000 jeeps and 4 × 4 trucks, 10,000 were unserviceable, and of 13,000 6 × 6 trucks only 4,441 were in running order." The supply situation was equally bad, with necessary supplies on hand lasting for an average of sixty days.[86]

John Michaelis recalls the situation on the ground in Korea. Commanding a regiment at the beginning of the conflict, Michaelis was not impressed by the material he received. The vehicles "were World War II surplus that had been junked, and we had to spend precious man-hours rebuilding them and servicing them to keep them rolling."[87] There was also a shortage of illuminating shells, and many of those that were available did not function. Added to this were tiny radios that were unsuited to the mountainous conditions in Korea, a shortage of 75 mm recoilless rifles, few C-rations and poor footwear.

None of the new weapons being developed got to Japan before the conflict erupted.[88]

When it came to air transportation there were only six of the workhorse C-54s available. A serious omission was in landing craft and other vessels. When the "balloon went up" the army had to resort to Japanese fishing boats and coastal bulk carriers for shipping many U.S. soldiers to Korea. Lyle Rishell got to Korea on a run-down, rusty ferry that he feared would not survive the journey.[89] The Eighth Army, the occupying force in Japan, in 1948 had an authorized strength of 87,215 while it actually numbered 45,561, with 43 percent of those in the Far East Command rated the lowest in capacity for service.[90] In what would seem to be the stupefied mentality of the high command, no one apparently saw that Korea was a most likely site of conflict and perhaps an exercise in transporting combat-ready units there (or at least having a plan for such an action) might be an appropriate activity. There was a 1948 Pentagon preliminary logistical study that obviously was not taken into consideration by the Far East Command and was never referred to when things happened. It apparently remained submerged in the dense debris of the command's archives.[91] Of course, even a small-scale exercise based on its proposal would have caused serious disruption of the very active sports program and other planned activities.

In 1949 MacArthur began reducing the policing role of the army, so, theoretically, all four divisions were reinforced for the purpose for which they existed.[92] F.R. Fehrenbach declares that these soldiers were utterly unprepared for action.[93] According to Max Hastings, MacArthur's "absolute lack of attention to the combat training of his divisions in Japan" can only be explained by MacArthur's oft-repeated belief that there was no danger of war.[94] A more authoritative voice was that of Matthew Ridgway, who declared in his memoirs, "The state of our Army in Japan at the outbreak of the Korean War was inexcusable."[95] Newly appointed as army chief of staff in 1949, Joe Collins went to Japan to inspect the Eighth Army there (the first such visitation since 1946). In his autobiography he said nothing about the results of his inspection, but was impressed by how he was received "most cordially," complete with "a magnificent military review in my honor." After an inspection tour in January–February 1950 the Joint Chiefs of Staff complimented MacArthur on "the present high standard" of his ground, sea and air units.[96] Who was going to give the five-star general a bad report? As well, high-level inspections of this sort are often little more than public relations exercises; moreover, the military has a predilection for elevated self-assessment. (How was morale? Required answer: excellent.) When Korea exploded into war and U.S. intervention began, Army Chief of Staff Joe Collins felt reassured that the location of this event was "fortunate" in that it was the one place in which the U.S. military was "well positioned" to respond. Respond it did, but as historian Kim Chum-kon noted, the United States "did not have so much as one combat-ready division to throw immediately into action." In *The American Occupation of Japan*, Michael Schaller strangely says nothing about the condition of the U.S. Army in Nippon nor anything about its subsequent involvement in Korea. Military forces occupy a place.[97]

In *Combat Ready?*, published in 2010, Thomas Hanson takes issue with the assessment that the Eighth Army was not ready for action. He points out that the various deficiencies of the Eighth were part of an overall condition of the U.S. Army at that time, especially the severe budget reductions of the Truman administration and the Congress. He takes note of the active training exercises carried on by the four divisions.[98] That may be the case, but the Eighth was essentially an occupation or garrison force. When the test of war occurred across the way, the army responded with an ad hoc, stumbling, thrown-together effort. With all that went before, and reversing the usual cliché, it seemed to have been a matter of wait, then hurry up.

On the eve of the Korean War Dean Acheson and Dean Rusk of the State Department advocated some sort of military action to shore up the U.S. position in Asia, particularly in regard to Japan, the assumption being that with Chinese Communists busily preparing an invasion, Formosa would be the focus of concern. Rusk, then Assistant Secretary of State for Far Eastern Affairs, declared on the eve of the North Korean invasion that South Korean forces could hold off a North Korean attack in the "unlikely" event that this should occur.[99] As has been seen, the strength of the U.S. Air Force in that theater had been temporarily depleted due to the transfer of many cargo planes for the Berlin airlift, the navy had experienced substantial budget reductions and the army certainly was not prepared for serious military action.

Despite initially dismissing the North Korean attack as merely another "border incident,"[100] MacArthur had some indications that North Korea was going to invade, but did nothing in response. In fact, all of the U.S. intelligence agencies were surprised when the attack came.[101] The South Korean Defense Ministry in May and June had warned that an attack was imminent, but these alerts were discounted in Tokyo as crying wolf.[102] When the U.S. military did intervene, overconfidence about its capabilities was obvious. At the beginning of the effort Douglas MacArthur, according to U.S. diplomatic representative to Japan William Sebald, was casual and confident. MacArthur believed that two American divisions would be adequate to "clear South Korea of Communist forces," and then the four divisions in Japan would be sufficient.[103]

This perception that the episode would result in an "easy war" was reflected down to the lower ranks, such as when PFC Robert Alip was told by his battalion commander that they should be back in Japan in two months (adding ominously, "Some of you won't be coming back").[104] Lyle Rishell recalls when he got to Korea in the first days of the conflict the "tremendous optimism" of the soldiers who were with him, summed up in the statement, "The American army would make short work of the 'gooks.'"[105] Some on the other side also anticipated a short war: there was a general assumption that the capture of Seoul would result in the collapse of the South Korean regime. For at least some American military people this kind of easy optimism was to be repeated fifteen years later regarding intervention in Vietnam.[106]

Various explanations have been provided for the poor state of readiness of the U.S. military in Japan. Much blame has been directed at the budget reductions imposed by the Truman administration beginning in 1949. Not surprisingly, the bulk of U.S. Army equipment were leftovers from the last war, notably the 2.6 bazooka, which had been already been shown to be ineffective against large German tanks.[107] But it does not take new equipment to generate basic combat readiness. Physical fitness, weapons training, field exercises and other ordinary army responsibilities are low-cost activities that are the minimum requirements of any military organization. Having spent a year in the Seventh Division in Japan just before the Korean War, Lyle Rishell experienced training programs that were "constant, well-organized and well executed." His division was in the far north of Japan, however, where there was plenty of space for field exercises, and it was cannibalized of equipment, troops and leadership at the beginning of the war, and was filled out by draftees and South Korean soldiers by the time it went into combat.[108]

Based on the evidence of that time, the occupation army in Japan was not combat ready. General Edward Almond, MacArthur's chief of staff, held that this condition was due to the inferior quality and resistance to discipline of peacetime recruits rather than the failure of army leadership, which, of course, included himself.[109] On the other hand, Thomas Hanson has concluded that the Eighth Army was in fine fettle at the time.[110] If this was the case, then the initial pathetic performance in throwing together a force to send to Korea was a failure of leadership, specifically that of the top brass.

General Walton Walker became commander of the Eighth Army in September 1948 — nearly two years before the outbreak of the Korean War — and tried to improve matters. How ineffective his efforts were was clearly demonstrated when U.S. Army soldiers were rushed into Korea in June 1950. If he was credited with being aggressive, forceful, indeed bullying, these qualities did not carry over to the state of his army on the eve of war. Walker's biographer notes the many difficulties that Walker faced in energizing his army, citing the fact that due to the lack of available land for field exercises, tanks were in storage.[111]

By all appearances it took the outbreak of war in Korea to break the lethargy, lack of discipline and general nonsense that infected the Eighth Army and its command. Then, everyone got busy, a common phenomenon in all organizations, not just military ones, in the wake of stark failure. After paying tribute to Walker's achievement in galvanizing resistance in the Pusan Perimeter, Max Hastings notes that Walker "was leading one of the least professional, least motivated armies that America had ever put in the field. Even many of its higher commanders seemed afflicted by bug out fever."[112] The initial group of U.S. soldiers thrown into the fight suffered the humiliation of being attacked by North Korean fighter planes and tanks. This was the force Walker had commanded for nearly two years before the war began.[113]

Along with other army leaders, Major General William Dean after Korea was scathing in his comments on the foolish mentality of the American troops in occupied Japan, where, he said, they had become accustomed to "Japanese girlfriends, plenty of beer, and servants to shine their boots."[114] What of the officer corps—looking forward to the next dinner or dance at the O Club (à la Pearl Harbor)? As the commander of the Twenty-Fourth Division, Dean shared in the failure of army readiness, which became clearly apparent when elements of his division were shattered by the attacking North Koreans. Together with other high-ranking officers seeking to rally the troops, Dean left his command post and joined in the combat, which resulted in the humiliation of his capture. After personally firing bazookas at North Korean tanks, he became detached from his unit and after five weeks behind the lines, was captured, thus becoming the highest-ranking American prisoner of war.[115]

Matthew Ridgway, who later took command of the Eighth Army, also was appalled by the poor condition of this force on the eve of the war and the almost inconceivable reluctance by Tokyo intelligence to recognize the clear indications that the North Koreans were about to do something serious.[116]

Then there was the position of Douglas MacArthur, who wore two hats— that of effective viceroy of Japan, reforming Japanese institutions of various sorts, and that of commander of Far Eastern U.S. forces. Deliberately avoiding any post-war return to the United States, with the likelihood of highly ceremonial but mandatory retirement, from all appearances MacArthur concentrated on his viceroy role, particularly the plan for a Japanese peace treaty that would provide for permanent U.S. bases there. Nevertheless, did it really take five years to re-order Japanese government and related matters? What about his military responsibilities? He repeatedly complained, rightly, about military budget reductions, but seemed indifferent or oblivious to the efficiency of his army. Was it that the great man was above being concerned about such mundane matters as troop readiness, or was it excessive preoccupation with his political responsibilities?

He was noted for having a cleared desk (without a telephone), but what, if anything, was going on in his mind during those years? He not only shunned staff meetings, but never attended army field exercises, restricting himself to occasionally reviewing meticulously ranked units who marched by him as he stood on the plaza of the Imperial Palace.[117] Now aged seventy, well past the retirement age for active-duty general officers, his career surely would come to an end with the looming Japanese treaty. John Muccio, U.S. ambassador to South Korea, compared MacArthur with Syngman Rhee and Chiang Kai-shek: "Ego was a dominant trait in each. As they grew older each became more and more isolated." Viewing MacArthur's leadership in Korea, Muccio noted that MacArthur "had gotten to the age where he was no longer in touch with the situation. And I think that was very, very evident in the developments in November and December in northern Korea." Muccio believed that when MacArthur during the conflict disregarded orders from President Truman, "he should have been removed long before — much earlier." In fact, for all his high-handed deportment and more, MacArthur was a time bomb primed to explode, which he finally did in early 1951. In the 1930s Franklin Roosevelt privately said MacArthur was the most dangerous man in America. In 1946 MacArthur twice fended off President Truman's suggestions that he come to Washington, and did the same in 1949. When the general was removed in April 1951, Averill Harriman, citing the 1949 episode, held that MacArthur should have been relieved at that time, and George Marshall agreed with him. The firing of MacArthur did not affect the military situation in Korea, but it certainly inflamed partisan politics at home.[118]

Anthony McAuliffe, of World War II Bastogne fame, while serving for a few months as commander of the Twenty-Fourth Infantry Division in Japan in 1949, noted that in that time MacArthur did not once visit his division. He told a reporter, "This army here is no damn good." Frustrated in his efforts to promote training in his unit, McAuliffe was pleased to being reassigned stateside. That reporter, Keyes Beech, observed that when the call to action came, soldiers "were almost literally snatched from under the quilts of their Japanese girl friends."[119] An officer in the occupation army, Charles Bussey, paints a damning picture of the Eighth Army at that time: poor discipline, almost nonexistent field training, drug and alcohol addiction, rampant vene-real disease, and black market operations.[120]

During the debacle of the retreat from the Yalu in late 1950 — except for a brief stop at Kimpo airport on December 11— MacArthur remained in Tokyo, but after things began looking up under Ridgway's command of the Eighth Army in early 1951 MacArthur began a series of mini-visits (sometimes of two hours' duration and much to Ridgway's growing annoyance), posing for pho-tographs and informing journalists about any good news there was to relate, even announcing offensive action before it took place. He never spent a night in Korea.[121] This was quite unlike the pattern of behavior of Dwight Eisenhower as supreme commander in Europe during World War II. After endless inspec-tions of training units, Ike liked to be up front with the troops, sleeping in a tent, and usually returning to his headquarters with a bad head cold. He also sometimes liked to take an ordinary soldier aside (outside the glare of the man's officers and sergeants) and ask him about conditions and complaints. How much Eisenhower's admonitions about equal treatment of enlisted men had an effect in lower headquarters is hard to say. In any case, this approach was clearly was not the style of "Dug-out Doug."[122]

The political role MacArthur assumed clearly led to his assumption that he was more than just an army commander, even if he was a five-star one. According to D. Clayton James, "It was as if MacArthur existed in Tokyo in a cocoon" and he was "quite shocked by the troops'" poor performances early in the Korean war.[123] More shocks, as well as triumphs, were to follow in due course. MacArthur told William Sebald that he considered that he held the status of a "sovereign." On August first he told Sebald that vast amounts of money "had been wasted upon frills and fancies which, in turn, mitigated against producing good soldiers."[124]

In his massive biography of the great man, William Manchester briefly mentions the flabby condition of American forces in occupied Japan and their initially incompetent performance in Korea, with the comment that their lack of readiness was because "no one dreamed that they would ever be needed," a strange comment to make about professional soldiers whose primary responsibility was to be prepared to practice their profession, which includes anticipating potential conflicts. Manchester quickly moves on to more exciting things, including page after page of MacArthur's musing on the Korean episode.[125] In his *First Call: The Making of the Modern U.S. Military, 1945–1953*, Thomas Boettcher briefly observes the "woeful unfitness" of the army personnel thrust into the fight, with no further commentary.[126]

MacArthur's failure to have his forces ready when the Korean War broke out is comparable to his disastrous preparation for the Japanese invasion of the Philippines before and after Pearl Harbor. Events quickly buried the questions about why there was this professional ineptitude. Was there any investigation, congressional or otherwise, of these failures? Rather than being censured for his profligate failings in the Philippines (where as a field marshal with a gold baton he had spent five years developing a Philippine army) he was awarded the (Congressional) Medal of Honor — for fleeing from the battle zone with his family. For that matter, was there any military utility for the reconquest of the Philippines begun in October 1944 and, island to island, extended for months into 1945, or was it more MacArthur vanity of the "I shall return" variety when the vital need was to strike, without diversion, at the Japanese heartland? In Korea he was hailed as a brilliant tactician for the Inchon invasion, but this was followed by catastrophe on the approaches to the Yalu.

In both cases political considerations dictated the decision to overlook MacArthur's repeated failings. If the Roosevelt administration had acted to lay responsibility for the quick defeat in the Philippines on MacArthur, in the wake of the Pearl Harbor disaster, this would clearly raise the matter of wholesale deficiency of the military commanders in those places, which inevitably would lead back to the involvement and responsibility of the administration. Better to sweep that all aside, under the carpet, and get on to the heroic, futile resistance on Bataan and the unfolding war.

The same phenomenon occurred in the matter of the gross lack of readiness of the Eighth Army when Korea erupted. Any detailed assessment of this condition would have focused on MacArthur and Walton Walker, but also would have led back to the severe cuts in military expenditures imposed by the Truman administration and Congress in 1949. There was no investigation here either; there was a war to be won.

From 1945 to the outbreak of the Korean War, MacArthur assumed the status of at least a mandarin, almost never traveling around Japan, leaving there only twice — a brief trip to the Philippines and a short visit to Seoul in 1948 for the launching of the Republic of Korea.[127] Omar Bradley later declared that MacArthur treated the Joint Chiefs "as if we were a bunch of kids" and while he acknowledged MacArthur's brilliance, he saw him as a "megalomaniac" who had "an obsession for self-glorification," almost no consideration for other men with whom he served, and contempt for the judgment of his superiors.[128]

With MacArthur in Tokyo was Major General Courtney Whitney, who had followed MacArthur to the pre-war Philippines, where he set up a private law practice until 1940 when he rejoined the army as a leading staff officer to MacArthur, a position he held until MacArthur was removed from command in 1951. In the Japanese occupation he was involved in the writing of the Japanese constitution, but his principal occupation was that of MacArthur confidant and adviser, indeed, his alter-ego. In Korea he accompanied MacArthur on his one-day sorties there. Some journalists regarded him as "abrasive, aloof, opportunistic, lickspittle and pompous, not to mention stupid"[129]; surely, he must have had some redeeming qualities. After MacArthur was fired Whitney followed him into retirement, where he became his secretary and wrote a wholly uncritical account of MacArthur's military genius.[130]

MacArthur's chief of staff was Edward Almond, who during World War II had commanded an all-black division in Italy, whose failures Almond blamed entirely on its troops, while absolving himself of any responsibility. Having served in the Philippines near the end of the war (and thus become a late-joining member of MacArthur's coterie of the "Bataan gang"), he was appointed chief of personnel on MacArthur's staff in Japan. From this relatively minor position he rose to be chief of staff to MacArthur. Perhaps a key to Almond's rise was his assessment of his superior: he believed MacArthur was "the greatest man alive." Extravagant praise of the boss is usually a good idea, but Almond's unbridled hero-worship would be seen as excessive and even counter-productive, although not by MacArthur.[131] Forceful and energetic, he became totally an instrument of MacArthur's will. Roy Appleman declares that Almond combined "a driving energy and a consuming impatience with incompetence," while David Halberstam, noting Almond's disastrous conduct of operations in northeast Korea at the end of 1950 and then later his muddled conduct of his corps in the central region at the beginning of 1951, declared that many of those who served with Almond believed it had been the "one big mistake" of Matthew Ridgway that he had not relieved or at least transferred Almond. Yet this would have been difficult, as Almond was still MacArthur's chief of staff.[132] Strongly opposed to racial integration of the army, Almond did nothing to implement President Truman's 1948 ban of racial discrimination in the army. In this matter, as in all others, he followed MacArthur's position: nothing was done.

When MacArthur put into operation his grand strategy of two maritime invasions, he assured direct control of his chosen instrument, the X Corps, by making Almond the independent commander of it. After leading a successful incursion at Inchon on the west coast in September 1950, Almond led a similar operation on the east coast beginning in October. The Inchon operation was a straightforward, direct twenty-mile thrust to Seoul, while the east-coast venture was a much larger, sprawling affair that proved to be well beyond Almond's ability. In both operations Almond clashed with O.P. Smith, the commander of the First Marine Division.[133]

Then there was MacArthur's chief of intelligence. German-born and with an originally German name, Major General Charles Willoughby, when he was not overseeing the preparation of a massive narrative of the victorious Pacific campaign (which would have featured his boss), is said to have tailored intelligence reports to suit the perspective of his boss, a not-unheard-of method employed by subordinates[134]; moreover, he has been charged with doctoring and distorting them. One staff member declared, Willoughby "falsified the intelligence reports.... He should have gone to jail."[135] Major General Robert Eichelberger has observed the many times Willoughby misread Japanese strengths during the Pacific war.[136] Willoughby had been MacArthur's intelligence head since 1941, and historian H.A. DeWeerd has noted that the usual practice was to change staff officers about every four years. DeWeerd's 1951 conclusion: "A few fresh minds on the intelligence staff in Tokyo seem called for even at this late hour."[137] It is chilling to note how often Willoughby's intelligence conclusions were wrong.

Generally speaking, military intelligence is not an oxymoron, as has been sometimes claimed, but a dysfunctional unit can lead to disaster. In the Far East on the eve of the Korean War such was the case. During the Pacific war Douglas MacArthur had kept the Office of Strategic Services out of his domain, and its successor organization, the Central Intelligence Agency, only had a minor presence in Japan — three members in a Tokyo hotel room.[138] Through its agents in North Korea and China, however, the C.I.A. came to the conclusion that the North Koreans "could mount a coordinated attack at any time," yet it believed that a North Korean attack would only achieve a limited, short-term incursion. Admiral Roscoe Hillenkoetter, the CIA director, sent such a report to Truman officials, including the president, five days before the attack came. MacArthur relied on his intelligence staff alone, and this probability was not accepted. According to Stanley McGowen, MacArthur's intelligence surmised that all the North Korean activity just above the 38th parallel at that time probably was some sort of agricultural project.[139] One difficulty in trying to figure out what was going there was that the North Koreans, in assembling their forces, used couriers rather than radio transmission. It must have been noted by some intelligence observers in the months leading up to the attack that the Soviets were pouring military equipment into the north and that the 7,000-man group of Russian military advisors there was a clear signal that something was afoot. But a major problem had arisen — the ability to read secret Soviet military transmissions had ceased in 1948. At that time, alerted to the situation by an American spy that U.S. cryptographers were reading their transmissions, the Soviets changed to a new and as-yet unbreakable cipher system.[140]

Another aspect of the intelligence situation was that resources for this function had been substantially reduced, while each of the four armed forces had its own intelligence unit that reported to its own high command. There seems to have been little coordination between them or with MacArthur's staff.[141] This dysfunctional state of affairs surely was a factor in the complete failure to anticipate that something was about to happen next door. There was no alert, there was no formation of a crisis response unit or whatever it could be called. Where was the contingency plan for this possibility? On that Sunday morning at the four army divisions in Japan all was peaceful and quiet. It was Douglas MacArthur in the Philippines all over again. During the course of the Korean War there were two important intelligence assessments that had to be made, the other one being the likelihood of Chinese intervention, and MacArthur's intelligence people got them both wrong.[142]

American intelligence operatives in North Korea seemed to be remarkably deficient, both before and during the conflict. The difficulties for American intelligence to penetrate Korea were many: due to "an alien land in which we had no ties of culture or blood or language, the work was often nearly impossible."[143] After the army's evacuation of South Korea, Willoughby retained a small intelligence group in Seoul (under the cover name of the Korean Labor Organization) with agents in the north, which he believed would keep him informed about developments, but, in the event, proved to be totally ineffectual.[144] According to John Dille, a notable exception to this picture of incompetence was an American officer ("Bill") who had spent six years— to 1951— traveling around Korea, learning the language, and had built up a tightly knit and loyal cadre of agents. Dille believes Bill's achievement was great: "He was our only solid link with North Korea, and it was his advice and inside information that were responsible, more than anything else, for our ability to stay there, against the tremendous odds and under the immense confusion which marked the early days."[145]

As we shall see, "Bill" most probably was Don Nichols, who fits this description perfectly. Nichols rightly claims that his unit was the only one that accurately predicted the outbreak. Despite the unit's previous accurate predictions, Nichols' signal was not acted upon.[146] As the war progressed, the U.S. military did create bases on the western islands in North Korea, from which intelligence and sabotage operations were launched. Unable to penetrate to the Communist main supply routes, these operations had little more than nuisance value, but they did tie up a lot of enemy troops.[147] John Singlaub recalls an air force sergeant operating out of the west coast island who cut a cable under the Yellow Sea, which disrupted telecommunications between the Chinese headquarters and Beijing, forcing Beijing to rely on radio communication, which was shortly penetrated by "our crypto specialists."[148]

In his examination of the intelligence failure, Singlaub has declared that the Central Intelligence Agency submitted several reports, forwarded by agents in Manchuria, of active northern military activities on the eve of the attack, but they were given the lowest designation of reliability by Willoughby.[149] This did not prevent Admiral Roscoe Hillenkoetter, the CIA director, from informing both the military and political leaders in Washington of the agency's dire information. After the fact, Dean Acheson claimed he had not received such information, but Hillenkoetter provided evidence, based on signatures on reports received, that Acheson and other leaders had got the reports.[150] Singlaub's account is in stark contrast to that of some chroniclers of the war, one of whom, David Esposito, asserts that the CIA gave scant attention to Korea in the six months leading up to the invasion and that it failed to anticipate the outbreak of the war.[151] Spencer Tucker condemns the CIA for not assessing Communist intent on its eve.[152] As well, the CIA report of June 19, 1950, held that even if the North Koreans attacked, under existing conditions, they would be unable to take over all of South Korea.[153] There had been a series of false alarms, some of which were transmitted by the South Korean Defense Ministry, which led Omar Bradley and, initially, Douglas MacArthur to believe that what began on June 25 was just another border clash. Yet based on the findings of the CIA would it not have been prudent to issue an alert by the Far East Command and the South Korean Army? At the least, this would have provided an exercise in preparation. In the event, it would appear that a scapegoat was needed; blame for the intelligence fiasco was heaped on the CIA, and Hillenkoetter was replaced as its director in October.[154]

Looking at the big picture and figuratively shaking his head, Max Hastings has commented, "Only five years after the end of World War II, the victors found themselves embarrassingly, absurdly pressed to find the resources with which to fight a limited war in Asia." The condition of the U.S. Army in Japan was so bad, he observed, "For months to come, as America mobilized, her military effort in the Far East would be a patchwork of expedience and improvisation."[155] In 1948 Omar Bradley had proposed the creation of a mobile strike force to address military emergencies, but this did not happen.[156]

One of the expectations for the North Korean invasion of the south made by Joseph Stalin and Kim Il Sung was that rapid and total success would be achieved before the United States could effectively intervene; Kim thought this could be achieved in three to four weeks.[157] Stalin had been informed by spies in the United States that the Americans would not take such an action. If the United States did take action, surely a further consideration must have been the ability of American forces in Japan to do so effectively. There were many Communist informants in Japan who provided assessments, and surely their reports would have noted the lack of U.S. military readiness, which must have encouraged the Communist leaders to proceed with their venture.[158] What was public knowledge was that some air transport capacity had been removed from MacArthur's command beginning in the autumn of 1948 for the Berlin airlift. One Communist estimate was that it would take at least fifty days before the U.S. military could effectively intervene.[159] No matter their state of readiness, there were four American infantry divisions, with air bases galore, just across the way in Japan; flight time: three to four hours.

Ten days after the beginning of the conflict the most that the Eighth Army could muster into Korea was a ragtag group of 500 infantrymen (sans tanks and artillery) in an *ad hoc* "task force" to face "a hundred times as many enemy troops, with T-34 tanks and artillery." The lack of U.S. armor was partially addressed by Col. Olaf Winningstad, 8th Army Ordnance chief, who shortly after the beginning of the conflict managed to rebuild three inoperative M26 Pershing medium tanks that arrived in Korea on July 16 but were soon destroyed and their crews killed or captured.[160] Things had reached such a sorry state that MacArthur told John Muccio, U.S. ambassador to South Korea, on July 29 that there were no further ground forces under his command and it would take four or five weeks to get reinforcements from the United States.[161]

It is most likely that there would have been no Korean War if the Truman administration and its military leaders had not followed a muddled policy. In the late 1940s the military high command had written off South Korea as an essential part of U.S. military security. This was followed by Dean Acheson's unfortunate January 1950 statement omitting South Korea as part of America's defense perimeter in northern Asia. With regard to South Korea, Acheson made the curious assertion that should it be threatened the United States could turn to the United Nations, which would call forth "the commitments of the entire civilized world" which "had not proved to a weak reed to lean on." The U.N. not a weak reed? In the post-war period what effective action had this international body taken to deal with one political entity attacking another? It should be recalled, however, that Acheson's statement also excluded Formosa, yet the Rhee government was greatly alarmed by Acheson's statement.[162] There was no uncertainty about South Korea in the mind of Senator Tom Connally, chairman of the Foreign Relations Committee, who in May 1950 declared that the fall of South Korea to the Communists was inevitable and since the place was "not absolutely essential" the United States should be prepared to abandon it.[163]

Already there were the administration's severe budget reductions of 1949. There were a variety of reasons for cutting back military expenditures. Based on his experience as chairman of a Senate committee that investigated waste and profiteering during World War II, Harry Truman was convinced that this pattern would recur with a big military buildup. The extent of the cutbacks was striking. The army had a total of 6.1 million soldiers in ninety divisions in August 1945, which plunged to 592,000 troops and ten divisions by June 1950, and similar reductions took place in the other armed forces.[164] Although much of the military was concentrated in northern Asia, in Japan the army had 108,000 personnel, in four divisions that were understrength, poorly trained and badly equipped.[165]

From Truman's perspective, more money for the military would mean less for his important social program objectives, including comprehensive national health insurance. After both active war and reserve service as an officer (retiring as a colonel in the Missouri National Guard in 1938), Truman nevertheless had an aversion to what he saw as the machinations of the top brass, and, as time was to show, this attitude extended to Douglas MacArthur, who found reasons to decline Truman's twice repeated invitation in 1946 to return to the United States for consultations. Truman made known his dislike of what he saw as the Marine Corps publicity campaign.[166] An overriding assumption concerning the need for maintaining conventional military forces was the predominant belief, shared by many civilian and military leaders, that any new war would be a matter of atomic weapons and the air force.[167]

Ex-army chief of staff Dwight Eisenhower was convinced that not enough money had been given to the military for defense needs. Yet the difference between what had been appropriated — 13 billion dollars — and what Eisenhower wanted — 15 billion dollars — was not so great. At the same time, however, the United States commitment to the new North Atlantic Treaty would soon require a greatly expanded military commitment to western Europe.[168] What was in the minds of Harry Truman and his advisors? That a greatly expanded American presence in western Europe would counter Soviet ideas about expansion in that direction? In any case, Korea was not completely ignored: in March 1950 the United States agreed to provide the Seoul government with ten million dollars' worth of military aid, but nothing of substance arrived before the North Koreans invaded.[169] The Communist regime in Pyongyang thus was provided with a window of opportunity: strike before the vital augmentation of the South Korean Army had occurred. Another factor was the lack of a clear policy statement that the United States would fight to protect South Korea.

On the very eve of the North Korean attack John Foster Dulles, in his characteristically pontifical manner, told the South Korean government, "You are not alone," but when Syngman Rhee asked for a defense treaty, Dulles said that was not necessary — the "free world" would respond to an attack on South Korea. Dulles had already conferred with the leaders of some countries about the possibility of a "Pacific Pact" security alliance.[170] By this time the Pyongyang strategists, obviously guided by their Russian advisors, went ahead, confident of a quick victory before the largely somnolent U.S. military in Japan could effectively respond.

Despite this picture of cutbacks and lack of preparedness, a major shift in global policy was in the works. In April 1950 the National Security Council produced an assessment (NSC-68) that recommended a massive increase in military spending, tripling the defense budget. With the Korean War already underway, President Truman approved the proposal in September 1950. Without doubt, it took the obvious example of Communist aggression in Korea to bring about a major financial turnabout and to rally support in the Congress and the public for such a program. For the immediate and short-term needs of Korea, however, it was too little, too late.

In the spring of 1950 there were strong indications of North Korean preparations for an invasion, but these were discounted by American military intelligence in Japan. When on May 10 the South Korean defense minister declared that Communist forces were gathering at the 38th parallel, the army high command at the Pentagon agreed with MacArthur that an attack was not pending.[171] A two-man Australian observation team, which seemed to be mostly concerned about South Korea attacking the north, concluded in a report completed on the eve of the war that despite some reports of increased activity north of the border, "No reports, however, had been received of any unusual activity on the part of the North Korean forces that would indicate any imminent change in the general situation on the parallel."[172] U.S. Army intelligence concluded North Korean movement just north of the 38th parallel was merely "a long-standing Communist practice of rotating the locations of their best-equipped units."[173]

The best that the Central Intelligence Agency could do was to provide contradictory assessments of the likelihood of a northern invasion. In its report of June 19, based on material dated May 15, it noted discontent in the north, which it believed would reduce the ability of the Communists to take over the south. Yet it saw the large military force assembled there: an army of 66,000, including 16,000 of Manchurian background, and a border constabulary of 20,500, while another 60,000–70,000 ex–Korean soldiers were "available" in Manchuria.[174] U.S. Ambassador John Muccio was confident about the prospects of the South Korean Army, declaring it had made "enormous progress during the past year." He supported the plan to reduce by half the U.S. military advisory group, from 472 personnel to 242.[175]

When the North Koreans struck, Harry S. Truman reversed years of apparent ambivalence about the U.S. commitment to South Korea by promptly ordering military support to stop this action. Had the Truman administration made it clear that this would be its response to such an event, there would have been no North Korean attack, no Korean War. In several penetrating observations about the Korean saga, John Wilz firmly comes to this conclusion. Furthermore, and surely correctly, he argues that if even a small U.S. Army force had remained in South Korea the Communists would not have moved.[176]

A First World Army

Some revisionist historians have questioned whether the outbreak of the Korean War was the sole responsibility of North Korea. Citing a variety of border incursions carried out by both sides in the run-up to June 25, 1950, Bruce Cumings is unable to conclude that it was initiated only by the Communist regime in Pyongyang.[177] The evidence, however, is overwhelming that North Korea, with the Soviet Union's direction, developed a thorough war plan and implemented it. This was the conclusion of the U.S. government and it quickly moved to gain acceptance of this assertion at the United Nations. Support for this position by the U.N. Security Council was expedited by the boycott by the Soviet Union (in protest of the exclusion of Red China from the organization) of its proceedings. Even if the Soviet Union had vetoed the resulting resolution, however, the General Assembly could have passed a similar measure.[178]

There would have been no North Korean attacks without the approval and support of the Soviet Union and the consent of Communist China. With the communist victory in China in 1949, the Korean communist movement saw this venture as further fulfillment of communist expansion in Asia. At the same time that the Soviet Union withdrew its forces from North Korea in 1948, it sent a high-level military advisory group to Pyongyang. In 1949 it gave the North Korean regime a forty million dollar credit to buy Russian arms, almost all of which were of World War II vintage. It did not make a formal military treaty with the North — this would link the Soviets too closely to any consequent actions by the North. For long, Joseph Stalin was reluctant to give his support, fearing the United States response. In January 1950 Stalin told Kim that the proposed attack "requires through preparation. It has to be organized in such a way that there will not be a large risk."[179] The following April, with Kim and his staff sequestered in Moscow, Stalin gave his direct approval, began pouring military equipment into North Korea, and dispatched more military advisors to Pyongyang to prepare an invasion plan.[180]

A factor that must have mitigated Stalin's concern was the achievement of the Soviet Union in exploding an atomic bomb in August 1949 (the development of the weapon being speeded by Soviet spies in the United States and Britain).[181] As John Gaddis has noted, that event gave the Soviets the opportunity to develop this weapon before the Americans could stockpile enough

An executed U.S. soldier, one of four found on July 10, 1950. Courtesy National Archives, 111-SC-343302 [PRS].

A-bombs to give them a clear superiority in a nuclear war.[182] Surely this was a factor in Stalin's giving his approval for the North Korean attack the next year. Communist espionage also was responsible for securing vital information on the development of jet aircraft. Beginning in November 1950, the U.S. Air Force was shocked when Soviet MiG-15 jet fighters not only flew rings around U.S. propeller-driven aircraft but were conspicuously superior to the first generation of American jets as well.[183]

White Allies

In the wake of the North Korean invasion, the United Nations sanctioned involvement and, moreover, urged member states to provide fighting forces to oppose North Korean aggression. With minor exceptions, only a few European countries and those with European populations did this, and their contingents were small. Britain sent the largest number, averaging about 9,000 from all services at any one time, followed by Canada with almost 27,000 and Australia with 15,000 (in both cases that number rotated at various times), New Zealand with an average of 1,000 soldiers and 1,300 sailors on two frigates, battalions from the Netherlands and Belgium, with South Africa proving a small air fighter formation.[184] The independent countries of European population in the British Commonwealth aligned their forces into a Commonwealth Division.[185] Its troops earned excellent reputations as effective fighters, but had one unique feature in that they usually declined to wear helmets even in combat, which surely increased the danger of shrapnel wounds.[186]

The much smaller, token number from France, Greece, Belgium, Luxembourg and the Netherlands could be justified by the need to expand western European military capacity under the terms of the new North Atlantic Treaty, with France being preoccupied with the Communist-led rebellion in Vietnam.[187] Few of these contingents arrived until the beginning of 1951, and even then only 9,000 arrived of the 29,000 promised. At their peak they amounted to about 4 percent of U.N. ground troops. The U.S. State Department without result sought additional support. The requirement of the Far East Command in the spring of 1951 that arriving forces must have their own artillery, logistic and administrative capacity hindered efforts to increase participation in the cause.[188]

From the edge of Europe came a 5,000-man brigade from Turkey, with all their knives and bayonets sharpened.[189] Only two Asian nations— the Philippines and Thailand — along with Ethiopia and Columbia (courtesy of its military dictator), provided any, albeit tiny, forces, while India, Denmark, Sweden, Norway and Italy volunteered hospital units. For political reasons it was important for the U.N. effort to have at least the veneer of international support. For a military viewpoint, however, these small contingents probably were more trouble than they were worth. There were many difficulties involved: language barriers, varying diets, unit coordination, differences in weapons and more. In October 1950, when all was going well, Omar Bradley asked MacArthur what he intended to do with the slowly arriving European contingents. "They are useless [now] from a military point of view and probably would never see action," was the reply, but MacArthur appreciated the political aspect of them. Due to diplomatic considerations, these offers could not be turned down.[190] With full success looming, in late October the Joint Chiefs proposed reducing the size of contingents from these other countries.[191] As events demonstrated, however, those who came certainly found action. The commander of the Philippine 1,500-soldier force was removed after he complained that his men had not been given winter clothing.[192] The language barrier and lack of effective communications led the Turkish brigade to initial disaster.[193]

Largely due to United Nations sanction of the action, political support for the U.S.-led campaign against the North Korean invasion received general support in Britain, yet Max Hastings makes this curious claim: "It was only with the deepest reluctance that the British government and chiefs of staff at last agreed to send a token ground force to Korea."[194] In the event, they provided two battalions, which, joined with an Australian battalion, constituted a Commonwealth Brigade of about 5,000 personnel present at a time.[195] Given Britain's deep dependence on American financial backing for the British currency and the British government's frequent claim of a favored and close relationship to the United States, as well as the need to support the decision of the United States to build a much enlarged military presence in western Europe, Hastings's assertion of reluctance can best be seen in the light of the meager British forces available for this involvement. Given these economic and political realities, the UK government had no choice but to respond to the American request.[196] The British contribution, however, did provide London with some leverage in determining U.N. policy. Certainly not alone in this regard, the British military had not prepared for the Korean outbreak: territorial army reserve units had to be activated; when the first small British contingent arrived from Hong Kong in late August, it lacked artillery, rations and adequate supplies.[197] With cobbled-together transport, others trickled in over the next months. The resulting two British regiments, combined with an Australian battalion and the small New Zealand contingent, formed the Commonwealth Division, comprised about 3 percent of the U.N force.[198] Due to initial difficulties, there was evidence of some lack of harmony within the unit at the beginning. A more serious difficulty stemmed from Lieutenant General John "Iron Mike" O'Daniel, the corps commander, who objected to what he saw as the division's level of independence and flexibility and tried to impose U.S. operating procedures. The division's leadership successfully resisted O'Daniel's efforts, and it was left to operate as it saw fit.[199]

Although there were many conscripts (draftees) in the ranks, the British regiments demonstrated a high degree of discipline and training, with attachment to one's regiment being fundamental in troop indoctrination. Their most valuable contribution was in their frequently employed role of providing bloody rear guard protection. One American officer greeting the first British arrivals declared, "Glad you British have arrived — you're the real experts at retreating." For their part, some British officers were appalled by the lack of military security in the American ranks, with, for example, casual relationships between officers and enlisted men, journalists with a free run of unit headquarters, and American soldiers telephoning their girlfriends in Japan. Disturbed by the determined informality of many U.S. soldiers, on one British post a message was prominently displayed: "Military courtesy enforced on this compound," which, among other things, meant saluting and addressing as "sir" any officer in sight. The British assessment of American military competence did not improve with time.[200]

France provided diplomatic support for the American action, but only a single battalion. The French military already were deeply involved in attempting to defeat the Communist-led insurrection in Vietnam and were increasingly dependent on U.S. military equipment and supplies. When the United States entered the Korean conflict, the Truman Administration substantially expanded this assistance.[201]

The growing French debacle in Indochina, including Vietnam, drew the attention of wise old George Kennan, who told Acheson on August 21, "We are getting ourselves into the position of guaranteeing the French in an undertaking which neither they nor we, nor both of us together, can win." Kennan argued that the French position was "basically hopeless"; he advised, "We should do everything in our power to avoid embarrassing the French ... and to support them in any reasonable course they would like to adopt looking to its liquidation."[202]

At the Wake Island meeting of October 1950 both MacArthur and Truman expressed their displeasure about what the French were doing in Vietnam. With a large body of troops facing apparently weak opposition, MacArthur declared, "I cannot understand why they do not clean it up. They should be able to do so in four months." He saw the need for an aggressive commander there. According to Dean Rusk, MacArthur "contrasted the Indochinese situation sharply with Korea and left the impression that our problem in Korea was more difficult from a military point of view than the problem faced by the French." Truman expressed his frustration in getting the French to move to Vietnamese independence. Admiral Arthur Radford put his finger on the problem when he declared, "The French seem to have no popular backing from the local Indo-Chinese." Averill Harriman, diplomat for all seasons, noted, "The French hold a key position both in Europe and Asia," but said, "The French must change their attitude relative to Indo-China." After the massive Chinese assault beginning in November the matter of Vietnam came up again, this time at an important meeting in Washington on December 3. George Marshall, now secretary of defense, raised the matter, pointing to what he saw as the "dilemma of the French there and the resulting French attitude." Dean Acheson declared, "The French are so weak and shell-shocked they are anxious for a deal which would give an illusion of safety." In the opinion of Dean Rusk, "The French would try to get a deal with Ho and then withdraw. They would not stay firm except with a solid U.N. front." This assessment of the French problem in Vietnam was offered at a time when U.S. forces in Korea had been driven onto the ropes by the Chinese.

Despite the dire situation, the French military was prepared to soldier on. Five days after this conference the French ambassador renewed his request that the United States provide an aircraft carrier "which might be used most effectively in the gulf of Tonkin." At the end of the month the French U.N. representative told Warren Austin, the U.S. representative, that France was only fighting in Vietnam to stop the spread of communism. If Red China gave full support to Vietnamese communists the fall of Indochina "was quite certain," and would mean that the "rest of SE Asia (Nepal, Burma, Thailand, Indonesia) would fall very quickly to Communists and in turn India would not be far behind." If the United States made the determination that Vietnam could be held this would require "very substantial help from the US." The situation dragged along, with the United States seriously considering sending in its air force, until the final French fiasco at Dien Bien Phu in May 1954.[203]

Most of the British military and the lesser contributions from France and a few other European countries did not arrive until late in the year, by which time it was obvious that the U.S. forces were in the process of crushing the North Korean invaders. Thomas Boettcher observes that their "leaders now eagerly wanted to have a role in the victory." When the tide turned with Chinese intervention in November 1950 American appeals for more troops from its allies were unavailing.[204]

What happened in Korea began as a violent internal conflict in an Asian country that was followed by the intervention of a mostly European-related nation (allowing a 10 percent mix of people of African descent), principally supported by European countries (Britain, and to a much smaller degree, France and the Netherlands) that had long intervened in and occupied a variety of Asian countries. Although European domination of large parts of Asia was in the process of dissolution, the history of European exploitation was clearly known to discerning Asians. Communist propagandists could make a plausible case this was European imperialism all over again. This was followed by the entrance in the war of another Asian people: the Chinese. Although there were many Asians (the South Koreans and the Turks) who, for their own reasons, fought alongside with the Europeans, the conflict can be seen as one of white people versus yellow people. In this respect the wartime motto of the Japanese — Asia for the Asians — was part of the mix that was the Korean War.

Looking at the early course of the conflict, when the American military was effectively employed in South Korea it soon defeated the North Korean Army and then faced the ominous decision about going north of the 38th parallel. Once that decision was made the United States was confronted by repeated Chinese Communist statements that it would intervene, which it did. At this critical juncture — in late September 1950 — representatives of the Soviet Union began proposing that the conflict should end with the defeat of North Koreans and their flight back to where they came from: the 38th parallel. The Indian government was also active in seeking in a halt to the conflict on that basis. Had that happened the Korean episode would have fulfilled the objective of firmly defeating aggression in a three-month campaign. Given the crumbling of North Korean opposition, the U.S. State Department did not choose to pursue this possibility.

Although America's allies were wary about the matter, the combination of military, political and public opinion to go north was, in William Stueck's words, "nearly irresistible." After the dramatic success of the Inchon action and the subsequent breakout from the Pusan Perimeter, and choosing to ignore the possibility of Soviet intervention and the much more likely Chinese risk, the United States (again in Stueck's words) "embarked on a dangerous course in Korea before exploring prospects for an advantageous settlement." Before the Chinese onslaught of late November 1950, the Joint Chiefs of Staff, concerned about the wide dispersal of U.N. forces and within their authority for providing guidance, asked Dean Acheson to request President Truman to issue a directive that military units should be consolidated. This was not done. MacArthur estimated that his forces could complete the occupation of the north in ten days, while the army head of supply (G-4) on September 26, declaring that "present indications are that hostilities in Korea may end at an early date (VK-day)," was concerned with reducing the oversupply of munitions and equipment. The prevailing opinion in the army was that the Chinese would not intervene in effective force, but some "low key" consideration was given that this might happen. An October 11 estimate by the Operations Division (G-3) held that if the Chinese attacked in force, U.S. and South Korean forces could meet this challenge, but it would be a "tight" situation. Although infantry "fillers" were still arriving, it noted that substantial reinforcements would not be available for months, which did not enhance the immediate position.[205]

The land into which American troops were being poured was a peninsula that began with low-lying land at its southern tip and rose up to rugged hills in the middle and mountains in the east. Marine Corporal Harold Mulhausen commented, "One thing never changed in Korea — the hills. They all looked about the same, and there was always one more we had to take." Army Sergeant James Hart had a similar experience: "Korea is just one hill and one mountain after the other, and since we also carried about eighty pounds of equipment, soldiering in Korea was pretty exhausting. Most of us required another six to eight weeks after arriving to get in top condition."[206]

When Rene Cutforth arrived in central Korea in December 1950 he noted the "extraordinary skyline. The hills— and they were not much more than 2000 feet high — were like nothing I'd seen in my life so much as the fantastic backgrounds to Walt Disney's fairy stories. They were the most improbable hills that went straight up and down like a row of spikes or sharks' teeth.... Wherever you were in Korea, the sharks'-tooth peaks encircled you. They might be close up or far away, but they were always visible and always the same."[207] A French soldier had the same experience. Jean Larteguy remembered, "How I sweated and struggled my way over those peaks of Korea! Forever climbing and crawling my way up, achieving one crest and then seeing from there all the other crests and mountains we'd have to take sooner or later; mountains that lifted themselves serenely into infinity all the way to Siberia."[208]

Weather conditions also were challenging, to say the least. American soldiers, many of them unfit, arriving in July 1950 were confronted with extreme heat as well as the pervading smell of rice paddies laced with all kinds of excrement. The monsoon season resulted in massive rainfall. In addition to other needs, fresh water was in great demand, the local water usually not being potable. In the summer the primitive Korean road system generated heaps of dust that clung to everything and everybody; in the rainy season there was deep mud to contend with. Four months later, as the troops drove north they were confronted with the bitter Korean winter. There seemed to be a pattern to it — two days of very cold but calm weather followed by three days of brutal Siberian arctic ones.[209]

Cutforth described the impact of the bad days: "Its effect on the human spirit was a curious one: it created fear — a quite generalized fear which sapped every kind of morale. I have stood in this wind feeling so small and helpless that I was ready to cry with self pity. It was such an implacable foe. It never let up. It sought you out and wore you down, it was like being nagged beyond endurance."[210] Serving in a Marine infantry company in the winter of 1951–52, James Brady recalls the bitter temperatures: "How could you ever get warm if the cold w[as] inside you?" He also saw a positive side to it: "Both snow and cold discouraged fighting and kept both armies calm if not actually peaceful."[211] This situation seemed to have prevailed one bitter night in an army infantry company who voted to "build fires and chance being shot" rather than "do without fires and chance freezing to death." They had a peaceful night with frozen opponents.[212]

The United States contributed almost all the material, but also about 90 percent of the manpower of the U.N. force, which about matched the number of South Korean troops. As was the case in the Pacific war against Japan, the alignments were essentially racial, with white and black Americans coming to the aid of the crumbling South Korea military, and, on the other side, all Asians opponents—first Koreans and later Chinese. From one perspective, the conflict could be viewed as a final effort of white men to maintain control in at least one part of Asia. The U.N. connection provided the political backing to the enterprise, while the military link involved little more than shuffling reports and other material back and forth between the American headquarters in Tokyo and the U.N. Secretariat.

The opening assault of the North Korean Army is usually seen as having a devastating effect of the South Korean military. Now that it had substantial Soviet equipment, the northern "People's Army" had a massive advantage: twice as many troops and artillery, seven times as many heavy machine guns, six and a half times as many armored vehicles and six times as many planes.[213]

Before the war, to make up for the lack of fighter aircraft, a public campaign in South Korea was mounted to purchase ten of them, but they arrived disarmed. To overcome in a small way the lack of bombers, light reconnaissance planes dropped boxes of explosives.[214] Some ROK units, although ill-equipped and poorly led, did effectively resist. For example, Jiyul Kim notes that the ROK Sixth Division blunted the initial North Korean attempts to envelop Seoul and, arguably, "the defensive success there brought time for the disintegrating front to consolidate, and the subsequent delaying actions allowed the entry of U.S. forces."[215]

Seoul was captured four days after the invasion began. North Korean officer Ju Young-bok was surprised to find that the South Korean Army had not prepared to invade the north, as he had been told, but that the "puppet troops fought well despite their inferior weapons."[216] American journalist O.H.P. King, who was on the scene, declares that many South Korean soldiers fought until they ran out of ammunition, with at least some of them retreating to rejoin forces further south.[217] Nevertheless, the rout was on. What defense plan the South Korean Army had quickly fell apart. Many of South Korean troops heading south did not lack transportation. King observed "convoy after convoy of ROK army vehicles loaded with begrimed infantrymen, artillery pieces, field kitchens, and every sort of appurtenance, but especially personnel, passed us in an unending stream." This indeed, he said, was a "bug-out."[218]

Anthony Farrar-Hockley comments on this situation: "Rumors, doubts, anxieties, lack of decision and organizational arrangements then brought about one of those events common in the opening days of a surprise offensive." He points to the premature blowing up of the Han bridge leading out of Seoul, with the result being "hundreds killed upon the demolished spans; almost half of the ROK Army, and more than half of their transport, heavy weapons and equipment, were lost on the northern bank."[219]

The next point of resistance was at Suwon with its airfield, twenty miles south of Seoul. C-54 transport planes began flying in supplies, U.S. jets provided some air cover and MacArthur flew in to survey the situation. North Korean Yaks periodically attacked the airstrip, then there were reports that North Korean tanks had crossed the Han, which resulted in a frantic and probably premature evacuation. In reality, only a few tanks had crossed the river and North Korean forces did not arrive at Suwon, without opposition, until two and a half days later. Obviously well-prepared, the North Koreans in their southern thrust had to cross three major rivers — the Han, the Kum and Naktong — which, if seriously defended, would have presented major obstacles. The South Korean Army started out with about 96,000 soldiers, which dropped a couple of weeks later to 57,000, with five battered divisions arriving in the south at what became the Pusan Perimeter. Over that time the ROK resistance took a toll on the North Korean forces. To its credit, the invading northern army forded the three major rivers in small boats at night, sustaining heavy casualties.[220]

According to U.S. Navy Capt. John Tarpey, on the very first night of their attack the North Koreans dispatched a troop ship towards the southern port of Pusan; it was sunk by a South Korean patrol boat. Tarpey cites an unnamed historian who declared that this action was "the most important surface engagement" of the Korean War. Had the North Korean sortie succeeded it would have stopped or seriously disrupted the subsequent flow of U.S. military support through that key southern port. Another early naval action occurred on July 2 when three U.N. destroyers (one U.S. and two British) tangled with four North Korean torpedo boats escorting ten trawlers down the east coast. That clash represented the end of North Korean efforts to control the sea — anywhere in Korea.[221]

Estimated at over 100,000, the substantial if chaotic flight of people from Seoul largely countered the Communist claim to be liberating the city from Rhee's gang. On the other hand, *The Reds Take a City* declares that this outflow represents only 7 percent of the city's population and that many of those leaving were government officials of all ranks and prominent supporters of that government. Two hundred ten members of the National Assembly fled south, with fifty-five remaining (who quickly swore allegiance to the new regime). The North Korean Army attempted to halt the embarrassing flow, offering a bag of rice to anyone who returned to the city; very few did.[222]

Another factor disrupting the Communist timetable (full conquest in a month) was the nonappearance of the projected indigenous rising: the substantial campaign carried out by the South Korean military and police against Communist supporters the previous year obviously had had its impact, although large South Korean Army units were still involved in this task. When the North Korean high command was planning its southern invasion Pak Hon-yong, the leader of the Communist movement in the south, had given Kim Il Sung, the "Great Leader," a guarantee that there would be a widespread revolt there, but this did not materialize. The chagrin felt by Kim about this major failure was intense. He later declared,

> Pak Hon-yong, that long-time spy of American bastards, claimed there were 200,000 underground SKLP (South Korean Labor Party) members in the South, and 60,000 in Seoul alone. Two hundred thousand? There was not a single revolt when we reached as far as the Kaktong line. If only a few thousand workers had risen up in Pusan, we would have clearly been able to liberate Pusan and probably prevented the landing of those damned Americans.

For his optimistic estimate, Pak was executed.[223]

To heap all the blame on Pak, convenient as it was, was to evade the reality of the failure of Communist informants in the south and the faulty expectations of Kim and company. Had there been a southern general manifestation of support for the northern "liberators" the rationale for American intervention would have been gravely undermined, but there was no revolt. There were plenty of supporters of Red revolution in the south, but seeing how fast the "People's Army" was rolling towards them, obviously they could afford to bide their time.

In planning its invasion the North Korean military had anticipated that the seizure of Seoul followed by a general uprising in the rest of the south would effectively mark the end of its campaign. When this did not happen it took some reorganization for its forces to drive south. In the eyes of John Muccio, U.S. ambassador to Korea, the great mystery of the war was the Communist military's one-week halt after Seoul when it could have swept south against crumpling opposition.[224]

At the beginning of American involvement in the conflict the desperate, makeshift rushing-in of U.S. soldiers to prevent a total conquest of South Korea resulted in confused and disorganized American actions. Having deployed its garrisons in Japan, to quickly mobilize, equip and transport a mass of young Americans five thousand miles away was a strenuous undertaking, particularly considering that the army, in effect, had been half dozing through most of the post-war years. Outdated and poorly maintained arms and equipment had to be renovated, rebuilt or junked. "Operation Roll-Up" had retrieved a large amount of material from the Pacific war and much of it had been renovated in Japanese factories, while much of it remained deficient.

Innovation was the order of the day. At the end of June Tokyo Ordnance located three desperately needed Pershing medium tanks in bad condition and needing extensive repairs. Although the tanks were quickly renovated and shipped to Korea, improperly sized fan belts proved to be their Achilles' heel. After some effective use in combat, the engines overheated and two of them had to be abandoned, resulting in the death and capture of their crews and supporting infantry.[225] Having spent a few months on active maneuvers in Japan before the war, Lt. William Funchess encountered a difficult situation when his unit was dispatched to Korea: "Our military equipment consisted of a few small tanks, some corroded hand grenades, old vehicles, and weapons left over from World War II." He also noted the lack of parachute flares and a severe deficiency of small arms ammunition.[226]

When the Second Division was sent to Korea, 20 percent of its vehicles had to be towed from Fort Lewis, Washington, to the port of embarkation, with servicing to be provided during the trip. En route, Ralph Hockley recalls, "We wound up training our soldiers to fire their weapons at tin cans thrown in the Pacific." When the division arrived "in theatre," there were examples of old radio batteries failing as well as, in one case, no ammunition for a 57-mm recoilless rifle for the first month.[227] These episodes could stand as representative of the early problems of the American military effort in Korea. So, it was more than a matter of soldiers unfit for active war duty, but it included failures to maintain an adequate flow of new materiel for such activity. To no avail, Douglas MacArthur repeatedly requested new vehicles and weapons. This situation leads back to two mistaken assumptions: no one would challenge the mighty U.S. military, resting comfortably on its laurels, and if that should occur, Uncle Sam had his atomic bombs and long range planes to deal with the situation.

At the very beginning of the buildup of American forces, a unit from Hawaii was airlifted, but the great mass of the nearly five million men (and women) who served in Korea over the next three years were shipped there by boat — across the wide, varying, and often turbulent Pacific Ocean. Few of those involved remembered the voyage as a holiday cruise.[228]

Some of the ships were army and navy transports, but commercial vessels were employed as well. The voyages, averaging from ten to fourteen days, varied according to ocean conditions—from stormy to smooth — but no ship sank. They all arrived at the Japanese port of Sasabo, then were transported to Fort Drake for processing, resulting in huge overcrowding with the great majority being processed as replacement troops across the way.[229]

Throwing in small ill-equipped infantry "combat groups" from Japan to slow down the rapidly advancing tank-led North Korean Army revealed the lack of readiness of the sequestered Eighth Army in Japan.[230] On July 9 Douglas MacArthur spelled out the dire situation. They were outnumbered ten to one, and to hold the southern tip of the country was "becoming increasingly problematical." He noted that North Korean armor and infantry were clearly superior at that point. He saw the urgent need for four more divisions.[231] Despite this state of affairs, he already was contemplating the employment of an amphibious maneuver, "to strike him behind his mass of ground force."[232]

In what turned out to be a three-year war, about 4.9 million Americans served in the Korean theatre (which included those stationed in Japan). The total for the U.S. Army was 2.8 million.[233] The troop rotation system, which began in April 1951, obviously was going full blast (35,000 a month by mid–1952) as this number was only 230,000 by June 1952,[234] which was about the same as the number of U.S. military personnel stationed in Germany by this time.[235]

The need to quickly create a large military force for Korea could not be met from the existing active duty forces. The first major component to be brought into the picture was the Army General Reserve, which was quickly stripped of half of its combat trained soldiers, about 50,000 troops.[236] The search immediately shifted to National Guard divisions as well as men in inactive reserve units (of men who had served a year of active duty), and World War II veterans who were listed in these organizations, often without the knowledge of the members.[237]

Eight National Guard divisions were activated, with two of them being sent to Korea. The administration (or was it the Defense Department?) decided to draw in these people rather than those in organized Army Reserve units, on the grounds that the latter might be needed to confront direct Soviet actions, particularly in Europe. This arrangement resulted in "the most controversial aspect of the mobilization of the Army Reserve." Based on their previous experience, most of those recalled to the military were sent as "fillers," replacements in depleted units.[238]

The next source of supply was the draft, which was quickly expanded; 50,000 were inducted in September 1950, which grew to 80,000 a month at the beginning of 1951, with 23,000 of them being shipped to Korea as replacements in January of that year. There were "generous" exemptions for some groups — college students, fathers and, as in World War II, many farm workers. As a result, about 40 percent of young men did not serve. Industrial workers were not exempted; someone had to fight the war.[239] "Whether intended or not," comments Paul Edwards, "the result was that the bulk of the combat forces in Korea were drawn from the lower-to-middle classes, with limited education."[240]

When American forces entered the fray there was an impression among some soldiers in Japan that this "police action" was not going to be a serious affair. Some thought they were only being sent over to help in the evacuation of American civilians; others wondered if they were being sent to Taiwan to head off the pending Communist invasion. Cpl. Lacy Barnett recalled, "Many of the men believed once the North Koreans discovered American troops had entered the war they would begin to pull back. No one yet had briefed us on the military situation or on anything else about Korea and its people and culture." In one unit soldiers were told to bring along their dress uniforms for an anticipated victory parade in Seoul.[241] This positive assumption was shared by Gregory Henderson, the U.S. consul in Pusan, who, observing the arrival of the first few U.S. soldiers, recalled, "No young man today can relive the feelings of utter confidence in victory.... Now we were there, we would win and the war would be over."[242] Dean Hess recalled that when American airmen arrived "in theatre" they believed the outcome of the struggle "was in the bag."[243]

It was the experience of journalist Denis Warner that army confidence in the outcome continued up until it met the North Korean invaders.[244] This assumption about the superiority of American military might was widely shared by those heading into the fray. For example, it was the belief of soldier Bob Roy that the troops would be back in Japan in a week or two.[245] Harold Noble, a diplomat in the U.S. Embassy who had spent a lifetime in Korea, believed that "just one United States division would knock those North Koreans back on their heels."[246] Some soldiers stationed in Hawaii were fearful that the conflict would end before they got there, thus, "We wouldn't get our Combat Infantryman's Badges."[247]

When he was rushed to the Far East, Lt. Richard Mack was surprised to find things at Fort Drake being carried on as usual — quiet Sunday afternoon bridge games at the Officers' Club, no noise from young officers concerned about the life and death struggle that was taking place across the way.[248]

But some things were stirring. Imprisoned soldiers were being offered release if they agreed to go to Korea. One officer recalls having finally got rid of five totally unfit soldiers, who left the company areas "in handcuffs" but were shortly returned; given the dire situation, someone in higher authority ordered that his company "could not do without these five thugs and they were shipped back to us."[249] John Jessup remembers that in order to quickly fill up the ranks of the Fifth Regimental Combat Team, 200 stockade residents were press-ganged into the unit; on the cruise to Korea aboard a Japanese coastal vessel trouble erupted: "Even aboard ship some of the thugs, who were no longer handcuffed, beat and robbed other GIs. What could we do with them? Send them to Korea?"[250]

At the beginning of August, after the fighting had been going on for a month, Richard Mack's first assignment was to command a (Japanese) boatload of stockade volunteers. PFC Leonard Korgie observed about sixty of them on his ship; his reaction: "How hard up can the 24th be?"[251] When Mack arrived at his platoon in the field he quickly encountered shortages — no first aid kits, no bayonets for carbines, no boots, no compasses, few M-1 rifles, rusty ammunition clips. He found discipline slack in the extreme; the prompt removal of his first sergeant for gross misconduct improved the situation.[252]

What can be judged as a typically inept initial performance of a rifle company in the Twenty-Fourth Division, fresh from garrison duty in Japan, can be seen when it was confronted with the reality of war. Many of the rifles were faulty due to dirt and improper assembly; there was a shortage of vehicles, signal equipment and ammunition for heavy weapons; the company even lacked grenades. When North Korean soldiers attacked, many riflemen at first failed to fire; stunned by being attacked, some panicked, dropped their weapons and fled.[253] All other failures aside, how can soldiers in a rifle company in an infantry division supposedly undergoing training not know about the care and operation of a rifle? As anyone who has undergone infantry training knows, that weapon, strapped to your shoulder, soon seems to become part of you.

Another example of failure to provide basic weapon training can be seen the experience of Col. Robert Martin, commander of the Thirty-Fourth Infantry Regiment, who found that he was the only man present who knew how to fire a 2.3 inch rocket launcher (bazooka). When he attempted to fire it at a North Korean tank he was killed, the shell from the tank cutting him in half.[254]

What was probably the most shocking experience of U.S. soldiers happened to personnel of a battalion of the Twenty-Ninth Infantry Regiment on quiet occupation duty on Okinawa. Together with 400 raw recruits just arriving on the island, the battalion was quickly shipped to Korea, where it was immediately sent into the war. Without any training in combat operations and ill-equipped, the result was a slaughter. Of the 757 soldiers who went into the fight, 313 were killed, with about 100 taken prisoner.[255]

In those early days, there was plenty of confusion and disorganization within both the American ranks and those of their Korean ally. Gregory

Henderson, U.S. consul in Pusan, noted that the alarm caused by the evacuation of foreigners was countered by the arrival of the first American soldiers—a single platoon in three trucks. People stood along the streets to cheer their arrival.[256] "Chaos" confronted Australian journalist Denis Warner when he arrived in the port of Pusan on July 1, but he was impressed by Korean efforts to keep operational a small, disused airstrip: "Hundreds of Koreans stood by with long baskets filled with rock and sand on their backs to fill in the holes knocked in the runway by each arriving aircraft, tamping down the repairs with their bare feet." At length, he managed to get on a makeshift train heading north. Spirits were high: "At all the stops new recruits pushed and shoved through the carriage. Most of them brought old long-stocked Japanese rifles, with five or ten rounds of ammunition in clips on their belts." As well, there were Korean girls in long white trousers—members of the women's auxiliary—who "brought us tea and fruit and rice cakes at each station." Along the way the train was joined by an American missionary and "a band of Korean first-aid girls." Not surprisingly, hymns were sung in the night, in which all aboard soon joined in: "We rattled to war to the tune of 'Onward Christian Soldiers.'"[257]

Initial optimism was soon to be replaced by defeat and despair. Less than a week later, Warner saw the drastic turn of the tide. The impact of North Korean T-34 tanks was decisive. After one setback a radio message declared, "Troops exhausted, throwing away their equipment, rifles, everything, even taking off their boots." When a puzzled officer asked why boots were removed, a soldier supplied the answer: "It's easier to walk in the rice fields, Sir."[258]

The Fourth of July, 1950, was a unique experience for Major Ambrose Nugent of the Fifty-Second Field Artillery Battalion of the Twenty-Fourth Infantry Division. Busy organizing firing positions, he saw five to six thousand South Korean soldiers fleeing south, abandoning all their equipment and weapons. Thus exposed, he was one of those in his battalion who were captured by the North Koreans.[259] At this early stage of the conflict, small groups of American soldiers everywhere joined with masses of South Korean troops in full retreat. Yet according to some reports all was not lost. The *U.S. Chargé* on July 9 reported, "ROK troops have won two small victories in past two days and their morale is rapidly returning." The next day Ambassador Muccio declared that U.S. air power "is taking a tremendous toll of enemy and definitely checking his thrusting power. Meanwhile US manpower and equipment continue to pour in in ever-growing quantities."[260]

An echo of that confused period occurred in 1999 when controversy erupted around charges that U.S. soldiers and airmen over a three-day period beginning on July 26, 1950, fired on masses of Korean refugees at a railroad tunnel at No Gun Ri, eighty miles south of Seoul. The refugees were obstructing operations and were thought to have disguised North Korean troops in their midst. The shooting resulted in the deaths of an estimated 400 people.

On that day Muccio told Washington of the mounting refugee problem facing the Eighth Army: "The enemy has used the refugees to his advantage in many ways: by forcing them south and so clogging the roads as to interfere with military movements; by using them as a channel for infiltration of agents; and most dangerous of all by disguising their own troops as refugees." According to Muccio this resulted in attacks from the rear, which he said "have been devastatingly successful." In this communication (which remained buried in the records of the National Archives for almost fifty years) Muccio related the decision of the Eighth Army about how this problem was to be addressed. If after leaflet drops, police supervision, and the banning of night movements of refugees the problem remained, then refugees "will receive warning shots and if they then persist in advancing they will be shot."[261]

Reports of this episode (which won Pulitzer Prizes for three Associated Press journalists) and the ensuing controversy about the scope of the incident were followed by the appointment by the government of the Republic of Korea of the Truth and Reconciliation Commission, which after a two-and-a-half-year investigation concluded that in more than two hundred incidents the American military had killed many South Korean civilians.[262] The U.S. Army for a long time demonstrated determined reluctance to reopen questions about these incidents, but in regard to at least a couple of actions it has done so. In almost all cases the fatalities were caused by U.S. Air Force bombardments of suspected enemy hideouts.[263]

The origins of these episodes are to be found in the context of the fear and disorganization of an inexperienced and unprepared American military as it desperately sought to blunt the North Korean forces pushing south. Based on the decision of the Eighth Army leaders, several U.S. commanders issued orders that the flow of refugees was to be stopped, using any means necessary. Some soldiers and airman obviously took the orders to mean they could bomb and shoot the people fleeing from the Communists.[264] That it was known at the time that these kinds of actions had taken place can be seen by a report on the front page of the New York Times on September 30, 1950: "Fear of infiltrators led to the slaughter of hundreds of South Korean civilians, women as well as men, by some U.S. troops." In some cases the U.S. military acknowledged that its agents were responsible for civilian deaths at that time. Bloody and confused as they were, U.S. delaying actions did provide time to form a defense ring around the southern port of Pusan, and for the large-scale buildup of troops and weapons that followed.[265]

At the same time American military personnel stood by while agents of the South Korean government, preparing to retreat, executed thousands of prisoners and others who were suspected to be supporters of the northern invaders.[266] Knowledge of these massacres was known to officials in the U.S. government, but Douglas MacArthur decided that the mass murders were "internal matters" to be left to the South Korean authorities. To protests from the British government, Assistant Secretary of State Dean Rusk responded that U.S. commanders were doing "everything they can to curb such atrocities," while Muccio later said that at the time he had urged South Korean officials to conduct executions humanely and only after due process of law.[267]

Particularly in the early stages of the conflict, disarmed American prisoners of war were killed by North Korean soldiers, notably when the Reds were in retreat. Of the estimated 370 American prisoners who were forced north in the Communist retreat of September 1950, only twenty-three survived. In Taejon advancing American soldiers found what could only be described as a massacre: beneath the floor of a jail they found thirty-two dead U.S. soldiers, dressed as Koreans. (One of the discovers recalled, "Two of the G.I.s were still alive, but nearly insane from the experiences they had endured." In a nearby well were the bodies of twenty-nine soldiers, and about three hundred dead Americans, most of whom had their hands tied behind them, were found in the surrounding hills. This was combined with the wholesale shooting of Korean men and the murder of Korean women in the basement of a church.[268] In Sunchon sixty-six bodies of executed American soldiers were found in a railway tunnel, while seven others had died as a result of starvation or disease. When the Chinese intervened they proclaimed a policy of leniency towards prisoners and made some effort to stop the North Koreans killing of them. For its part, the U.S. Army had to deal with a mass of surrendered North Korean troops, whose numbers greatly increased as the conflict turned against the north.[269]

The ongoing human cost of the war was apparent to Denis Warner even at its beginning. He arrived at Taejon, a key midlands city, on July 20 on the eve of its chaotic U.S. Army evacuation:

> The streets were abandoned, the shops shuttered and deserted. Along the whole mile of the main street, jammed the week before with thousands of people, there was no man or woman, and only one child, a naked girl, not more than three, coated with dirt and trickling with dysentery, left on the pavement in front of a shop.[270]

In mid-summer the battle of the Pusan Perimeter was taking shape. Anthony Farrar-Hockley makes the insightful point that had the North Korean Army concentrated on battering into Pusan, rather than spreading its forces occupying the southwest, by the third week in July, before substantial American support had arrived, it probably would have resulted in a total Communist victory.[271] Criticizing poor Soviet planning, Nikita Khrushchev declared that the lack of Soviet control at the front and the failure to concentrate attacks deprived the Communists of victory. Yet, in his opinion, it was a close call: one more tank corps was all that was needed to crush the perimeter.[272]

As events transpired, the Communist occupation of almost all of South Korea lasted little more than two months. Although the expected "people's revolt" to coincide with the arrival of the North Korean Army did not occur,

Communist supporters quickly emerged to lead a purge and, frequently, execution of Rhee officials and other "reactionary upholders of capitalist imperialism." Following the mass release of political internees from prisons in the capital, a series of show trials by *ad hoc* "People's Courts" were staged in Seoul, usually followed by executions.[273] The flavor of the Communist message can be seen in this announcement: "Chieftains of the traitorous clique who engaged in various kinds of exploitation and killing in the name of the so-called National Assemblymen have surrendered themselves and are now under the warm protection of the Democratic People's Republic government." Warm protection did not extend to a posse of "reactionary bureaucrats" who were marched off to the north, with those unable to walk being shot.[274] Obviously the opposition underground had been keeping track of events all along as, according to one informant, hundreds of girls who had fraternized with American soldiers during the earlier occupation were put to death.[275]

The Communist occupation obviously was a carefully planned operation, with loudspeakers, posters and leaflets covering every town and village, where "people's committees" were organized to rouse local support. An estimated 5,000–6,000 Communist party personnel descended on the South. The new power in the land provided free admission to Russian and Chinese films in the capital and urged people to move north, where they would be provided with "ample food, housing, furnishings and places of occupation."[276] In some districts of the city people were simply rounded up and shipped to the north. An Hong-kyoun recalled the free movies that the Communists provided, which sometimes ended with the hall doors being locked and many of the audience "forced into trucks and hauled away." An's family protected him from this misfortune by digging a hole under their house, where he remained during the day.[277] Along with three young female Communist "guests," two men were hidden in Connie Kang's house at that time. Every house gate was required to have pictures of Kim Il Sung and Stalin; households were equipped with bamboo spears, with mandatory drills on their use to fight the "American imperialists." Neighborhood organizers constantly recruited people, particularly women, for meetings and labor crews.[278] For the members of families who had joined the "Volunteers' Force," meals were provided twice a day at special feeding centers.[279]

Since many people had opposed the Rhee government for its corruption and economic injustice, there was substantial support for the new regime in Seoul. Large numbers of people began to wear red armbands. In Inchon the "Korean People's Army" was greeted with a "grand celebration."[280] One national assemblyman who fled Seoul reported that the North Korean Army was "very kind" to the civilian population and "does not conduct any of its executions of undesirable civilians but left this dirty work to the guerillas to perform." As well, he declared, the North Koreans "are using every means possible to stop the southward evacuation of South Korean civilians in their occupied areas."[281] Elections were held on August 15 with only Communist-sponsored candidates on the ballot. A major undertaking was the gathering of millions of signatures in support of various causes: the withdrawal of American forces and the trial of Syngman Rhee and other "national traitors." Communist propaganda declared that there were hated Japanese soldiers in the enemy ranks and even that Pusan had been captured.[282]

Announcements of sweeping measures of land reform, improved working conditions, educational opportunity and the liberation of women were joined with political promises. Many left-wing supporters and university students (the C.I.A. estimated that half of the university students in the capital actively gave support) were motivated to support the new government, with some of them going so far as to join the conquering army.[283] Historian Bong-young Choy declares that "some prominent political and military leaders cooperated with the northern regime."[284] A few ministers formerly in the Rhee government broadcast their support.[285] The North Koreans arrived with new school texts ready for distribution.[286]

The invading force secured the undamaged radio network based in Seoul, and managed to lure back some of its staff, including announcers. Its first announcement declared: "Your government has fled, the People's Republic is now in control, go back to your work. Everyone will be forgiven if he goes back to work."[287] Housewife Lee Hyaan Sook recalled, "The North Koreans made Communism sound so wonderful that many thought it must be like heaven. It seemed to have a special appeal for both those with very little education and those with a lot of education."[288] Early in the war a captured American soldier recalled his reception by some South Korean villagers, who "began throwing rocks at me. They hit me with sticks and spat at me. I was never so glad of anything as I was to get out of that village." To complete the episode, a bit later he was guarded by a very young North Korean soldier with a little English who requested that he sing the American national anthem, which he gladly did.[289]

Despite what he had been told would happen, a North Korean officer noted, "Many of the southern Koreans did not greet their liberators."[290] Yet one study indicates that the personnel of the new regime "gave manifest evidence of sleepless hard work and general industry. Both in city and country areas Koreans reported that they were impressed with the businesslike conduct and the courteous behavior of Communists officials."[291]

From the beginning the North Korean occupation of Seoul had some negative aspects. Soldiers confiscated rice and local men and women were forced to work on rebuilding the bridges across the Han River. Promised labor benefits did not materialize, and the eight-hour workday was extended if assigned tasks had not been fulfilled. With large-scale removal of teachers, the educational system was disrupted.[292] Moreover, under the cover of a barrage of propaganda, the new authority began recruiting and drafting young men to shore up the

Communist forces besieging Pusan. An estimated 200,000 members of the Democratic Youths' League soon found themselves in the Volunteers' Force. With little training or equipment, these "volunteers" were rushed to the battlefront to cover the heavy losses being experienced by the "Korean People's Army."[293] Lee Young Ho went through the experience of being impressed into this force: rounded up in his native village, tied together with other conscripts, he was marched north, given three weeks of basic training and allowed to fire three bullets. He was then employed to serve in the cause of Great Leader Kim Il Sung.[294] The Communists also used captured ROK troops, who, after a period of "re-education," were termed "Liberation Soldiers" and were initially employed in service and labor units. According to Kevin Mahoney, many of these recruits as well as dragooned ROK soldiers "surrendered at the first opportunity" to the other side.[295]

When the North Koreans had to rapidly retreat in September, many others of the conscripted southerners deserted, while the Rhee government, when it regained control, conducted a purge process in reverse. But the Communist program of giving small peasant farmers ownership of their land was not reversed by the renewed Rhee regime; its land reform program — which finally had been under way on the eve of the war — proceeded to broaden its efforts to do the same thing, with the transfer of land to small farmers (with a 30 percent government subsidy) being completed just after the war.[296] In January 1951 the South Korean government was once again driven out of Seoul, and despite the restrained deportment of the Chinese occupiers, all but about 200,000 of a million people fled, which obviously demonstrated a rejection of the Communist program and its operation. Conversely, when the South Korean allied forces regained control of the capital two and a half months later, there was a huge return of the refugees to the city. E.J. Kahn saw this return: "Every night, from five to ten thousand of them were straggling back across the Han." He saw the motivation for the return trek as at least partly based on sentiment: despite massive damage, it was their home and the center of their country.[297]

With the South Korean government in near total disarray, the U.S. Information and Education Agency stepped into the breach. Through the use of radio broadcasts, various publications, and the mass distribution of leaflets, the agency claimed it achieved credibility with the Koreans on both sides of the line.[298]

The damage inflicted on the North Korean Army in the early stages of the war, by air attacks on supply lines as well as from opposition by South Korean and American forces, eventually resulted in losses of an estimated 58,000 soldiers. This dire situation required reinforcements from the north. Here too problems quickly arose. Draft-dodging became widespread and military police were forced to sweep into villages in attempts to round up potential soldiers. The Pyongyang government got Chinese cooperation in conscripting Koreans living in Manchuria.[299] Probably it was at this point that the Soviets sent several hundred Koreans living across the border, soldiers or otherwise, to join in.[300] The proud army that had launched its great venture in late June had degenerated to a battered remnant fleeing north by mid–September, but it was to be heard from again. If South Korea found a savior in the United States, North Korea was to find one across the Yalu.

Just before the Communist seizure of Seoul, the Republic of Korea government fled to Taejon and then was forced to evacuate further south to Taegu. With continued North Korean assault, the U.S. commander of the Eighth Army, Walton Walker, ordered all remaining ministries to withdraw while he prepared to pull his army further south. Cho Pyong-ok refused to evacuate his Home Affairs Ministry, where it remained during the bitter but successful defense of the city.[301] All the other battered ministries retreated to the tip of the peninsula at Pusan, where, faced with miserable living conditions, their staffs struggled to revive operations amidst rudimentary conditions.[302] Historian W.D. Reeve describes the scene: "Offices, of sorts, were somehow found — often partly roofless and windowless — hastily refurnished with odds and ends of boards, packing cases and cardboard." Often with no fuel and temperatures sometimes falling to zero degrees Fahrenheit, office staff worked in mufflers and overcoats. The headquarters of President Rhee was "a weathered and somewhat dilapidated old brick residence on a hillside above the harbor. With the building heated by a single oil stove, his staff were crammed into a few rooms." Being cooped up in the Pusan perimeter lasted less than three months before U.S. action swept almost all of South Korea from Communist control, which required a rapid effort to restore the administrative responsibility of the southern republic. Because the U.N. (American) Command opposed the move, the central government did not return to the capital until the summer of 1953. There it was faced with the same conditions as in Pusan, but things rapidly improved, and not only for the government. Driven by a mass of returned civilians, Reeve declares, "In an incredibly short time a dead and deserted city was transformed into a hive of activity."[303] That, however, is looking ahead.

Connie Kang, who arrived in Pusan from Seoul on the top of a train with her mother, recalled the scene: "Pusan was crowded and dirty. Homeless urchins in tattered clothes, with gaunt faces and lice in their hair, roamed the streets, carrying tin cans to collect leftovers. Sometimes they ran after American jeeps, which showered them with dust and dirt, hoping to get a piece of chewing gum or a candy bar." One revelation she had was American canned food: "I had my first taste of canned Chef Boyardee spaghetti, which we mixed with rice. I loved it. My favorite was corned beef hash. I still like to eat it the way we did it then — mixed with a bowl of hot steamy rice." With frequent power outages and water shortages, "We used kerosene lamps and stood in line for hours with buckets to draw water from a public water pipe." A nightly routine was picking lice "buried in the folds of our clothing like monkeys in a zoo."[304]

Robert Oliver, who was there at the time, declared, "The streets of Pusan offered teeming testimony to gross human hardship and deprivation, but not misery." With the massive influx of refugees, its population swelled from 400,000 to 1.2 million, converting Pusan "into a gigantic slum." Based on Korean tradition, distraught refugees were given shelter by their Pusan relatives, the result being great overcrowding. Oliver was impressed by the prevailing spirit of the besieged mass of people: "Yet desperate as the situation became, the amazing fact is the general atmosphere of cheerfulness that prevailed." Moreover, he said, "Perhaps no other people at any time ever received such a prolonged and severe test of their innate good-nature and optimism." Through it all, he noted, "It is a sheer miracle that no mass starvation, freezing or epidemics occurred." He attributed "a large share of the credit" for avoiding these situations to the U.S. Army's Civil Assistance Command, but he said it was also due to the Korean characteristics of demonstrativeness, resilience and effervescence.[305] On the other hand, Pusan's port was filled with war orphans begging and stealing.[306]

As U.S. forces greatly increased in the Pusan enclave there was mounting apprehension in Communist ranks in Seoul about an American onslaught. U.S. planes were already striking at known Communist facilities. Before the North Korean forces were driven out of the south about 20,000–22,000 civilians were executed, with most of them being killed as the tide turned against the Communists in the last days of their control.[307] In early January to March 1951 the North Koreans (propelled by the Chinese) again occupied Seoul, but by that time the city had been reduced to a mere shell of about 100,000 people.[308] There were no grand celebrations this time. In early 1951 under the determined direction of Mathew Ridgway, a revived U.S. Eighth Army drove north, and once again — and for the last time — Seoul was liberated. Although the process began slowly, the capital was to bloom into a modern metropolis.[309]

This development was paralleled by that of South Korea as a whole. Given the carnage, destruction and brutality of what went on in the war of 1950–1953, this eventual transformation can only be viewed as vivid testimony to the courage, intelligence and determination of its people. Within the same country, however, there stands in stark contrast another political entity that has been characterized by famine, dictatorship and a virulent ideology. These developments unfolded essentially during the half century since the land was torn by war.

It is now time to go back to that miserable conflict and examine it from the bottom up. There are various accounts of the overt military aspects — battles fought, etc. This is a study of the foundations of that episode of warfare — the people who were involved, their motivations, the mechanisms and equipment of war, logistics, supplies, propaganda, and intelligence, and the other things that constitute the foundations of organized violence at the top.

CHAPTER TWO

Participants in War

Conflicting Koreans

At the beginning of the North Korean invasion some South Korean Army units did put up effective resistance, but overall that force was characterized by flight and desertion. American intelligence operator Don Nichols noted the wholesale run made by Korean security forces in Seoul, and he observed the mass execution of political prisoners in Suwon.[1] When what was left of the South Korean Army, battered and bruised, retreated to the Pusan enclave in July 1950, its prospects were grim. A huge influx of U.S. soldiers and equipment allowed the ROK army to reorganize and revive.[2] In fact, soon some ROK units became adept at tank hunting, which they treated as something of a sport.[3] Surprised and disappointed that there was no supporting uprising to greet its invasion (complaints later voiced by Kim Il Sung), the North Korean Army, after impressing as many young men as it could find in its southern area of control, had no alternative but to repeatedly hurl its forces against the Pusan perimeter. According to the account by the Korean Institute of Military History, what ensued was a battle of sheer determination: "The predominant South Korean will to fight against the invaders overwhelmed that of the enemy's." With their backs to the sea, "the Naktong [River] became a watershed for the South Koreans to keep their freedom and their adamant will to fight against Communism." The Institute's narrative did not understate the situation when it declared, "The ROK Army swore to punish the North Korean Communists invaders at any cost to regain the lost territory by making a counterattack against them."[4] The breakout from the perimeter and the defeat of the "North Korean People's Army," however, was largely an American achievement.

There were bitter relations between the soldiers of the two Koreas, with each side generally convinced of the righteousness of its cause. The killing of prisoners of the other side was frequent and apparently expected.[5] A sight that became common to advancing U.N. forces was to find South Korean soldiers and some civilians with hands bound and bullets in the back of their heads.[6] When three South Korean soldiers attached to an American infantry unit were ordered to bring back four North Korean prisoners for intelligence interrogation, they killed them, which resulted in a severe reprimand from the company commander, but that was all.[7]

There were glory days for the South Korean Army following in the wake of the rushed and disorganized North Korean retreat from Pusan, with two ROK divisions sweeping up the east coast, passing through Wonsan before the Americans, held back by sea mines, could get out of their boats. One unit reached the far northeast corner approaching the frontier with the Soviet Union. As it did with the Americans, the advent of the Chinese Communist military totally turned the tide for the ROK.

Based on a strategy advocated from Sun Tzu to Liddell Hart, the Chincoms (Chinese Communist army) launched concentrated attacks at the weak points of the other side. In this case, the weak point was the South Korean divisions. When the ROKs collapsed, U.S. units were rushed in to fill the gap, providing excellent opportunities for ambushes. Why were the South Korean forces so often inadequate? There was the traditional Korean anxiety about the China giant looming over their peninsula. They also were subjected to powerful Chinese spearheads. Both of these combined to create a terrified reaction by Korean soldiers when they encountered the Red Chinese mass attacks. After the first Chinese assault — that of late October — Walton Walker observed amongst South Korea soldiers "an intense, psychological fear of Chinese intervention" along with "previous complacency — and over-confidence in all ROK ranks."[8]

A week after he arrived in Korea, Matthew Ridgway experienced the panicked flight of one group of South Korean troops: "They had abandoned their heavy artillery, their machine guns— all their crew-served weapons. Only a few had kept their rifles. Their only thought was to get away, to put miles between them and the fearful enemy that was at their heels."[9] He declared that the ROKs "had a very deep fear of the Chinese." On occasion when he got some sleep beside a ROK division, "it would be gone by morning. They would pull out during the night and be ten to twenty kilometers to the rear by daylight."[10] On the other hand, Anthony Farrar-Hockley makes the point that after the immediate impact of the North Korean invasion and once the Pusan Perimeter was established, the South Korean units generally fought well with few defections.[11] Yet there were repeated episodes when South Korean units just left the scene without informing adjacent (American) units.[12]

In the wake of the Chinese intervention in late November 1950, the two South Korean divisions on the northeast coast were evacuated by sea to become part of the South Korean Army being assigned to the east central area just north of the 38th parallel. In January 1951 it encountered understrength North Korean units who had successfully broken through the southern lines and penetrated deep into the interior, posing a threat to the U.S. Eighth Army, then fully occupied in responding to the Chinese offensive in the west. Units of the U.S. X Corps were brought in to close the gap, and in a month-long battle centered on the junction town of Wonju, the North Koreans were driven out of the area.[13]

The Chinese attack beginning on New Year's Eve, 1950, once again threatened the loss of Seoul. Attempting to prevent the male population from again falling into the hands of the enemy, Rhee's government tried to organize a national guard of all males between seventeen and forty years of age.[14] This effort quickly foundered. Yong-ho Ch'oe recalled the situation: "The severe mistreatment of these men during the evacuation later became the single biggest scandal that rocked the Rhee government during the war." When the South Korean government was reestablished in Seoul in September 1950 it conducted a purge of its opponents. Despite that action, in December while South Korean military police carried on large-scale arrests, a Chinese occupation loomed that American reporter John Denson believed would reactivate Communist support: "At the very lowest estimate there are 10,000 Communist agents and informers in the city, and perhaps many more thousands of collaborators." With a renewed and massive exodus of people from the city, however, there was not much to occupy, and Chinese control lasted less than three months.[15]

At that time journalist Hanson Baldwin presented a dismal picture of the condition of the country and its people. From the air "Korea presents a curious cartography ... a tangled, twisted mass of rugged mountains, stubbed with small timber, snow-capped in the north, laced with many streams and rivers—ice-locked now — and in the valleys and up the terraces of the hills the fantastic patterns of rice paddies, green and golden and yellow, broken now and again by wasteland, red as the clay of Georgia, corrugated like the mountains of the moon." From the ground things looked different: "The same impersonal destructiveness of war has blasted bridges, filled streets with rubble, reduced freight yards and factories to twisted steel and water-filled craters." This was the background to the mass of refugees: "Clustered round the wreckage, poking through the debris, moving endlessly down the streets and roads, toiling from dawn to dusk in the rice paddies the peasant masses struggled to survive."[16]

Once the Chinese onslaught had been contained by the spring of 1951 General Ridgway turned to the rebuilding of the battered South Korean Army. In order to create a professional officer structure, groups of South Korean officers were shuttled to advanced infantry and artillery schools at army bases in Japan and the United States, while the Korean Military Advisory Group was expanded. The artillery component in Korean units was increased, and the Korean Military Academy was reopened. Despite the pleas of Syngman Rhee for a larger force, Ridgway concluded that a South Korean army of 250,000 trained soldiers in ten divisions would suffice, although he believed that if the war continued it would be three years before that force would be completely effective.[17]

James Van Fleet, Ridgway's successor as Eighth Army commander, acknowledged that South Korean divisions lacked the equipment of American units, but needed time to learn the effective use and deployment of modern military machinery, "so don't expect our ROK friends to pick all this up in a few months." Under his direction, entire South Korean units were pulled out of the line and put through vigorous infantry training. He became a strong advocate of retraining and expanding that army, which would allow for the reduction of U.S. forces. Van Fleet went further in publicly advocating a twenty-division South Korean Army. In a March 1952 interview published in the right-wing *U.S. News and World Report*, he held that the manpower was available and the cost to the United States would be less if the bigger army was built. This was not to be the last time that, while on active duty, Van Fleet publicly made known his views on military matters.[18]

Another factor in the Korean relationship was that many North Korean and Chinese soldiers had been subjected to lengthy propaganda conditioning that continued during the war, and thus most of them appeared to be highly motivated. Although two-thirds of the Chinese soldiers were illiterate and about another 16 percent had only basic schooling, they clearly were receptive to the concentrated political conditioning. Alexander George has set out the extent of Chinese troop indoctrination and subsequent political control.[19] Due to serious political divisions up to the eve of the war and the lack of heavy weapons, South Korean soldiers did not have this preparation. Its officer corps was filled with political appointees lacking in military ability but who also frequently were corrupt. There were also those who had English and knew how to type, known as "swallows," whose abilities spared them from the rigors of war. This latter situation, however, is common in all military organizations. An indication of how the two contending positions were viewed by conscripts on either side may be seen by the fact that many more switched to the southern side than to the other. It is likely that food, supplies, equipment and the like, however, were more motivating factors than any ideological assumptions.[20]

Since almost half the forces under U.N. command were South Koreans (about 235,000 versus 270,000 U.S. and allied by April 1951) it was not possible to relegate ROKs to rearguard activity, such as chasing after guerrillas in the mountains. This problem was partially addressed by assigning Koreans to U.S. units—the KATUSA (Korean Augmentation to the U.S. Army) program or "buddy" system. It originated when MacArthur saw the need to build up the understrength Seventh Division in preparation for the Inchon operation. To meet this need, Korean police rounded up 8,637 young men, 7,000 of whom were shipped to Japan for a bare three weeks of training. To Major General Edwin Wright, who was in charge of planning for the operation, the involuntary recruits were "right out of the rice paddies and have nothing but shorts and straw hats." Lt. Colonel Charles R. Scherer, a training officer in the division, described the draftee cohort: they looked

> as though they had been herded together to get them off the streets of Pusan. They spent their first week in Japan in quarantine, since they had to be deloused and cleaned. They could not speak English and we had few interpreters. Our instruction was given primarily in sign language.... They had no idea of sanitation, let alone the more complicated activities of military life.... They ate our rations, rode our trucks, used our supplies. But except for menial tasks, they were a performance cipher.[21]

According to Robert Smith's diatribe about MacArthur, many of the Seventh Division's instructors "considered the Koreans a lesser breed, referred to them freely as 'gooks' and sneered to see them mistaking toothpaste for something good to eat and wearing one uniform over another to make sure of holding on to it. Poverty that deep was clearly un–American. Why, you even had to show them how to use a latrine."[22] Without mentioning these problems, in its account of the war the Korean Institute of Military History blandly states, "Many American units employed the KATUSA soldiers to best advantage as security guards, in scouting and patrolling, and in performing various labor details."[23]

When the Inchon operation began, the Thirty-Second Regiment of the

South Korean soldiers extracting a 57mm anti-tank gun, August 1950. Courtesy Truman Library, 67-7415.

Seventh Division was composed of 1,873 Koreans and 3,241 Americans. Although the KATUSA program was praised by GHQ press releases and later MacArthur claimed it as one of his achievements, historian Stanley Weintraub declared that these men "were not soldiers but refugees swept up off the streets of Pusan, bewildered, hungry, ragged and scared"; and were, even after some training, a "hopeless component in the 7th Division, many of whom, when in a combat situations, never fired their weapons." Journalist E.J. Kahn observed of these participants that "many of them had become so accustomed to traveling about in vehicles" that when they returned to ROK units "it took them a month to become toughened to the point where they could keep pace with their fellow-citizens."[24]

As commander of an infantry platoon in the Twenty-Fifth Division, Lyle Rishell had a most positive experience with KATUSAs: "They went on patrol, shared our meager rations, stood long, lonely hours at night, fought our battles, and were wounded and died with us, and they never complained. They were brothers in arms, and they didn't let us down."[25] Korean soldiers were also assigned to the Third Infantry Division, which in November 1950 joined the east coast venture at Wonsan. Having trained with the division for two months in Japan, the KATUSAs knew more about the division than did the American replacements who arrived just before its departure for Korea. In one of its operations it was clear that the Korean contingent had not fired their weapons. Each American company usually had attached to it a half-dozen translators, infiltrators ("Blue Boys") and a contingent of porters comprising what James Brady called the "gook train," which brought up ammunition, food and other supplies.[26]

It took experience for many South Koreans to be effective soldiers. Not having tank or anti-tank training, they initially had a great fear of tanks, of which their North Korean opponents had many, but over time some of them became adept at tank hunting. They also had to go through a lengthy learning experience about the use of mines. But having KATUSAs on hand could also prove useful in unusual ways. Encountering some Korean men in civilian clothes walking down a road, the KATUSA soldiers quickly concluded that they were North Korean combatants—their hair was cut, a military requirement. Two other indicators were tanned necks and calloused feet. Sometimes they could identify northerners by their accents. Because they were Koreans, the KATUSAs could pick up a wide range of information from the people they encountered along the way.[27]

Inadequately trained and motivated South Korean soldiers remained a problem. When the jerry-built U.S. Seventh Division came under devastating attack by Chinese forces in November 1950 in northeast Korea, many of the newly recruited KATUSAs, who composed about one-fourth of the division, did not resist. When the Chinese struck the two U.S. regiments (700 of the 3,000 men involved being Koreans) on the east side of the Chosin reservoir, David Barr, commander of the division, described the attached Koreans as being "stunned, confused and exhausted." Some of the American soldiers thought the Koreans tended to behave more like prisoners of war than soldiers. During the Chosin withdrawal, some scared South Korean soldiers huddling in a ditch were urged by a Marine officer to fire on the heights; one Korean merely fired his eight-round clip in the air and crawled away. Another Marine officer discovered that the thirty Koreans attached to his unit had slipped away during the night.[28]

At the end of October 1951 the maximum number of Korean soldiers attached to U.S. Army companies was reduced from 100 to 25. Due at least to cultural and language differences, the program was considered a failure, but the KATUSAs did provide useful labor in their assigned units, and many became proficient soldiers; the program was continued after the war.[29] Even in U.S. divisions that had few Koreans as infantrymen or laborers there were Koreans attached as agents and translators.[30]

At that time there were not enough American troops to man a full front when facing the estimated 750,000 Chincoms and North Koreans. As has been seen, during the advance north, and while ragged North Korean units were hastily being reorganized, ROK divisions ran up the east coast almost to the Soviet border, but were shortly evacuated when the Chinese struck.[31]

The effectiveness of the retrained South Korean force was put to the test in the topsy-turvy struggle with the Chinese for White Horse Mountain in October 1952. In what proved to be the largest Chinese offensive of the year, the fight for the summit went back and forth (a total of twenty-four times) with the South Korean Ninth Division, now fully equipped, holding it at the end. Army PFC Rudolph Stephens, who observed the fight, comments about the determined and bloody South Korean effort: "We knew that the days when they would break and run when the Chinese attacked were over." Later, an ROK division passed another vital test when it defeated a similar North Korean unit on the east coast.[32]

The small but well-trained Korean Marine Corps won the respect of many American combatants, including Marines Edward McAleer and James Elkins. In a battle for control of some rugged hills in June 1952, an attached Korean Marine regiment was "faced with the toughest assignment.... Their zone of operation was a maze of ridges defended by an estimated NKPA regiment.... As the KMCs launched their attack, the enemy met it head on — Koreans facing Koreans, each side considering the others traitors, and little mercy expected from either side." After an inconclusive struggle of five days, the Korean Marines borrowed a page from the Communist book and launched a night attack, which, catching their fellow countrymen by surprise, proceeded to kill many of them while the rest withdrew. In the following mop-up operation the "bitterness existing between the two forces," was apparent when Korean Marines found the bodies of ten of their men who had been shot in the back of the head.[33] In Chris Sarno's view, the Korean Marines never

Refugees leaving the Taegu area, July 1950. Courtesy National Archives, 111-SC346721 [PRS].

retreated, although they were undisciplined in fire control and radio communication.[34]

The leadership provided by Matthew Ridgway and then James Van Fleet, Ridgway's successor as commander of the Eighth Army, turned the southern army into an effective fighting force. Two leading Russian officers had high praise for him. In their *Alien Wars* Oleg Sarin and Lev Dvoretsky declared that Ridgway "was an extremely competent commander with rich combat experience.... This enabled him to change the course of the war and to save the world from another Communist victory and another foothold in Asia." Pat Frank was strongly impressed by Van Fleet's effectiveness in molding the South Korea Army. Indeed, "to the ROKs he was a semi-god, because he had compassion for the Korean people, and confidence in the Korean Army." The designation "gook" was not used in Van Fleet's headquarters. As far as Frank saw it, this successful training program had far-reaching effects: "It was a factor which not only had the immediate effect on the course of battle, allowing the steady rotation of American troops, and later the withdrawal of large units from the line for service elsewhere, but eventually it may shift the balance of power in East Asia." He also noted that, because of his previous work in Greece helping to defeat a communist insurgency, the small Greek contingent in Korea were Van Fleet's enthusiastic supporters. He also believed Turkish soldiers "revered" Van Fleet. It was clearly a remarkable achievement to get Greeks and Turks on the same side about anything.[35]

Then there was the Korean civilian response to the conflict. When the North Korean Army rolled over most of the south, a small Communist underground quickly emerged, and there is evidence of enthusiastic if limited support for the "People's Liberators," but that is all. There seems no clear evidence of substantial disruption by these people. When the South Korean forces retreated, however, government agents killed thousands of suspected supporters of the invading army.[36] The scramble out of Seoul was such that the entire radio network facility was left untouched, and the Communists were pleased to put it back into operation, even recruiting some of the original broadcasters.[37] American soldiers had the opportunity to hear the latest popular American songs provided, with appropriate commentary, by Seoul City Sue.[38]

Even as American and South Korean forces were being driven out of the north (all in three weeks), anti–Communist opposition was mounted on the islands on the west coast, an effort that was given logistical support by the U.S. Navy. These partisan forces reportedly grew to several thousand and were sustained until the end of the war. Further evidence of popular sentiment was the mass of refugees moving south, with few (if any) going north.[39] When Chinese soldiers began pouring into North Korea in November 1950 a village headman near the Yalu, at potential danger to himself, sent a messenger bringing this information to a U.S. unit: the Seventeenth Regiment of the Army Seventh Division. Subsequently one of its units, now rapidly withdrawing south, found it could not load its heavy equipment on an available train, whereupon local people, working through the night at temperatures of 30 degrees below zero, built a ramp of railroad ties.[40] In a life-saving act, a wounded American soldier wandering in the hills was fed by a Korean farmer who directed him to the south.[41] When South Korean and American soldiers came into villages, towns and cities in the north they were given rousing receptions.[42] At the town of Anak the local people had rebelled against the Communist administration before the allies got there. As well, there were a variety of examples of local people assisting arriving soldiers in rooting out fleeing North Korean troops.[43]

There was a bitter relationship between the two Korean forces. South Korean general Sun Yup Paik recalled that at the time of the exchange of prisoners after the armistice of 1953, there were very few officers among the thousands of returning South Koreans. "The Communists," he commented, "singled out the officers for persecution, and the only ones to survive captivity were those skillful enough to pretend to be enlisted men, and maintain that fiction throughout long months of captivity."[44]

There were many examples of brutal treatment meted out by Koreans to other Koreans. As it had been the policy since U.S. intervention, the American military effectively kept out of matters relating to Koreans alone. In his history of the war, Max Hastings addresses this depressing matter: "U.N. soldiers' sense of alienation from the Koreans was intensified by observing their brutality to each other." British journalist James Cameron was outraged by what he heard about the South Korean police: "the beatings-up, the crucifixions, the attachment of genitals to terminals of field telephones." He pointed to the opinion of the London *Times*: "All the complaints against the People's Government of North Korea could be leveled against the democratically elected South Korean Government. Acts of persecutions and reprisal have been committed under both." When Cameron brought his complaints to the U.N. Commission, he was told that nothing could be done: "These are Asiatic people and congenitally different; their standards of behavior are different from ours."[45]

As has been seen, there was strong political opposition to the government of Syngman Rhee, but he managed to remain in control. Rhee observed some of the proprieties of representative government; he also employed coercion, arrests and whatever else it took to remain in power. His was not a full dictatorship, and he always had to take into consideration American pressure to adhere to at least some democratic practices. He had to contend with substantial and outspoken opposition in the National Assembly. Under the special circumstances of war, there was little evidence of substantial Korean dissatisfaction with his regime. This should be seen, however, in the context of a wartime situation. Using a variety of means, constitutional and otherwise, he succeeded in gaining reelection in 1952 and 1956, and remained as president until after a clearly rigged election public pressure forced him from office in 1960.[46]

His northern counterpart, Kim Il Sung (as he was named by the Russians), ran a tightly controlled totalitarian Communist state until his death in 1994. Although his initiation of war in the Korean peninsula wrought death and destruction in both parts of the country, of course no free elections were possible. The North Korean government retained, through ideology and practical achievement, a substantial body of support. Despite initial defeat by the Americans enough of the North Korean army had gotten across the Yalu where it was reequipped and trained. Overriding the widely-held belief that the North Korean military had been shattered, on the eve of the major Chinese attack in late November Far East intelligence estimated that North Korean forces totaled about 83,000 personnel (while the Chinese numbers came into the wide range of between 40,000 and 71,000). Emboldened now by massive Chinese support, elements of four of its infantry divisions reappeared in the war in December

1950. Combined with remnants of its forces left behind in the north, it expanded to become an increasingly important factor in the conflict. After the war the northern regime had the audacity to claim its plunge into war had reaped great benefits for the Korean people. To solidify this claim it developed a "personality cult" that asserted that the people were fortunate to have Kim Il Sung at their helm. With 34,000 monuments dedicated to the "Great Leader," the cult of Kim easily matched that of Josef Stalin in his heyday (with the remnant of statues of Comrade Koba being restricted to his native Georgia). The best measure of popular support for this regime can be seen by the many Koreans who fled from the Democratic People's Republic of Korea. Despite widespread famine and poverty, as well as a consistent effort to develop nuclear weapons, to date this government stands as a model of paranoid Stalinist communism.[47]

By 1951, with potential opposition in the north effectively quelled, efforts to insert South Korean agents by airdrops and infiltration were generally unsuccessful, although some penetration from islands on the west coast did keep a large number of North Korean troops in defensive positions there. There also was the ongoing concern, particularly by the Communist command, about a U.S. seaborne attack on that coast. In the south, there remained Communist insurgent activity throughout the conflict. After the U.N. forces drove into the north, Communist irregular operations continued in the north, particularly in the Wonsan area. An overall impression is that among those Koreans who were strongly committed to their cause, they were about evenly matched. It is also most probable that a large majority of the people were just trying to survive the maelstrom in which they found themselves.[48]

On balance, the autocratic government of Rhee, with all its failings, provided at least the veneer behind which the U.S. government could claim its efforts there were based on a fight for freedom and democracy. This was good enough for Harry Truman: at the Wake Island meeting with MacArthur in October 1950, he declared, "We are supporting the Rhee Government." From that ragged foundation, and after the twenty years of military dictatorship that followed Rhee, free, representative government eventually blossomed.[49]

Americans and Koreans

Very few American soldiers welcomed the chance to fight in Korea. General John Hodges, commander of the small advisory body of American forces on the eve of the war, once declared that there were "only three things the troops are afraid of. They're gonorrhea, diarrhea and Korea."[50] Thrown into rearguard efforts to stem the tide of an invading Asian army, most Americans saw around them a poor, rural countryside in the boiling heat of the summer of 1950. They encountered a people whose language, customs and heritage

were markedly different from their own. There had not been a period of awareness and contemplation of the unfamiliar people as had been the case prior to
the American clash with the Japanese and Germans.

Given the miserable conditions then prevailing in Korea, derogatory racial
stereotypes flourished. The English journalist Philip Deane observed, "No
American seems to call the Koreans, friends or foes, anything but Gooks."
According to Reginald Thompson, another English journalist on the scene, the
American military had a contemptuous attitude towards all Koreans: "They
never spoke of the enemy as though they were people, but as one might speak
of apes. If they remarked a dead Korean body of whatever sex, uniformed or
uniformed, it was simply 'dead Gook' or 'good Gook.'"[51] An additional English
journalist, James Cameron, shared the same view of the American-Korean
relationship, noting that American servicemen, having nothing in common
with the Korean people, did not attempt to learn their language. Cameron
took a decidedly negative posture on Korea, which he saw as a "doomed place,
a country of despair," yet he could not fail to note its relatively high literacy
rate, which he attributed to the Japanese occupation.[52]

One U.S. Marine officer remembered distinguishing South Koreans from
the other kind by calling them "our gooks."[53] Hanley, Choe and Mendoza, in
their study of the No Gun Ri massacre, later declared, "American soldiers
almost universally pinned the crude word 'gook' on all Koreans, whether enemy
or allied, soldier or civilian."[54] It is of interest that *me-gook* in Korean means
American.[55] It is not surprising that American soldiers, observing the retreat
of the battered, exhausted South Korean Army, formed a negative opinion
about the allies they had intervened to save from destruction.

At the beginning, Hobart Gay, commander of the First Cavalry Division,
told a press conference that he did not intend to take the ROK Army in his
calculations "at all," but quickly found that a South Korean unit had effectively
blocked an attack on his right flank.[56] Three days after the United States got
into the conflict, Keyes Beech remembers seeing a middle-aged Korean trotting
through a rice paddy carrying a wounded American flyer on his back.[57] American soldiers also had to contend with all the difficulties of entry into combat
as well as the flood of Korean refugees who often were seen as obstacles to
their often desperate defensive efforts, as well as sometimes harboring enemy
troops in their midst.

There remained a contrasting relationship. An American officer about
to lead a group of Korean partisans into enemy territory brought them to a
Red Cross canteen for coffee only to be told, "Sorry. We don't serve Koreans."[58]
A group of Korean refugees heading south from the Chosin reservoir disaster came upon wounded U.S. troops and in the presence of Chinese soldiers
stopped to melt snow and give water, as well as cover, to some of the injured
and dying men.[59] Some South Koreans slipped bits of food to American POWs
being marched north, while above the 38th parallel there were examples

Search of a Korean civilian by Corporal James G. Gilman and Sergeant Tony F. Haluska, February 4, 1951. Courtesy Truman Library 2007-470.

where children, probably encouraged by adults, spat and threw stones at them.[60]

The most direct connection between American and Korean soldiers was through the KATUSA (Koreans Attached to the U.S. Army) program, which employed 30,000–40,000 young Koreans almost from the beginning of the conflict to fill the gap in U.S. troops. There were many problems with this relationship, but several benefits as well. Korean participants in the program by an overwhelming margin had a positive view of the experience, which they clearly found better than service in their own army. Under pressure from the South Korean government the number of KATUSAs was gradually reduced. According to David Skaggs, "KATUSA duty was looked upon with such favor by the Koreans that they knew that continuation of the duty was dependent upon outstanding performance."[61] PFC James Cardinal recalled one related incident: "At the dike I saw my KATUSAs were disorganized and beginning to falter. They were as brave as the next man, just needed firm leadership. Cursing and kicking, I got them back on the firing line." William Anderson became close to his KATUSA "buddy" Lee Sang Yu, who during adventures in

Manchuria and North Korea had taught himself English. The same thing happened with James Bolt, who trained Che Chon on the howitzer. Bolt became known to some in his infantry company as a "gook lover," but when Bolt rotated the two men shed tears. Having been rescued by Herman Brummer from an exploding tent stove, his houseboy Pakee became devoted to him; for Brummer's part, Pakee "became like a son to me." Soldier Charles Lonsford found the Korean replacements to be "good soldiers." When Lieutenant Kim, the Korean interpreter in infantryman Allen Wilkinson's company, was wounded and sent to the rear, Wilkinson was sorry to see him leave: "We classify him, along with us, as a pro, an old hand, a veteran."[62]

Other American soldiers had different experiences. Soldier Glen Justice discovered that during combat some Korean augmenters merely fired their rifles in the air. As far as Francis McGrath was concerned the KATUSAs he encountered were lazy, disloyal, dishonest and thieves. The Seventh Infantry Division had been infused with a large number of South Korean soldiers; Sgt. James Chatham's platoon was almost half Korean. Chatham had a most negative recollection of their performance in combat: "The Katusas were the worst in their undisciplined rout, but in truth, some green American soldiers were no better." Aware of the reputation of ROK stragglers for "killing and looting if no one is around to see them do it.... They would kill Yankees too." James Neely encountered three of them, to whom he gave cigarettes while covering them with a Thompson machine gun (which he called a Chicago piano). When they did not seem to want to leave, a smack on the side of Neely's gun and some strong words sent them on their way.[63]

While in North Korea in October 1950, Signal Corpsman Paul Noll participated in a campaign to secure Korean recruits. When he arrived in his designated village he was overwhelmed by volunteers who piled into his three-quarter-ton truck. Of the forty-five who volunteered only two were rejected, one being blind and the other having only one leg.[64]

Some basic difficulties soon arose about Koreans in American ranks. The U.S. Army did not have boot sizes small enough for Korean feet. Rushed production in Japanese factories soon addressed this matter. Another problem was with food. GI C-rations (at $2.00 a can) did not suit Korean appetites. The solution was the J-ration ($.79 a pack) composed of rice (of course), biscuits, fish, peas, kelp, tea, important condiments such as red pepper, garlic and soybean paste, and (strangely) chewing gum, with a few Japanese cigarettes included.[65] What was usually missing was *kimchi*, the Korean favorite, which was spicy pickled cabbage allowed to ferment in ceramic jars buried in the ground. When the Quartermaster Corps began providing *kimchi* in cans the mixture ate through the bottom; a plastic liner dealt with the problem.[66] There are few records of American soldiers acquiring a taste for the Korean national dish. An exception was one hungry teenager (seventeen years old), Army PFC William Anderson, who got to like a *kimchi* and rice combination.[67]

On occasion, a very small amount of money was provided for Korean soldiers to buy locally grown food. To break the monotony of continual C-rations, some American soldiers got local women to cook them rice, in exchange for a couple of cans of C-rations, which were prized by many Koreans. Sometimes GIs traded C-rations for eggs.[68]

At the beginning of American involvement in the Korean conflict there was an almost unanimous American negative assessment of the South Korean Army. The initial glaring inadequacy of that force was due to the lack of provision of heavy weapons by the U.S. Army. When the North Koreans struck, some ROK soldiers had never seen a tank. With masses of heavy weapons being salvaged around the Pacific, at least some these could have been sent to Korea. The reason that this was not done was inflated concern that Syngman Rhee would use them to attack North Korea. Surprisingly, neither the Central Intelligence Agency nor Tokyo Army Intelligence knew of the huge flow of Russian weapons into and the military mobilization in North Korea on the eve of the war.[69]

U.S. Army commanders had such a low opinion of ROK military capacity that for long they shunned any opportunity for joint operations. General Sun Yup Paik remembers the proud day when the first such operation took place, which he said was a clear affirmation of American confidence in the ability of their Korean allies. Paik also recalls what he termed was the T-34 disease — fear of Russian tanks — but all that was changed in August 1950 when the ineffective 2.6 bazooka shell was replaced with the armor-piercing 3.5 one. With just a few of the new weapons in hand, Paik's soldiers went hunting T-34s. Honest soldier that he was, he recalled his shock, disappointment and humiliation on the occasions when his troops panicked and ran away. He graphically describes the defeat of the North Korean Army at the end of the Pusan campaign, where, for example, "enemy machine gunners in every fighting position on every important strong point were chained in place by their wrists, condemning these men to continue fighting until they were killed."[70]

As others have observed about the South Korean response to the Chinese intervention, Paik noted that his division "seemed to regard the Communist Chinese Army with unreasoning terror. I must acknowledge that a pernicious aspect of this fear was widespread defeatism. My men seemed to be psychologically defeated even before the battle began."[71] Moving above Wonsan on the east coast in November 1950, Marine Warand Kirsch encountered South Korean soldiers streaming by, exclaiming, "Many, many Chinese."[72] On the other hand, Paik recalled the extreme docility of captured Chinese soldiers, formerly "mysterious supermen," who willingly provided information about their units, which calls into question the effectiveness of Chinese troop indoctrination.[73]

Throughout Paik's autobiography there is not a hint of disrespect shown to him or his soldiers by the American military, although he does discreetly raise the matter of the occasion when Ned Almond, noted commander of the X Corps, put lightly armed Korean divisions at the point position of a major anticipated Chinese assault.[74] When their field artillery unit was prevented from moving forward by the passage of an ROK infantry division, the GIs involved, to their "chagrin and dismay," observed the South Korean convey contained several vehicles "crammed full of furniture, comforts and personnel for the officers," including two loads of "Sheebie-Sheebie" female entertainers.[75] Other problems regularly surfaced. When typewriter repairman Richard Harris was about to bring two Korean technicians into a mess hall, he was told by the mess sergeant that the Koreans would have to wait until everyone else was fed. The difficulty was quickly resolved when Harris brought the matter to the company command level.[76]

The level of proficiency achieved by the ROK army and the disarray of the North Korean force, as indicated by Paik, was such by the autumn of 1950 that it raises an important question. Could a fully equipped ROK army have occupied North Korea on its own? The Communist Chinese declaration was that the Americans not cross the 38th parallel, not South Korean soldiers. In the ill-fated joint invasion of the north, ROK troops demonstrated great mobility and determination, reaching close to the Soviet border before things were all turned around by the Chinese intervention.

Particularly in the early months of the war, South Korean units more than occasionally broke and ran, leaving behind weapons and equipment. As far as he was concerned, Marine officer Louis Buttell held that South Korean divisions were untrained and unreliable.[77] As has been seen, when Mathew Ridgway took over the Eighth Army at the end of December 1950 he was greeted by South Korean soldiers streaming past him. Camped near the front, he found that a South Korean company had disappeared overnight.[78] British journalist Noel Monks remembered the performance of at least some South Korean soldiers: "I lost count of the times they ran and left gaping holes in our lines."[79] The Far East Command fended off Syngman Rhee's request for the formation of additional South Korean divisions by noting the poor performance of existing units.[80] As long as many ROK soldiers abandoned weapons, efforts to impose tight control of weapons in U.S. units proved to be ineffective. There was, however, a gradual and sustained improvement in combat effectiveness when, under the strong arm of Jim Van Fleet, the Republic of Korea's military was reorganized, retrained and reequipped.[81]

American military appreciation of at least some Koreans quickly developed when confronted with the disciplined, effective force of the North Korean Army. The slaughter of American POWs by North Korean troops while they were advancing and when they were forced to retreat in the Pusan perimeter in September 1950 conditioned most U.S. soldiers to show no mercy for their North Korean opponents. Unlike the Chinese when they came into the conflict, the North Koreans were not interested in accumulating prisoners.[82] When a

convoy of the Thirty-First Regiment of Seventh Division was destroyed east
of Chosin, Donald McAllister remembers North Korean soldiers laughing as
they threw gasoline into trucks holding immobile American wounded. Able
to hobble along, McAllister was put in a hut with other captives, while North
Korean and Chinese soldiers argued about their disposition, with the Koreans
wanting execution while the Chinese wanted prisoners.[83] Another POW, Donald Barton, recalled that "the Chinese treated us fairly decently. Decency ended
... when we were turned over to North Koreans.... The guards were merci-
less."[84]

In forced marches to the north conducted by North Koreans, those POWs
who were unable to keep up were killed. At various times the North Koreans
simply killed groups of American POWs. While being herded by North Korean
soldiers P.O.W. William Funchess remembered, "We came on some wounded
GIs lying on the ground. The enemy soldiers kicked and prodded them with
bayonets in an effort to get them on their feet. When the GIs were unable to
stand, the enemy soldiers forced us to walk past the wounded. In a few seconds
I heard rifle shots. I turned my head and saw the GIs had been killed.[85]

There were many examples of sustained Communist opposition. Taken
prisoner in the early days of the conflict, Edward Gregory was marched through
a village where "people spit on me, hit me with sticks, threw rocks and dung."
It was Lloyd Pate's experience that he received abuse while still in South Korea,
but had a more positive experience in the north.[86] American military police
sometimes found grenades buried in bags of rice belonging to "refugees," and
women with long dresses with shells and tubes strapped to their legs.[87] Michael
Njus's infantry company discovered a Korean woman whose A-frame concealed
an artillery radio; she was executed "on the spot."[88] In the north some children
unexpectedly threw grenades at American soldiers. A group of children being
coaxed out of a cave suddenly fell down with burp guns strapped to their backs,
while the men behind them opened fire.[89] One Marine retained regret over
having to kill boy soldiers ten or twelve years old.[90]

All through the conflict there was a mass of refugees moving north and
south — but always away from the Communist controlled parts of Korea. Control of this human flood continued to be a major difficulty for American soldiers. On the other hand, over time American soldiers developed a recognition
that many of their South Korean counterparts were capable of effective military
operations, this despite a wide variety of misadventures, of which the Americans also had their share. By mid–1951 the area along the east coast became
an all–Korean conflict. Although the corps led by General Paik still lacked adequate armor, it was greatly assisted by U.S. Navy batteries, which kept the
North Koreans out of the immediate coastal area. Paik's force succeeded in
driving his Korean opponents above the 38th parallel.[91]

One area where effective bonding between Koreans and Americans took
place was on coastal islands where guerrilla operations were directed against

Communist-held territory. According to Michael Haas, there developed trust and confidence between Korean partisans and U.S. Navy sailors who supported partisan efforts. This bonding also was a necessary requirement between the partisans and U.S. personnel, including helicopter pilots, in attacks not only on the coast but particularly on dangerous ventures into the interior.[92]

Given that almost all tonnage was moved to the front by rail, an American transportation officer was impressed by the hard work provided by Korean railroad workers, noting, "I marveled at the ingenuity of the Koreans as they put freight cars back onto the rails with little or no equipment. Everything considered, the Korean railroad personnel have done extremely well." Testimony also came from a cable laying company about the extraordinary rapport Sgt. Van Atta had with his Korean workers. Atta's commanding officer observed of them, whenever the cable was broken "they fixed it — regardless of whose territory it was in." As an example of the strong bond that developed between Atta and his crew, Col. Thomas Pitcher remembered,

> Once, north of Seoul, Van Atta went ahead of the infantry into enemy territory to get started on the cable. He was surrounded by Korean civilians and communications men. Suddenly several North Korean soldiers came on the scene and, seeing an American soldier, asked the civilians why an enemy soldier was there. The communications men replied: "He's a prisoner. We're using him to repair the cable." The enemy soldiers moved on.[93]

With the need to rebuild masses of bridges, U.S. Army engineers went to work with a plethora of machinery, while Korean work crews achieved amazing results with shovels, sandbags and manpower. An army engineer recalled the difference: "To an army almost helpless without its mechanized equipment, Korean methods seemed quaint and simple but surprisingly effective." From human conveyor belts to hand splitting logs to precision, the Korean workers employed traditional construction practices to great effect. The American engineer was particularly impressed by the Korean three-man shovel: "Its beauty lay in its simplicity of concept: the chief operator thrust the shovel, to which two lines were attached, into the ditch; his two assistants, ahead and to either side, pulled the lines; up came the shovel and its load. Working in unison, they were poetry in motion. They also moved dirt."[94]

Under the impact of massive air bombardment, the other side also had a great need to constantly rebuild battered transportation facilities and achieved equally effective results. North Korean workers were joined by a massive Chinese labor force. Repair of rail lines and road commenced immediately after bombardments. Although it did slow down supplies and reinforcements, the best efforts of the U.S. Air Force could not effectively stop the flow. Although there was a lot of talk about hordes of Communist troops attacking American positions, the real hordes were masses of Asian laborers matching and often confounding expectations about American machines and technology.[95]

Both sides used huge numbers of Korean laborers to carry all kinds of supplies to the front lines. Using a wooden frame strapped to their backs they trudged forward with heavy loads. The A frame (or H frame), Phillip Knightley observed, was "perhaps the decisive instrument of the war."[96] On the South Korean side the Korean Service Corps, whose members were sometimes called "choggie boys," grew to number 100,000 workers by 1952, many of them drawn from the moribund Korean National Guard.[97] Jim Brady well remembered this group: "The gook train, and no one called it anything else, was made up of Koreans, service corps personnel, men for one reason or another unsuited to active soldiering. I was surprised how old some of them were, literally old men. They carried tremendous loads on A-frames: rations, ammo, oil, rolls of barbed wire, shovels, tents, empty sandbags, the stuff of the army. I was sure their burden weighed more than mine, and when we'd been on the march for an hour, climbing all the time, I wondered how the old ones cut it."[98] Lyle Rishell was "amazed" that the porters could so easily climb the hills that had exhausted him. In addition, the Koreans also cut timber, built bunkers, strung barbed wire and, most importantly, were stretcher-bearers, often at the risk of their lives.[99] Another Marine, Martin Russ, who called the Korean supply column the "yo-bo train," was impressed at the "yo-bos'" capacity for work: in building bunkers, "the amount of digging they accomplished was almost unbelievable."[100]

Climbing a steep hill for the first time, Army artillery officer Alfred Gale took a break on the way up only to be shortly passed by a "coogie bearer" carrying two five-gallon cans of water on an A-frame — more than eighty-five pounds in weight. "Since I was carrying nothing but a carbine and a canteen," Gale recalls, "I was immediately shamed into pushing on."[101]

There was some communication between American and North Korean soldiers on the battlefield, but the messages seemed to be only in one direction. Some North Korean troops quickly learned to mimic the American voice and, seeking to reveal the other side's positions, would cry out for a medic or other assistance. Sometimes the message was designed to intimidate: "Mansei! G.I. die!," "Die, Yankee Pig," "Go home, Yankee son of a bitch." The only evidence of American responses were shouts of violent and, sometimes, racial abuse.[102]

There was a general perception that North Korean troops, initially at least, were better trained and equipped than the Chinese soldiers who followed them. Unlike Chinese soldiers, the North Koreans rarely surrendered. Also as in the case of the Chinese, there were women combat soldiers in the "People's Army," something that did not occur in the ROK Army.[103] After a brief firefight, Gene Robinson's Marine unit found two North Korean women in a foxhole, one with a baby strapped to her back, all dead.[104] Marine James Elkins, among others, recalls that some of North Korean women were very good with mortars and that on occasion a heavily pregnant woman carrying a white flag would approach his position "knowing that she would get medical attention."[105] Although rarely noted in subsequent accounts, each U.S. infantry company had a couple of Koreans, from the KATUSA element, who were useful in encouraging North Korean soldiers to surrender.[106]

In a once-in-a-lifetime experience, Richard Aiple was credited with capturing three North Korean soldiers. Supposedly covered by his buddy, Aiple was filling canteens in a stream when he looked up to see three North Korean soldiers with burp guns. Resigned to his imminent death, he was surprised to see them surrender. His startled shout woke his dozing cover-mate.[107] While urinating behind a bunker an unarmed corpsman heard a series of clipping sounds. A strong exclamation from him revealed two young North Korean soldiers cutting communication wire, who promptly surrendered.[108]

One area where help for Americans was virtually ruled out was in Communist prisoner camps. Even here, there were exceptions. An old North Korean woman supplied a blanket for a wounded American. While sentenced to isolation, William Funchess managed to strike a relationship with a young Korean boy whose family had some connection with the United States— postcards from the 1920s. Through the good offices of his mother, on one occasion the boy provided Funchess with a feast of scrambled eggs.[109]

Another aspect of the Korean-American relationship had to do with the huge number of Korean prisoners, who, along with some Chinese POWs, eventually were concentrated on Koje-do Island, off of Pusan. There were few troops to provide for prisoner control, administration was indifferent, and initially there was no effort at reeducation. There is evidence that Communist agents infiltrated the camps; underground areas were created where "people's democracy" enforcement was meted out. As a result, Communist agitation riots swept the camps, at one point bringing about the kidnapping of the prison commandant, all grist to Communist propaganda mills.[110] A common complaint of many South Koreans in confinement was that, dragooned into the "People's Army," they should not have been lumped in with the other inmates. Violent action was required to stifle these disturbances. Unlike the situation of South Korean prisoners in the north who were deemed "liberated soldiers" and put to work under guard in labor gangs and then mostly integrated in the Communist army, the Korean POWs in the south were kept penned up under guard.[111]

As for the civilian population, there was a general American perception that many Koreans, south and north, viewed them as liberators from Communism. Wounded U.S. Marines fighting in Seoul in September 1950 were cared for by civilians; when the litter supply was exhausted, the Koreans used doors to evacuate the wounded. Jack Wright was impressed by this activity: "For a people who could, at times, be so cruel and crude, there were other times when they could be gentle. A mother couldn't take care of her baby better than those civilians took care of our wounded." Having been wounded, Joseph Saluzzi lay out beyond his lines all night only to be greeted at daylight by four Korean boys, who placed him on a straw mat and carried him back to his side.

There were several examples of North Korean civilians helping escaped American POWs.[112] Some GIs, however, saw an underlying hostility by many Koreans, who were out to cheat or rob American soldiers. Veteran William Dannenmaier makes the point that "not all Americans serving in the rear areas were paragons of virtue. Some of them were sincere workers—like us—doing their jobs to which they had been assigned. Others were loudmouthed, bullying braggarts who used every opportunity to demonstrate their superiority by intimidating a battered and homeless people."[113] Without apparent provocation, an American soldier had taken an old man behind his hut and killed him. A unit formation soon followed with people from the village pointing out the perpetrator, who was court-martialed and imprisoned.[114] While on mess duty, Marine Leonard Martin dumped refuse down a hillside so that hungry Koreans had to run down to retrieve it.[115]

French soldier and journalist Jean Larteguy observed the American soldiers in Seoul: "In that city of Seoul, three-quarters destroyed, everything was up for sale.... The GIs came in from the front and threw themselves with their dollars upon anything alcoholic or female, placing a premium on the market in schoolgirls—students either real or made to look real with their braids, their blue dresses, their flat shoes."[116] Ahn Junghyo remembered as a child hearing of the reputation of Americans: "Americanism and the popularity of Americans in South Korea were already widespread when the giant Americans, General Megado [MacArthur] and his soldiers came to rescue South Koreans from the North Korean aggressors." He saw the arrival of American troops in his town:

> For us, the grass roots people of the hermit kingdom, the American liberators were like Santa Clauses.... But it did not take long for us to realize how the big-nosed liberators behaved after nightfall. They terrorized the villagers with nightly visits to molest our mothers, aunts and sisters. Every night my mother and other village women had to run and hide in the bushes, in rice boxes and under the floor to escape the U.N. forces of the night.

There were three clear examples of rape in Jim Brady's Marine unit.[117]

Out of fear, some refugees would not report Communist infiltrators in their midst. On the other hand, working with his KATUSA comrade Che Chon, James Bolt found that nearby villagers would tell him if strangers appeared in their village. Like almost all American servicemen in Korea, Bolt was struck by the poverty of the people, noting the clear evidence of extensive disease, including elephantiasis.[118] When a group of American Marines about to cross the Han River found that the Quartermaster Corps had provided them with inflatable rafts but no paddles, local farmers shortly carved them a supply.[119] Lee Leguire remembers that his squad, fighting its way into Seoul in September 1950, caught some ducks, which they strapped to their packs until they found a Korean woman who cooked the ducks for them, along with some rice.[120]

While reorganizing in the Pusan area following their withdrawal from North Korea, units of the X Corps undertook deep patrols to scout out Communist guerrillas and leftover North Korean soldiers. Although regularly bracketed by enemy mortars (mortars set to strike at designated approach points), very few captives resulted. Barry Jones remembered: "Bands of guerillas would appear, and disappear just as quickly.... They had the terrain plotted. When you moved into their zone they'd nail you. They wiped out a whole army battalion that way."[121]

Given this frustrating situation, one company commander tried a different approach. He spread the word around surrounding villages via scouts that the Americans were "crazy," profligate in dishing out food and cigarettes. In response, some of the opponents came in to get some, surrendering without apparent "loss of face."[122]

Through it all, there remained an uneven, shifting balance of GI opinion about Korea and its people. Due to the language and cultural gaps, few longstanding relationships developed. There were, of course, examples of understanding and consideration shown by American soldiers for Koreans, especially for children.

Everywhere there were clusters of abandoned children. This situation was brought home to PFC James Cardinal; he wrote to his parents, "I feel terribly sorry for the refugees. They seem so miserable and all are hungry and cold. Six little girls, none older than seven, just came down the road. Three are without shoes or socks; they are all homeless orphans. We are letting them sit by the fire and are feeding them. They'll probably wander along till they freeze or starve to death."[123] Infantryman Curtis Morrow recalled coming upon a small bridge which he approached with great caution. Rather than just throwing in a grenade he discovered that under it there was a small boy in rags holding an ox. He arranged for the eleven-year-old to be put to work with the Korean labor force at battalion headquarters, and whenever Morrow encountered him the boy gave him a smile and a salute.[124] An orphaned Korean boy encountered a six-foot-eight U.S. Army dentist, whom the boy thought was a giant. The dentist turned out to be a giant in another way: he arranged for the boy to be brought to the United States and settled with a Korean family in Seattle; the boy grew up to be a dental surgeon.[125] Marine fighter pilot Jerome Wilson not only lined holes with cardboard and newspapers along his airstrip for abandoned children but also had his family send clothes for them.[126] Headquarters soldier Herman Brummer found he was being followed by an autonomous group of orphans (not an adult in sight) and for good reasons— he gave them clothes, food and candy, and also played with them.[127]

With poorly equipped orphanages scattered around the country, N.F. Jeffers recalled that people, apparently both Japanese and Americans, in the Tokyo-Yokohama area contributed clothing, with the Air Force Combat Cargo Arm providing transport; "One load carried was 880 pounds of winter clothing for the kids at the Ba Hwa Orphanage outside of Taegu." The United Nations relief agency provided most of the help for the refugees.[128]

There were repeated instances in which American soldiers reached out to help Korean children. A further episode: acting as a guard on Koje-do Island, Rudolph Stephens recalls finding "a little boy all alone, in a bundle of rags sleeping in a rice field," where upon his group brought "Little Kim" to their tent, cleaned him up and gave him the semblance of a uniform. Soon the boy was joining them in the mess hall, but this happy arrangement was brought to a halt by an inspecting officer who, citing regulations, ordered the boy out of the company area. Stephens' group responded by repeatedly slipping food to the boy along a fence. A similar situation happened in Jim Brady's Marine unit when its houseboy was forced to depart, but did so "with stage tears and forty bucks in script."[129] Sometimes American soldiers had uniforms cut from GI blankets and other material for their "house boys," but one of the cooks in an army mess crew went one step further and had his wife send him child-size jeans, a cowboy shirt and boots for his little companion.[130] Another small boy hooked up with an infantry platoon; one day he left, and so did some of the soldiers' money, wallets, watches, etc.[131]

Another vignette: American soldiers were rightly concerned about enemy soldiers mixing in with refugees, but during the fighting retreat from Chosin, Lt. Ralph Abell rescued a baby that he found behind a burning hut. "We gave her some powdered milk. That didn't go over too well. We gave her some licks of our C-rations, and that hit the spot." Eventually, the baby was handed over to the care of the unit chaplain. Abell has thought back about the matter: "She would be pushing fifty now. I've always wondered how she made out."[132] In the same movement Sgt. H.D. Bales and another soldier took a toddler each from a mass of refugees and sheltered them in their parkas.[133]

British actor Michael Caine recalls that during his time in Korea he was involved in "one of the saddest things I have ever done in my life": rounding up lost children, including infants. When an American train, called the Mickey Mouse Express, decorated with cartoon characters, came through an area, soldiers were sent to find this flotsam of children and bring them to the train, "which was a cross between a hospital and a children's nursery."[134] In a more modest episode, army medic Allen Scott decided to introduce baseball to Korea. He organized a group of young Korean boys, who laid out a smooth field; then he poured flour to make base lines. Unfortunately, his unit moved before he could complete his instructional league activities, but surely other soldiers carried forward his efforts.[135]

Not all these encounters had happy endings. In the same frightful withdrawal, Capt. William Hopkins saw a little brother and sister (who had bangs like Hopkins's sister at that age) pass by with other refugees; "a little later the girl, shivering and distraught, came back up the road." As she passed by his bunker "she fell over in the snow and lay there." Hopkins brought her inside, gave her hot tea and a C-ration, but had to send her down the hill where the other refugees had gone. Moving forward later, "he caught sight of a frozen body beside the road and recognized the girl with the bangs who had reminded him of his sister."[136] Retreating in a convoy out of Pyongyang, soldier William Anderson saw a small girl crying over a dead woman, who obviously was her mother; the convoy kept moving. "I have had this sight haunting my mind ever since," recalls Anderson. "I can still hear her crying."[137] Standing guard duty in North Korea while a flood of refugees passed by, Cpl. Paul Noll was approached by a young couple holding a freezing baby. He offered them what he could — all his money and some food, but that was all: "They eventually moved on and I stood there and cried because of my helplessness as what to do.... I am haunted by this memory and what might have been."[138]

In addition to individual acts of compassion and caring, there were concerted efforts by American soldiers. During his relatively brief time in Korea in 1952, novelist Pat Frank noticed "Give a Hand" posters around the First Corps area, which were part of an effort to raise $100,000 from GIs to help children who had lost hands or legs or both. That amount was quickly donated, with another like amount being collected the following month. Frank discovered that "there was hardly a unit in the 8th Army, or Fifth Air Force, that didn't operate its own private charity." Based on his wide experience, Frank concluded that U.S. servicemen had a particular quality: "It is a simple thing called kindness."[139]

Not only was air force officer Dean Hess responsible for patching together a bit of a South Korean air force in the early days of the war, but he also joined with Chaplain Russell Blisdell and Chaplain Assistant Merle Strang in effecting the air evacuation of about a thousand orphans and the eighty orphanage staff from Seoul to the southern tip of Korea just before Christmas in 1950. The "Kiddy Car Airlift" was widely reported in the United States, and contributions flooded in from American civilians as well as soldiers in Korea.[140] The next year airmen brought gifts to the children with funds provided by members of the Fifth Air Force.[141]

There were instances when North Korean people, in extremely dangerous circumstances, helped American soldiers in distress, for instance, during that eventful Marine/Army encounter with Chinese troops at Chosin. Following the destruction of the army convoy (Task Force Faith) east of the reservoir, many surviving soldiers fled across the ice, with the Chinese not firing on them. Other soldiers, mostly wounded, skirted along the shoreline. One of these was William Hingston, who forced his way into a house with the occupants, who, at real risk to themselves, "helped him as much as they could." Hingston had a wounded soldier with him, and the elder of the household used his oxcart piled with blankets to move the wounded man to the Marine perimeter at Hagaru-ri.[142] Exhausted and bleeding, Crosby Miller broke into a house and collapsed into sleep, to be awoken by a surprised Korean woman, who gave him something to drink and dressed his shattered hand. Miller then staggered to a small settlement where a Korean man led him into a house,

After action: Marines of the First Marine Division, September 24, 1951. Courtesy National Archives, ARC 532424 [NA].

where, after some GI coffee, members of the family wrote out, in broken English, directions for Miller. Not to be outdone, one of the men led him in that direction. Three wounded American soldiers had the distinction of being delivered to safety by sleigh, provided by a family of Korean farmers.[143]

Had these North Koreans been found to have done so, the punishment for assisting American soldiers was execution. Discovering that Korean villagers, by hand signals, often informed American units if there were guerrillas in the area, Pat Frank believes that "thousands of Americans have kept their life and liberty because they were helped by Korean civilians for no other reason than they trust us, and believe in our essential goodness."[144]

In his *Substitute for Victory*, John Dille provides a sensitive assessment of the relationship between the two groups. There were many episodes of American racism, casual destruction and violence, but Dille believes that most U.S. soldiers behaved properly. The Koreans endured the many slights and much worse with Oriental stoicism and a general understanding that the Americans were there to help them.[145]

Under the leadership of Mathew Ridgway, the Eighth Army Public Affairs

Office tried its best to impose good behavior towards Koreans with a series of mimeographed messages: "Swearing at the driver of an ox cart will not make the ox move any faster," "Remember that to our Korean allies personal dignity ('Face') is as important as a healthy bankroll is to most Americans," "No amount of aid will mean anything unless accompanied by a friendly smile and a little courtesy." It also produced a short history of Korea. The army imposed strict speed limitations on traffic. To address GI impatience with slow-moving Korean pedestrians a poster soon appeared: "Keep your shirt on! After all it's his road."[146] An old woman who had experienced repeated occupations declared that the Chinese troops were the best — disciplined and polite — while the American soldiers just barged in and grabbed whatever they wanted. Dille concludes, "Most Koreans accepted the Americans, faults and all, with a good deal more patience than we accepted them."[147]

The flood of refugees was almost always moving south. There was a recurring American suspicion, not always justified, that enemy soldiers were moving through American lines in the midst of these people. Sgt. Bill Menninger remembered the situation early in the war: "The enemy was often mistaken for friendly ROK troops and vice versa. Fleeing civilians blocked the roads. They cut up our phone wire to tie bundles of belongings. Many of these civilians were actually enemy soldiers. Once they got behind us, weapons would appear and we'd have another roadblock to fight our way through."[148] The masses of refugees often obstructed the field of fire of American units. South Korean police frequently were used to move these people away, but they were not always available.

One U.S. Army officer graphically described the dilemma he faced when confronted with an advancing mass of refugees: "I instructed the roadblock to fire full tracer [rounds] along the final protective line, then to fall back onto the high ground. If an enemy unit was in and among those refugees, well, then they simply would be in our rear in the morning. I could not order firing on those thousands upon thousands of pitiful refugees."[149] PFC Victor Fox remembered coming upon a freight train in Pyongyang "piled high and crammed with refugees, stoically waiting for whatever fate their God held for them. When I found some English-speaking civilians, I discovered many of them were highly educated and before the war had held prominent positions in their communities."[150] Escaping refugees often clung to any train moving south. While traveling on a box car train in bitter weather heading south, Anthony Herbert noted that Koreans clinging to the outside had frozen to death. They had to be removed with crowbars.[151]

The key port city of Pusan was the center for displaced Koreans. What E.J. Kahn saw in Pusan in mid–1951 was a scene of mass displacement: "Clinging to the sides of the hills that rise in the center of the city are hundreds of shacks, built out of cardboard and paper."[152] Lt. Eddie Deerfield, attached to a broadcasting unit, remembered a market scene there in 1952: "The local folks displayed a variety of legal and black market goods, from vegetables to dried squid to tires and diesel generators." His attention was drawn to "a cluster of very young children in short jackets cut from GI wool blankets, their legs and feet bare in the near-freezing temperatures, seemingly impervious to the cold." Half a century later, "My thoughts turned to the packs of homeless children that wandered the streets of Pusan along the waterfront, without shoes or warm clothing, begging and stealing to survive from day to day."[153]

Pat Frank had a similar impression of Pusan when he arrived there the same year: "Pusan itself is a cauldron of misery. Naked children, their bellies swelled with starvation, grub in the filth. The pocked streets eddy with the sick, the half-clothed, the leprous, the mutilated and the beggars.... Ever since the first Communist drive, when a million refugees fled into the corner of Korea known as the Pusan perimeter, it has been this way."[154] Michael Caine's introduction to Korea, with Pusan in particular, was as his ship approached the coast: "A faint but very unpleasant smell gradually started to permeate the air in our quarters down to the bowels of the ship"—from the Korean farmers' practice of using human excrement for fertilizer. In Pusan he saw buildings that were "made out of every available piece of scrap and waste materials that the inhabitants could get their hands on." Conditions were so bad "you could almost see disease in the air."[155]

The South Korean government was overwhelmed trying to provide for the many refugee centers. The problem was particularly acute in trying to assist the many war orphans. E.J. Kahn visited one of these places, a former cattle research center in Pusan: "In one cattle shed, a school was in session, with a student body of four hundred and a faculty of four. The teachers, themselves refugees, had hardly any textbook, but they did have a few blackboards, and the lessons they chalked on these were being diligently copied by their pupils into notebooks made from the cardboard sides of ration cartons." In fifteen tents scattered around the camp, there were only six Korean doctors, "with extremely scanty equipment" to care "for as many as two hundred and forty incoming patients a day."[156]

After twelve months of war there were more than three million refugees. United Nations agencies saved these people from starvation — a pound of rice per day apiece, with most of the rice being donated by the Philippines and Thailand.[157]

Hugh Lafferty experienced the dire health hazards of military service in Korea: "Our drinking water supply was limited. Our medics and I were concerned about sanitary conditions.... Washing hands and mess gear was practically impossible. We ate soggy C rations or went without." As well, he was aware of the ongoing health problems around him. Due to the use of human and animal excrement for fertilizer, all kinds of aliments existed. He estimated that "the average intestinal tape worm in one of the natives or a ROK soldier with a gut blown open was about six feet."[158] This condition also applied to

American POWs, one of whom remembers discovering his large tapeworm upon his release.[159] Another soldier found that chewing tobacco prevented him from getting stomach parasites.[160]

Another aspect of the American-Korean relationship was the reception given to American units occupying places formerly controlled by the Communists. There were repeated episodes of Koreans lining a town street shouting "*Man-se*" (long life) as the Yanks rolled in. This was certainly the case in Seoul in September 1950, when following the fierce struggle to regain control over the city, the liberators and South Korean government representatives got a tumultuous reception. According to Harold Noble, "The battered streets were lined by citizens of all ages, small children and aged men and women, many holding small South Korean flags." He noted, "All the adults looked gaunt and drawn from hunger or disease," and he was sure that the reception was spontaneous: "There was no one available to make them come out and cheer."[161]

Some GIs harbored a suspicion that such receptions were not simply an effort at accommodation. When American soldiers entered the important city of Suwon, "The huge entrance gate ... was decorated with evergreen garlands and boughs and large banners written out in English," recalled Victor Fox. "Civilians waving South Korean flags and shouting 'Man-se' lined the streets of our advance. Some troopers wondered whether the people held North Korean flags in their other hand — just in case."[162] In one North Korean town local people gave eggs and produce to American troops, unlike in the south where they were offered for sale. Based on his experience, Second Lt. Adrian Brian concluded if there was a welcoming committee greeting his unit, there were no North Korean troops nearby. On one occasion in the spirit of a happy reception and as a precaution, he put a willing Korean boy on the hood of his jeep: "I knew the civilians wouldn't let the kid ride with me if the road ahead was mined."[163]

A North Korean soldier in the process of withdrawing from Seoul in September 1950 was confronted with a sweeping change in the people's demeanor: "I was so surprised to see the same residents who warmly welcomed us a week before now welcome the ROK troops back into the city with cooked food and the ROK national flags." A similar phenomenon occurred in North Korea, where crowds greeted American and South Korean troops in the fall of 1950; after that November when American POWS were led through those places, they were subjected to strong abuse. A clear possibility was that people of differing political alignments attended those occasions. In contrast to the first evacuation, there was a massive evacuation of the South Korean capital city before the Communists again regained Seoul the following January.[164]

One of the many sad episodes of the conflict took place as the Army X Corps was working its way up to the Chosin reservoir in November 1950: the people in one village unearthed their forbidden Bibles and other religious materials, only to have to bury them once again when the American force was driven south. John Y. Lee, an ROK liaison officer with the Marine Division, observed their reaction to this turn of events: "Through the window I saw many crying while the services were conduct[ed]. I knelt down in the snow outside the window and prayed for them." As has been seen, when the U.S. Army units were retreating from the Yalu, there were instances where North Korean civilians freely provided valuable assistance. On the eve of the evacuation of Pyongyang an American reporter noted the drastic change in the demeanor of some of the population: "Unconcealed fear marked the faces of those whose houses until this morning sported flags of the Korean Republic or the United Nations blue and white."[165]

A strongly negative view of Americans in Korea was provided to Rene Cutforth, an English journalist, by a Korean Catholic priest who told him that if a plebiscite was held in South Korea, "the Communist vote would be more than seventy-five percent." This was due to "the bombs and the burning and the raping behind the lines," which the result being "we dislike you all cordially." Thus, "your cause is good, but you have lost our good will, and though you all appear to despise us, that is a big thing to lose." There are many examples to sustain this judgment, but, despite all the massive death and destruction, on balance most Koreans appeared to understand and appreciate what the Americans were doing there.[166]

One American officer, Melvin Voorhees, was unstinting in his praise for the Korean people:

> The sense of dignity, self-confidence and pride possessed by the average Korean was notable. He did not cringe or grovel. Despite forty years under political and economic domination of Japan and centuries prior to that of mistreatment by foreigners, he remained conscious of his rightful place and of that of his people. He did not bow and scrape and cater to the American in the calculated manner of the Japanese and the German.[167]

On the other hand, Rene Cutforth recalled episodes of jeep stealing and looting by Korean civilians, all of this taking place, it should be noted, in the midst of chaos and destruction.[168]

When a chance to get out of war-ravaged Korea opened up, U.S. servicemen *en masse* opted for a few days in nearby Japan. They would not have received this hospitality in Japan (or Germany) just a few years before. Yet at the end of the war in Europe, American soldiers greatly preferred the people of defeated Germany to those of Allied France. A similar view of the Koreans and Japanese marked the attitudes of American troops in the Korean War. American soldiers were in Korea to fight a war, however, and the training and employment of young Korean men were vital parts of that effort. By the end of the war South Korean troops were the majority of combatants on the allied side. Moreover, a small number of U.S. military (about 33,000 army and air force personnel in 2010) remained in Korea almost sixty years later as part of the commitment of the United States to prevent a renewal of war in that divided country.[169]

From the beginning of the summer of 1950, hundreds of thousands of Americans poured into Korea. Part of their relationship with the Korean people was sexual. Very few American servicemen married Korean women, a relationship that was actively discouraged by the U.S. military. Prostitutes were part of the scene in every Korean city and larger town. In over three hundred accounts by American servicemen of their time in that country, the great majority of them declared they had nothing to do with prostitutes and many of them claimed they had no direct knowledge of this matter. It is not surprising that many servicemen said nothing about this potential relationship. In fact, only one American explicitly mentioned having intercourse with a Korean woman. Evidence for Americans resorting to Korean prostitutes is provided by the frequent treatment for a variety of sexually transmitted aliments, for which a shot of penicillin was the usual remedy.

With intercourse commonly occurring between Americans and Koreans, it is surprising that there were so few offspring. Although it is probable that many American soldiers used condoms, the Korean women involved in this activity surely employed birth control methods, either traditional or modern. In any case, few biracial offspring were apparent. Although traditional Koreans were committed to maintaining their racial identity and thus opposed American-era prostitution, there was constant sexual activity between "*me-gooks*" and "gooks." An American soldier arriving in Korea in 1959 was surprised to see so many fair-haired young boys clinging to the backs of U.S. Army trucks.[170] Probably for purposes of deflecting public concern, the American military did not view the whole matter as being of considerable import. In the experience of one woman born of an American-Korean relationship, there was considerable antipathy exhibited by Korean people towards the half-breeds; this was a common condition. In her case, members of her family killed her mother for giving birth to the child of an American soldier, and the off-spring was shuffled off to an orphanage.[171]

Despite the efforts of the U.S. Army and Korean authorities, kijich', or prostitution, was a common occurrence during the conflict; this continued after it was over, but the gradual decline in troop numbers also brought about a reduction in this activity. In a nation of nearly fifty million people, a 2009 estimate has it that there were 18,000 registered and 9,000 unregistered prostitutes. "Camptown" prostitution at least limited the activity to specific locations, which the great majority of Koreans completely avoided. Beginning in the early 1990s a whole new dimension in this activity was the influx of some Russian and a large number of Filipino women. In all this, South Korea was caught in a bind: it needed American military security, which meant, as a practical matter, that it had to endure concentrations of prostitution.[172]

When American soldiers first arrived in Korea they were met with blazing heat, high humidity and all the realities of a country in turmoil. Later, as they moved north, they encountered bitter wind and plunging temperatures. Spring resulted in torrential rain, which left infantrymen wet and muddy for weeks. When Michael Caine first got there, a U.S. Marine informed him of the prevailing weather conditions: "Hot as hell in the summer, below zero in the goddam winter and in the windy season you breathe human shit dust from the dried-up manure on the fields." The Marine also provided information about vermin: "There are more rats than there are flies and there are more mosquitoes than both of them put together." Caine recalls being assaulted by all kinds of insects during nighttime patrols, on one occasion, he said, "I could only just see through the slits in my eyes as my lids and surrounding face had swollen from the bites and almost completely closed off my field of vision."[173] As a result, U.N. participants often had a negative view of the place. Above all, they had the physical reality of hill after hill, rows of them reaching to the Yalu.

Removed from the face of battle and the circumstances of camp life, however, some of them discovered a land of great natural beauty, which a few of them recorded. On his second sojourn in the country, Korea in the springtime struck army advisor S.L.A. Marshall:

> From a point of no man's land, our fighting front looked like a rhapsody in pink, so thickly covered were the slopes and saddles with wild plum and chindoe.... For three weeks this radiant flush relieved the normal monotony of an otherwise drab countryside. Above the pink sea the profiles of the ridge lines also had temporary look.... From grass-green sea in the valley bottom up to the blue sky, it was layer on layer of vivid color, the sweetest front that anyone ever smelled.[174]

Grizzled Marine Martin Russ had the same experience. Shortly after dawn one day he "watched the mist disperse, and then the strings of fog that hover over the gullies. Very beautiful. Land of the morning calm is right. Despite the occasional rumblings in the distance, early mornings in Korea are almost too much to take."[175]

Jim Brady remembered looking at the scene from a mountain top in midwinter: "Sometimes I just stayed out there somewhere sheltered from the wind and looked at the country, those serried rows of hills.... In a country this lovely, unless someone was shooting at you or sending you out on patrol, if you could stay dry and warm, and you knew there was one more little can of sweet peaches or pears back in the bunker, the war wasn't so bad."[176] Moving up at dawn to "Bloody Ridge" in September 1951, Marine machine gunner John Genrich observed, "It looked like too beautiful of a day for so many young men to die."[177] A final recollection, that of Anthony Herbert: "Dawn broke across the sky as we made our way back. The hills emerged from the darkness like rolling blue swells on a winter ocean of white and gray. At the horizon, earth and sky blended in a pale blue-green mist. The taller, nearer ridges and peaks appeared sharply etched in white. Everything but us stood still and calm, just as it always did in this country when the war was elsewhere."[178]

From the perspective of the arid desert of the American West, an illegitimate Korean-American girl, who had been adopted by a childless evangelical minister and his cold-hearted wife, fondly remembered her childhood home: "The tiny village was breathtaking in its beauty: a verdant, lush valley on the outskirts of Seoul, surrounded by Korea's million mountains. Visually, it was the embodiment of Korea's name: Land of the Morning Calm."[179]

Chinese and American Soldiers

When the Chinese Communists barreled into Korea, its "volunteers," although often deficient in garments and weapons, almost invariably had been subjected to indoctrination. Included in this was being instructed to pursue what they called a "lenient policy" towards their captured opponents. The release of fifty-seven wounded American and some South Korean soldiers shortly before Thanksgiving in 1950 was held by the Chinese leaders to be a manifestation of this policy. One of the released U.S. soldiers recalled that when they were captured, "a Chinese major, the only officer they saw, apologized for their close quarters." When a North Korean soldier took the watch of an American prisoner, that major "had the Korean Red shot dead."[180] After his Chinese guards allowed another POW to keep his nail clippers and watch, a North Korean soldier took the watch, which was retrieved for the POW.[181] Another substantial release of POWs occurred on February 8, 1951, when forty-eight of them were freed.[182] There was no equivalent action by the other side.

Another account relates that a Chinese soldier, in conformity with the lenient policy, interceded in an effort by a North Korean soldier to execute a captured American. At the end of the Chosin campaign the Chinese military took a group of 250 army soldiers and 45 Marines to an area called "Happy Valley," where the prisoners were subjected to intense political indoctrination whose purpose was to spread the good news of the wonders of communism. Loaded up with propaganda material, nineteen of them were released.[183] This appears to be the same experience that a group of a group of Marines related: they were told if they provided their Chinese captors with information about their units, they would be released. Having provided the Chinese interrogators with a realm of false information, nineteen of them were brought south to the Imjin River for release, which was disrupted by an air attack.[184]

There were several other occasions when the Chinese released groups of American prisoners. One of these occurred on February 17, 1951, during the extended battle for the Wonyu area when thirty members of the Second Division were turned loose. Six days later the same thing happened to twenty-nine of them. On that St. Patrick's Day a tank-infantry patrol came upon sixteen wounded Americans, who told them that after capture they had been relieved of their money and valuables ("involuntary contributions" to the Chinese Communist cause) but were left behind when the fit prisoners were sent north. At that time the wounded group was provided with three letters dealing with their status—one each for encountered North Korea, Chinese and Americans. A North Korean unit which came upon them, with due respect for the Chinese injunction, left them "strictly alone." Five days later in the same area, twenty-nine of 152 captured Yanks were released. Soon thereafter two U.S. officers after being captured managed to escape and while moving south encountered a North Korean security policeman whom they told that they had been released "up north," whereupon he gave them a safe-conduct pass. Two more such incidents occurred the following May—on May 4 and May 21. The occasional release of small groups of newly captured American POWs clearly was part of the Chinese political posture in the war. Commenting on one of these occurrences and similar episodes, Roy Appleman has declared, "Such was one of the many quixotic and generous actions" that Chinese soldiers "were capable of during the war." There is only one example of North Koreans releasing enemy POWs, when on the night of February 8-9, 1951, they freed 22 American and 15 South Korean soldiers. With prior knowledge of released POWs, Anthony Farrar-Hockley's group of prisoners decided to show interest and appreciation for the accounts provided by their Chinese captors in hopes that this would earn them release, but when an exchange of sick and wounded captives took place in the spring of 1953 he noted that "a not inconsiderable" number of active collaborators were among those the Chinese released.[185]

During the Chinese onslaught on the Eighth Army in the west and the X Corps in the east in November-December 1950, massive fatalities were inflicted by both sides. Principally during the retreat of the lead elements of the Seventh Division from Chosin, Chinese soldiers slaughtered many wounded Americans. Yet there were surprising episodes of Chinese consideration for their opponents. After one firefight, Chinese soldiers let American walking wounded go back to their lines, while laying those badly wounded along a road to be retrieved by jeeps. One of these recalled being carried by Chinese soldiers on a stretcher marked, "Donated by the American Red Cross." Another veteran remembered that during the Chosin retreat, Chinese soldiers in hills on both sides of a road allowed wounded Americans to move along the road to safety. Others recalled how Chinese soldiers permitted American troops to crawl across the frozen reservoir.[186] After Chinese troops had destroyed an army convoy (Task Force Faith) attempting to retreat from Chosin, a group of wounded U.S. soldiers struggling to restart one of the trucks were captured by Chinese infantrymen who, according to a witness, "gave morphine to several men, bandaged their wounds and, after caring for them for several days, freed them."[187]

In at least a couple of instances, Chinese soldiers formerly in the Nationalist armies, who had been dragooned into the Communist "volunteers," showed kindness to wounded Americans. In the Chosin retreat a Chinese officer, formerly in the Nationalist Army and a Christian, told wounded Americans lying along a road that he would pray for them, also mentioning that he would be killed if his concern was observed by political officers, who were attached to all Chinese units. Several American POWs noted that some Chinese doctors and "political indoctrinators," among others, were helpful and sympathetic towards them. In William L. White's estimation, "among the ordinary Chinese there still remained a considerable reservoir of good will towards Americans."[188] One estimate was that 30 percent of Chinese soldiers in Korea had formerly been in the defeated Nationalist forces. Related to this was an estimate that there were 60,000 women in the Chinese forces, acting as nurses, clerks, translators, propagandists (singers, theatrical performers and related), security guards and sometimes as combat soldiers.[189]

Another Chinese-American encounter during the bitter winter retreat from Chosin occurred when a huge Chinese force in the dead of night surrounded a Marine unit that had many wounded and was almost out of ammunition. A English-speaking Chinese political officer sent word to the Marine commander that if his unit surrendered, the wounded, lying on the frozen ground, would be sent back to "friendly lines." The offer being accepted, the first thing the Chinese soldiers did was to strip the Marines of "every scrap of food they could winnow out of the pockets and packs of the men." Most likely, they also collected prized GI boots. A Chinese colonel congratulated his Marine equivalent for putting up a good fight. True to their word, the Chinese, one way or another, sent the wounded back to the scattered Marine lines.[190] This apparently was the same episode when a group of twenty Marines, with rifles slung and surrounded by a mass of Chinese soldiers, were sent to retrieve a few wounded GIs and two British commandos who had been left in a small house. Placed on stretchers, the rescued soldiers were brought back, including a GI who was clutching a bag of mail that he insisted on carrying back for delivery. This surely must be the most striking example of the injunction, "The mail must go through"![191]

During the heroic fighting withdrawal of the First Marine Division from Chosin, the weather was so brutal there were times when the usual operations of warfare were suspended. While looking for a missing officer a Marine search party came upon several Chinese soldiers huddled around a blazing fire. Major Hal Roach: "They pretended not to see us and we pretended not to see them, and all the while I was calling out at the top of my voice" the name of the missing Marine, who was never found. During that march to the coast, Marine Alan Herrington discovered he was being accompanied by a Chinese soldier carrying a wounded comrade on his back. Obviously this mixture was outside the bounds of usual military protocol, so the Chinese twosome were detached from the line of march, and they struggled off into the mist. Rather than shooting a wounded Chinese soldier he encountered on the road, Marine Bob Young bound him up and put him in the back of a truck, with the Chinese soldier shortly returning the favor by helping to push disabled vehicles out of the line of march.[192]

Part of the rearguard pulling out of Hagaru, PFC Richard Stewart came face to face with three Chinese soldiers sharing a can of food. Surprise was not matched by hostility: "I just backed away, and they returned to their meal."[193] During that retreat army PFC James Bolt noticed a Chinese soldier, with rifle strapped on his back, was riding along on Bolt's howitzer trailer. When questioned, the soldier explained that his feet were so badly frostbitten that his officers suggested that he go to the Americans, who would take care of him. Indeed, they did — wrapping up his feet and shipping him to the rear in an ambulance.[194] In the same march Marine Richard Bohart saw a pathetic sight — three Chinese soldiers in a line coming down a hill guided by tree branches. They were almost blind, and after being napalmed their bodies were blackened with erupting red blotches at which maggots were at work. In what Bohart saw as a humane action, they were led away and shot.[195] In releasing a wounded American soldier a Chinese officer said to him, "No more petroleum," that is, napalm, which he obviously deemed to be outside the rules of the game of conventional warfare.[196]

During the retreat from Hagaru, Marines found they could not take along 160 Chinese prisoners, so, after proving them with some food and fuel, they released them. Although most of the Chinese were reluctant to be cut loose, many of them were killed in a subsequent Chinese bombardment on that position.[197]

During the same pull-back, Marine Lt. Dave Peppin encountered a striking example of Asian stoicism. Standing in the road he found three Chinese officers of obviously high rank (they were wearing scarlet-lined capes). Obviously unable to flee, they silently refused to surrender, so Peppin's Marines shot them down.[198]

In the middle of the Chinese assault on the army convoy of elements (Task Force Faith) of the Thirty-First Regimental Combat Team east of Chosin, Chinese soldiers moved along the halted trucks, killing all the wounded aboard who could not get off, while sparing those who could walk. Having destroyed the military effectiveness of that unit, most Chinese soldiers seemed to have had enough killing for the time being. Not only did some provide medical help to wounded GIs, but they failed to fire at the hundreds of soldiers fleeing across the ice to the Marine perimeter at Hagaru-ri. Seeking to escape along the shoreline, Crosby Miller had repeated encounters with Chinese soldiers. Lying wounded in a hut, Miller met two Chinese soldiers, who only each took a cigarette from him and laughed at his bleeding. Soon two more Chinese soldiers came in and this time took all his cigarettes and his lighter. A third twosome only took a can of C-rations and also left. Having moved forward, he was shoved into a shed by two more Chinese troopers. Miller surmised that he was not being shot due to his deathly appearance: "Unshaven, dirty, covered with blood and with frozen fingers now beginning to blister and turn black, I believe I was being left to die." His final encounter came when two more Chinese "volunteers" dragged him out of a shed and proceeded to tear up his ID card and take his wallet, while returning his family photographs. One of the soldiers pointed a rifle at him for "what seemed to be an eternity," but then turned and walked away. Having had enough contact in those circumstances with his Chinese contemporaries to last a lifetime, Miller soon found succor with a Korean family, who led him to freedom.[199]

An American soldier recalled a time, in April 1951, when as part of a supply group he encountered Chinese soldiers: "They were only 200 feet from us. They did not fire at us, nor we at them. As we left on our truck the CCF waved good-bye to us, perhaps because we were loading dead and wounded while throwing off 81 mm mortar ammo."[200] While on a patrol in the central mountains in 1952, James McAleer relates a distant encounter with a Chinese forward observer: they waved to him and he waved to them. Since Chinese mortar fire was so inaccurate, they decided not to disturb him, as he might have been replaced with a more proficient observer.[201]

During the struggle for "Old Baldy" in October 1951, army Lt. Morton Wood watched American wounded and dead being brought out. There was a lull in the fighting: "An eerie calm lay over the valley. The Chinese on Hill 346 were plainly visible, scurrying about, repairing their bombed and napalmed trench line. They had obviously been ordered to withhold fire." In another encounter, having crawled forward to drag in a wounded soldier, W.B. Woodruff observed, "The Chinese, I noted, had kept their record intact of never firing on a rescue effort."[202] A British regiment experienced an example of Chinese restraint. Anthony Farrar-Hockley recalled being in a group of soldiers who were completely covered by Chinese machine guns—"They could have mown us down like grass before a scythe"—but did not fire. Recognizing the hopelessness of their situation, the British soldiers surrendered.[203] An Australian doctor remembered a battle in April 1951 during which Chinese soldiers stopped firing to allow some of the Australian wounded to be withdrawn.[204]

An American soldier was about to kill a disarmed Chinese soldier who started to cry and took out a photograph of his young wife and child, whereupon the GI sent him to the rear. Having killed a wounded Chinese soldier, Marine Ernest Gonzales found a folder of family photographs in the dead man's pocket; "I never again killed a wounded Chinese soldier."[205] Coming upon a badly wounded Chinese soldier, an American lit a cigarette and put it in the mouth of the dying opponent.[206] After an extended firefight, Marine Albert Styles zeroed in on a single Chinese soldier running up a hill who turned and waved at him, upon which Styles held his fire, with his squad members nodding in agreement at his inaction. Enough death for one day.[207] A striking episode occurred when U.S. and British Marines, retreating in the east, left behind fifty wounded Chinese soldiers, after providing them with "first aid, food and water in a heated house" as a "thank you" gesture for similar treatment accorded United States prisoners on the northwestern front. In the bitter retreat another 160 captured Chinese soldiers were provided with some food and released.[208] There were episodes when American soldiers held fire while Chinese troops retrieved their dead and wounded, and vice versa. Encounters such as these were atypical, but there were a least a few gestures of mutual concern and respect.

Anthony Herbert recalls the respect he had for the fighting capacity of one Chinese soldier he encountered in the spring of 1951. While the rest of his comrades had retreated, a Chinese machine gunner refused to pull back, continuing to kill and wound soldiers in Herbert's unit. When the Chinese soldier at last was cornered Herbert called upon him to surrender, whereupon another American immediately killed him. This action angered Herbert: "Chinese or no Chinese, the dead machine gunner had been a hell of a trooper.... I would have been proud to have had the guy in my outfit."[209]

In other instances, Chinese soldiers killed without restraint. During the Eighth Army retreat in November 1950, Herbert came upon 29 dead Americans who had been strung up and their stomachs ripped open.[210] Michael Czuboka, a Canadian infantryman, came upon a "scene of horror" in February 1951: "Something like 68 black and mostly naked American bodies were scattered all around us. They had been bayoneted and shot by the Chinese, and their weapons and clothing had been removed. They were frozen solid and looked like black marble statues." Czuboka noted that their ring fingers had been cut off. Apparently these soldiers had only posted a single sentry and had not dug slit trenches. His company commander issued orders: no sleeping bags on the front line and multiple sentries, especially at dawn, the time the Chinese invariably attacked.[211] A report of the incident appeared in a Toronto newspaper, whereupon MacArthur requested an immediate report, querying why the story had "passed your censor."[212] In February 1951 soldier Carrol Everist evaded death by pretending insanity. After the other ambushed members in his group had been executed, Everist put on his act. He recalls, "I had heard that the Chinese believe if you are insane, you are worse than if dead." The Chinese soldiers stripped him of his watch and billfold, but returned his prayer book. Then, "the Chinese pulled out, leaving me."[213]

In the process of destroying the Thirty-First Regiment of the Seventh Division east of Chosin, Chinese soldiers ordered off trucks all who could move, then killed all those who were not ambulatory. In the same encounter American soldiers threw phosphorous grenades and killed a hut full of Chinese soldiers immobilized from frozen extremities—toes and fingers.[214] In one retreat Chinese solders left behind four wounded Americans in a hut. These are examples of consideration and even compassion on either side. Back and forth the pendulum swung, with both sides exhibiting extremes of behavior. There were also singular cases of killing. Jim Brady remembered the time when four Marines sunning themselves on top of a bunker were hit by a single mortar shell. One of his sergeants began vigorously calibrating his mortar over and over, then fired, hitting four soldiers on other side: "Dodge had evened the score."[215]

As were some North Koreans, Chinese soldiers were adapt at both mimicking American sounds and getting U.S. passwords. To forestall this effort, American soldiers learned to employ some words in English which were difficult for the Chinese to replicate. For example green came back from the Chinese as "gleem."[216] Marines used code words when calling for medical assistance from their corpsmen. In addition to the clamor of bugles, drums and whistles, the Chinese also delivered clearly intimidating messages. During the fight at Chosin, Marine Ted Heckelman heard Chinese loudspeakers asserting the claim, "Tonight you die, Marines; tonight you die!"[217] One way that U.N. soldiers on patrol could ascertain if any Chinese soldiers were in the vicinity was to note the smell of garlic left by them.[218]

A clear advantage that both the North Koreans and Chinese forces had was in the matter of troop indoctrination, which, in most cases, was reinforced by repetition. In contrast, at least initially, political conditioning for American troops virtually did not exist. A lot of soldiers claimed they did not know why they were there or what the war was about. When Mathew Ridgway took command of the Eighth Army in April 1951 he addressed this matter in a short statement, which was followed up with a series of informative bulletins.[219] At the beginning of the conflict American soldiers, from far and wide, were simply rushed to Korea. The Chinese, in particular, were successful in including ordinary soldiers in projected operations and also effectively diminished rank and privilege, a condition which only existed in American ranks through the informal, democratic character of the American experience. When the first few Chinese soldiers were captured, U.S. intelligence officers were amazed and doubtful about the knowledge that these Chinese captives had about the operations in which they were involved.[220] Paul Edwards commented, "The average Chinese soldier was far better informed than an American enlisted man would be about the activities of his army." The fact that many ordinary Chinese soldiers were so informed was used by U.S. frontline intelligence units to counter planned enemy assaults. Considering the extreme privations that were the fate of ordinary Communist soldiers, it is impressive how high their morale remained, clearly testimony to the effectiveness of their indoctrination.[221] At the very front and on the eve of battle, political officers would encourage soldiers to declare they would conduct heroic actions, and, in some instances, "propaganda girls would join in, singing and banging pans." The usual practice was to have a political officer for each platoon.[222]

The marked enthusiasm with which Chinese soldiers attacked led several

American troops to surmise that their opponents were stimulated by narcotics. Marine James DeLong recalls that he could tell when Chinese soldiers were about to attack by the smell of what he believed to be marijuana, cocaine and heroin. Soldier Arthur Smith remembered that many Chinese troops were "high on opium," while Marine Jon Genrich was sure they were "drugged." Another soldier, Kenneth Kendall, found a bag of opium on a dead Chinese officer. Marine general O.P. Smith held that "a great many" of the Chinese soldiers "carried benzedrine pills and opium."[223] Some soldiers believed their Chinese opponents attacked while stimulated by rice wine.[224]

An experienced Marine infantry company commander, John Chafee, provides insight into the contrasting North Korean and Chinese approaches to combat. The North Koreans, he believed, "were more like the Japs in the islands than like anyone else. You had to dig them out of the caves, you had to kill them. They don't surrender, not very often and not in bunches." James Brady, a lieutenant in Chafee's company, saw the Chinese as different: "The Chinks were better equipped than the North Koreans, their communications were better, their artillery, too, very soldier-like. But they did surrender. They had more sense than the gooks, and if you could prove to them they were finished, well, they gave up. Of course it wasn't their country they were fighting in, and that may have made the difference."[225] Army soldier William Anderson has a similar experience.[226]

A continuing concern for the Chinese leadership was the huge number of former Nationalist soldiers brought into the "People's Army." These "liberated soldiers" initially were subject to lengthy indoctrination, but despite this effort, which was continued during the fighting, ex–Nationalists were by far the most likely to surrender and later led the group who elected to go to Taiwan at the end of the conflict. The failure of the last great Chinese offensive in the spring of 1951 to be immediately followed by a U.N. counterattack convinced many Chinese soldiers that victory was not to be had. According to Alexander George, there was a "high state of demoralization and disaffection among ordinary soldiers," which was compounded by the loss through combat of many Party officers.[227]

In stark contrast to the piecemeal rotation system employed in the U.S. forces beginning in the spring of 1951, the Chinese military practiced rotation of entire armies. While there was little augmentation of American forces by that time, the shifting of Chinese soldiers allowed for their battered units to be replaced by masses of fresh troops. At that time, while small numbers of GIs left Korea when their time was up (from nine months to little more than a year), the Chinese rotated two-thirds of their field forces, said to include 25 field corps, 70 artillery divisions, 10 railroad engineer divisions and more.[228]

Compared to the generally brutal North Korean treatment of captured Americans, the Chinese usually shunned physical abuse, instead employing methods of measured but increasingly intense indoctrination and rewards for cooperation and punishment for resisters. Conversion to the ideology of communism apparently was more important to the Chinese (surely reflecting their pride both in great cultural heritage of their country and the New China in the process of construction) than a desire to punish the Americans for their intervention in Korea, which, understandably, seemed to be the prime motive of North Korean Communists. Despite the continuing efforts of the Chinese personnel involved, very few American prisoners collaborated (those who did were termed "progressives" by their Chinese captors).[229]

When a full exchange of prisoners finally took place in mid–1953, only twenty-one of 3,597 U.S. soldiers chose not to return. One of the former POWS commented that this handful probably feared what would happen to them when they returned to American lines.[230] At least one of those who chose to remain had given pro-communist lectures to the POWs and later made radio broadcasts. One of the twenty-one later died in China, but all of the others eventually left there, with most returning to the United States.[231] So, despite all the ensuing journalistic commentary about the matter, only a handful made the decision to stay.

When this large flow of POWs was released, the army made the decision that there would be only limited access by the swarms of journalists to the released men until all POWs were returned, which extended to the following September. Counterintelligence officers lectured to the returnees at rest camps and on troop ships. From this decision sprang press speculation about the impact of communist indoctrination of the prisoners, so-called "brainwashing." This in turn led to a rash of pompous outbursts from cranks, blowhard patriots and armchair militiamen about the weakness, softness, failure and more of young male Americans. The evidence for these statements was the supposed cravenness of the POWs. One army major concocted the unsupported claim that one-third of the POWS had been conditioned by communist indoctrination.[232]

Here was a clear case of blaming the victims. Reflecting this perception was the production by the U.S. military of the Uniform Code of Military Justice (which to some people was very close to being an oxymoron) in which captured American servicemen were ordered to provide only their name, rank, serial number and date of birth. This mindless constraint demonstrated a totally unrealistic comprehension of the POW experience and was put into effect when Dwight Eisenhower, who had never spent a minute in combat, was president.[233]

When, at last, the fighting ended in July 1953, at one site, while a barrage of flares from both sides filled the air, Chinese soldiers responded with songs and proceeded to bring small presents and candy to the front. The Marines opposite did not know how to respond except to belt out the "Marine Corps Hymn."[234]

For what it is worth, and recognizing that the conduct of war does not require courtly behavior, anecdotal evidence seems to indicate that Chinese soldiers had a more positive attitude towards their American opponents than the other way around. In a pathetic incident a Chinese soldier slipped some Christmas cards into a MASH unit in 1951, but was killed crossing a minefield when returning to his lines.[235] There seemed to be an element of Chinese humanity or a form of *jeu d'esprit* about some of their actions. In any case, Chinese soldiers clearly had an appreciation of American clothing, footwear, food, beverages and weapons.

Communist Bloc: Russians, Chinese and Koreans

The mid-twentieth century history of North Korea is one dominated by Russian influence followed by that of the Chinese, while the northern state struggled to remain autonomous. The late nineteenth century Russian advance across Siberia to the Pacific and onwards to Korea was halted by Russia's defeat by Japan in 1894, but the incursion was resumed at the end of the Pacific War in 1945 when the USSR made a full entrance into Korea, taking control of the territory north of the 38th parallel and organizing a communist state there. As has been seen, it was with Soviet planning and military equipment and training that the North Koreans launched their invasion of the south in June 1950.[236] The Russians, in fact, were latecomers to the Korean scene: the adjoining massive Asian country had for many centuries loomed over little Chosin.

The historic relationship between China and Korea is one between a huge, dynamic civilization and a small, marginal but original society. The fundamental task of an independent Korea was to resist Chinese and then Japanese domination. One important mark of distinction was a separate Korean language. In the communist upheaval in northern Asia, Korea became a pivot. In the struggle against the Japanese a Korean volunteer corps was formed in Manchuria.[237] During the culmination of the Chinese civil war in the late 1940s the new communist state of North Korea provided Chinese Communist forces with a place of refuge, rest and recuperation.[238] In the midst of that conflict exiled Koreans established organizations both in China and the Soviet Union to promote the formation of a communist Korea.[239] With the victory of the Chinese Communists in late 1949 a substantial number of soldiers (estimates varying from 20,000 to 70,000) of Korean origin, with their equipment, were transferred to the new northern state, where they provided a trained cadre for its army. Douglas MacArthur declared that this transfer constituted "a vast pool of combat-seasoned troops." This action could be viewed merely as part of the process of the demobilization of the massive People's Liberation Army. In any case, it was an extremely beneficial to the developing military, which grew to about 200,000 personnel by the eve of the North Korean invasion of the south in June 1950, twice as large as the South Korean military. Beyond not opposing the North Korean plan to invade the south, the Chinese Communists, fully preoccupied with their work of forging a "New China," did nothing more to further that venture. A negative factor in the relationship was a 1949 dispute about water rights along the Yalu, which the Soviet Union resolved that year.[240] Soviet Russia provided the training, plans and equipment for the attack. The communist government in the north was dominated by Koreans who had served in the Russian armed forces, eventually removing from power those who had been aligned with the Chinese.[241]

With the intervention of the United States military the North Korean enterprise came to grief. Having routed the North Koreans in the south, the United States and its South Korean ally headed north, where they met popular support but only crumbling conventional opposition, although in the broad, mountainous northeast some guerrilla action emerged.[242] As the allies swept north, the Marxist regime collapsed, with an estimated 80 percent of party members abandoning their party identification cards. North Korean soldiers surrendered *en masse.* Following its flight from the capital of Pyongyang, the remnant of the government was based at Sinuiju on the Yalu and then in the deep mountains near the river further to the east at the town of Kanggye.[243] Already, in September and October, most ROK prisoners were being moved into Manchuria, where they were indoctrinated and trained to be joined by newly drafted northerners. As well, large numbers of soldiers in broken formations also crossed the Yalu, there to be reorganized and reequipped by the Chinese Army. They were followed by the departure of the Soviet military advisors. Robert Leckie has estimated that only 30 percent of North Koreans who had attacked across the thirty-eighth parallel remained in action by mid–September while Soviet advisors withdrew.[244]

Confronted with this dire situation North Korea's leader, Kim Il Sung, on September 30 appealed to both the Soviets and the Chinese for help.[245] Having seen the plan that he had sponsored come to disaster, Joseph Stalin, claiming his military was fully committed in Europe, now urged his communist ally in China to intervene, declaring that the North Korean military could hold out "for at most one week," and proposed that the small area of Soviet territory adjoining Korea be employed as a hospital zone while the much longer area above the Yalu be used to reorganize and reequip the North Korean military refugees. If the Chinese would intervene, he promised substantial equipment and weapons.[246] Believing that China had an obligation to help its fraternal comrades in Korea, but also that American control of the Yalu region was a serious threat to the unfolding Chinese communist revolution, and, obviously in retaliation to the United States' action in blocking its invasion of Taiwan, after further maneuvers with Stalin, China's leaders took the plunge. This was done without the promised Soviet weapons, but with a wealth of U.S. small arms captured from the Nationalists in the Chinese civil war.[247]

China's extraordinary success in rapidly driving the American and South

Korean forces out of North Korea by the end of 1950 gave a new lease on life to the North Korean Communists. North Korea first had to deal with the humiliating fact that many of its people had rejected its system. The Chinese Army undertook the task of rebuilding the defeated northern force and by January 1951 some understrength North Korean army units reappeared at the front, the Chinese being responsible for the reorganization of at least two Korean divisions in Manchuria. Although these units had initial success against equally ill-prepared South Korean divisions in the central front, by the end of the month they were shattered and driven north by the revived U.S. Army X Corps. Nevertheless, pleased by this evidence of Chinese support, Stalin took the extraordinary step of canceling the debt for 20 of the 64 infantry divisions that the Soviets had helped to equip. According to Andrei Lankov, the North Korean military only played a "modest role in the continuing conflict, acting as auxiliaries, securing communications and rear security," but, in fact, it developed fully equipped infantry divisions.[248]

There was also the reality of a huge Chinese presence in North Korean territory. A joint military leadership led by the Chinese commander Peng Dehuai and Kim Il Sung had at least nominal control of operations, but the Chinese element was by far the dominant partner.[249] In his biography of Kim Il Sung, Dae-Sook Suh declares that the Chinese military "pushed Kim aside and took over management of the war."[250] The Chinese forces quickly rose to about a million personnel, with an accompanying immediate demand for food. North Korea was the immediate source of supply. Moreover, the Chinese launched their campaign with a lack of a supply stream and inadequate logistics. This situation was clearly apparent when the Chinese sent an army of 100,000 soldiers to attack the Marines at Chosin based on the faulty assumptions that they could be fed by "collecting" it from the "very lightly populated" area and could get ammunition from "retreated enemy positions." In addition, they had totally inadequate clothing for the bitter weather.[251]

There were complaints that Chinese soldiers treated Korean civilians and soldiers as inept inferiors, but, out of necessity, the North Korea government stifled such matters. Tensions developed when Chinese troops appropriated Korean food and enlisted Koreans into their formations. Alan Millett goes so far as to say, "The Chinese soldiers punished the Koreans for starting the war, largely through the confiscation of shelter, fuel and food." Chinese political officers combated this tendency, and nominal joint food committees were formed to deal with Chinese food shortages.[252]

When the Chinese forces had driven the American and South Koreans out of the north, Kim Il Sung began the process of reviving his battered government. At a party conference at its refugee capital at Kanggye on December 21, 1950, he told the assembled remnants that everyone had failed, except himself, of course, in the invasion venture. There was no promised uprising in the south. The commander at Pyongyang had fled before the advancing Americans.

Kim removed many of the leading government officials. His purge was so drastic that under Chinese pressure many of these were reinstated.[253]

During the ground warfare along the 38th parallel, the U.S. Air Force bombed to rubble every city in North Korea, in response to which the northerners dug huge underground facilities (in one of which Mao's son was killed). In an effort to force the Communist side to agree to an armistice, the U.S. Air Force launched two major attacks in 1952 on Pyongyang: On June 11 it flew 1,200 sorties that dumped 23,000 gallons of napalm on the capital, and on August 2, it fielded 1,400 sorties that dropped about 700 tons of bombs. These attacks were followed beginning in September with major assaults on cities in northeast Korea, near the Russian and Manchurian borders.[254]

The Soviet Union provided not only masses of equipment and weapons to both its Chinese and Korean comrades, but also a large contingent of military personnel, principally in support of the Chinese air war but also thousands of soldiers in the land campaign. In fact, the initial Communist effort to blunt the U.S. bombing along the Yalu was for a long time entirely conducted by Russian pilots and support formations. The Russian air support forces also were deeply involved in training Chinese pilots and in repair work. Although the United States was aware of this situation, it chose not to raise the matter to prevent an outcry by the American public about the serious loss of U.S. airmen and planes, which undoubtedly would have the effect of an unwanted confrontation with the Soviet Union.

The Russians also participated in land actions. An estimated 6000 Soviet advisors were attached to frontline Chinese and North Korean units. Difficulties with this relationship seemed to be mostly with the Korean language, including translation; Korean sensitivities; lack of technical knowledge; and serious deficiencies in supplies and ammunition. Ongoing problems for both sides were the rugged terrain and scant road network. Isolated Soviet advisors had to subsist on a Korean-type diet, which led one Russian advisor to complain that while Korean soldiers could survive by eating "insects and plant roots," Soviet personnel required three meals a day.

As the conflict dragged on and with all the assistance provided by the Soviet Union not achieving the desired results, Stalin at length demanded to know why the Communist forces appeared to be "helpless" in the circumstances. At a top-level meeting in December 1951 he declared that he was "ready to take any measures ... to increase military supplies two or three [times] if need be," but said, "Decisive success must be achieved in the near future." Despite near-frantic activity by Kremlin cohorts, this was not achieved. The very considerable financial and political drain on the Soviet Union, and the military stalemate, continued. With victory out of reach, it is claimed, Stalin "lost all interest in the conflict."[255]

Although Stalin, ignoring huge human and material losses, had earlier asserted that North Korea had only suffered casualties, at this point Kim Il

Sung began to urge his Soviet and Chinese masters that the conflict be ended. In one of his last acts, Stalin — just before his death in March 1953 — reportedly decided to stop the war, a position which was promptly assumed by his successors.[256] For their part, having concluded that nothing further could be gained by continuing the war, Mao and company eventually agreed to an armistice, which went into effect in July 1953.[257]

As in the south, North Korea had the mighty task of rebuilding its economy. Both the Russian and Chinese governments provided massive aid, which included exchanging valuable assets like oil and gas for inferior Korean products.[258] Elements of the Chinese army remained in Korea until 1958. To assure that there would not be a renewal of the conflict, the United States has maintained a garrison of 30,000 army troops as well as air force bases in South Korea.[259]

When the war ended, North Korea, with the resources provided by its Communist allies, embarked on a major rebuilding program, which resulted in substantial achievement in developing the mining and manufacturing industries. When the help given by their neighbors was exhausted, economic production stalemated.[260] On repeated occasions Kim Il Sung managed to oust from the leadership anyone whom he saw as a threat to his supremacy, which led to a cult of the "Great Leader," a Korean equivalent of Mao Zedong, with thousands of Kim statues and an accompanying blatant rewriting of history about the importance of Kim, going back to the conflict with the Japanese in the 1940s.[261]

Beginning in 1967 North Korea undertook a comprehensive campaign to undermine the other Korea, which combined kidnapping, espionage, murder and explosions to an extraordinary degree, by any measure of interstate relations. The scope of this activity can be seen in the extensive tunnel system dug under the armistice line, one of which is now a major tourist attraction along the Demilitarized Zone.[262] All of this was matched by occasional and abortive efforts at cooperation between the entities. When Kim died in 1994 at the age of eighty-four he left behind a personal dynasty, with his erratic son as his successor, and, more ominously, a nuclear arms program. A devastating famine swept across the land, with the government only reluctantly allowing humanitarian aid supplied from abroad.[263] The shift of Communist China to something of an open market economy increasingly isolated the last avowedly Stalinist system. The former Soviet Union has for long disavowed any connection with the Kim government.[264] North Korea stands in marked contrast to the flourishing economic, social and political development of its rival to the south. What has happened in the Republic of Korea was indeed "the great leap forward." On the other side, the Communist regime, isolating its population from outside influence and maintaining a police state system, retains tight control of its people.[265]

United States and Other United Nations Supporters

With the mandate from the United Nations Security Council to oppose the North Korean invasion of the south, the U.S. government asked other countries to contribute military forces. The response was almost entirely from western European American allies and from countries of European domination. The principal exception was from Turkey. Another exception was Thailand, which in addition to providing two naval corvettes donated 40,000 tons of rice. In all, 29,000 troops were offered, with only about 9,000 having arrived by September 1950. The Pentagon believed that they shortly would not be needed; however, as events were to prove, there was lots more of war to come.[266]

The government of Turkey responded with a force that averaged 5,000 soldiers at a given time. Turkish support was undoubtedly based on historic antipathy towards Russia and a desire to retain American backing for what the Turks viewed as their vulnerable geographical location. Due to inadequate preparation and language barriers, in the first operation into which they were thrust, Turkish troops attacked a South Korean formation. When the Chinese launched their onslaught, Turkish troops suffered heavy casualties, for which they blamed the Americans for not providing fire support and for failing to inform them of withdrawal plans.[267] Its troops, however, soon proved to be effective fighters. Moreover, the Turkish government remained a staunch ally throughout the course of the war.

In later confrontations with the enemy Turkish troops had astounding successes, which became legendary. On one notable occasion a Turkish battle report declared: "Enemy attacks. We attacked. Send more bread." After a heavy artillery bombardment on a Chinese position some Turkish troops complained that there were not enough of the enemy "left to make a decent fight." S.L.A. Marshall, however, held that the exploits of the Turks were overrated.[268] There was a continuing need to provide the kind of food the Turks wanted, including meals without pork, but one unique problem arose when they declined to use mass shower facilities. Individual cubicles were provided.[269]

When British forces arrived on the scene they cast a critical eye on the conduct of the American military. As we have seen, the British military leaders who watched the rapid and hurried retreat of American forces were appalled by unit disintegration and the collapse of morale. Moreover, the small British units were called upon to provide rearguard protection for the running Americans, which they did — at bitter cost. Jeffry Grey recalls the "sticky situations" in which his comrades found themselves. This resulted in the decimation of one regiment: the Ulster Rifles. Grey noted a general propensity among these units: too proud "to call for help," British regiments "assumed they could do what Americans could not." American Bob Ondrish recalled the heroic rearguard fight conducted by British units who "received the brunt of the Chinese initial attack" on the first day of their offensive in April 1951. Noting the "great numbers of casualties, both killed and wounded," he was deeply impressed by their deportment: "They were a truly professional army unit that stood second to none on that day."[270]

Why the difference in combat mentality? The American military only knew how to advance and secure ground, while the British had the experience and organization for going forward and backwards. What allowed the British units to operate effectively in the dire circumstances of retreat was the cohesion built into the regimental system, which was effectively lacking in the American ground forces, with the notable exceptions of airborne troops and the Marines. The repeated employment of British troops for rearguard fighting was a source of resentment in their ranks.[271]

The next notable involvement of British soldiers was when they came upon ROK military and South Korean gunmen killing groups of civilians. While the British units were able to halt this murder on occasion, position of the Tokyo high command was that these matters were under the exclusive authority of the South Korean government. According to a U.S. Navy chaplain, mass executions of civilians by the South Korean military "happened all over the front."[272] The condition of the Korean population was noted by journalist Noel Monks: "In nearly two years in Korea I never heard or saw a Korean man, woman or child laugh as though they meant it."[273]

Through it all, the relationship between the American and British soldiers was generally good, but the stark reality in the disparity of pay and supplies was always there, just as it was in the previous war. British pay for ordinary soldiers was so low that the reality resulted in a modest increase during that time. Due to the disinclination of the American military to face the problems of providing such facilities, as been seen, many American soldiers took advantage of British "wet canteens," where they usually provided the funds while the Brits added the comradeship. There were beneficial exchanges: British rum was swapped for American Old Gold cigarettes. A British shortage of field stoves was immediately addressed when cases of gin were exchanged for "dozens of U.S. stoves."[274] Inevitability, relations where not always amicable. In Ginza, Japan, where American and Commonwealth soldiers, the latter including the Australian contingent, were seated at different sides of a beer hall, the evening often ended with fights among allies,[275] but that was not unusual among soldiers of all distinctions; U.S. Marines-versus-soldiers punch-ups were only of serious interest to the military police.

What many British soldiers, and not only among officers, could not comprehend was the democratic ethos that prevailed among the Yanks. The British regimental system did bond all members as members, yet the rank and class differences remained. The typical GI Joe wasn't having any of that, despite posted notices regarding observation of "military courtesy." In fact, American enlisted men sometimes called their officers by their first names.[276] One British observer, in surely an exceptional experience, heard an American lieutenant remonstrating an enlisted man about having a dirty rifle; the soldier told him to "fuck off," whereupon the officer left the scene.[277]

Undoubtedly the most memorable recollection concerned the profligate American supply of food and equipment. John Grey remembered, "The Americans lived in the lap of luxury compared to us."[278] This abundance was distasteful to Alfie Fowley, who found the Yanks were "untidy bleeders" with tins of half-eaten food thrown around everywhere. The Americans had a wealth of ice cream, steaks and film; Stanley Maud watched one U.S. unit depart with "their chewing gum and ice cream machines," but was best pleased when the ice cream trucks "paid a visit."[279]

While British soldiers were required to pay for lost equipment, "the Yanks "could replace just about everything." One of the very few British items that many Americans sought were British service revolvers, "because they looked like cowboy pistols."[280] After a U.S. sergeant instructed some British soldiers on the operation of a BAR, he dumped out his kit bag: "Help yourselves, Lads." Bob Walding was astounded: "If we lost anything we had to pay for it and here was this guy giving equipment away that was worth a fortune to us."[281] American largess extended to the use of ammunition. A British soldier saw a U.S. infantry unit being relieved, which, not finding any opposition and for "a bit of fun," fired off all its ammunition. At least one British unit was viewed as "very honorable" by Chinese opponents, who informed its members that they would not fire on stretcher bearers nor use phosphorous shells against them as they did against Americans.[282]

Through the dark days of the end of 1950, despite alarm about the muted U.S. threat to use atomic weapons, British support for the war effort remained firm. It appears that British prime minister Clement Atlee was not completely reassured about the potential use of atomic weapons, and some in the State Department believed that his apparent hankering for a "deal" with Communist China could undermine the American position. For his part, Atlee agreed with one of his cabinet colleagues that American leaders were "dangerously hysterical" about the situation.[283]

Race in War

If some Koreans were brought into the American forces for the purpose of improving their combat effectiveness, another kind of integration, of much greater significance, was taking place at the same time: American racial integration, which had the same effect. Despite President Truman's 1948 order ending racial discrimination in the military, there were still all-black regiments in the army. It should be noted that Truman's executive order banned discrimination but not segregation.[284] MacArthur, who had an answer for everything, later said he had inherited his black units, but at the time he did nothing to foster actual integration.[285] By law (repealed in July 1950) in a post–Civil War mandate, the army was required to maintain four all-black regiments. Known as "Buffalo soldiers," they were stationed as far as possible from the bulk of the civilian population, in the far West where they fought another minority: Native Americans.[286]

When the war began the air force, as a newly-independent service, which started out with only one segregated unit, led the way in integration. The Korean War resulted in a dramatic turnabout for the Marine Corps, which began with a very small number of blacks, half of whom were stewards; the number rapidly grew in course of the conflict.[287] In this process the air force and, somewhat reluctantly, the navy led the way, while the army did not even accept "in principle" gradual integration until January 1950, with full implementation beginning in April 1951. On the eve of the Korean War 98 percent of blacks were in segregated army units; ten months into the war the percentage was the same.[288] Serving in a black airborne unit in Germany on the eve of the war, then–Major John Singlaub observed the "downright impractical and terribly wasteful use" of personnel and facilities that segregation entailed, but he found his own efforts to break through this barrier blocked by long-standing racial policies.[289] In early accounts of the conflict black soldiers usually were identified by their race. S.L.A. Marshall always made this distinction, while a photograph in Marguerite Higgins's combat account saw fit to identify some American soldiers in a rice paddy as "Negro infantrymen." Observing the North Koreans' use of deception in the early days of the war, she reported, "In engagements with our Negro troops, Communists went so far as to black their faces with charcoal and don the uniforms stripped from dead or wounded Americans. So disguised, they managed to walk right up to our positions."[290] She had nothing to say, as had others, about the apparent failings of all-black units.

One all-black unit that failed to hold together in the early days was the Twenty-Fourth Infantry Regiment of the Twenty-Fifth Division, which was plagued by many desertions to the extent that it soon was used as an "outpost" force to indicate North Korean attacks and then be backed up by a reserve regiment. The initial poor performance quickly became a blame game, with the Eight Army pointing to the Twenty-Fifth Division, which "passed the buck" to the Twenty-Fourth Regiment. Its Seventy-Seventh Engineer Company appeared to have serious problems with "bug-outs" and "straggling"; its commander claimed that soldiers in his company were "very bitter" based on the proposition that "they felt they were stupid to risk their lives unduly because when they got home they didn't have the rewards citizenship should have provided." The "sickening reputation" of the unit spread around the army in Korea.[291] Charles Bussey, then a captain in the regiment, noted that, like other American soldiers, its members had not been trained for night fighting or for dealing with the varied tactics of the North Koreans.[292]

When Curtis Morrow joined the regiment as a replacement in December 1950, his platoon sergeant quickly informed him that although black people had been subjected to discrimination in the United States, "That's another fight we'll have to deal with when, or if, we return to America. Here, we are fighting for our lives." Pending the regiment being broken up and its members being transferred to integrated units, Morrow recalled one of his fellows wondering, "Maybe that's why the government is breaking up the Deuce-Four. Maybe they don't like the idea of us black soldiers fighting as a team in a war." He also heard the claim that "given an even chance, we could out-soldier and out-fight any white soldier. And there was no way they [whites] could justify their racist attitudes towards their fellow American comrades in war or peace."[293] But now the all-black units were to go.

Giving a contrary view on the effectiveness of black combat soldiers, S.L.A. Marshall points to performance of the Ninth Infantry Regiment, saying they "had fought as well as any such unit ever in national history." When Marshall met with Secretary of Defense George Marshall in April 1951 he told Marshall that integration "was the only way," to which the secretary responded that "he had believed ever since he was a second lieutenant that this was the right answer." During the battles of the Pusan Perimeter one all-black regiment had performed very poorly, with the eventual result being the transfer of its soldiers to other regiments, hence, integration, army-style.[294]

Earlier, during the later stages of World War II, despite qualms and complaints (such as the view that the military should not be used to engineer social or racial changes), necessity at that time — the stark shortage of infantry by 1944 in Europe with eighteen-year-olds being drafted out of high school as early as February of that year — began the breakdown of the racial caste system.[295] Despite this initial pragmatic integration, all black units remained in place. At the end of that war a black unit guarding a group of German prisoners humorously referred to their captives as "white Negroes."[296] But in 1950 Korea segregation was weakening but still in place. While white units were crying out for replacements, there was a backlog of thousands of African American soldiers in Japan. Another oddity was that basic training companies at this time were gradually integrated.[297]

As the Korean War heated up, with draftees pouring into his basic training post of Fort Jackson, South Carolina, at a rate of a thousand a day, Brigadier General Frank McConnell, in the name of efficiency, abandoned segregation — on his own authority. Rudolph Stephens had a rude introduction to racial matters when a busload of draftees from east Tennessee arrived at Jackson to be greeted by a "big black sergeant" who heaped abuse on the boys. This was a new experience for Stephens as "very few of us had even spoken to a black person in our lives, and the way he was carrying on made most of us have second thoughts about the U.S. Army."[298]

Because of a series of complaints about the treatment of black soldiers in

Korea, many of whom were given quick courts-martial and sentenced to life imprisonment for fleeing from the front lines, Thurgood Marshall, chief lawyer for the NAACP, traveled to Korea and, after reviewing the court-martial convictions of several black soldiers, concluded, "The men were tried in an atmosphere making justice impossible." Marshall also criticized Douglas MacArthur for not implementing Truman's order banning discrimination. Marshall's allegations got extensive treatment in the black press, and he wrote a book about the matter.[299] An investigation by the Far East Command, not surprisingly, concluded that most of Marshall's charges were groundless, but this controversy clearly drew attention to army segregation.[300]

Once the Korean War was underway the U.S. Army leadership found continuing difficulties with troop integration. Now head of army administration (G-1), Anthony McAuliffe argued that based on prior experience the racial impact of such a move might have a bad effect on "overall American efficiency," but later allowed, "We didn't do it to improve the social situation.... It was merely a matter of getting the best out of the military personnel that was available to us." Mark Clark, chief of Army Field Forces, believed the matter should be dealt with in some other way, which meant doing nothing. The problem of racially segregated units in Korea convinced Joe Collins, army chief of staff, among others, that integrated units were the solution. In his autobiography he declared, "It was no surprise to those of us who were familiar with the success of integrated black platoons in World War II that the integrated units performed well." There was some concern that the breakup of all-black combat units would simply result in black soldiers being transferred to all-black service units, but this did not happen.[301] "Commanders in Korea," declares Morris MacGregor, "had already begun to apply the only practical remedy. Confronted with battle losses in white units and a growing surplus of black replacements arriving in Japan, the Eighth Army began assigning individual black replacements just as it had been assigning individual Korean soldiers to under-strength units."[302]

The pressing need for replacement troops was real. The Pentagon estimated that it would need 25,000 replacements a month beginning in the spring of 1951; a sharply rising percentage of them had to be drawn from African Americans. Steven Casey comments: "There was just no way all these men could be placed in blacks-only units."[303]

Due to the heavy losses of officers in the Twenty-Fourth Infantry Regiment, replacement officers were placed in positions where they were needed, and in some cases black officers were in command of white officers, which marked a major change in unofficial policy for assignments. Although there were white officers in the regiment who strongly disliked being in black units, many others found their troops were effective and quickly adapted to the situation.[304] Lt. Lyle Rishell recalls the close bond he formed with his platoon sergeant: "He was the consummate noncom. I couldn't have asked for any better. He was indispensable, and I loved the man." When replacements arrived in his platoon, "many of them expressed surprise that I was white — after all they had been assigned to a black unit — but there was never a hint of animosity as they faced me that first time." The relationship grew stronger through the shared experiences of combat. One day he overheard some of his soldiers threatening to kill a black lieutenant whom they considered to be reckless and grossly incompetent; if he ever reappeared, he would be "one dead nigger." "The incident stands out," Rishell remembered, "because it was the only racial slur that I heard voiced the entire time in Korea." He was apprehensive when the first KATUSAs arrived in his platoon: they looked like small boys playing at the game of war. He quickly came to appreciate them: "For the time they were with us, the ROKs never betrayed my trust." Probably due to their efforts to stop soldiers from unauthorized retreats, Rishell's regiment had the highest officer casualty rate in the Eighth Army.[305]

Casualties in the ranks of the noncommissioned officers were also great. James Brady recalls that in his Marine infantry company, when a black sergeant was made platoon sergeant there was grumbling among some Southern white soldiers "about a 'nigger' taking over." The company commander addressed the platoon in "his soft Virginia voice": 'Sergeant Keefe is the new platoon sergeant. He runs the platoon. I don't care about anything else. To me, and to Keefe, you're all just marines.'" Brady also noted that in "1951 and 1952 you never saw a Negro officer. Maybe there weren't any. I suppose that should have bothered me, aroused decent, liberal instincts. It didn't. I accepted the status quo." Jack Daley, commander of an infantry company, remembered when in October 1951 black soldiers were assigned to his unit: "I found these men to be excellent soldiers and they added to the combat effectiveness of F Company." When black soldiers were transferred from the Marine Combat Service Group, some of them arrived at Dave Koegel's infantry company: "In my squad one of the new Negroes was assigned to share a hole with an Alabaman. Knowing looks went around. They were for nothing; the two men soon became fast friends."[306]

During the war there were two episodes of large-scale surrenders of American soldiers, and one of these happened to 138 soldiers in Company C of the Third Battalion of the Twenty-Fourth Regiment. This took place during the Chinese onslaught on the western front beginning in late November 1950. On November 27, while other units were pulling back, this company, out of radio contact, apparently was left behind, was surrounded and faced annihilation. The decision to surrender is a matter of dispute. A white platoon lieutenant recalled that the decision was a command one: "There was no vote and little discussion," while one soldier remembered that the company's commander, Capt. Milford Stanley, allowed its members to decide. One sergeant, declaring that he had five children to look after, obviously decided not to die. Another soldier recollected one lieutenant who "wanted to hold out but ... a Chinese negotiator arrived while he was making his plea and shot him dead on the spot."[307] Chinese general Ping Dy attributed the surrender to successful persuasion of his psywar unit, but as has been seen there was a lot more than persuasion that brought about this situation. This was the only time such a group surrender happened to black soldiers.[308]

Even before the Korean War, some U.S. Army units were already in the process of being desegregated. As has been seen, Fort Jackson, South Carolina, was so overloaded with draftees that the post commander on his own initiative decided to train blacks and whites together.[309] In Korea the commander of a quartermaster company in the Second Infantry Division noted that his unit "was integrated and that at least a third of my men were Negroes. I believe these were my best men. They held more than their share of the NCO ratings. They did the skilled jobs. They knew they were getting a break on rotation points and were not being discriminated against in any way. They were good soldiers."[310]

During the conflict the great majority of black soldiers initialed were in segregated service units—with the largest group being truck drivers, as was the case with the acclaimed "Red Ball Express" in World War II. Rene Cutforth recalled an occasion when a black truck unit helped to bridge the bruised relations between British and American units then being hammered by the Chinese. Cutforth encountered a unit he called "Captain Wagner's Famous Negro Trucking Company," which drove to the front lines to pull out the remains of the devastated Royal Ulster Rifles battalion retreating above Seoul in January 1951. In the process, the company "went further forward and stayed there longer than anybody had a right to expect of them," which earned it the lasting gratitude of the British Twenty-Ninth Brigade. The company maintained an excellent relationship with the brigade until it eventually was transferred elsewhere. In Cutforth's view, this black unit's effective but diplomatic achievement was important: "I don't suppose that unit will ever get a mention from military historians, but it deserves a very special one, because at that time in the war the ties which bound the United Nations together were at their most frayed."[311] It is getting that mention now.

In prisoner of war camps Chinese agents attempted to divide black and white Americans, but with little success; under pressure concerning racial inequality in the United States, a black American captain repeatedly maintained, "I am an American, not a Negro." North Korean soldiers obviously were informed about race relations in America. While being tortured, one black soldier recalled that English-speaking Communists harangued him: "Why was he in Korea, fighting them in their own country, while his people in America were constantly being dehumanized, raped, hanged and killed just for sport by the same (white people) he was fighting with against them, here in Korea."[312]

The Chinese shortly separated black soldiers from white ones and constantly lectured the blacks on racial inequality in America. Robert Fletcher recalled the frequent contents of the lectures: "You know white people will never let black people accomplish anything in the United States. They're always going to control the money, control the jobs, make sure their friends will always have a job, and black people will go just so far. What you need to do is go back to your country and help start a revolution."[313]

Jerry Morgan had a vivid recollection of his POW experience: "The Chinese could not understand the black Americans. We were always laughing and talking and singing. The Chinese just couldn't comprehend that. We had them completely befuddled. We would be doing all that and right next to us would be a company of whites. They would be sitting around dejected, not laughing or talking. And there we were acting foolish. I say foolish in the eyes of the Chinese, but to us this was a means of survival. Back in the United States we were used to being down, and the only way for us to go was up." He also noted that his fellow black POWs cared for each other, the result being that none of the ten members of his group died. He also stressed how religious conviction saw them through, with the blacks in his POW camp forming a choir and appointing their own ministers.[314] An unusual development was that black soldiers suffered from frostbite to a greater degree than white ones.[315]

At the end of war 4,439 American POWs were released, with twenty-one of them electing to remain on the Communist side. The fact that this tiny number made that decision became part of the controversy, almost entirely motivated by cheap partisan politics, about the conduct of American prisoners in the hands of the Communists. Three of those who remained behind were black, another tiny minority. After living in China for fifteen years and having made at least one broadcast to black Americans during the Vietnam War, eventually disillusioned with communism, Clarence Adams returned to Memphis, Tennessee, in 1966. Like other POWS, the blacks were subjected to lengthy interrogations, but the racial bar remained: the ship sending them home was segregated.[316]

Among black soldiers, particularly in all-black units, there was a widespread awareness about racial inequality back home, while they were fighting and dying in Korea. According to Curtis Morrow, a common theme in their conversations was, "The Chinese, the North Koreans and every other fighting man in this war must be telling each other that we (black Americans, Negroes, Niggers, colored people or whatever the f___ they chose to call us) must be the biggest fools in the world." As for the poor performance of black units in the early days of the conflict, Morrow was told by "old timers" that that was a common occurrence in all U.N. forces at the time, with the blame being heaped on all-black, Puerto Rican and South Korean companies. Army veteran Samuel King recalls, "It was an embarrassment for us to have someone in a foreign country know how we were being treated." Despite all the negative feeling, there is no example of black soldiers demonstrating against segregation or refusing combat on that score. For some, civilian mores had not caught up with the new military standard. In 1952 when Morrow returned home with a shipload of soldiers, a San Francisco bartender refused to serve him (which was followed by a general melee).[317]

Related to this whole subject is the response of Japanese people to black soldiers in the wake of the American occupation. According to Curtis Morrow, the mother of his Japanese fiancée recalled that her people "had been bewildered by the American whites' attitudes toward their fellow American countrymen. She and her friends never perceived any difference between the white and black soldiers." She also mentioned that in the immediate period of occupation near the Kobe military base there was a colony of Germans, and that area was off limits to black soldiers.[318]

Matthew Ridgway, who became Far East commander after MacArthur, was firm in his views on race relations: "Segregation has always seemed to me both un–American and un–Christian for free citizens to be taught to down-grade themselves this way as if they were unfit to associate with their fellows or to accept leadership themselves." In October 1951 he ordered total integration of all forces in Korea. To match the ratio in the U.S. population as a whole, the number of blacks in combat units was set at 12 percent. The Korean War finished off segregation in the American military.[319]

The process was slow and limited, yet, as Morris McGregor observes, "the conversion to integrated units was permanent." Moreover, "the Korean expedient, adopted out of battlefield necessity, carried out haphazardly, and based on such imponderables as casualties and the draft, passed the ultimate test of traditional American pragmatism: it worked. And according to reports from Korea, it worked well."[320] Despite the fears of some, there seemed to be little friction or tension; at least, it did not work its way into official reports. One practice from the days of segregation persisted: in company rosters black soldiers continued to be listed as "Class II Personnel," separate from other troops.[321]

There were episodes of racial difficulty. One soldier remembered one of them: "While we were in reserve a black man, Sergeant Williams, was promoted to platoon sergeant. In November, when we moved up on Heartbreak Ridge for the second time, our assistant platoon sergeant had to share the Third Platoon Headquarters bunker with Sergeant Williams, and he made it clear he wasn't happy about the situation. He would "rather go over and sleep with the Chinese," he said. When word of this got back to Sergeant Williams and went up the chain of command, "our 'assistant platoon sergeant' became an 'assistant squad leader.' He did manage to hang on to his rank, but it was still a demotion."[322]

Another Marine remembered only one racial incident in his platoon, but it was a nasty one. He and some of his buddies were gathered together in a bunker to celebrate his birthday, handing around a bottle of whiskey. A black

Marine, who had been standing fire watch, joined the party and was about to take a swallow when a white sergeant from Texas knocked him down. He shortly returned with a BAR and opened fire before being subdued. Both participants along with another sergeant were court-martialed and sentenced.[323]

There was a low-key example of racism remembered by a Marine. In a company of mostly white Southerners, he became friendly with a black Marine, and between them they managed to build a comfortable bunker, whereupon his commanding officer "requested" that he move from that bunker. When he declined to move, the CO "warned that I would be ostracized by many of the Marines. He was right."[324] A black officer in a company who fought at Pork Chop Hill in 1953 recalled the situation: "Prejudice existed in the company, as it certainly did in the Army; however, any impact it had on our combat efficiency was not apparent. The prejudice was transparent to most of us, but where it existed, it was dealt with between those involved, not breaking out into the open."[325]

Anthony Herbert recalls when the first black replacement arrived at his company. Opposition, he believed, came from the headquarters people, but the objections were quelled when the company commander was told there would be no rotation until black replacements were accepted. As Herbert saw it, "Most of the troops didn't care one way or the other." The black trooper, whom Herbert considered to be a "super soldier, probably one of the finest sergeants in the whole damn Army," was shortly killed in action.[326]

There were other vignettes. The commander of an infantry company remembers a PFC Tyrone, a barely literate black, who was knocked off the back of a tank and apparently was severely injured. About a month later Tyrone climbed up the mountain to be welcomed where his company was dug in. Years later the CO looked back at the episode:

> When I now think of the Korean War, I am reminded of soldiers like Tyrone and others who were drafted and barely able to read and write. I wonder where his share of the Great American Dream was. Soldiers like Tyrone were unlikely to find a good education or economic prosperity in the foxholes. Then I think of all the people who, for whatever reason, evaded military services and did enjoy a good education along with economic prosperity without ever hearing a shot fired in anger.[327]

In an infantry company hunting guerrillas, black soldier "A.C." was noted for falling behind the troop on the march, but when the company was under attack that night he vigorously covered its position, firing his BAR. One of his fellows questioned his change in deportment: "Yesterday, you acted like a yeller nigger.... Tonight, you're all over the place." The explanation: "Hell, white boy, can't you tell the difference? In daytime I stand out like a sore thumb. At night I got it made." An efficient pattern was established: "When we went into the assault in the daytime, A.C. dropped back. When we set up at night, A.C. went the front."[328]

Integrated units fought better, and that was that. From there the matter of desegregation moved on to the wholly different world of civilian America, but, despite the special circumstances of military life, the abolition of racial division in the armed forces could be, and was, held up as a major example of how it could work. The discipline imposed by military law, of course, did not translate to civilian life.

On one occasion Chinese soldiers found their advance was halted by their vanguard squad, who reported that "they had seen ghosts on the hill. Actually, they were black American soldiers sleeping in the trenches. Our new recruits had never seen black people before." A group of American POWs trapped in a barn were filled with fear when they heard tanks approaching, but were relieved: One of them shouted, "They're American. There's a black soldier with them." When Chinese soldiers overran an artillery battery at night, it was hard to tell who was who. A GI recalled yelling to a silhouette rushing by: "Halt! You Chinese?" The soldier replied "Man, where'en hell you ever see a black Chinese?" It was the GI's buddy Pugh.[329]

Recalling the high incidence of fatalities among white officers in otherwise all-black units, Curtis Morrow explained: "They stand out like sore thumbs, which is why the less daring ones prefer fighting in an all-white or mixed unit."[330] A final vignette from the black combat experience in Korea: a Chinese soldier, having decided to surrender, stood in a road holding his surrender pass until an American tank came along, whereupon two black soldiers jumped down. His reaction was one of fear — he never had seen or heard of black Americans. But all ended well: the soldiers gave him cigarettes and gum (the latter also surely unknown to him) and directed him to the rear.[331]

By the end of the war 90 percent of black soldiers were in integrated units. By April 1951 the percentage of black soldiers in transportation and service units had greatly declined, with the result being that the ratio of blacks and whites serving in combat positions (41 percent) was about the same.[332] The chance to die for your country was now equal. In January 1952 soldiers in all–Puerto-Rican units were assigned to other outfits in the 8th Army.[333]

How it all happened is well stated by Melvin Voorhees. In the spring of 1951 the all-black Twenty-Fourth Regiment was deactivated and its members were spread around the Twenty-Fifth Infantry Division: "But that merely ratified a policy already adopted by the soldiers of EUSAK. Long before, in the heat and cold and mud and dust and tears and blood of Korea, they had decided to judge each other not as to race or color but as to individual worth. And so they did."[334]

A minor aspect of the racial situation in the American military was the presence of a few Sino-American (Nisei) soldiers in the U.S. Army, which led to Communist charges that Japanese troops were fighting with the Americans. A wounded Asian-American remembers lying along a frozen road with American soldiers passing by, assuming he was one of the enemy, until he was helped by another Hawaiian.[335] When encountering soldiers he did not know, army scout Herb Wong took care to identify himself and remember the current password.[336]

In a subsection of his account of his time in Korea, "The Death of Segregation," novelist Pat Frank provides his assessment of the process of army integration in Korea:

> The results were immediate and happy. The Negro soldier dropped the chip on his shoulder. When an unpleasant work detail was assigned to his unit, he no longer suspected it was because of the color of his skin. And the white soldier, discovering that he could, and indeed must, depend on the Negro soldier at his side for his very life, abandoned his prejudice. The result reached far beyond the operations of Eighth Army. It strengthened America's whole position on race before the world.[337]

GI Joe and Other Soldiers

It is a general characteristic of twentieth century American military history that great emphasis is placed on the activity of the high command and the movement of armies, while only passing references are made to the condition and existence of the ordinary soldier. This situation probably is due to the predominance of two kinds of people who write on the subject: on the one hand, would-be Ivy Leaguers who prefer war in the abstract while leafing through tidy official reports, and, on the other hand, retired military officers who are consumed with the doings of the activities of the high command. Despite the flurry of paperwork and important staff meetings in rear areas, wars are fought by ordinary soldiers in the dirt and grime of the front where bullets, shells and explosives kill and mutilate. One of the few military historians who have looked at the requirements of the ordinary soldier in Korea was S.L.A. Marshall, who, among other things, examined the overloading of infantrymen and fatigue factors in combat. Obviously, the uniforms, weapons and gear of the troops in Korea were of World War II vintage, as they remained for training purposes (as this writer recalls) through the late 1950s.[338]

Another matter, which has been given little attention but was of great importance to those who were involved, is the forging of an effective fighting force for the conflict — largely based on those who were drafted or called out of the reserves. In many accounts there is the impression that fighting units come into being largely to provide grist for the direction of the upper ranks.

At the beginning there was only a limited amount of field rations available in Japan, but the Stateside Quartermaster Corps quickly began sending huge amounts of C-rations, mostly left over from the previous war.[339] As things stabilized, it appears that, despite all the difficulties, food of some sort usually was provided to the troops. An officer in Quartermaster claimed that soldiers were fed "two hot meals a day whenever it is tactically possible," a claim that was supported by another Quartermaster officer, which is probably evidence that they never missed a meal themselves.[340] But when forty-four soldiers sent a letter of complaint about the food to the Tokyo edition of the *Stars and Stripes*, MacArthur's office prevented it from being printed.[341] Infantryman John Graham remembered the menu for his company at one time: "We had plain corned beef hash for breakfast, corned beef with mustard at noon, and corned beef hash with catsup for supper — and we were in the rear."[342] Another soldier described the food as "terrible."[343] One of the things that stand out in the memory of Curtis Murrow about demanding physical activity and combat is constant hunger and thirst: "There was never a sufficient amount of food or water. And there were many days when I would've given a month's pay for a canteen of water." While in combat Allen Wilkinson waited a month before he got a hot meal.[344]

In most cases opinions about food were determined by circumstances. Tony Kondysar recalls arriving in Korea cold, wet and hungry, to be given a meal of the often-derided chipped beef on toast (often referred to as SOS), which he found to be "hot and never tasted as good as it did that day! I can still recall the warmth it generated in my stomach and the rest of my body."[345] In the early days of the American involvement, U.S combat troops were given a monotonous supply of C-ration corned beef (which became the Spam of the Korean War), but improvements in variety and quality gradually were achieved. James Huston appears to overstate the food situation when he declares, "After conditions more or less stabilized, it could almost taken for granted in combat units that plenty of good food would be forthcoming daily." One new food preparation was the five-in-one ration, which was unsuitable for infantrymen who ordinarily did not carry mess gear and lacked equipment for heating up food. The Eighth Army soon requested that no more five-in-ones be sent.[346]

During the bitter weather at Chosin many Marines found energy from Tootsie Rolls. One Marine recalled, "I saw many others do as I did — eat six or eight large Tootsie Rolls within a 10 to 15 minute period." During the bloody withdrawal it would melt (in the mouth) when nothing else would. Fortunately, this chocolate candy was available "by the truckload." One explanation for its ready supply is a radio request for ammunition, probably for rifle bullets, which disguised this need by calling the needed ammo by the name of the candy.[347]

The demand for water was constant. James Brady's Marines and Curtis Murrow's soldiers were not the only ones craving this basic fluid. At the beginning of U.S. involvement troops were confronted with broiling heat, which could best be addressed by water. Jack Wright recalled the situation: "Guys almost went mad for water. I never felt the kind of heat I felt in Korea. I just burned up." Climbing hills all day to meet with the enemy was thirsty work, and Lyle Rishell recalled that in his infantry company the water supply "was almost nonexistent." His men "did not complain about the rations or their dirty clothing or even the lack of a field jacket to keep warm at night, but they craved water above everything." One day on the mountain where they were stationed it rained: "The men went crazy, using every container they could lay their hands on…. They stood and danced and turned their faces to the sky, like an ancient Indian rain dance."[348] Lacking water, Jim Brady recalled that those in his Marine unit never washed and that a couple of ounces of left-over coffee was used for shaving.[349] Upon joining a new infantry company, when Anthony Herbert asked where the mess kits were he was directed to a pile of unwashed kits. When he asked where the water was, other soldiers laughed — there was no water.[350]

Another infantryman, Allen Wilkinson, craving some fresh water, was filling his canteen in a stream when he was warned off: "Get the hell away from that stream! Don't you know you are snipers' bait." A new recruit shortly was drawn to the same stream and was killed. Chinese soldiers were told by their North Korean counterparts as evidence of U.S. troops "could not endure hardships in Korea" that Americans through harsh experience had learned not to drink the local water, which resulted in dysenteric diarrhea, but in some places the water was safe to consume. Melting snow to make a canteen cup of water was an extremely slow process.[351]

A propensity of combat soldiers in various wars is the ability to sleep at every suitable opportunity; it was no different in Korea. Infantryman John Graham remembers this phenomenon: when a combat soldier stops, "he takes a nap. He sleeps. He can learn to go to sleep in less than five seconds and to sleep for as little as one minute at a time. He can even learn to sleep while he is walking."[352] Allen Wilkinson has described the same phenomenon: "We take ten and literally throw our bodies to the ground…. Some of us lie about on rocks and stones and fall asleep automatically. Other just sprawl themselves out on the flat surface." Andrew Barr recalls his condition after brutal combat followed by a non-stop seven-day withdrawal from the north in December 1950: "I don't remember being afraid. I don't remember fear, ever. There was just an overwhelming craving for sleep. An hour's nap. Half an hour."[353]

Anyone who has served in the military remembers long chow lines, sometimes in rain, cold and wind. On one occasion, Charles Brown found he had unexpectedly moved to the top of the food chain. Having lost his mess kit, he had anticipated a long wait, but incoming mortar rounds had scattered most of the soldiers ahead of him, so he found he now had a choice of mess kits and was near the top of the line.[354] A sad food experience happened to William Anderson, who had been anticipating the promised deluxe Christmas 1950 meal. This hope was dashed when North Korean shelling destroyed his company's field kitchen.[355] Having lived on C-rations for weeks during Chosin, Marine Charlie Carmin found that his stomach had shrunk so much that he could not do justice to the Christmas feast.[356] One soldier received the Purple Heart through an unusual set of circumstances. As he sat on his helmet on top of his bunker a shell struck above the bunker and hit a large stone, which rolled down on top of him, fracturing his skull. Combat area rule: helmet on at all times.[357]

The life of a combat infantryman is vividly recalled by Allen Wilkinson: "The GI lives so miserably that at times it is beyond human endurance. He live, eats, sleeps, washes, curses, fights and dies in his foxhole.... Actually, he does not live at all; he just exists."[358]

Much of the war, especially when there were largely static lines at the end, was fought out of bunkers. They not only flooded and collapsed under artillery barrage, they also were occupied by rats, some of them "big as cats," as soldier William Dillon remembered. It was most inadvisable to use poison against the varmints as, their mites, believed to be the source of hemorrhagic fever, could spread to soldiers' clothing. A partial solution was found by using flashlights within a bunker, shooting the rats and then burning them.[359]

British infantryman and actor Michael Caine had an interesting experience with rats. Tired of being overrun with them, he and his bunkmate dug out the area around the entrenchment. In the process they discovered why their tobacco and dried milk packs were disappearing from their rations. "Our rats were clever": leaving behind the sugar packs, they were taking the tobacco to line their nests and the dried milk for their offspring.[360] Another British soldier, Alfie Fowley, recalls sleeping with a blanket across his face to keep the rats off it.[361] There also were field rats. Awaiting another Chinese assault, Allen Wilkinson saw them "crawling about the dead" in front of his position.[362] British trooper Gerald Kingslad observed that explosions did not bother rats in this activity.[363]

Volmer Warner's Twenty-Fourth Division rifle company had a series of unusual incidents as it moved north beginning in August 1950. For the cost of a couple of cartons of cigarettes, his company obtained machine guns from retreating South Korean soldiers. After crossing the 38th parallel and running far ahead of its mess crew the company replenished its food supply by robbing a bank, one bazooka shot opening the vault, which supplied ample funds for many chicken dinners. Sometimes when darkness drew near, his company would attack and occupy a village, which provided indoor housing for the night. When its mechanics managed to restart a disabled T-34 tank, it was put at the head of the advancing column until some spoilsports in the air force held it was confusing that an American infantry unit was being led by a Russian tank. Fun and games for Warner's company — but that was while it was heading north. On an earlier occasion North Korean soldiers drove a captured American tank into combat.[364]

A wildly popular innovation was the mobile field shower, with which, another army quartermaster officer explained, at least "every man could bathe and change within four days. Normally, however, the men had a shower once a week."[365] Many combat participants have a very different recollection. Fighting in a Marine infantry unit, James Brady recalls that his company was on the line for forty-six days, with so little water that its members could not wash, before it had a shower.[366] James Dill, in an artillery unit east of Chosin, had to wait for a mere forty-three days before he got a bath.[367] Driving to get supplies, signal corps soldier Paul Noll spotted a "Quartermaster Shower Unit," and not having had a proper shower in over a year (only a "whore's bath" using a helmet), not only was he treated to the real thing but his ragged fatigues were exchanged for new ones. Having been alerted by Noll, everyone in his company made repeated trips to the unit that day, but after that he "never saw another shower unit."[368]

Having lived in the same clothes for weeks at a time, Marine PFC Bruce Lippert remembers washing out of a helmet and having a shower about once a month.[369] Army soldier Rudolph Stephens got a shower every three weeks. John Sullivan's infantry platoon were so dirty that after they finally got a shower they were almost unrecognizable.[370] These experiences probably were typical for those in combat. The lack of showers even extended to some non-combat soldiers. Harry Bauser, a member of a meteorology unit, managed to get a shower at an air force facility on Thanksgiving 1952, whereupon the local air force commander, judging Bauser's group to be "too dirty," banned them from the place. His next shower: March 1953.[371]

As part of a clothing exchange, which eliminated soldiers' having to haul around duffel bags, there was a vital sock exchange program. The experiences of many combat soldiers surely differed from that of the providers of these services. During 1951–1952 James Brady, for example, vividly recalled a single shower experience, but his company was very dirty for many weeks at a time.[372] When soldier Charles Brown had the opportunity to visit his father, a captain on a freighter at Inchon, he smelled so bad that he was immediately sent to the head and his clothes were stripped off.[373] Tired of dirty clothing, one soldier while on leave in Seoul bought a set of fatigues for twenty dollars. With his bullet-riddled boots disintegrating and no Marine supply available, in his ratty fatigues Frank Muetzel approached a clean, neatly dressed army major who informed him that his supply was exclusively for an incoming airborne unit. Armed with a submachine gun and a pistol, Muetzel declared he wanted boots "right then and there"; he got the boots.[374]

Distasteful as it was, soldiers often would take badly-needed cloth gloves and mittens off dead GIs; in bitter weather, military-issued leather gloves gave almost no protection, with the frequent result that where fingernails joined skin, "deep furrows" there "bled almost constantly." Jim Brady's Marines found a partial solution to sore and bleeding hands when some families sent over good old American Jergens Lotion, which some of the troops called "Jerkoff Lotion."[375] There was great reluctance to examine the contents of the pack of a dead soldier, but Americans frequently foraged for enemy caps and blankets.[376] A few went further than that, stripping gold fillings from dead enemy soldiers. When one soldier was given a filling with the tooth attached, he decided that if he were captured it would be most inadvisable to have this in his possession, so he threw it away.[377]

It was not until deep in the winter of 1950-1951 that fur hats were issued; when they were, recalls James Dill, they "made everyone look like an illegitimate son of Mao Tse-tung." He also remembered when a company aidman came up with a solution to cracked, bleeding lips: "White paste that made everyone look like a character in a minstrel show."[378]

A great boost to morale took place when five-day furloughs to Japan were instituted. Preparation for "Operation Relax" was underway by November 1950. Studies dating to the last European war showed that soldiers subjected to 180 days of combat experience had increased casualty rates. The "R and R" (rest and recreation) policy was implemented on New Year's Eve, 1950, just at the time of a massive Chinese offensive. The five days did not include the time it took to reach Japan or some brief orientation after arrival; it was a full five days of leave.[379] The operation was suspended during subsequent large-scale Chinese attacks, but by the end of the conflict 800,000 delighted soldiers had made this trip.[380] In at least some units a five-day bonus was offered for the capture of an enemy soldier.[381]

A troop rotation system, whereby front-line soldiers, "depending on the availability of replacements," could exit Korea after nine months with 36 combat area points, went into effect in April 1951. There was a precedent for the release of military people after war experience in the later stages of World War II, when, beginning in October 1944, soldiers with lengthy involvement in service, combat, or other factors (such as expiration of length of enlistment) were discharged.[382] In Korea there was a sliding scale of points assigned: four points per month for frontline service, three points for those in combat areas (including artillery), two points for those in rear service roles and one point for those who were stationed in Japan. Additional points were awarded for combat wounds. Rotation meant that a very large number of young Americans served in Korea — up to four million, with many serving a single year.[383]

The negative side of the rotation system was that it deprived frontline units of experienced soldiers, often when they were most needed. John Singlaub is strongly critical of the rotation policy on two counts: it destroys unit morale and esprit de corps "by making each individual soldier acutely conscious of his time remaining in combat and it removed soldiers just when they had acquired skill in their tasks.[384] Anthony Herbert strongly endorsed Singlaub's position on the matter, but at least "he who fought up front went home up front."[385] Facing a shortfall of "live bodies" as replacements, in October 1952 the Far East Command raised the rotation points for combat soldiers from 36 to 39 points, but due to a public outcry the secretary of the army restored the level to 36 points. Rudolph Stephens recalls that the points were raised to 40 by the spring of 1953, by which time, after twelve months in Korea, he was stuck at 39½ points.[386] A factor that could delay rotation was if a serviceman had a MOS (military occupation specialty) for which there was a "critical" need. A radio operator, anticipating rotation, found himself in that category.[387]

While the U.S. military was undertaking its rotation system, the Chinese began a rotation process on a much larger scale, with whole divisions taking part. Of an estimated 2.1 million soldiers in the Chinese army, two-thirds of them rotated through Korea.[388]

By the spring of 1951 with 15,000 to 20,000 military personnel leaving, there had to be about the same number taking their place. A continuing problem, left unresolved from the Second World War, was that of replacements. A series of replacement depots, from the U.S. west coast to Japan then on to Korea, processed the green soldiers. According to Harry Summers, "This system was enormously wasteful, for either by accident or design troops would spend months lost in the replacement depot system."[389] What Summers does not refer to is what training or conditioning, if any, took place in these places. In the early days of the war, many soldiers were rushed pell-mell as individuals into combat with little weapons training or conditioning. As was the case towards the end of World War II, the greatest need was for riflemen. Soldiers who had been assigned another MOS in reserve units found that when they were called to active duty and sent to Korea they were assigned to rifle companies, which, of course, was bitterly resented by many of those involved.[390] When the U.S. Second Infantry Division was sent to Korea it had already experienced a personnel turnover of 139 percent, its regiments were only 60 to 65 percent combat-ready, and its ranks were filled out with people from headquarters units and replacement training centers. The same general condition applied to the Third Infantry Division, with General Mark Clark, then head of Army Field Forces, declaring that the force was at one-third of its strength and "had to be filled up from almost every source, scraping the bottom of the barrel to get men in order to send it over." Army sergeant W.B. Woodruff's comment could be applied to the replacement situation in general: "They were good enough men, but young, confused, bewildered, and with no conception of infantry combat." Allen Wilkinson remembers the fate of inexperienced replacements arriving in his company: "They drop like flies, for they do not know enough to take cover when they should.... The newcomers huddle together frightened, not knowing what this is all about."[391]

By March 1951 the situation had improved to the point that at least partially trained infantrymen were being shipped over. Another change was made in September 1951: where possible, replacements were assigned to units while the units were in reserve and were not directly sent to the front. Not for the U.S. Army was the German system, extolled by Martin Van Creveld, whereby replacements were trained together in units of common regional origin and then together were assigned to divisions with that identity. This also was the pattern in British regiments and, for that matter, in many Chinese divisions. Peter Watson has made the eminently sensible suggestion that soldiers should be linked together in groups of four from basic training to combat, thus providing the emotional reinforcement and practical assistance that would, at least in part, overcome the isolation of the newcomer tossed into an existing band of soldiers.[392]

As the conflict continued almost all of the reserve and National Guard personnel in combat situations rotated home, which resulted in an increase of draftees to replace them. This became more of a factor when additional guard and reserve units being called up were sent to Europe. The U.S. military there grew from 80,000 in 1950 to 250,000 in 1953, well beyond the reality of warfare.[393] Draft quotas were greatly increased until by October 1950 the conflict appeared to be drawing to a close. At that time Carl Vinson, chairman of the Senate Armed Services Committee, declared that, in order to attain his goal of increasing the armed services from two million to three million, the principle of universal service should be adopted, which meant an expanded draft and the elimination of almost all exemptions.[394]

To meet the manpower shortage in Korea, the army in 1952 expanded its incorporation of Korean soldiers in American units—the KATUSA program. By late that year two to three Koreans were in most nine-man rifle squads, a percentage that was sustained until the end of the conflict. During the darkest time of the war, in many cases even after having been wounded, as long as a soldier could fire a rifle he was kept on the line.[395]

Turnover in the military created problems in continuity and leadership. Jim Van Fleet, Eighth Army commander, lamented, "It is a damn hard job to keep an army ever fit, ready and eager to fight — especially when they go home faster than we can train them." Hanson Baldwin of the *New York Times* held that "rotation and turnover, and the Army's replacement system, have made the fine old regiments ... merely numbers on the roster, not living, breathing parts of a continuing tradition." What needed to be done, he believed, was to "build up unit *esprit*" and restore "unit integrity and cohesiveness." There was a widely held perception that the quality of the enlisted soldiers was declining. This was made more apparent when the army was forced to lower the minimum score in mental tests of draftees and even allowed some into the service who scored below that standard, while at the same time many potential draftees were given deferments for college attendance and protected occupations, and others managed to get into reserve units. In general, this created a class division, with those with less education sent to war, while the middle-class and above "college-types" were deferred until it was likely the conflict would be over. One bit of solace to those who were actually doing any fighting was combat pay of forty-five dollars a month, retroactive to the beginning of American involvement.[396]

Soldiers of whatever rank gave at least occasional attention to the goings-on of the leadership at the top. The removal of Douglas MacArthur from the Far East Command in April 1951 left many soldiers with mixed feelings. He was never popular with the troops (and reportedly was hated by Marines).[397] Everyone knew that he had directed one great triumph — Inchon — and one great disaster, the rout of the Eighth Army beginning in November 1950. One soldier, Anthony Herbert, recorded how he saw the change at the top: "Ridgway replaced MacArthur and we began to get an unlimited supply of ammo. Up until then, it had been pretty skimpy and every new clip had to be accounted for in reports and other paperwork. But with General Ridgway running the show, we settled down to fight — fight we did."[398]

Herbert also observed change at other levels at that time. He recalled: "We started getting in replacements, most of them from the Reserves or the National Guard, and there was definitely a difference. They were guys who didn't have to cover their asses at any time, because their careers weren't on the line. They were the real citizen-soldiers that have always been the strength of this country." He noted, with regret, that this element was to be missing in the subsequent campaign in Vietnam.[399]

When the war reached effective stalemate in mid–1951 there were a series of bitterly contested mini-battles over a few barren hills at the front, which resulted in a huge increase in American casualties. To many combat soldiers these were senseless fights over tiny bits of terrain that would make no substantial difference in the outcome of the war. In at least two instances— at Old Baldy in July 1952 and Jackson Heights the following October — there were combat refusals by soldiers, which quickly brought forth courts-martial, further evidence to the high command that morale was in a bad way. Yet, there was not a serious discipline problem, except, of course, with those soldiers who objected to what they perceived to be suicide actions.[400]

Fragging, the killing of hated officers and others, generally did not come along until Vietnam, but Rudolph Stephens experienced the killing of a much disliked officer when two sticks of dynamite were put under the officer's cot when no one else was around.[401] Although relations within and between ranks was generally good, the stress of combat was great. Jim Brady recalled a machine gunner who shot his bunkmate with a .45-caliber pistol.[402] Then there were SIWs— self-inflicted wounds. At the brutal fighting at Yudam-ri in the Chosin encounter, a Marine shot a finger off to get out of the fight, but "lost so much blood that he froze to death before he could be carried off the hill."[403] A Marine who stepped on a mine had both legs blown at the knee and died before he was brought back to his lines.[404] Since all soldiers were required to wear their helmets in combat areas, a new replacement shot and killed a soldier entering his bunker who was only wearing a cloth cap, the usual head garb of the Chinese.[405] A Marine in Jim Brady's company killed two Marines who he thought were Chinese infiltrators. Overcome with remorse, he refused to have their bodies removed from the company area and stood over them all night holding a drawn .45-caliber pistol until he was finally led away.[406] Inevitably there were those who could not take the enormous strain of combat. A young soldier put the point of his rifle in his mouth and would not take it out.[407] Another soldier, oblivious to any punishment, constantly ran from his position.[408] Soldier Kenneth Kendall came upon two soldiers shooting pistols at about twenty-five feet at each other's legs. Not SIWs (self inflicted wounds); in this case they could be called MIW (mutually inflicted wounds). Two soldiers on guard played an abbreviated form of Russian roulette, for which infraction they were required to dig a six by six foot hole in frozen ground and at various locations as their platoon changed locations.[409]

There were other non-combat casualties: "We were killing ourselves and breaking our legs and falling sick and cracking up and being carried away," recalls Jim Brady. "It was how it was in a mountain war in deep winter."[410] When a soldier in Canadian R. Bruce Wareing's tank company contracted the dreaded hemorrhagic fever and died, Wareing amazingly recalls that it did not set off any general alarm in his unit.[411]

Combat enlisted men had a keen awareness of the capability of both their NCOs and officers. Sergeants, who generally had combat experience, were much valued. Able, considerate officers were highly praised, while incompetent ones seemed to be quickly dispatched to other duties. Charles Brown recalls that his company commander, approaching time for rotation, barricaded himself in his bunker, appointed guards and did not emerge even for meals.[412] Another Marine recollects a second lieutenant who remained in his bunker day and night, but after enemy shelling ceased would emerge firing his .32-caliber pistol and shouting, "Now take that!"[413] For a similar disinclination to exposure to the front, another CO was given the name of the "bunker mole."[414] After a severe fight with Chinese troops, Marine Eldon Stanley recalls a CO "who sat on his ass in his bunker and didn't come out until three days after the firefight."[415] Soldier James DeLong had a platoon leader who never got out of his foxhole: "He didn't want to stick his neck out."[416]

In an unusual incident, another company commander, about to enter combat, shot himself in the foot, while a lieutenant, having declared that "he wouldn't be in Korea long," on his first day on the line also shot himself in the foot, something that was a fairly common occurrence among ordinary soldiers. Marine Paul Welsh vividly remembered a battalion major of unusual incompetence who avoided visits to the front line at all costs.[417] At least two company commanders collapsed under the pressure of combat.[418] George Zong recalls a company commander who issued orders which would have resulted in "people getting killed for nothing"; the CO "later went crazy." Then there was a regimental colonel who had an extremely deep foxhole from which he refused to come out until ordered by his division commander to emerge. An army patrol in North Korea in November 1950 was ambushed. Sergeant James Chatham recalls the scene: "Men were running, screaming, bunching up like lambs for the slaughter," which resulted in the relief of the company commander. Chatham's judgment: "Rightly so. He had set no flankers, no point, nor did he fight his company as he should have done."[419] John Michaelis, who commanded the Twenty-Seventh Regiment of the Twenty-Fifth Division as the beginning of the war, found he was confronted with "some officers [who] got jittery almost immediately and began to imagine that the enemy was coming in on them at night." He called them "grasshoppers" and had them replaced.[420] These occurrences were, of course, uncharacteristic of the scores of combat company commanders.

After the brutal retreat of the Marines from Chosin, an officious X Corps staff major with a thin mustache and swagger stick was exclaiming at Hungnam about the unshaven, dirty condition of the survivors huddled in a line. Marine Anthony Biebel recalls: "I heard a smack, and when I turned around he was out cold. Somebody had decked him. Never heard anything about it."[421] Confronted with the usual dire shortage of water, a Marine carrying a five-gallon can of water up a hill was approached by a "certain command person" who, after a long drink, proceeded to wash his face, hands and hair, and then ordered the enlisted man to go back for another can. Shortly thereafter the "certain command person" was shot, reportedly by a sniper.[422] Then there was the not infrequent occurrence of the newly assigned officer who gave a lecture on morale, discipline, etc., to the troops. Infantryman William Dillon recalls such an occasion: standing on the hood of a jeep while giving his oration, the officer dove for cover when a shell landed nearby. The men did not move; knowing the sound that the incoming shells made, they knew it was not going to land close to them.[423] John Graham has described what various incoming mortar and artillery shells sounded like and how to anticipate their time of arrival.[424]

There were frequent episodes where allied fighter planes and artillery fired on U.S. and South Korean troops. Army mortar man Harold Reinhart recalled a time when his unit got a double dose, both due to incorrect coordinates—first an aerial strafing by U.S. planes; the second an artillery barrage by a French company.[425] The result: 55 dead, 120 wounded. Horrendous incidents took place when napalm was inadvertently dropped on the same Marines and soldiers.[426]

Around mid–1951, with the front lines effectively stabilized, the army command decided that an accurate measure of frontline effectiveness was to be based on the number of enemy captured. By then the intelligence that captured soldiers could provide was slight, and high casualties were endured by the many patrols sent out to get them. This obsession led to the establishment of unit quotas and, from the perspective of rear headquarters, kept the frontline troopers on their toes. Sometimes an incentive was provided: if the members of a patrol captured an enemy soldier they would get an R and R furlough.[427] The Chinese employed a similar reward system.[428] John Sullivan, among others, doubted the utility of getting captives for intelligence purposes; in his situation, he said, "We felt that any information would not tell us anything we didn't already know."[429] After endless dangerous patrols and battling up and down Old Baldy, soldier Rudolph Stephens wondered why spotter planes would not be more effective in determining enemy dispositions than the carnage he experienced on foot.[430] Apparently, the compilation of statistics and "ticket-punching" came to dominate.

With effective stalemate and only a few frontline soldiers doing any fighting, the rear-guard officer corps had to find something to do to be useful or at least appear busy. The result was over-supervision, with what looked like flocks of officers prowling through the ranks, clipboards in hand, inspecting this, that and the other thing. Had this group ventured to the front lines they surely would have found soldiers who were ragged, dirty and worn, but it is most likely they concentrated their efforts in rear areas, checking on such matters as the proper alignment of footlockers, and military courtesy.[431]

In this period of declining encounters, Joe Collins weighed in with a statement that was astounding for the chief officer of the army. Based on his observations, he declared that there was a dire need to revive "the basics of American offensive doctrine." In his view, attack tactics were ineffective, and there was little proper coordination of fire support. In November 1952 the word went out: commanders at all levels were to begin instruction in fundamentals in these matters, right down to the squad and platoon levels. This order surely must have created unease, if not alarm, at some rear echelon officers' club gatherings.[432]

The renewed emphasis on basics probably accounted for the experience of Rudolph Stephens, who recalled that when his company was sent into reserve it was first provided with a very welcome real breakfast and then immediately was subjected to a twenty-mile hike in full battle gear, followed by mountain maneuvers. This experience turned out to be necessary for overall conditioning after the relatively static status of close-quarter combat, but an immediate twenty-mile hike![433]

Seventeen-year-old replacement Curtis Morrow quickly got a full dose of wartime experience when he joined a frontline infantry company in December 1950 as the allied forces were continuing their retreat from the north. In the bitter cold, the soldiers he joined were bundled up in rags; the only things clean about them were their weapons. This was a cardinal rule in infantry companies: you may be dirty, but keep your rifle clean. Morrow's new associates first showed Morrow how to kill body lice. Advice on other kinds of killing followed shortly. Morrow does not mention ever seeing any inspecting officer arriving on the scene. One method to keep dirt from getting in a rifle barrel was to cover its top with a condom.[434]

When he joined a Marine rifle company as a replacement, Richard Bohart was struck by the appearance of his new colleagues: they all had beards and were filthy; and more frightening, they all looked crazy, "with wild looks in their eyes," but three or four days later, "they looked normal to me."[435] James Dill speculated that his grizzled appearance (and, according to his Korean translator, a murderous mentality) motivated some North Korean villagers to build a needed ramp. When Jim Brady joined his Marine unit in the mountains he was surprised to see the nonregulation garb: "Some men wore knee-length parkas, other pile vests or field jackets, one a forest green overcoat to his ankles. There were stolen army jackets, turtleneck sweaters, a plaid mackinaw made respectable by an issue green scarf tossed jauntily over one shoulder." One of his men wore cowboy boots. He also observed that "military courtesy," at least in his combat area, was minimal: saluting once in the morning and once at night.[436]

In a beneficent gesture, the army provided the troops in the combat zone with free cigarettes, beer, other beverages, candy and the inevitable gum. During the steamy summer of 1950 there was a severe shortage of potable water for the troops. A brief episode of attention to the life of GI Joe occurred in September 1950, when the army cut off the beer ration for enlisted men. As happened in other wars, some hometown vigilantes and armchair patriots became alarmed about the moral temptations encountered by young soldiers, Marines, sailors and airmen, in this case alcoholic beverages provided to fighting men from public funds.[437] According to the account of one (and only one) Marine, there was a regular ration of alcohol at least in the Marine headquarters he was in, with enlisted men getting twenty-four cans of beer a week, while NCOs and officers received two bottles of whisky. In fact, some of the beer was donated by American brewers.[438] The water in Korea was so bad in many places in Korea that it had to be imported from Japan, but beer was seen by some as the essence of the Devil's buttermilk.

Since so many soldiers were under the (U.S.A.) legal drinking age of twenty-one, the American public questioned whether our armed forces should be pouring it down the throats of our fine young men. As a result of this flap, many soldiers now had to buy their own beer (and wine) at nominal cost at post exchanges, usually at ten cents a can. By 1951 enlisted men were provided with two cans of beer a day.[439] Seeking convivial settings for beer consumption, American soldiers sometimes visited British units, which had "wet canteens"; the Americans had the money and were liberal in their use of it, while the poorly paid British soldiers welcomed the generous Yanks.[440]

U.S. servicemen had been warned that Korean-made distilled spirits were "practically poison," but this did not deter some troopers from trying the near-toxic and banned Korean whisky, or "Skoch," which at least one soldier said tasted like molasses; Rene Cutforth said it was "a horrible drink and its effects cannot be predicted."[441] By 1952 soldiers returning from rest and recreation sorties to Japan were allowed to buy and bring a case of whisky, which could then be sold for from five to fifteen dollars a bottle. The NCOs in John Sullivan's platoon revealed to him that they had built a supply of whisky and beer, for special occasions, in a cavern in his command bunker.[442] Marine Lt. Jim Brady recalls that in his battalion a liquor run periodically would be organized to Japan, while Pat Robertson, later a noted evangelist, was known as the "liquor officer" in his rear-based Marine unit, with frequent sorties to Japan.[443] In any case, there was no public outcry at home about the liquor allotment for officers and NCOs, in part because it was assumed that they were of legal drinking age, and in part because the allotment was generally unknown. Since the "Class VI ration" came from non-appropriated funds, it is difficult to determine if this was official policy and how the bottles were distributed. It appears that NCOs got one bottle a month while officers got two.[444] There were several recollections in which officers gave some of their liquor to enlisted men in their unit. One of them recalled that he gave half his monthly ration of a case of scotch to soldiers returning from patrols.[445] In any case, on special occasions ordinary soldiers got hold of distilled spirits and sometimes with the necessary ingredients made their own "applejack" or "moonshine" (combining fruit juice, sugar and yeast). Some of the juice was thoughtfully provided by the American Women's Temperance League. In the middle of the grim situation at Chosin, Sgt. Bob Corley was grateful to "Chesty" Fuller when the colonel gave him a shot of Old Grand Dad, which "was like something from heaven, not just a drink of tanglewood."[446]

Beer raised the hackles of some folks back home, but what would the watchdogs of public morality have made of the relationship of soldiers with Asian women in Korea and Japan, with masses of U.S. troops taking advantage of R and R trips to Japan? In a program that was fully operational by April 1951, after six months "in country" two enlisted men per company and one officer per battalion could participate, with the leave time averaging five full days after arrival in Japan plus a day of uniform changes and brief processing, so the escape from Korea could easily exceed a week.[447] It is not clear if preference was given to those in combat units. For poorly-paid personnel from countries supporting the U.N. effort, the Eighth Army paid their expenses.[448] During these brief breaks from war, most GI's spent little time visiting art galleries and other cultural facilities. It would probably have been comforting for the home folk to know that often the leading desire of combat soldiers was to sleep in a warm, clean, soft bed, followed by hot, clean food, with other priorities to follow.

To some participants, the R and R sojourn was known as "I and I"— intoxication and intercourse.[449] Prostitutes in Korea had a toxic reputation, but an army report held that venereal disease had not been a major problem. The initiation of the R and R program coincided with the outbreak of this malady. One alarmed division commander declared that any soldier with such an ailment would automatically be placed at the bottom of the rotation list.[450] In any case, some considered going on R and R as a prelude to bad luck upon returning to Korea, even leading to death.[451]

At no time in this war or in the previous two European wars did the U.S. military provide facilities for regulated sexual activity. This was unlike what occurred in World War II with German soldiers, who were provided with regulated brothels, as well as with Japanese troops, who were supplied with "comfort women" from Korea, which experience remains a bitter memory for many Koreans. In Korea sexual encounters, on a large as well as a small scale, were common, principally in rear areas. Informed by a pimp that sex could be had for the cost of a carton of cigarettes, an American soldier joined a line including Turkish and Dutch troops. When his turn came, no fondling was allowed; it was all brief business.[452] Another soldier encountered another large-scale operation, this time in Seoul. "A building the size of a basketball gym" was partitioned in small sheeted enclosures, with the girls talking and laughing with each other while servicing the servicemen.[453] An intelligence unit spotted some young women on a ridge; while escorting them to the rear, the soldiers had to carry five of them across a stream, to be met with an angry, hooting bunch of troopers, shouting, "You have taken our girls!"[454] Michael Caine was informed by an American Marine about Korean hookers: "100 percent gonorrhea." An army soldier recalled standing guard outside an officers' club while prostitutes in kimonos were brought in.[455] Sex was sometimes procured at the point of a rifle. Two army soldiers broke down the door of a Korean home and had forced sex with the young female inhabitants.[456] Another Marine stopped one of his own from assaulting a woman.[457]

There was leave time to go to Seoul. Marine Martin Russ recalls a short 1952 visit, which was preceded by a warning speech by an officer, "something or other about venereal diseases and conduct yourselves according as befits United States Marines." Russ was struck by his entrance into Seoul: "The capital city appeared, as out of nowhere. The road became a precipitous mountain pass and then, abruptly, there is Seoul ... which, in the early morning is indescribable. It is beautiful, ugly, breath-taking; the most intriguing, moving sight I've ever seen." Once in the city he was surrounded by a "phalanx of wild children, armed to the teeth with chewing gum, shoeshine kits and other more curious wares." After a couple of beers (three dollars minimum for each), followed by a swarm of beseeching children he ventured into a whorehouse, where his visit was disrupted by a female member of the Korean vice squad.[458]

Pat Frank has also recorded his impression of Seoul as he saw it that year. From the top of South Mountain he could see why the city had been called the "pearl of the Orient": "wide avenues and sweeping circles, and the more modern buildings and the lordly Capitol dome shone white in the sunlight, and the ancient palaces were like oblong-cut rubies and agates resting in the emerald clusters of their parkland." Closer examination presented a different picture:

I saw most of the modern buildings gutted by shell and bomb, and the Capitol hollowed by flame.... The vacant spaces were acres of rubble in which children gone wild slept and fought and sometimes ate.... The brown splotches were burlap-covered markets sprung up where once had stood stores. Four tides of war had rolled over Seoul, and it was ninety percent destroyed.[459]

Michael Caine had vivid recollections of his visits to Seoul. Not only was the city "smothered in hookers," but there were violent encounters, "literally murderous," by soldiers from different units and countries. U.S. soldiers fought Marines, Greeks took on Turks, but the deadliest brawls were between French Canadians, most of whom had been lumberjacks, and massive New Zealand Maoris, who for some unknown reason hated them. Australians "would fight anybody who was as drunk as they were." He found the place so dangerous that he only went there in a group of his mates, frequently adorned with Red Cross armbands.[460]

It is a convention of journalists and other commentators to describe those who were in military service during a war as having "fought" in that conflict. In World War II, so often compared favorably to what went on in Korea, the great majority of the total of sixteen million in military service at one time or another did no fighting, were in fact very safe from the deadly violence of combat. In that war the support "tail" of service personnel was about seven to every frontline soldier. During the Korean conflict, excluding the very safe support personnel in Japan and the United States, there was about a four to one ratio between the rear echelon and those who actually were in combat.[461] Communications specialist James Christiansen sometimes shed a figurative tear as he sat in his warm hut when he thought about the infantry experiencing brutal cold and ice, not to say the threat of death or mutilation.[462]

Because of the poverty of the country and massive destruction of buildings, there was to be no repetition of what occurred in mid–1944 France when the Service of Supply, abandoning its mass of prefabricated buildings in Normandy, rushed into Paris in the wake of its liberation and took over most hotels for its members. D.D. Eisenhower responded by ordering the removal of all nonessential personnel from Paris and shortly informed his field commanders that he was "chasing the SOS out of Paris" to provide rest facilities for combat soldiers on leave, but J.C.H. Lee, the general in charge of this supply empire, "ignored Eisenhower's order." In defense of this action and others like it, Lee declared that "the rear echelon have their morale problems too." If boredom was a problem they could have requested transfer to the front lines, but when a "clean-out" of the rear echelon to fill the growing gap in infantrymen was attempted, many of those who would have been affected strongly defended the important work they did behind the lines.[463]

As in other wars, support personnel in Korea were in an enviable situation.

They experienced plenty of discomfort and inconvenience due to the weather (those cold mornings were tough) and some other things, but they had first call on supplies and clothing intended for frontline soldiers. Three "hots" and a cot for them — always. By the nature of their employment, those in combat arms— the infantry, artillery and tanks— were, at the least, usually dirty, worn, lice-ridden and exhausted (in extreme cold, no lice). Anyone who has any doubt about this assertion should at a minimum try a bit of rough living, sleeping in a foxhole, trench or even a tent in the woods for a few days. Above all, the rear guard did not have to confront the reality of bullets, explosives, death and mutilation as well as the continuing threat of another massive Chinese attack.

Anthony Herbert could always tell the difference between frontline troopers and "rear-area commandos" when they were on leave in Korea. When combat soldiers had some leave "in country" they always got cleaned up, while those of the rear echelon "ran around as dirty and as unshaven as possible, trying to look like Willie and Joe, carrying burp guns or other 'captured' weapons on slings around their necks."[464]

Although greeted with great enthusiasm by the rear echelon, live performances of singers, musicians and actors put on by the United Service Organization (USO) met with a mixed, and sometimes depressing, response from frontline troops.[465] One veteran recalled coming to a casualty station and wandering over to a USO show in his blood-spattered fatigues, where he glumly sat through a program of happy songs and vivid dancing. On the other hand, Jim Brady enjoyed an act from a Broadway drama performed by Paul Douglas and his leggy wife Jan Sterling on a snowy, windswept wooden stage.[466] In *Psywar*, Stephen Peace concluded, "The juxtaposition of a lively show and men dying on the battlefield could be more than some men could handle, resulting in depression or other psychological problems."[467]

At least in this war soldiers were not pressured to publicly glorify their commanders. In the previous war the most notorious example of this was credited to Mark Clark, who traveled with a band, had a group of journalists on hand and required that all press releases begin with his name and rank. A song was produced in his honor, "The Sons of the General Clark," which began, "Stand Up and sing the praise of General Clark; Your hearts and voices raise for General Clark." A soldier recalled an entertainment staged in wartime Italy: "As we went in we were all handed little slips of paper by a warrant officer who muttered as he gave out each slip, 'It's sung to the tune of God Bless America, I think. Please give it all you've got.'" He does not note the degree of audience participation.[468] In regard to public recognition, George Marshall informed Eisenhower in May and June 1944 that both Clark and Omar Bradley were being given undue attention, while subordinate commanders were not mentioned. For that matter, Ike had a personal public relations officer in his bloated staff of 3,000 personnel.[469] To top it all, and in both wars, the name of Douglas MacArthur headed just about every press release originating from his headquarters.[470] Doug, the one-man band, was winning the war in the Pacific and now in Korea. Mark Clark, without his previous fanfare, was connected to the latter part of the Korean War when in April 1952 he succeeded Ridgway as Far East commander. There were no songs in praise of "Dugout Doug" in either war.

Medical care for wounded soldiers was considerably improved over that provided in the previous war. The mortality rate was reduced by half. Eighty percent of the wounded eventually returned to duty. Immediate medical care was provided by combat medics, with seven of them being attached to each infantry company.[471] For more effective immediate treatment of wounds, medic John Kamperschroer believes twice as many medics should have been provided.[472] Time after time in their memoirs, soldiers extolled the bravery and effectiveness of this band of intrepid men.[473] Acting as a medic, army dentist Morton Silver recalls a memorable episode. Coming to the aid of a badly wounded Marine who had been given up as lost, he began to wipe away massive clots and bloody effusions that were soaking his entire upper torso. Quickly sizing up the situation, Silver "plugged the facial wound, applied pressure and stopped the arterial flow." Filled with relief and satisfaction, he shouted to the Marine, "You're not going to die! Damn it, you're going to live!"[474]

Surgical units in forward areas (MASH — Mobile Army Surgical Hospitals) were vital in keeping the mortality rate very low. Military hospitals in Japan were greatly expanded. In the view of Albert Cowdrey, "Many of the patients who should have stayed in Korea were hastily evacuated to nearby Japan," although it is most unlikely that the wounded objected to this.[475] An important development was the ready availability of whole blood for transfusions. The shortage of doctors was addressed by a draft focused on them. All-volunteer nurses were welcomed not only for their professional expertise. Cases of psychiatric illness fell and rose with the fortunes of the war.

There was the pressing need to combat a wide variety of infectious diseases. The most fearsome of these was hemorrhagic fever, which first struck along the front northeast of Seoul in the spring of 1951 and then returned with a vengeance that autumn. Vigorous action by the medical service reduced the mortality rate from its effects to 5 percent, but the cause of this virulent Asiatic fever was not identified.[476] The people who worked in Dr. Harold Secor's MASH unit had such a high regard for his services that when he was ordered to the rear they awarded him, unofficially of course, the Combat Infantryman's Badge. Evacuated for further medical attention, soldier Jack Jaunal had visions of being transferred to a Swedish hospital ship, with its blue-eyed, blonde nurses, but that was not to be, while British soldier Alfie Fowler looked forward with pleasure to being sent to a Norwegian hospital ship, but to his embarrassment a most attractive blonde nurse coolly shaved down every part of his body in front of his onlooking colleagues.[477]

A development confronting American soldiers was the use that the Chinese military made of a wide variety of musical signaling devices—horns, bugles, whistles, cymbals, flares, colored smoke bombs, etc.—for its nighttime attacks (and thus overcoming the lack of radio communication). These, together with mass singing and beating of drums, also were designed to rouse its troops and instill fear in its opponents. The use of such devices had a long history in Asian warfare, but was new to the young Americans in Korea. What sounded like "Taps"—played for the dead—to many American soldiers, was, in fact, a signal for reassembling troops.[478] Early in the conflict U.S. troops, noting that North Korean units sometimes fired green flares before an attack, responded by firing their own green flares, which caused confusion on the other side.[479] The U.S. Cavalry may have used bugles when it charged the Indians in the American West, but the Chinese clamor was much more insidious than that. According to Samuel Griffith, this cacophony chilled South Korean troops "to the bone." Anthony Farrar-Hockley provides a description of the first serious encounter that South Korean soldiers had with Chinese troops on the pivotal night of November 25: "That night, battalions of the ROK 7th and 8th Divisions heard drums, clanging gongs and clashing cymbals. The South Korean soldiers knew that presaged an attack. The warning sacrificed surprise but aroused dread."[480]

One U.S. unit countered the Chinese signaling by turning on its siren; others drowned out the din with artillery barrages and star flares. After studying the matter, S.L.A. Marshall concluded that the Chinese used bugles to signal attack movements. He arranged to have similar bugles produced, which had to add an element of confusion for the other side, although it is not clear how widespread this tactic was.[481] Apparently independently of Marshall, using captured instruments and learning what the various sounds indicated, one infantry company was ready for the next Chinese serenade, with its commander declaring, "The next time they attack blowing their 'charge' we are going to blow their retreat. Every time they blow a whistle we'll blow six. Every time they shoot up one flare we'll shoot up three."[482] At Chosin some Marines figured out that one blast on a Chinese whistle indicated advance, while two called for a retreat, so the Marines used their whistles to confuse the Chinese. Another response of some Americans was to charge "yelling and shouting." A Marine company being overrun near Chosin counterattacked; one survivor recollects the scene: "They attacked abreast with marching fire, sweeping across the low ground where the tents were, howling like wild Indians the whole time."[483] Preparing to assault a hill called Gillis Island, Army PFC Rudolph Stephens recalls his anticipation: "I began to notice the tanks were firing away at the top of the hill, and soon everyone was firing his rifle and yelling as loud as he could. That had a calming effect on one's nerves, and soon I was yelling as loud as the rest."[484]

S.L.A. Marshall believes that due to the Chinese clamor, American troops in Korea were much more demonstrative in attack than were those of World War II. As another soldier related that when confronted with attacking yelling Chinese, "We started yelling back."[485]

A common practice for attacking Chinese was to blow what was taken to be "Taps," which many Americans believed to be a clear indication that death was approaching. On the grim Christmas Eve of 1950, however, a few Chinese buglers provided ragged renditions of "Jingle Bells" and "Silent Night," but on a very different occasion, as Chinese soldiers overran a U.S. artillery position one GI thought he could hear Chinese buglers playing "Silent Night."[486] Marine Martin Russ recalls getting a full treatment of Christmas music, including songs by Bing Crosby, broadcast by Chinese loudspeakers.[487] Rudolph Stephens recollected that to arouse Yanks' concerns about the womenfolk they had left behind, Chinese loud speakers played "I Wonder Who's Kissing Her Now" and the great Hank Williams song, "Your Cheating Heart," followed by maudlin statements about Sino concerns on the matter.[488]

For its part, the only seasonal music that a Marine platoon could provide in 1952 was a single song on a worn record played on a windup Victrola; "Jingle Bells" was played over and over.[489] The Chinese also sent over Christmas cards, some of which declared that while American soldiers were freezing in the trenches at home, millionaires were enjoying their holiday dinners. Another message, with an appropriate female image, declared, "Darling, I will dream that you are coming back to me this Christmas. I can't think of a Christmas without you."[490] By all evidence the impact of these Chinese efforts was slight at best.

The outbreak of the war required a major adjustment of the U.S. Army's morale support unit from the peacetime situation, which formerly dealt with basic education about the responsibilities of citizenship, etc. The Office of the Chief of Information responded with a series of pamphlets, radio programs and films—of varying quality and effectiveness. The principal message was that American soldiers were fighting the dire threat of communist expansion. It also provided information about Korea and its people, matters that were almost universally unknown to those who were now thrust into the clash of arms in that country. To address the flood of reservists, National Guardsmen and draftees, in August 1950 the army high command instituted its Pre-Combat Orientation Course.[491]

When Matthew Ridgway took command of the Eighth Army at the end of December 1950, one of the changes he made was in basic provision for soldiers. After the war he declared that his top priority as a commander had been to provide this for his soldiers. During his regular inspections at the front he constantly asked soldiers if they were getting an adequate supply of socks and gloves, whether they were getting hot meals and even if they had writing paper. He went so far as to carry a supply of gloves for soldiers with lost or torn ones. A second priority was to share their "hardships and hazards." He slept in a tent and was all over the forward areas. The troops quickly realized his commitment to their welfare. He took a particular interest in troop information and indoctrination and was dissatisfied the efforts of the Troop Information publications. He proceeded to put forth his own views on why the United States was fighting in Korea, which were transmitted throughout his army. Using simple, direct language, Ridgway emphasized that the confrontation was not only between evil communism and the glories of democracy, but God versus Marxist atheism. Although the Eighth Army distributed the statement to all commands, it is doubtful if most soldiers ever saw it.[492] In any case, he led by example.

The rapid withdrawal of army units from North Korea had resulted in the wholesale abandonment of helmets, bayonets and web equipment to such an extent that many units had to be almost completely reequipped before they were again combat ready. Soon combat deficiencies drew the attention of the Army Field Forces Headquarters in far-off Monroe, Virginia. Its report of March 13, 1951, noted little use of hand signals in combat, lack of bayonet use, weak patrol operation, poor collection of battlefield intelligence, dirty handheld weapons, poor use of camouflage, need for night fighting training, and, not least, wasteful use of resources, with soldiers leaving items on the battlefield "including tanks and vehicles."[493]

Later, in 1952 the army brought forth a requirement of "minimum standards" of army knowledge for all personnel in the following order of priorities: present individual mission, unit history, names of commanding officers, price of individual equipment used and, apparently last, why U.S. troops were fighting in Korea. There was considerable rejection of the information and indoctrination efforts by many army commanders, who saw them as ineffective and a waste of valuable time. Some soldiers claimed they never heard of these matters and did not know why they were in Korea (a common enough position of assumed ignorance in all such activities), while many others held that, due to prior conditioning, they did not need adamant denunciations of communism. If the impacts of these efforts were slight or minimal, faced with effective communist troop indoctrination, they certainly were better than nothing. The great majority of soldiers seemed never to have bothered to read the variety of leaflets produced by Troop Information, yet having an hour or more a week to gather for a film, an oration or a "discussion" session provided a break for many in the rear areas from the mundane routine of military life, while those at the front were understandably preoccupied with combat operations. Subjected to a barrage of orders and other pronouncements, the attention of enlisted men was not increased when the title "Troop Information" was changed to "Command Information."[494]

One element in the U.S. Army that could benefit from efforts at troop indoctrination was foreign-born young men, not yet eligible for citizenship, who were caught up in the draft. A U.S.-Ireland agreement of January 1950 exempted Irish-born immigrants from mandatory military service but came too late for those who had already been drafted or had volunteered. A notable experience for one young Irishman was that of Frank McCourt, author of *Angela's Ashes*, but instead of being sent to Korea he became a dog handler in Germany. Although totals for such Irish persons is unknown, about thirty-five of them were killed in Korea, including five priests and a nun. In 1952 the remains of nine soldiers were shipped back to Ireland, while another group was buried in a Bronx cemetery. In 2005 a modest memorial monument was constructed at the village of Lixnaw in County Kerry for those who had been killed.[495]

CHAPTER THREE

Aspects of a War

Uncle Sam's Supplies

At the beginning of the U.S. entry into the Korean conflict, almost everything the army used — uniforms, weapons and all the rest — was left over from World War II. Much of it had been collected around the Pacific and renovated in Japan. This deficit was gradually overcome with new production in the United States and also, importantly, output from Japanese factories. As the U.N. forces moved north in September 1950, the U.S. Army experienced substantial supply problems. This was an armed force that required enormous amounts of supplies of all sorts. One logjam was created by MacArthur's insistence on sending the X Corps back through Seoul to be shipped to Wonsan on the east coast. As a result the port of Inchon was sealed off from needed supplies for the Eighth Army, which remained responsible for logistical support for the X Corps adventure. An alternative supply route was from the southern port of Pusan, but the decimation of the Korean rail system required supplies from there to be sent by truck over battered roads.[1]

Reaching back to its main base on the U.S. West Coast, by all appearances the Quartermaster Corps was overwhelmed by the growing need for supplies combined with the ever-increasing supply routes as the Eighth Army moved north. In his history of the U.S. Army, Russell Weigley declares that the Quartermaster Corps made a "heroic effort to approximate the American standard of living among the Korean Mountains." As a result of "lavish supply," including "ample provision of warm clothing when winter came," it "came about as close as possible to succeeding in that impossible task."[2]

This was not the perception of many of those who served there. The experience of one officer in the Marine Corps probably was typical of the problems it confronted: "Shoes are tied with scraps of cord and kitchens are using toilet soap received from home by mail.... It was understandable that supply confusion should exist at first, but I do not understand why the supply authorities should resist our legitimate requests telling us that we are using too much."[3] On the other hand, Americans, and not just their soldiers, were and are notorious for waste. The minimum total supply requirement for offensive action by the Eighth Army was 4,000 tons daily, which was ten times the amount needed for an equivalent Chinese force.[4] A serious problem that existed from the beginning was Korean pilferage of supplies. The matter was addressed by having MPs and Korean police guarding supply trains at all stops heading north.[5]

With all kinds of bottlenecks and breakdowns, and with supply personnel continuing what seemed to be their longstanding tradition of dragging their heels about releasing "their" supplies, expedients outside the turgid chain of command were resorted to. From far into North Korea, Major James Spellman explained one way this worked: "So long as Pusan remained within truck distance, it was possible to bypass approving authorities and go directly to the mountains of supplies in the port. Often we obtained supplies in Pusan that were impossible to get through the red-tape maze of proper channels." Viewing the matter from the end of the food chain, Spellman declared, "Even now, if a unit is willing to send its trucks 230 miles to Ascom City (outside of Seoul) or 400 miles to Pusan, supplies can be obtained. But the price in broken springs and dead-lined trucks is prohibitive."[6]

The cost of the breakdown in the supply system can be seen in the long delay in resupplying the Eighth Army as it prepared to move above Pyongyang in what was billed as the "final offensive." Lack of supply required this action to be delayed for about three weeks in November, and even then that army moved without full provision, while the temperature plunged and Chinese forces flowed across the Yalu. The inefficient organization resulted in the near-criminal failure to provide winter clothing for many of the soldiers.[7] According to Roy Appleman, "All elements of Eighth Army were short of, or entirely without, winter clothing on the eve of the advance."[8] Supply bungling, for example, resulted in twenty truckloads of winter gear, along with tons of other supplies, being destroyed as American forces soon raced south out of Pyongyang. Lack of spare parts made half of the vehicles inoperative in one of Walker's divisions.[9]

James Cardinal, a rifleman in the chaotic situation, provides a grim recollection: "When the retreat began, the winter clothing that had not been issued and food, ammunition, gasoline and other equipment and supplies were still in vast supply dumps awaiting distribution.... As is probably true of every war, we saw rear echelon personnel wearing winter equipment of the sort that had not been issued to us." He passed by fenced-in supply dumps surrounded by guards who had orders to shoot anyone who tried to get to the supplies. Due to severe weather and the lack of proper clothing, "At night we had to sleep with our rifles, grenades and canteens of water inside our sleeping bags.... It was extremely dangerous to touch anything made of metal unless you wore gloves." This pattern of gross mismanagement, he concluded, "was one of the reasons for the poor morale that beset [the] Eighth Army in the weeks that were to come." Victor Fox had a similar experience, with an emphasis on hunger: "In actual fact, the company at this time began to starve," to such an extent that "many of us even scrounged around other regimental trains looking for biscuits — it was like something out of the Depression." Yet he was told that "great amounts of equipment, fuel, ammo — even rations ... had been torched or dynamited."[10] Leonard Korgie said that when he was withdrawing through Pyongyang at night, "The whole city looked like it was burning. In one place the engineers burned a rations dump about the size of a football field."[11] When a major tried to prevent a group of soldiers from salvaging some winter gear from pending destruction, a carbine was pointed at him while the clothing was taken.[12] On the other hand, another soldier recalled handing out food and gasoline to passing trucks leaving the North Korean capital. During the withdrawal from Chosin in December 1950, some Marines removed needed gloves and mittens from their dead.[13]

In the run-up to the offensive, the Quartermaster Corps airlifted in large quantities of winter clothing, but, as Stanley Weintraub observes, "Airlift ... could not outfit all forward troops, even badly." The lack of winter clothing as cold weather set in in the fall of 1950 was an emphatic complaint. In the vital matter of protecting feet from severe weather, notes Weintraub, "Many winter shoe packs were too large and all were poorly designed. Their airtightness caused them to retain body moisture, encouraging frostbite."[14] Weintraub probably is referring to the "Arctic" boots worn by Marines, which Ray Vallowe recalled froze sweat within, unlike army leather boots, which "could breathe and evaporate that water and sweat. To keep the water out we supplemented with rubber overshoes."[15] To Jim Brady, "Frozen feet were a continual fear," which could only be addressed by dry feet: "How the socks smelled didn't matter, only that they were dry."[16] The best boot turned out to be the so-called "Mickey Mouse" one, which had an ungainly size with a wool-lined interior and several layers of rubber outside.[17] These were shades of the problems at the end of 1944 in Europe. At one point GIs encountered Chinese soldiers wearing U.S. winter gear, while the Yanks were shivering in warm-weather clothing.[18] Some soldiers claimed they did not receive winter clothing until they had been driven out of North Korea, when, almost miraculously, their supply sergeant reappeared and presented them with an early "Christmas present" in the form of seasonal clothing.[19]

Because of the frequent need for urination and bowel movements, combat soldiers wearing layers of leg clothing were presented with a serious problem. Marine Jim Brady recalled how in bitter weather he endured a severe case of the "runs," but as John Chafee, his company commander, told him, everyone had been through that.[20] Although all the nearly mandatory long johns had a flap at the back, it is a wonder that the Quartermaster Corps never thought of this practical matter by providing rear zippers for outer grab. No doubt, zippers would have frozen in Arctic conditions, but Corps personnel sitting in heated rear echelon facilities apparently did not consider the matter.

To provide for better protection against shrapnel in the winter of 1951-52, the military introduced new field jackets that were lighter and warmer but lined with Fiberglas. A rumor soon spread that if hit with a bullet, the fiberglass fragments would burrow deep into the body. According to Jim Brady, many combat soldiers wanted nothing to do with them, but Marine Martin Russ declares that by 1952 every Marine outside of his bunker was required to wear one of the armored vests. Marine Edward McAleer said he never heard of it while he was there.[21] In 1951 the Marines led the way in introducing body armor, followed by the army later that year, which began distributing an inferior sort.[22] By the spring of 1952 the vests were widely available for both branches. Optional equipment included mid-section armored shorts, used on patrols and assaults. Given the plethora of mines, servicemen looking forward to becoming fathers found good use for them.[23]

At the beginning of the conflict a unit of South Korean Marines trapped on the southeast coast had to be evacuated by the U.S. Navy, but was forced to leave all its vehicles and equipment behind. Thus, the North Korean soldiers realized a source of supply that was to be a continuing feature of both American and South Korean withdrawals throughout the war.[24] One of the benefits the Chinese derived from their initial successes, as at Pyongyang, was the heaps of material left behind by their retreating opponents. As on other occasions, many Chinese soldiers were highly appreciative of the GI food, clothing and footwear they found cast aside or, in the matter of footwear, they stripped from dead or wounded Americans.[25] One Chinese officer recalled, "Without the American sleeping bags and overcoats that we captured, I am not sure we could have gone on." Another allowed that Chinese troops were driven by high morale "but their real purpose was to get the enemy's biscuits, canned food, chocolates and clothing." The propensity of Chinese soldiers to seek GI food was addressed by one group of Americans, who had "a great idea, best of the war": to booby-trap left-behind rations.[26] A Communist spokesman at the time declared that the wealth of weapons and equipment that fell into the hands of the winners of the Chinese civil war was so great that Chiang Kai-shek "came to be the head of the transport department of the People's Liberation Army and the United States our arsenal."[27]

The lure of American equipment, clothing and supplies was such that it often interfered with sustaining Chinese attacks. Frequently Chinese soldiers stopped to strip wounded or dead Americans of their footwear, coats and food.[28] There were problems—GI boots were much too big, as were their steel helmets. The Chinese soldiers admittedly were poorly clothed and equipped with deplorable footwear for the bitter winter of 1950-51, and their supply system was grossly inadequate, so the American material was greatly appreciated.[29]

A unique feature of Chinese garb was strips on leggings that could be used as tourniquets to stop bleeding.[30]

There was also the problem of theft of American equipment by Korean civilians. According to Rene Cutforth, it was a common practice of American soldiers in inhabited areas to padlock and chain jeeps and remove the rotor arm. "Motor vehicles were worth their weight in gold at that time to the South Korean gangs and racketeers. A stolen jeep would be rushed off to some alley in Seoul's maze of mean streets and swiftly repainted. They would give it a new number, paint out the unit signs and stencil a large R.O.K.— Republic of Korea on the front and back of it." The jeep involved was not put to military use but would be crammed with "panic-stricken middle class refugees from Seoul and Kaesong — they could get twelve of them on each jeep — and carry them southwards," for a very hefty fee. There were episodes of truckloads of refugees being robbed while being taken south. Looting and theft of luggage were also endemic. Cutforth decided not to write about jeep-stealing at the time largely because it would provide more grist to the mill of "a great many dazed and shamed individuals in the American forces who had begun to find the cause of all their disasters and defeats in the behavior of the South Koreans."[31] E.J. Kahn points out, however, that during war all sides readily "appropriated" wherever they could. "Theft in a war zone is always considered almost as much a sport as a crime," he noted, and Koreans, who had so little to start with, "went in for it with somewhat greater gusto than any others on the scene." American troops also participated. Short of vehicles just before the Inchon invasion, some Marines purloined a variety of army ones, including the jeep of the commander of a military police company, which after a quick green coat of paint and phony numbers were applied was presented to the battalion commanding officer.[32] Theft on U.S. Army bases in Korea after the war remained a continuing problem, with the "slicky boys" active in night infiltration.[33]

Many Koreans assumed Americans always carried small personal items. An American POW recalled being led in a group that crossed a group of ROK prisoners, who beseeched them for some of these things, "still sure *all* American soldiers *must* have candy bars and cigarettes."[34]

Chinese soldiers often entered the war with little training and sometimes only equipped with hand grenades. One American combatant recalled that the Chinese threw grenades, many of which were duds, "by the bucket." In some instances they were told they could get enemy rifles on the battlefield. Although Chinese soldiers valued American food, clothing and footwear, they secured many abandoned weapons from South Korean units.[35] That American soldiers also lost more than weapons can be seen in a situation in February 1951 in the First Cavalry Division when enlisted men abandoned helmets, bayonets and other gear. Ridgway was aghast at this condition, which was endemic in the Eighth Army at the time. He issued an order that this was to cease immediately.[36]

The acquisition of American supplies went a small way towards overcoming the serious problem that the Chinese had with logistics. The Chinese had entered the war at the beginning of a long bitter winter, when the scarcity of cold-weather clothing proved to be a brutal burden. One astounding statement has it that Chinese forces initially only brought enough food for a quarter of their minimal needs.[37] It is also stated that the Chinese originally only had 800 trucks, with half of them being regularly disabled.[38] To address this problem, at the end of 1950 Stalin pledged to provide 2,000 trucks, but most Soviet munitions arriving in Korea were either too old or too poor in quality to be of any use (which brings up the question of the adequacy of Soviet aid in the conflict). The logistical situation resulted in shortages not only of food and clothing, but also of everything else, including ammunition, weapon repair and medical facilities.[39] This situation was substantially overcome by the employment of a vast force of "coolie" labor combined with pack animals of various sorts. Later the Soviet Union provided a huge fleet of trucks, but these became fair game for the intensive U.S. Air Force interdiction campaign. The

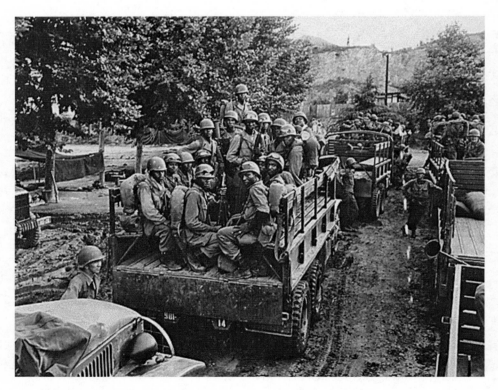

U.S. soldiers being trucked to the front. July 18, 1950. Courtesy National Archives, ARC 531362 [NA].

problems of supplying the front lines were spelled out afterwards by several Chinese generals, with Nie Rong Rougzhen declaring, "Transportation, trains and motorized transport alike, was extremely difficult to provide, if not impossible, throughout the war," while Hong Xuezhi held that their "logistical situation was extremely difficult to maintain" after Chinese frontline troops "were doubled and redoubled" during the fourth and fifth campaigns in 1951.[40]

The continuing handicap of Chinese logistics was that Chinese forces could only sustain major advances, due to lack of food and ammunition, for a few days at a time. Even for the rugged Chinese soldier, the very limited diet provided to the troops resulted in a variety of digestive tract diseases. Frostbite disabled more Chinese soldiers than did American weapons. The lack of medical facilities added to the toll. With all of these handicaps it is a wonder than the Chinese were able to sustain effective military performance, but they did. Given its vast population, the Chinese political leadership, without qualm, committed it to a war which killed or mutilated about a million of their people, but that proved to be a relatively small loss compared to the macabre, devastating events that followed in China, principally the Great Leap Forward and the Great Proletarian Revolution.

Contrasting Tactics and Weapons

Given their differing resources and traditions, the two sides varied widely in tactics and weapons.

Making a virtue of necessity, being effectively barred from main roads by American air attacks, Chinese military formations approached battle by advancing at night overland and using back roads, effectively employing camouflage, while bringing along a tail of animal-borne supplies. This approach made it most difficult for U.N. intelligence to locate them. With its huge retinue of vehicles of all sorts, there was no disguising American unit movements. As David Halberstam observed, "Hiding an American division on Korean soil would have been comparable to hiding a hippopotamus in a pet store." Chinese battle tactics varied from a mass direct assault to the indirect envelopment approach. The latter involved slow, creeping movement forward to the edge of American lines, probing for under-defended spots between units. Chinese soldiers, often without firearms, extensively used grenades, sometimes attached to long poles. Frequently Chinese grenades and other combustibles failed to explode. While the center of an enemy line was being held down, Chincoms moved around the flanks and to the rear of the unit to cut off retreat and reinforcements. The Chinese employed a similar technique in luring opposing formations to advance.[41] Experience showed that the tactics employed by the Chinese were predictable. This was the clear impression of a Captain Barber: "We were attacked in the same places at almost the same time of night,

Victim of war at Taejon, September 16, 1950. Courtesy National Archives, ARC 531374 [NA].

and they always made lots of noise before they charged.... They made no attempt at all to surprise us." In fact, in their attacks the Chinese usually employed envelopment and the cutting off of a rear contact while employing the frontal assault to hold the opposing soldiers in place. They already had successfully used these against their Nationalist opponents in the just recently concluded Chinese civil war.[42]

Although the Chinese employed a variety of tactics, the one most noted by their opponents was the mass frontal assault. Michael Caine's most memorable combat experience was confronting one of the "human wave" attacks. With the battlefield illuminated by search lights which made it a "*son et lumiere* in hell," he saw what he called "suicide squads," composed of old men and boys, who ran through minefields followed by efforts at barbed wire, which resulted in piles of dead soldiers who formed a human bridge over which armed infantrymen crawled.[43]

When they intervened in the war the Chinese achieved a unique tactical advantage when, switching from concealment and disguise, beginning around December 2, 1950, they suddenly lit up the hills with hundreds of campfires, which had the effect of making their opponents estimate that they were facing huge numbers of the enemy. To add to their combat effectiveness many wore white coveralls in winter. To meet the matter of the huge fatalities caused by enemy mass attacks, American infantrymen used dead opponents as human sandbags to reinforce their positions; in extreme situations, dead Americans were used for the same purpose.[44]

Having seen huge areas with what seemed to be infinite rows of hills, this writer agrees with S.L.A. Marshall's statement: "Korea — being an unending complex of steep hills and sharp-faced ridges — is natural mortar country."[45] This topography often limited the employment of artillery.[46] After seeing Chinese ability with mortars, Paul Leyva, among others, was impressed: "The Chinese were very good with mortars. Mortars are usually not an accurate weapon because what you're doing is lobbing shells high up in the air and letting them fall on something. It's like throwing a baseball over a high fence and trying to hit something you can't see. But the Chinese were very good." James Elkins remembers that North Korean women were proficient with that weapon, while Barry Jones declared that the North Korean mortar men could put a shell "in your back pocket."[47]

There were also snipers to contend with, some with captured M-1 rifles with sniper scopes. Allen Wilkinson recalls the omnipresence of the sharp-shooters: "They hide behind rocks, trees, bushes or shrubbery, in buildings that have been bombed out, or in the tops of trees. They are all around us, picking us off occasionally, one by one." He said experienced soldiers learned not to linger in the open, something replacements often failed to do.[48] The Chinese produced a copy of the Thompson submachine gun. One Chinese infantryman was amazed that his counterparts called in artillery and air attacks to deal with a single sniper rather than confront him themselves.[49]

The Chinese also had specialist combat units, known as bayonet companies, who were used for deep and rapid penetration and for assaulting key enemy functions, such as command posts and artillery positions. They often employed ruses to deceive the other side, such as wearing South Korean uniforms. One of these formations, known as the Sharp Swords, posing as South

Koreans, managed a deep penetration through American lines, with devastating effect. This ruse was employed on several occasions.[50]

U.S. soldiers spent much time climbing from one hill to another some of them gave themselves the name of "ridge runners."[51] One of the most difficult tasks noted at the beginning of their involvement was the need to lug equipment and supplies up the innumerable hills of the country. During the previous war, mules (brought in from the American West) had been provided to deal with mountainous Italy, but this practice did not carry forward to Korea.[52] The problem was shortly addressed by the employment of many Korean laborers, who demonstrated extraordinary ability to carry heavy loads, which were often *greater* than their own weight.[53]

Deficient in motor vehicles, to move their supplies, the Chinese employed not only manpower but a variety of animals—mules, oxen, even camels. A unique feature of the Chinese military was the use of units of horse cavalry, employing the rugged Mongolian pony. Although they were most often used for reconnaissance, rather than direct attacks, more than a few American soldiers remembered hearing the hoofbeats that signaled the arrival of the opposition, but there were few episodes of a mass attack by the horse cavalry.[54] The cavalry also accompanied advancing infantrymen who were moving at a dogtrot, while the horsemen urged them on.[55] The most effective transportation method that the Chinese employed was the human kind, of which they had an abundant supply. Piled high with supplies, the A-frame on the backs of Chinese laborers was what Don Nichols declared was the enemy secret weapon. Being a light infantry force, the Chinese did not use a lot of petroleum at the front, but to move it forward cross-country, Nichols observed, the Chinese would wrap a barrel of fuel in rice straw bags and then attach two ropes that a single porter could use to roll it along.[56]

The Chinese were effective in moving supplies of all sorts by using human labor and animals, but, no matter how rudimentary, both had to be adequately fed and cared for. Both Chinese and North Korean soldiers could subsist on a hugely lower weight of food than their opponents, and pack animals required about twelve pounds of forage a day, but all of this had to be brought forward, and there was little opportunity to secure any from immediate sources and in the face of continuing U.S. air interdiction. This situation presented the Communist side with serious and continuing logistical problems, but these were essentially overcome. By the end of the conflict it not only had considerably increased its available ammunition but also had greatly improved its food supply.[57]

Based initially on his observation of Communist forces in the Chinese civil war, Robert Rigg knew that they were "most skillful" not only in disguising the movements of their soldiers but also in the camouflaging of their field equipment.[58] Don Nichols was very impressed with both the North Korean and Chinese ability with camouflage, which he said they employed "so everything blended in with other things in the area. In thousands of cases you could not detect their equipment and/or personnel until you were within a few feet of them." He also noted their use of mine shafts and caves, as well as small villages, the houses of which were filled with supplies or soldiers; to further avoid detection, a few women and children would be kept around the villages. Having studied many aerial photographs, Nichols declared that these "showed nothing when there were actually many troops and equipment in the area." In addition, Nichols was impressed by the enemy's ability to carry out rapid and repeated repairs to roads and bridges.[59] William Anderson remembered unknowingly passing by camouflaged Chinese ambush parties who waited for the main body of the patrol.[60] Remembering traveling to Pyongyang, Wilfred Burchett declared, "An astonishing first impression was the number of bridges still intact on that single north-south road" that crossed dozens of rivers and streams. He noted that horse-drawn wagons hauling artillery were covered by masses of greenery.[61] Another tactic employed by the Chinese was when one of their long pack trains was in danger of being spotted by U.S. planes, a Chinese soldier would drop under a horse and hold one of its rear legs, thus making it immobile.[62] In snow-covered areas Chinese soldiers employed another method of camouflage — white coveralls over their uniforms; other times they reversed their jackets to expose the white lining.[63]

When the Chinese armies poured into North Korea beginning in October 1950 its soldiers initially had barely adequate clothing and headwear, with the serious disadvantage that their mustard-colored and light green cotton uniforms, warm in winter, were impossible to quickly dry after frequent rains.[64] Their greatest deficiency was in footwear, described as brown rubber and canvas tennis-type shoes. What also was lacking was an adequate supply of gloves. The bitter winter of 1950–1951 took a devastating toll of Chinese soldiers. Poor footwear in the Chosin campaign was held to be the principal cause of casualties. Had Chinese troops had adequate footwear undoubtedly they would have added to the defeat of the U.S. Army's X Corps.[65] After a night fight while coming down from Chosin, Marine Charlie Camin viewed a pile of dead Chinese, all of whose feet were swollen and black: "It was hard to believe that these men could even walk, let alone assault our position."[66] In breaking into American-held lines Chinese soldiers often not only headed for the galley and supply areas but also stripped boots and heavy clothing from wounded or dead opponents. In bitter weather army and Marine parkas were prized items. These quests were a source of anger for their officers as such actions disrupted tactical advances.[67]

American ground forces also experienced severe problems with footwear, particularly in bitter weather. Wearing the standard combat boot, soldiers moving forward found their feet perspired and when stationary their feet would freeze. Shoe packs, à la World War II, were ungainly in marching through rugged country and snow. What emerged as the best footwear was the so-called

Mickey Mouse boot, which had a wool-lined interior and several layers of rubber outside.[68] To avoid frozen feet infantrymen were urged to change their socks daily and usually carried a spare pair tucked against their upper bodies. While in combat and in below-zero temperatures, the ability to removed heavily-iced boots and change socks was severely limited. Despite the Quartermaster Corps's large scale sock exchange effort, trench foot was an endemic problem. At least for some time platoon leaders were given letters of reprimand in their personnel files if one of their soldiers got frostbite.[69]

Always seeking improvements in technique, S.L.A. Marshall noted the inadequacy of nighttime security of U.S. infantry companies. Not only did they frequently neglect to lay out mines and barbed wire enclosures, but given the usually rugged terrain, the infantry company was too small to deal with substantial Chinese nocturnal attacks. Based on the Marine model, Marshall urged the employment of battalion-sized nighttime security arrangements. He observed that infantrymen used their rifles more often than in World War II.[70] Unlike Marines, all of whom received thorough infantry training, some soldiers outside of the infantry seemed at a loss when required to serve as riflemen.[71]

Both the North Koreans and Chinese almost always attacked at night, thus avoiding U.S. air attacks and taking advantage of the general lack of American training in nocturnal combat. To counter the nighttime assaults, the devices commonly used were flares and illuminated shells, but on a limited basis giant searchlights were mounted on trucks and tanks, or, less effectively, on bombers.[72] From the time of his arrival in Korea, Matthew Ridgway was interested in illuminating the battlefield. Beginning in April 1951 each division was equipped with six huge seachlights.[73] Lt. Lyle Rishell recalled the first time he saw the use of battlefield searchlights: "I had never seen such brilliance in my life. When they were turned on, the battlefield was not nearly as frightening for the men. They would look for an enemy on the move and then bring devastating firepower on the unwelcome visitors." Occasionally the Chinese would also use searchlights, but, probably for lack of supply, they were not regularly used by the U.S. Army. Rishell fondly remembered the use of flares: "How we loved having those flares. They made all the difference during the night. They provided us with insurance whenever we used them to gain sole advantage over the attackers." These were ground-fired flares, which included short-range flares launched from rifles and mortars.[74]

The air force employed a variety of parachute flares. On the battlefield these "Firefly" flares dispensed a million candlepower and from low altitudes could illuminate about a square mile. The air force also used this device as a prelude to fighter and light bomber sorties on truck convoys on roads. Probably due to lack of supply, apparently these flares were not often employed. Because of the success of these tactics the other side resorted to transportation cross-country by mules, humans and even camels, but these methods slowed down the flow of material. To disguise nighttime troop movement the enemy often kept campfires burning, a few soldiers making noise and cowbells ringing at previous locations. The Chinese generally employed different means of communication at different levels of command: radio for regiments and above, telephone and signal flares for battalions, bugles for companies and whistles for platoons. For troop movement the Communists also used colored smoke bombs, which American soldiers often successfully imitated to the confusion of the attackers.[75]

To add to the vocal scene, Army 2nd Lt. Charles McAtee recalls that when the Chinese launched their spring offensive of 1951 the soldiers attacking his position, amidst all usual clamor, were singing "Open the Door, Richard," a popular United States song leading up to the war.[76]

During daytime movement Chinese soldiers often carried tree branches and stood still when under aerial surveillance. They also built stone bridges across streams just below the water line.[77] A low-technology but effective weapon, difficult to stop, employed by the other side was the "bed-check Charlie" propeller plane, made of wood and canvas, low-flying and slow moving, that not only disrupted troop sleep but also managed to penetrate airfields where its crude bombs achieved occasional destructive effect. The Japanese used the same technique in the Pacific from the beginning of the conflict with U.S. forces on Guadalcanal in August 1942, where America troops called them "Washing Machine Charlies"; their effect was recalled by Robert Leckie: "Charlie did not kill many people, but, like Macbeth, he murdered sleep."[78] The Charlies directed their attention to supply areas and airfields, even dropping empty sake bottles for their explosive effect. The Germans employed a type of this annoying craft during the Normandy campaign in mid–1944.[79] In Korea singular Charlie attacks began in mid–November 1950, when one of them dropped a string of fragmentation bombs on one of the Pyongyang airfields, damaging eleven Mustangs. The almost nightly visitations continued throughout the conflict, achieving their most spectacular success when one of them ignited a dump containing five million gallons of fuel at Inchon in early 1953.[80]

Due to the fact that American forces initially had to use leftover communications equipment, there were frequent breakdowns in radios and telephones. As well, there were major problems with land-laid wires, with Chinese soldiers regularly cutting them and sometimes following the land lines to company command posts. To counter this, Volney Warner's infantry company used battery-operated radios whenever possible.[81] The Chinese did not have these problems, as they did not have modern communications equipment in combat areas; there they operated with horns, flares and runners (messengers), which at least provided some flexibility to rigidly imposed attack plans.[82]

Douglas MacArthur obviously had not learned about effective withdrawal techniques. His prior experience in this matter was in the Philippines at the time of the Japanese invasion in December 1941. MacArthur had spent five

Winter war, circa December 1950. Courtesy National Archives, ARC 542213 [NA].

years "training" a Filipino defense force which promptly collapsed under Japanese assault. What followed was a disastrous run back to the unprepared Bataan peninsula during which the remnant of the fleeing Filipino force was joined by the disorganized U.S. military units, resulting in the surrender of 74,000 combatants in April 1942. Despite his incompetent leadership in this fiasco, MacArthur was awarded the Medal of Honor. (When Dwight Eisenhower was offered this award he declined, declaring he had not done anything.) During the major withdrawal from near the Yalu, MacArthur, who remained in Tokyo, never used the word retreat in his communiqués, decrying what press reports said was a disorderly and confused retreat, citing "irresponsible correspondents at the front, aided and abetted by other unpatriotic elements at home."[83]

The imposition of press censorship quelled most of these reports. Others, including Walker's only biographer, have asserted that Walker's rapid pullback ("tactical withdrawal") was well-planned and effective. S.L.A. Marshall, who was not there at the time, adamantly denied that there was any panicked run to the rear.[84] Roy Appleman presents abundant evidence that the withdrawal was hectic and disorganized. Michael James, a *New York Times* reporter on the scene, said "the 'withdrawal' looked very much like a rout," observing what was happening at the two Pyongyang airports: "Today, everything of value was being burned: new control towers, repair hangars, barracks and stocks of supplies, food, clothing and ammunition," while masses of American personnel were "begging for 'rides the hell out of here.'"[85]

In their studies of the British involvement (which averaged 5,000 men on site at any one time), three British historians — Michael Hickey, Callum MacDonald and Brian Catchpole — cite the dismay and disgust expressed by many British soldiers at the flight of U.S. troops, but few American soldiers had any knowledge of defensive warfare, whereas, through experience, it was part of British military doctrine. Hickey points out that the American response to serious assaults was to mount up and drive out in long lines of vehicles, with resulting pileups, ambushes and casualties, rather than to mount defensive counterattacks. The basic problem for the U.S. Army was it did not train its soldiers in withdrawal techniques or defensive warfare in general.[86]

Because of their defensive fighting capability, British units often were given rear-guard responsibilities, whose bloody results were felt keenly by British soldiers. Max Hastings points out that it was not just British officers who observed the poor performance of American soldiers in this regard; that opinion was shared by some of the outstanding U.S. Army field commanders.[87]

Writing as an enlisted man, Englishman Julian Turnstall observed the "utterly disorganized havoc" of American convoys in retreat; he wrote home that the Americans "have no idea of what to do in a withdrawal except get up and run. They are hopeless in retreat, a state chiefly inspired by their hopeless lack of discipline." On one occasion when British soldiers retreated on foot they were not prey to Chinese ambushers, who focused on vehicle convoys. In stark contrast to the wide gap between officers and men in British units, Turnstall was astounded by the casual relations he saw in American ranks.[88]

The U.S. Army's lack of defensive preparation had been demonstrated by the only other substantial experience the American military had of retreat during the European war: the chaotic initial response to the German Ardennes offensive in December 1944. In Korea the initial delaying retreat of U.S. Army units was seen as only a makeshift tactic, not a full-scale withdrawal of a whole army.[89] Only the First Marine Division won high praise from a Chinese military historian for its ability to form effective battalion-size defense perimeters when surrounded in the northeast sector.[90] It was S.L.A. Marshall's timely recommendation that all army units employ the larger size defense perimeters.[91] This was one of the deficits addressed by Matthew Ridgway when he took command of the Eighth Army at the end of 1950. Based on Ridgway's orders, troops were ordered out of their trucks and sent climbing the hills, while officers were evicted from their heated tents to prowl the battlefield. To meet North Korean and Chinese tactics of envelopment (including the cutting off of retreat routes), all-round defensive practices and deep patrols were instituted, with effective results. As Ridgway pointed out, the only advantage possessed by the Chinese was in numbers.[92]

The North Koreans began the war with a full complement of weapons—tanks, artillery, some planes and a variety of handheld weapons. These were principally old Japanese rifles and Russian submachine guns in which the original attached round cylinder had been replaced by the more efficient curved box magazine — the "burp" gun, named for the staccato sound it emitted when fired. Although the burp gun was simple in construction and easy to maintain, its firing was wasteful in ammunition and was inaccurate. The basic Communist rifle was the 1918 single-shot clip Mauser, which was produced at a high standard in China.[93] Both the North Koreans and the Chinese acquired a wealth of U.S. weapons, some from South Korean Army units. For the majority of American infantrymen the basic weapon was the M-1 Garand semiautomatic rifle, which had earned a reputation for range, power and reliability in World War II. It generally would fire even in bitterly cold weather. Infantryman Victor Fox did not understate its virtues: it was "incredibly reliable and durable. It could be dragged in mud, laid out in the rain, dropped, or run over by a truck, and it would still come up firing."[94] Then there was the quad-fifty: four machine guns mounted behind a steel shield, fired by one soldier. Here was an effective weapon with a wealth of firepower to counter Chinese superiority in numbers, but maintaining an adequate supply of ammunition was a continuing difficulty.[95]

South Koreans generally used the M-2 carbine rifle, lighter in weight, range and impact, which tended to jam in severe weather.[96] Lacking in both

Combat in Seoul, September 1950. Courtesy Truman Library, 2007-457.

armor and heavy artillery, the Chinese relied on mortars, rifles and grenades. In some Chinese infantry companies only one-third of its soldiers had rifles. They employed a wide variety of rifles, which resulted in continuing problems with ammunition, with Roy Appleman describing the situation as a "logistic nightmare."[97] Including rifles, the largest proportion of weapons were of American origin. Most Chinese soldiers advanced only with "potato mashers" (grenades with a small wooden handle), which had a limited explosive force and were often defective, as were their artillery and mortar rounds. The Chinese grenade had a limited concussive effect, as opposed to the American fragmentation type, which had a wider impact. Lacking in baseball experience, the Chinese threw tossed grenades in an underhand looping motion and were known as "inept and weak-armed throwers."[98] For attacks on bunkers Chinese soldiers sometimes wrapped sticks of TNT around their grenades.[99] From the Chinese perspective, it was largely a grenade war, and they had a huge supply of these inexpensive devices, while it has been estimated that only one Chinese soldier in four or five began combat with his own rifle.[100] Some American soldiers considered that the Chinese were poor shooters; another one noted that the Chinese were deficient in hand-to-hand combat.[101]

Engineering officer Charles Bussey experienced a capacity in North Korean soldiers in dealing with U.S. land mines, which demonstrated what he saw as the ingenuity of all Koreans: They would carefully dig up the American explosive, reshape it and then bury it behind U.S. lines. Bussey countered this effort by rounding up stray cattle and running them down suspect roads, resulting in exploded mines and a goodly supply of beef for his troops.[102]

Tony Kondysar had a different experience with mines. His combat engineer unit had the task of protecting bridges along the Imjin River. Upriver, the other side floated mines downstream. The engineers managed to destroy some of the mines, whereupon their opponents put dead America soldiers in the flotsam "knowing that we would try to recover the bodies. This was not a very pleasant task." Mine fields were scattered all over the front lines. The random placement of mines was a continuing source of apprehension for both sides, but they filled Jim Brady with fear: "I was going to have to do something about this phobia of mines. Easy to say. I kept seeing myself without legs."[103]

Before the war was over the Chinese, like the North Koreans before them, did a lot of retreating. In the process, the Chinese employed land mines, a weapon that was common in all armies, but in Chinese hands had a distinctive feature. First deployed by the Germans, who developed plastic explosives in wooden containers, for which metal detectors were ineffective, they were planted in Seoul when the Chinese withdrew in March 1951. Rene Cutforth noted their unique effectiveness: "They were ingenious mines, constructed so as to have the most devastating moral effect, inasmuch as it was quite difficult to be sure of exploding them. Not the first truck, but the hundred and first which went over was the more likely to be blown up. Some were so constructed as to be quite safe for forward-moving traffic but deadly for returning vehicles."[104] Each of them contained fifteen pounds of high explosives. The Chinese employed the box mine in many other places. This kind of mine could damage the tread of a tank but did not penetrate its armor.[105]

Edward McAleer encountered another approach by enemy mine-layers. Roads across rice paddies were built on elevated ground, so enemy soldiers would remove a stone from the supporting wall and tunnel in a mine beneath the road surface, which would be depressed by heavy traffic, causing an explosion.[106] U.S. troops also had to contend with the casual implantation of mine fields by their South Korean allies.[107] The Chinese often planted booby traps. Some American soldiers used hooks and chains to pull dead comrades from suspected locations.[108]

From the beginning the Chinese had a wealth of mortars, while their artillery capacity increased as the war went on. A decided advantage of the Chinese was that their mortar rounds could fit into U.S. mortar tubes, but not vice versa.[109] The Chinese also possessed a 120-mm heavy mortar, superior to anything the Americans had. Roy Appleman sings its praises: "It had long range and could be sited well back from the front and in defilade. Its burst was almost equal to that of US medium artillery, and it got results."[110] On occasion they also employed a T-34 tank. Heading up to the Chosin reservoir in early November 1950, Howard Mason's Marine company encountered one. Believing that someone was making off with his wire-laying "weasel" vehicle, a communications sergeant, standing in the road, challenged the approaching tank. Machine-gun fire convinced him this was not the case. After being hit by various weapons, "The tank withdrew, spouting sparks and flames, disappearing around a road bend."[111]

For its part, the American military employed a weapon only coming into use at the end of World War II: napalm. Infinitely more destructive than mines, it was capable of killing whole masses of its opponents, which greatly added to Chinese soldiers' fear of U.S. air power.[112] Robert Bunker describes its effectiveness for close air support against armor: when 500-pound bombs filled with thermite and napalm were "dropped against the Soviet-built T-34 tank even a near miss would result in this incendiary mixture igniting the rubber parts of the treads, which would then catch the rest of the tank on fire."[113] A special deep penetration napalm bomb was used against enemy bunkers. Then there was the "Golden Rain," which sprayed napalm above ground troops, showering them in flame. For its part, the army employed the deadly gel in flame-throwing tanks, portable flamethrowers, special landmines and 55-gallon

Destroyed North Korean T-34 tanks, September 6, 1950. Courtesy Truman Library, 2007-609.

drums wired with explosives in defensive positions. The air force used a total of 32,557 tons of napalm ordnance during the war.[114] As air force pilot Carl Brunson remembered, employment of this weapon was dangerous to airmen: "For maximum effectiveness we had to fly low and 'drag off' the napalm tanks. Very vulnerable to ground fire."[115] The other side never came close to developing a similar weapon.

The employment of this weapon was the first occasion of the Korean War that generated opposition in Britain. Ever the traditionalist, Winston Churchill, who had supported the mass bombardment of German cities resulting in thousands of civilians being killed during the previous war, privately expressed his dislike of spraying liquid fire over enemy emplacements. On a few occasions, misdirected napalm struck U.S. and South Korean troops. One such incident occurred during the Chosin withdrawal of December 1950. Infantryman James Ransone recalled the happening: "Men all around me were burned. They laying rolling in the snow. Men I knew, marched and fought with, begged me to shoot them.... Where the napalm had burned the skin to a crisp, it would be peeled back from the face, arms, legs."[116] In one incident, on December 1, 1950, east of Chosin, a navy Corsair prematurely released a canister on an American unit. The explosion engulfed 10–12 soldiers, who were burned alive. The injunction to roll in the snow did no good. At the same place four days earlier an early napalm release burned 15–20 soldiers so badly that several of them charged straight into Chinese fire so they would die quickly. Earlier in the conflict a Chinese officer about to release an American soldier requested that the United States not use petroleum, that is, napalm.[117]

Then there was the hand-held anti-tank rocket (named the bazooka by the Americans, for no other reason than to give it an identity), which was widely employed by both sides in the late European war. By all accounts, the German *panzerfaust*, with its greater penetrating power, was superior to the U.S. 2.3-inch version, whose shell bounced off heavily armored tanks. At the beginning of the Korean War the American military had only the 2.3 weapon, which was ineffective against Russian-built tanks. A heavier 3.5-inch model was just coming into production and supplies of these were rushed to Korea. When combined with other weapons, they devastated the North Korean tank force. Despite the fact that the Russians had captured a large supply of German *panzerfausts*, no weapon of this type was supplied by them to their Asian allies in Korea.[118]

On the Sea and in the Air

During the war the U.N. forces had complete control of the sea and effective control of the air. Due to the decision to seal off Formosa from the anticipated Chinese Communist invasion, the U.S. Navy had its hands full. Indeed, the commitment of the navy into the Formosa straits was largely a bluff, in Robert Simmons' words, "a show of words," due to inadequate ships, as the fleet had been drastically reduced from a wartime high of 1,200 ships and 42,000 aircraft to 237 ships and 4,300 planes, while personnel plunged to almost nine-tenths. Thus, the navy was in no position to defeat a serious Chinese invasion force. While a rapid expansion soon followed (with personnel almost doubling), the strength mounted by the navy was able to completely contain Red forces on both coasts of Korea, with four World War II battleships as well as five heavy cruisers blasting the coast.[119]

Its renewed capacity was evidenced when the navy was able to provide both protection and transport for 105,000 Marines and soldiers, plus 90,000 civilians, evacuated through Hungnam in December 1950.[120] Communist shore batteries sometimes presented danger: eighty-five ships were hit (forty-four of them being in the blockade off Wonsan) but with minor damage, although a British destroyer did suffer substantial damage in one encounter, with thirteen sailors being killed. The navy was able to supply offshore islands as centers

Two captured North Korean boy soldiers, Sindang-dong area, September 18, 1950. Courtesy National Archives, ARC 531377 [NA].

of opposition to the northern regime.[121] Aircraft carriers not only employed piston-driven Corsair fighter planes and the Douglas Skyraider light bomber to attack coastal areas but also provided interior combat support, with the Marine Air Arm being most effective, specifically during the Marine march to the sea from Chosin in December 1950.[122]

Another serious deficiency which arose as a result of post-war cutbacks was in minesweepers. At Wonsan in October the planned landing of a Marine force was delayed for a week until all available minesweepers and some recruited Japanese ones cleared the approaches of a huge variety of Soviet magnetic mines. There was also serious delay due to the same situation at Chinnampo, the port to Pyongyang, later that month. It was fortunate that the North Koreans had failed to lay a planned minefield at Inchon, but they did conduct limited mine activity there; a navy vessel came upon an American corpse floating above a drifter mine.[123]

During the course of the conflict allied nations, principally Britain and Australia, provided substantial naval support. The British navy sent a fleet — four carriers, five cruisers, and five destroyers, as well as smaller craft — while the Australian navy dispatched a carrier, two destroyers and a host of frigates. A few destroyers and frigates were provided by Canada, Columbia, France, the Netherlands, New Zealand, and Thailand. In the course of operations the U.S. Navy and Marine air contingents lost 559 planes shot down and 664 to non-combat situations. Navy air alone lost 493 killed, died of wounds or missing in action, combined with a large total of 4,043 non-battle deaths.[124]

An ongoing navy operation was the blockade of the North Korean coast. This had a devastating effect on local fisheries and fishermen. With a severe food shortage of all sorts, the North Korean government's response was to force fishermen under guard to put out to sea. Many fisher folk took the opportunity to sail their sampans out to U.S. Navy ships and defect. On the east coast a continuing contest at Wonsan took place, navy planes and ships contending with Communist coastal artillery and floating mines.[125]

During the course of the conflict the navy provided piston-driven fighters for close combat support, while the air force had jet-driven fighters for deep penetration of supply lines. At the beginning the air force did not have the responsibility or training for close combat air support, but it slowly developed this capacity. Due to the fact that its opponents increasingly used back roads and trails, the air force's lack of targeting capacity and concentration on main roads and transportation junctures early in the war had very limited impact on enemy troop movement and supply replenishment. In the prelude to the war Soviet supplies were shipped to the port of Wonsan, but this ceased with the outbreak of hostilities. Now the supplies were transported by rail down the east coast and were met with regular air and naval bombardment.

The conflict saw the employment of a new aircraft — the helicopter, which was being developed by German and American engineers during the previous

B-26 light bomber prepares for take-off, November 27, 1952. Courtesy National Archives, ARC 542253 [NA].

war, but now came into wide use. Originally used for observation, it soon was employed for medical evacuation. The noted television series *M*A*S*H* always had helicopters bringing in wounded soldiers to the forward medical facilities. In fact, only a very small number of the wounded (4 percent) were moved out of the immediate battle area by copters. All the others were brought back by bumpy road and ramshackle rail.[126] James Huston describes the latter method: "Some units used self-propelled railroad cars ('doodle bugs').... Some improvised rail buses, that is, they fitted metal wheels with flanges on to the front and rear of the buses."[127]

Except in the very first days of the war, the United States had the advantage of total air superiority. For close combat support both the Marines and the navy employed the Corsair/Mustang fighter, a propeller-driven craft. At first the air force found not only that its F-80 jets flew too fast for effective close support, but its planes could not operate on the primitive air fields in Korea, so remained based in Japan, although they could refuel at the airfield at Taegu. The basic solution was found when the propeller-driven F-51 Mustangs proved to be effective in both regards. Always there were difficulties as the air force worked to coordinate with carrier-based Navy and Marine fighters over designated targets. Particularly in the early stages of the conflict, there were repeated episodes, due to lack of training in close infantry support, where air force fighters attacked U.S. and South Korean troops.[128] To avoid such incidents all U.S. infantry companies carried identification panels, sometimes on their backs.[129] Important air force contributions were dropping proximity bombs and the use of the fearful weapon of napalm by B-26 bombers. Improvements in camera technology, even including color photographs of terrain, greatly increased the results from air reconnaissance. One simple device that was employed was a four-pointed barbed object dropped on roads, but this was promptly countered by labor crews sweeping them off the roads or with brushes attached to the front of trucks.[130]

At the beginning the air force proceeded to attack main roads and rail lines, but, due to several factors—lack of targeting intelligence, the other side mainly using trails with porters and pack animals, night movement, rapid repair of roads and U.S. lack of coordinated intelligence in the matter — the air force campaign was largely in vain. It adopted various means to meet this challenge but despite great effort did not succeed in stopping an adequate flow of troops and supplies. For its part, the enemy effectively countered by the employment of huge labor gangs, camouflage and deception and, ultimately, anti-aircraft (AA) guns.[131] It even used smudge pots (à la Florida citrus protection) to obscure troop dispositions. "Flak traps" were employed to lure enemy planes into heavily defended AA sites. Air force pilot Carl Brunson remembered the flak traps: "Out of a hundred close air support interdiction missions, I only got trapped 4–5 times. Shot at a thousand times, shot up a few, but never shot down."[132] Another effective means the Chinese used to counter U.S. interdiction efforts was to develop a network of road sentries who gave the alarm of an approaching air attack by firing a set series of rifle shots.[133] By April 1951 the Soviets provided a much more effective means to counter U.S. attacks on supply routes. Two AA divisions were stationed along the Yalu while mobile units operated as far south as Pyongyang.[134] By the autumn of 1952 the Soviets had provided 2,000 long range anti-aircraft guns.[135]

A particularly dangerous area for U.S. planes was "Death Valley," the road from Wonsan to Pyongyang, a route with many tunnels and revetments for sheltering trucks along which the Reds erected spanning cables, dummy trucks, mock parachutes in trees and hidden flack guns.[136] Cables were sometimes encountered in narrow valley roads as well as in other areas. To deal with the threat of decapitation, some jeeps had steel columns welded perpendicular to their front bumpers.[137]

U.S. air power, including bombers, had a free run over Korea until the very beginning of November 1950. By that time the B-29s had smashed almost every sizeable North Korean industrial complex.[138] Coinciding with their land intervention at that time, the Soviets introduced the MiG-15, a jet-propelled fighter that was faster and more maneuverable than any American plane. After

T/Sgt. Charles Ledbetter returns from night bombing mission. Third Bomber Wing, Fifth Air Force, July 1951. Courtesy National Archives, ARC 542358 [PRS].

World War II Russian jet plane development had been greatly assisted by the capture of German advanced aircraft and the engines modeled on those produced by the English Rolls-Royce firm, a supply of which were sold to the Soviets in 1946.[139] As in the case of the atomic bomb, additional knowledge was provided by American communist scientists.[140] Although it was in the process

Medical evacuation by helicopter, December 1952. Courtesy National Archives, ARC 542317 [NA].

of improving its jet aircraft technology, the U.S. Air Force appeared to be oblivious to what was emerging from its rival in the Soviet Union. Some B-29 bombers became the victims of this superior weapon and were thus deployed in nighttime bombing only. By the fall of 1952 the Chinese had countered with a night fighter.[141]

The introduction of jet fighters at that time — on November 1, 1950, when Chinese land forces had mysteriously withdrawn — would appear to be an indication that the Chinese were going to assume a major role in Korea and that the Soviet Union would provide at least one high technology weapon to its Chinese comrades. There were 32 MiGs in the first flight, 150 of them by April 1951. With the Chinese air force in its infancy, all of the initial MiG pilots were Russians, and that condition remained for many months. As a lure to get the Chinese to intervene, Josef Vissarionovich had promised Soviet air support, but as time was to show, this was only provided for defending the Yalu zone and did not extend to close air support for Chinese land forces, as the Chinese leadership reportedly assumed it would.[142] The Soviets set out to train and equip Chinese pilots for combat, with the assumption that the Chinese eventually would assume the bulk of the air effort. The lengthy process of training tried Stalin's patience, and Russian pilots remained heavily involved almost to the end of the conflict in July 1953. The Soviet leadership anticipated that

155mm Long Tom artillery, north of Seoul, May 1951. Courtesy National Archives, 111-SC-365570 [PRS].

the introduction of its advanced jet fighters would have a powerful impact on the course of the struggle. At most, however, the MiGs were an alarming wake-up call for the U.S. Air Force and did not substantially impede the American assault on Chinese troop and supply movement. In any case, Stalin was adamant that Soviet air involvement would remain limited to well above the 38th parallel.[143]

Employing it at this time was a move to counter the massive U.S. bombing. The first major jet confrontation took place over Sinuiju on the Yalu opposite the Chinese base at Antong on November 8, 1950. This marked the end of clear American air superiority in the borderland. As the number of MiGs increased, they began to focus on the slower, lumbering B-29 bombers, most of which initially lacked electronic countermeasures.[144]

For their part, Soviet MiG pilots initially lacked onboard radar, pressurized flight suits and air-conditioning. One veteran recalled, "We had to sweat in our cockpits for many hours on alert and simply wait. The Americans could always choose the most advantageous moment." Some general criticisms were that Soviet planes were too slow in taking off, failed to achieve high air levels for combat and lacked effective coordination. Airfield facilities were deficient and pilots had to contend with U.S. fighters attacking ascending and descending

MiGs, as well as raking fire on parked planes. Entering the conflict with only a small number of pilots, crew exhaustion soon followed. Due to "severe losses" of pilots, replacements were of inferior quality.[145]

In what has been called an "organized panic," the U.S. Air Force's response to the MiG was to rush deliveries of the higher performance F-84 Thunderbirds and F-86 Sabre jet fighters.[146] The U.S. Navy was "shocked" by the appearance of the swept-wing MiG-15, which was clearly superior to the navy's highest performance jet fighter, the straight-wing Grumman F9F Panther.[147] The British Meteor jet fighter, flown by a unit of the Australian air force, was "badly outclassed by the MiG-15" and was shifted to lower level duties.[148] Although the MiG had some areas of technical superiority, the proficiency of American pilots more than made up the difference. The rivalry for air supremacy in "MiG Alley"— the territory from the Yalu south towards Pyongyang —continued to the end of the conflict.[149] During September 1951, for example, the U.S. 4th Fighter-Interceptor Wing recorded sightings of 1,177 MiG sorties and engaged 911 of the MiGs in combat, with the American planes being at a three- or four-to-one disadvantage. As time was to show, U.S. pilots frequently were tangling with Soviet ones, flying thinly disguised jets. An estimated 2,000 Soviet pilots were involved, with instructions for speaking in Korean on a clipboard attached to their knees; in furious combat they reverted to Russian in communications. They provided an estimated 75 percent of the Communist fighter sorties.[150]

Soviet sources claimed they had a two-to-one advantage in "kills" over the Americans, while the balance shifted to a 13-to-one U.S. advantage when confronted with Chinese and some Korean pilots.[151] Some Soviet pilots recalled that they considered Chinese pilots, lacking in experience, to be dangerous in the sky, while North Korean anti-aircraft guns often fired at any planes that were nearby. On more than one occasion Soviet pilots refused to fly until Chinese-manned planes were grounded.[152] To counter continuing U.S. success, the commander of the tiny revived North Korean Air Force organized a special regiment to conduct a low-level flight to attack U.S. bases around Seoul, but his plan was vetoed by the Soviets, who obviously did not want to extend the air war.[153]

The employment of air power during the determined march of the First Marine Division from Chosin in December 1950 was responsible for the survival of that force. Not only did the close support of Marine and navy planes beat back Chinese attacks in the narrow corridor, but transport planes dropped vital supplies along the route.[154] Parachuting supplies to cut-off units was a regular feature of the war. From early 1951 thirty-five air force C-119s in Japan delivered pre-packed supplies every day. To mark the spot where the supplies were needed ground forces laid out a large T panel, but when some Chinese began to duplicate the same, the air force had its Mosquito fighter on hand to guide a C-119 to the correct drop zone.[155]

About 72,000 Soviet airmen rotated through bases in Manchuria during the war, with 26,000 of them being stationed there at the peak of their involvement in 1952.[156] Some of the Russian pilots believed they had shot down over 1,000 U.S. planes, while some historians believe the figure was about 350. The U.S. Air Force also made expansive claims about kills by their side. Part of the problem in establishing that a plane had been shot down was the means of determining this, with the Russians taking a broad view of the case. There was also the matter that glowing reports of Soviet air prowess were pleasing to Head Comrade J.V. Stalin. Just to show that they were doing something, North Korean pilots sometimes asserted kill claims.[157] In regard to the slow and outmoded B-29, only seven were lost out of a total of over 21,000 sorties, less than one-third of 1 percent.[158]

The impact of the Chinese air attacks ended U.S. daytime bombing along the Yalu. For all their ability to counter MiG attacks, the air force Sabre jet fighter could only spend 15–20 minutes on site.[159] The air force did make some improvements in anti–MiG methods, but Curtis LeMay, head of the Strategic Air Command, opposed using all the technology that had been developed for this purpose, arguing that this should be reserved for an all-out war.[160] For example, although this technique had been used in a massive bombing attack on Hamburg in 1943, the Strategic Air Command prevented the dropping of chaff (bits of metal) to confuse ground- and air-based radar until September 1952.[161] LeMay also effectively stopped the introduction of the advanced B-36 bomber as well as the jet-propelled B-47 and B-52. Fortunately for the U.S. air campaign, the Chinese did not develop a radar-equipped night fighter.[162]

The Chinese certainly sought to expand their air arms. A major limitation was that the MiG had a range of only a hundred miles. To overcome this condition, in early 1951 the Chinese air force began an ambitious program of building airfields south of the Yalu. These airstrips apparently were to be employed for rearming and refueling fighters, not as permanent facilities. This new air power was planned to supplement the Chinese spring offensive. If the Chinese had succeeded in this effort it would have allowed their planes to attack frontline allied forces and thus drastically altered the conditions of combat. Construction began of eight to ten of them, some of them with pierced-steel plank runways supplied by the Russians.[163] The three major centers of construction were at Sinuiju just below the Yalu opposite Antong and at Pyongyang, now densely defended by anti-aircraft guns, and just north of the Chongchon River.[164]

Fully alarmed by this development, the U.S. Air Force struck back beginning in April 1951, not only preventing any of these airfields from becoming operational but also keeping the Chinese from acquiring the air control necessary for this task. Failing in both endeavors, the Communists gave up airfield construction in mid–July—for the time being. China made a renewed effort beginning in September 1951 with the greatest air battle of the conflict taking place over Namsi in MiG Alley, one of the places where an airfield was being built, beginning on October 24, 1951, which effectively stopped this development. The Chinese ceased construction at the end of November, by which stage there was only one serviceable airfield in North Korea, that being the one along the Yalu opposite the Chinese base at Antong.[165] Not only did airfield construction come under continuing air assault, but the Chinese were incapable of providing ground control and supply facilities. They certainly kept trying: with a truce anticipated, by May 1953 the U.S. Air Force had identified no less than thirty-five Chinese airfields under construction and over the next month had proceeded to "neutralize" all but one of them, that being a site on the Soviet border.[166]

The Reds countered with radar-directed AA guns, searchlights, night fighters and attempts at deception. Despite their determined efforts, the Chinese did not succeed in building a fully operating combat airfield in Korea. Some accounts of this situation indicate that the Chinese had achieved this; Stanley McGowen stated the Chinese air force "never based substantial numbers of aircraft south of the Yalu River," probably based on the Chinese air force statement that of the 69 airfields it attempted to build only thirty planes were ever employed at any of them.[167] With U.N. truce negotiators insisting that no new airfield construction should take place after a cessation of warfare, a few days before a cease-fire had been agreed the Chinese managed to insert planes into grass landing strips; the U.S. Air Force attacked these.[168]

With truce negotiations in deadlock, in May 1952 the Chinese leadership assumed a posture of "protracted war." As part of this approach, it decided to double the size of its air force. There were serious obstacles to be overcome, which proved to be largely intractable. With heavy plane losses, a shortage of them soon developed. Urgent requests for advanced Soviet MiGs were met with the claim that Russian productive capacity could not meet this demand. With a mass of new pilots being thrown into combat, serious morale problems soon arose.[169]

The Chinese already had attempted to blunt the U.S. air attacks by means of camouflage, site deception and anti-aircraft guns, but two high Soviet military men, Oleg Sarin and Lev Dvoretsky, have claimed that the air defense technology provided by the Russians was of outmoded World War II vintage, requiring a "major revamping and modernization." As the contest went on, however, the Soviets introduced a variety of new measures.[170] By April 1951 the Soviets had provided two anti-aircraft divisions, which had centrally-directed ground radar systems and electronically-controlled searchlights.[171] Like the U.S. Air Force, the Soviets did not want to reveal all their advanced electronic gadgets in Korea, but they did allow the employment of their vastly improved "Token" radar system, which could detect enemy fighters out to a hundred miles from its principal base at Antong, just across the Yalu.[172]

By late 1952 the fighting had reached a stalemate, with Chinese frontline forces deeply entrenched. In order to effectively use air power in this situation the U.N. high command mounted a determined deception effort centered on the east coast at Kojo above Wonsan. Hoping to lure Chinese ground forces into rushing to the coast, naval guns pounded coastal targets while the air force hit interior ones. The opposing side had been anticipating an amphibious thrust on either coast so the results of the hoax were slight.[173]

The North Korean air force had been dispatched very early in the conflict, but it had kept back a few planes, as American soldiers discovered when they captured Kimpo airfield in September 1950, finding several North Korean fighter planes in a hangar "in perfect flying condition." With the Chinese intervention the Pyongyang government sought to build a jet-based air force — to be equipped by the Chinese and Soviets. It also was a strong advocate of attacks in South Korea, including Seoul. In the event, due largely to the lack of trained pilots, the North Koreans did not mount this force.[174] In addition, both the Russians and eventually the Chinese opposed bombardment south of the 38th parallel.[175]

As has been seen, the most the North Koreans employed was a slow moving and low flying Russian-built PO-2 or "bed-check Charlie"— a wooden and fabric biplane, which had been employed by the Russians in the previous war, provided an irritating night-time element, and did some occasional damage. Apparently the first time such a craft launched an attack was on November 19, 1950, along the Chongchon River. This was followed by almost nightly episodes at the Pyongyang airport.[176] The most destructive of these occurred on November 28 when a single intruder dropped a string of fragmentation bombs damaging eleven Mustang fighters, three of which were beyond repair. With the retreat of the Eighth Army the little marauders centered their sorties on the Seoul area. As many as fifteen of them were employed on occasion, but usually it was just a single intruder. A major and successful raid by fifteen of these planes caused a huge fire after oil storage facilities at Inchon were hit on June 16, 1953.[177] Given their slow speed and nighttime constraints, they were based on small, hastily repaired strips in obscure grass fields not far into North Korea, although the North Koreans unsuccessfully tried to build an airstrip in the wreckage of downtown Pyongyang. After two months repairing 69 airfields, the Chinese construction unit involved confessed failure; the repaired fields, it said, could only facilitate 30 planes, surely just the little "night hecklers."[178]

Although various methods were used to deal with them, some of these little raiders continued their operations until the end, with Kimpo airport outside Seoul being pestered by them. The Charlies dropped not only small bombs but also occasionally propaganda leaflets. One radar technician came up with an effective method to deal with them. Although they usually flew very low, going over a ridge the Charlies had to rise up, which momentarily brought them into radar detection, which provided an intercept vector directing a night fighter after the little craft.[179] The best solution was provided by the navy, which contributed the relatively slow-moving Corsair night fighter. At the end of June 1953, Lt. Guy Bordelon is credited with shooting down five of the craft, and Charlie was seen no more in the days leading up to the cease-fire.[180]

At the other end of the spectrum was the air conflict of advanced jet fighters of both the Russians and the Americans. A serious constraint on the American air war was that U.S. planes were under orders not to attack the home bases of the MiGs across the Yalu in Manchuria, although there were frequent episodes where U.S. planes did so. This general limitation had the important effect of precluding not only enemy retaliation at exposed U.S. military bases on land but also attacks on ships involved in the naval blockade along the coast; it also prevented the opening up of a wider war.[181]

Believing that such action would have a major impact on the course of the conflict, Douglas MacArthur and others strongly supported the bombing of Chinese bases in Manchuria. This action would come at a significant cost. The Chinese could pull back to airfields deeper in the interior, and they now had radar equipped anti-aircraft guns; longer range attacks would have exposed U.S. aircraft to increased enemy fighter opposition. Declaring that it was already operating on a "shoe-string," air force commander Hoyt Vandenberg declared that the air arm did not have the capacity for such action. He also cited the limitation of air bombing he recalled from World War II: "We used to bomb and close the Brenner Pass every day, and the Germans opened it every night."[182] Air force pilot Carl Brunson observed the same thing in Korea: "We frequently destroyed key rail lines, etc. and *the next day* they would be back in operation. Those labor gangs were effective."[183] Concentrated air attacks on transportation facilities not only failed to stop the basic flow of supplies, but were conducted despite the huge loss of planes. Repeated bombing of key transportation centers lured fighter-bombers into "flak traps," manned by masses of enemy anti-aircraft guns.[184] Through it all, with one rare exception, no allied frontline unit was subjected to air attack by its opponents. Substantial improvement in Soviet-provision and dispersal of anti-aircraft guns, however, resulted in a U.S. Air Force shift from interdiction of enemy supply routes to a concentration ("strangulation") at points of arrival of the supplies.[185]

Beginning in April 1952 as the truce talks dragged on, U.S. fighter planes unofficially, but in "hot pursuit," often crossed into Chinese territory with two to three minutes' jet flying time allowed.[186] Carl Brunson remembered the situation: "We fought in their back yard! Why not stray a bit?"[187] Although the U.S. military declared that American planes crossing beyond the Yalu was most exceptional, Soviet pilots flying "Chinese" fighters claimed the U.S. penetration was constant, with some attacks taking place as the Russian craft were taking off or landing.[188] The major Chinese airfield at Antong, just across the Yalu, was attacked in mid–1952. There was an important limitation: no attacks on Soviet bases in Manchuria. In the course of the rivalry the Soviets managed to secure a largely undamaged F-86 as well as a prized Sikorsky helicopter, while the Americans did not recover an intact MiG.[189]

One of the preconditions of Russian air involvement was to prevent seizure of Soviet planes or capture of their pilots. Their craft were restricted to territory held by the Communists and, for the same reasons, they were ordered not to venture off course. Determined to maintain the charade that the Soviet Union was not directly in the war, Stalin made plain his insistence that this be maintained. At an August 1952 meeting with Zhou Enlai, he declared that the seizure of downed Russian planes would remove this cover, as "the air force belongs to the state," that state being the USSR.[190]

Probably in response to strafing attacks by a U.S. Air Force fighter on the Chinese airfield just over the border at Antong on August 27, 1950, followed by two U.S. planes doing the same to a Soviet airfield on October 8, on September 4, 1950, a twin-engine bomber bearing a red star began flying towards a U.N. naval task force off the west coast of Korea. After the bomber was shot down recovery action revealed that one of its crew was in the Soviet air force. Other incidents followed later. In May and July 1952 "Chinese" planes attacked single U.S. craft in the Yellow Sea.[191] The only major Chinese maritime attack occurred the following November and probably was a response to the repeated American air raids into Chinese territory. A force of MiGs attacked planes of the U.N. Naval Task Force 77 group of ships, which included the aircraft carrier *Oriskany*, off the northeast coast of Korea. The MiGs shot down seven U.S. Navy planes.[192] This singular episode "goaded the Navy into subsequent development of two superlative fighters, the Vought F-8 Crusader and the McDonnell F-4 Phantom II." Just as the Soviets earlier had vetoed a plan by the revived North Korean Air Force to use low-level flights to attack Seoul, so Zhou Enlai personally stopped a project of February 1952 to launch Soviet-built Tu-2 bombers against Kimpo airfield outside Seoul. All along Soviet pilots had wanted to be able to attack U.S. air bases in Korea, but the Russian high command opposed this, knowing it might provide evidence of direct Soviet involvement in the war. For the same reason, it also banned flights over water, so the attack on Task Force 77 was a sole episode of such. Yet it was a warning that there were limits to limitations.[193]

The Soviets had advanced jet bombers in Manchuria (and more at Soviet air bases next door in the Port Arthur peninsula) and undoubtedly had missiles that could be fired from them. In World War II the Luftwaffe had such a weapon — the Fritz-X missile. In September 1943 a German bomber fired radio-controlled missiles sinking the Italian battleship *Roma*. Despite the danger of losing planes over water, the Russian and Chinese pilots could have most effectively used these missiles against the American and allied ships ringing both coasts of the peninsula.[194]

As American combat deaths rose during the period of what seemed to be interminable truce talks, with atomic bombs already on the island, the air force responded by staging a series of mock atomic bomb runs out of Okinawa over North Korea in the fall of 1951. After the operation the air force concluded that "with identifiable concentrations of Communist forces being rare, the exercise was considered operationally unsound."[195] As matters dragged on further, more was to be heard of the utility of atomic weapons to force an end to the conflict. The new Eisenhower administration, pushed along by its campaign rhetoric, seemingly moved in that direction. An "atomic cannon" was fired in an American western desert in May 1953.[196] A Fifth Air Force fighter-bomber wing was equipped and trained in Japan for delivering tactical nuclear weapons.[197] The Chinese leadership apparently was not perturbed by such indications. Beijing seemingly took the view that this was a bluff. Since the U.S. campaign in Korea was under the banner of the United Nations, participating allies surely would have opposed the United States again using atomic bombs in Asia or anywhere else. Evidence of this anticipated opposition could be seen in the alarm of the British government when in December 1950 President Truman refused to rule out the use of such a weapon.

With the realization by early 1952 that interdiction was having inadequate effect in choking off the flow of troops and supplies, the U.S. Air Force began concentrating on enemy supply dumps located close to the immediate combat zone. The Cherokee program, named in honor of the heritage of Vice Admiral J.J. "Jocko" Clark, who originated the tactics, appeared to have a major impact of the supply situation of the other side. The volume of fire from Communist forces slackened and they were forced to run daylight supply convoys, with disastrous results.[198]

A final major air force operation began in June 1952 with the bombing of the massive hydroelectric dam complex centered at Suiho on the Yalu as well at Kojo, Fusen and Kyosen. The participating pilots were instructed to hit not the superstructure of the dams but the transmitters at their bases; the attack on Suiho was met with a "low level of flack."[199] According to Soviet air personnel, they had not provided air defense at the sites as these were in the North Korean air defense area. In addition, there was an assumption that these facilities were, if unofficially, off limits to U.S. attack, and bad weather prevented the dispatch of Chinese planes from Antong.[200] The assault, undertaken to pressure the Communists to conclude truce negotiations, succeeded in massively damaging the facility and greatly reduced electrical power for both North Korea and Manchuria for months. As the North Koreans attempted repair the dams, the bombings were repeated in September 1952 and February 1953. North Korea experienced a two-week blackout and then only 10 percent of power was restored. These attacks were followed up by the bombing of the Namsan-Ni chemical plant on the Yalu in September 1952.[201] For all the damage that was done, these efforts apparently did not hasten the negotiations. The same applied to attacks on agricultural water systems. For only the second time in the war, these actions caused substantial public opposition in Britain.[202]

In its last major air operation of the conflict, in September 1952 the U.S. Navy sent 144 fighter planes from the decks of three aircraft carriers to attack the oil refinery at Aoji. This facility was tucked away deep in northeast Korea, four miles from the Manchurian border and eight miles from Soviet Siberia. North Korean authorities must have determined that the refinery was out of reach, both politically and tactically, to B-29 bombers, which if they attacked would be forced to cross one or both frontiers. Thus, there was no anti-aircraft or MiG opposition; at their leisure, the navy planes destroyed the refinery.[203]

Due to dissatisfaction among many Russian pilots on the scene, new, younger and inexperienced substitutes were brought in during the early part of 1953. As a result, Soviet air losses mounted.[204] In a policy decision by the immediate post–Stalin rulers in Moscow, Soviet pilots were withdrawn from Manchuria beginning in April 1953. With the full burden now on Chinese pilots, MiG losses rocketed beginning the next month. Not a "Marianas turkey shoot" of the 1944 Pacific, it was close enough. The Soviet decision obviously was a message by the Russian leaders to their Chinese allies that it was time to wrap up the Korean episode. The Russian economic cost of the war could now massively be reduced and it implied that it would be thus be in a better position to support Chinese economic development.[205]

The same applied to Red China — its participation in the war was costing between 30 and 40 percent of all government expenditures. There was apparent dissatisfaction among some of the population with this burden, with the Communist regime being required to take strong measures to stifle dissent.[206] Confronted with panic among some in the North Korean leadership about continuing destruction of North Korea, Kim Il Sung now wanted to end the conflict.[207] In his very last days, Stalin reportedly decided to call a halt to it, a position that was confirmed by his successors two weeks after his death on March 5, 1953.[208]

At the conclusion of the conflict, U.S. Air Force spokesmen asserted that air power demonstrated a vital capacity in defeating Communist aggression. They carried the conviction that their type of warfare was effective into the conflict in Vietnam that boiled up a dozen years later.[209] Among those who criticized such claims was Mathew Ridgway, who on one occasion in Korea responded to an air force report of extensive interdiction success by saying, "If all the enemy trucks you report as having been destroyed during the past ten days or so were actual kills, then there would not be a truck left in all of Asia." When there was a move afoot to use the U.S. Air Force in Vietnam to prevent French defeat in 1954, Ridgway declared, "The experience in Korea, where we had complete domination of the air and a far more powerful air force, afforded no basis for thinking that some additional airpower was going to bring about decisive results on the ground."[210] Moreover, the air force high command concluded that air strikes in the mountainous area around Dien Bien Phu would not save the French base.[211]

When in 1964 the Johnson administration was considering launching a bombing campaign in North Vietnam, Dean Rusk was dubious about its effectiveness: strategic bombing in Korea had not produced the anticipated results of drastically halting the flow of men and supplies to Chinese forces. Charles Shrader has concluded that although U.S. air power did not succeed in stopping an adequate flow of men and material coming down from North Korea and the Communist forces were better equipped the longer the conflict continued, it did prevent its opponents from effectively massing their resources for another major offensive.[212] The defeat of the Chinese "fifth offensive" in the spring of 1951 made that position clear.[213]

Jean Larteguy saw the drama in the Korean air combat: "The two sides came together and clashed as in medieval lists, and the dance began." An American colonel told him, "MiG Alley was a test-bed for both sides.... We are all not so much combat pilots of this war as research pilots for the wars of the future."[214]

John Halliday presents a balanced picture of the losses and gains of the two sides in the rivalry: He concludes that although Soviet pilots and ground artillery shot down many U.S. planes, that side was not able to prevent massive U.S. interdiction of supplies nor could it prevent destruction of hydroelectrical installations and agricultural dams; on the other hand, the U.S. Air Force could not effectively stifle Communist supplies and soldiers coming into Korea.[215] Although it was never used in ground combat areas, the Communist Chinese air force grew as the war went on, reaching the position of being the third largest in the world.[216]

In the area of electronic warfare, Daniel Kuehl has declared that the U.S. Air Force, largely due to loss of institutional memory and budget cuts, failed to retain and learn lessons from World War II. At least one air force report — that of the Far East Air Forces — recognized the overall loss of procedures and techniques between the wars. A similar situation was to arise in Vietnam.[217] As so often is the case, by the time another conflict arose, the people who had learned these operations in the previous war usually were no longer there. The key to institutional memory is the written word.

A final aspect of the air war was secret flights mounted by the CIA and air force into Chinese territory. This was "Operation Tropic," begun in April 1952, whose purpose to monitor Chinese troop movement and start guerrilla actions. There were also clandestine air force sorties, using "crash boats" in coastal areas.[218] The intelligence flights into Manchuria came a cropper in November 1952 when a CIA Civilian Air Transport spy plane, using the innovative harness retrieval method, was lured into an area by Chinese counterintelligence and was shot down. Both pilot and copilot survived, a situation that was not revealed by Chinese authorities until after the Korean War ended. In 1954, amidst great fanfare, John Downey and Richard Fecteau were convicted of espionage and given long prison sentences.[219]

Intelligence and Special Operations

The effectiveness of American intelligence operations during the conflict presents a very mixed picture. After the withdrawal of the U.S. Army from Korea in 1949 there remained the small 400-man Military Advisory Group, whose responsibility was to stimulate the development of the South Korean Army. There was an even smaller unit — the secret Korean Liaison Office, operating under the cover of the Korean Labor Organization, whose job was to keep an eye on the potential threat from the north. If it had sixteen agents in the north by late 1949, as Charles Willoughby, MacArthur's intelligence chief, claimed, they failed to warn of the North Korean assault of June 1950.[220] In Tokyo, MacArthur's intelligence unit regularly provided estimates that presented conclusions that MacArthur believed to be the reality of the situation. The Far East G-2 operation failed to anticipate both the North Korean attack and the Chinese intervention the following November.[221]

When Matthew Ridgway became Far East commander in April 1951 he recognized the failures of MacArthur's intelligence unit, but he retained Willoughby as intelligence head, noting that Willoughby's organization was proficient at assembling intelligence, but saying nothing about its judgments and conclusions.[222] Known by his critics as "Sir Charles," Willoughby soon followed his deposed chief, retiring from the army later that summer.[223]

During the post–World War II period, like many other specialized services, military intelligence was substantially reduced. In 1949 the Armed Forces Security Agency (AFSA) was formed to coordinate the cryptology findings of the three military branches, but shortage of resources and lack of cooperation from the three military organizations made its operations largely ineffectual. At that time attention was centered on the Soviet Union and, to a lesser extent, the Huk rebellion in the Philippines, with very little attention given to Communist China. As a minimal gesture, in April 1950 the Army Security Agency (ASA) assigned two specialists and one of its two Korean linguists to follow activities in North Korea. About 200 transmissions had been acquired, but few had been processed by the time Korea exploded. The Army Security Agency did pick up a couple of interesting developments— the Soviet listening post in Vladivostok was targeting South Korean communications and the Russians were sending large amounts of medical supplies to North Korea and Manchuria — but that was about it. It was all quiet on the communications front.[224]

Once the United States intervened in the Korean conflict, historian John Finnegan declared, army intelligence responded with "desperate improvisation." Due to aging World War II equipment, mountainous terrain and a shortage of Korean linguists, it got off to a slow start, with field commanders preferring to rely on locally acquired intelligence from Korean contacts. "Confronted by an almost complete intelligence void," Finnegan comments, "the Army at last took steps to enhance its human intelligence collection capabilities."[225] In what Matthew Aid calls "the Thirty Day Miracle," the Armed Forces Security Agency was able to break the codes of all North Korean transmissions, which proved to be of unlimited value to Walton Walker as he conducted the defense of the emerging Pusan Perimeter. Decrypts also were vital to the success of the Inchon venture, as they revealed the location of all North Korean units at that time. A major failing of intelligence was its inability to realize the extent to which its opponents were laying mines in the harbor of Wonsan, which delayed the landing of the X Corps for two weeks in October 1950. North Koreans, with substantial Russian assistance, deposited a wide variety of maritime mines under the cover of darkness. The failure implied that Far East intelligence surprisingly had no reliable agents in that location. South Korean army units had occupied the city on October 11, but, intent on heading north, obviously were not in communication with X Corps about the matter. As well, naval intelligence lacked knowledge about mines at Hungnam and Kojo, two other east coast ports, so alternative landing sites were ruled out.[226]

The Armed Forces Security Agency (AFSA) as early as July 1950 intercepted messages indicating Chinese forces were moving north to Manchuria and the Soviet air force had established a communication net to cover air bases in North Korea and Manchuria. Although the Chinese armies moving north observed radio silence, beginning in July 1950 an army listening post on Okinawa indicated that the Chinese were moving hundreds of thousands of soldiers to Manchuria. Two communications in November were most ominous. One, in early November, was a radiotelephone call made by an Eastern European reporting that Chinese soldiers were being urged to volunteer to fight in Korea, as "we are already at war there." A transmission in mid–November requesting 30,000 copies of maps of Korea clearly indicated that the Chinese were about to make a move. Then there was the explosive report of Karl Rankin, U.S. ambassador to Taiwan, on November 6 to the State Department, in which he reported that Chinese Nationalist intelligence, whose reports had already been sent to Washington, "lends strong support to the assumption that the Chinese communists plan to throw the book at the United Nations forces in Korea." His explanations of why the Chinese had not intervened earlier (which were borne out by events) were several: initially the Chinese believed North Korea would prevail, the need to replenish supplies for the North Koreans, preparation of units for the campaign, delaying action until close to the Yalu, thus beyond U.S. reconnaissance and interdiction. MacArthur and company obviously refused to credit these reports.[227] In Matthew Ridgway's judgment, if MacArthur did not want to believe something, he wouldn't.[228]

The new Central Intelligence Agency, operating largely out of Formosa and directed by the dynamic Desmond FitzGerald, made various claims about penetrating Communist communications and mobilizing anti–Communist elements in North Korea. With a few exceptions, however, its operations were failures. A small CIA unit, under the direction of Hans Toft, who had extensive

OSS experience in Asia, was finally established in Japan on the eve of the war, and then rapidly expanded. Friction with MacArthur's intelligence unit soon arose. The agency got off to a faulty start, particularly about the vital matter of potential Chinese intervention. Although it did note that a few Chinese soldiers were turning up, it failed to detect two Chinese army groups moving into North Korea. It believed that Chinese troops coming in simply had the mission of protecting the Suiho power complex and similar facilities along the Yalu.[229]

On November 7 MacArthur told Washington that he "had been confirmed in his belief" that there had not been a full-scale Chinese intervention.[230] When the Chinese did pour in, the CIA initially declared that these soldiers were composed of unmotivated and untrained draftees, thus were of low combat readiness. When it expanded its estimate to 200,000 Chinese troops, MacArthur did not seem to know about it, or, at least, did not acknowledge it.[231]

With the advent of the Chinese into the war beginning in late October 1950, army intelligence found itself with some Cantonese linguists but only a handful who knew Mandarin.[232] During the two-week period when the Chinese forces drove the Eighth Army into rapid retreat, no SIGINT (signal intelligence) unit was able to provide any substantial information about the movement and strength of the pursuing Chinese forces. Matthew Aid comments, "The result was that as of mid–December, senior U.S. military commanders found themselves in the embarrassing position of having to admit that information from all sources was 'vague and indefinite on the exact disposition' of Chinese forces." The Far East Command intelligence surmised that the two major Chinese forces were waiting for reinforcements and had the need to reorganize. Roy Appleman commented, "Both were wrong. And they continued to be wrong in this matter for the next three months." What halted the Chinese divisions on the western sector was crippling frostbite, which also had a major impact on those in the east.[233]

Not being able to directly pick up much about Chinese operations, SIGINT continued to try to follow these while continuing to exploit North Korean transmissions, but in July 1951 the North Koreans switched to an effectively unbreakable code system and began greater reliance on landline communications. Intercepted radio communications proved to be of great value in January 1951 when they revealed that although the Chinese high command was preparing to launch a new offensive, its forces had been weakened by massive casualties, supply shortages and disease. Through it all, an underlying problem in intelligence operations was that only 7 percent of those in intelligence positions at various army levels had any training or experience in the field. When lax security and mismanagement were included, Finnegan concludes, "Even towards the end of the war, deficiencies abounded."[234]

A CIA operation directed out of Seoul beginning in April 1951 seemed to have achieved considerable success. In mounting numbers, forty-four units totaling 1,500 agents were involved not only in gathering intelligence but also in harassing enemy communications and supply lines. One agent claimed he had identified details of enemy troop strength of every North Korean and Chinese unit at the front. The Tokyo intelligence organization was duly impressed: this agent's findings were "one of the outstanding intelligence reports of the war."[235]

There were some potential problems. None of the CIA agents at the station spoke fluent Korean, and the whole operation was in the hands of Korean "principal agents." In early 1953 John L. Hart took charge of the unit, and his investigation of the operation revealed that the agent reports were bogus and, moreover, mostly produced by enemy intelligence. He also concluded that many agents employed by army intelligence were equally unreliable. Rather than scrap the entire operation and reveal CIA incompetence, W. Bedell Smith, the CIA director, ordered that the operation be rebuilt from the bottom up. After careful screening and training, a new batch of agents were sent north.[236] The results were equally dismaying. According to Christopher Andrew, under Hart's direction none of the agents "succeeded in maintaining radio contact for more than a brief period. All were believed to have been caught and executed."[237]

Two early, small army operations to penetrate deep behind enemy lines quickly came to disaster. They were Operation Virginia I, of March 15, 1951, and Operation Spitfire, of the following June. In January 1951 a much larger effort, Operation Green Dragon, was mounted by the Combined Command Reconnaissance Activities Korea, which was designed to establish semipermanent bases in the enemy interior. One hundred fifty-three partisans were parachuted into an area about forty miles west of Pyongyang. Radio transmissions indicated that a base had been secured and more messages were received.[238] For seven months supplies were dropped there, but lack of activity resulted in the conclusion that Green Dragon was controlled by North Korean counterintelligence. All of the participants were captured.[239]

David Hatch is confirmed in his judgment: "SIGINT (intercepted radio transmissions) was almost the only intelligence worth having." The difficulty was that the Chinese rarely used radio transmissions, either from lack of facilities at the local level or, for long range communications, from awareness that their messages were being monitored by the other side.[240]

Despite all the difficulties, one small and irregular army intelligence unit apparently achieved effective results. Journalist John Dille relates that a unit headed by "Bill," a soldier with six years' prior experience in Korea, had substantial success in operating a small group in North Korea.[241] "Bill," as noted earlier, undoubtedly was Don Nichols, an air force master sergeant who developed an agent network in the north in the years before the war. Rejecting the usual military protocols and procedures, Nichols was a man for all seasons of military activity. Casual in dress and fluent in Korean, he demonstrably had the complete trust of his agents. Even before the war began, in May 1950, Nichols' group secured and was dismantling a Soviet Il-10 fighter-bomber, but before the wreckage could be shipped out it was seized by North Korean soldiers at the beginning of their invasion. Within days of that event Nichols signaled that this was pending, but his warning received no reply. With the war now underway, he was responsible for acquiring a Russian T-34 tank and later recovered a partially destroyed MiG-15. In addition, he directed his agents behind enemy lines. He was involuntarily promoted to warrant officer, declined rotation and continued his operations throughout the conflict.[242]

Following the U.N. forces' withdrawal from the north, in 1951 a partisan infantry unit began activity on coastal islands, principally on the west coast. This organization succeeded in gathering intelligence and attacking enemy communications and transportation, but failed in its attempts to establish guerrilla bases in the interior.[243] Its activities at least had the effect of tying down enemy forces along the cost.[244]

There were a variety of units involved in intelligence and special operations and these were getting in each other's way. The U.S. Army mounted an expanded albeit modest guerrilla force, led by Col. John McGee, at the beginning of 1951. Having observed strong opposition to the Communist regime in the west coast province of Hwanghae during the army's advance into North Korea, the new outfit planted small bases on four islands there. As anti–Communist actions mounted, the North Korean military offered bounties for the capture or killing of American advisors. It also succeeded in inserting its own agents into partisan groups.[245]

Before he arrived on the scene Lt. Ben Malcolm had noted that in the Basic Infantry Officers course there was "very little relevance to what was going on in Korea." During the six-month course about thirty minutes addressed guerrilla tactics and unconventional warfare. During the ten months he helped to direct partisan operations Malcolm was impressed by the performance of the 16,000 guerrillas who risked their lives in conducting sabotage and intelligence gathering operations, all with minimum reward in rice, acquisition of weapons and loot. He was struck by how little support this operation received from the Eighth Army high command or anyone in Tokyo. The partisans had to approach their coastal objectives in slow moving junks, except for a single week in June 1952 when PT boats were provided. Malcolm estimated that "a single squadron or two of fast-moving, heavily armed PT boats" operating in conjunction "with partisan units on the ground would have created incredible havoc" with North Korean coastal defenses.

As Malcolm was to observe later in Vietnam, intelligence reports were sent up to higher command, but very little response came down. Another problem he encountered, one not restricted to his base, was the lack of coordination between intelligence units, including those of CIA personnel, who

North Korean and Chinese prisoners. Pusan, April 1951. Courtesy National Archives, ARC 541956 [NA].

remained aloof from the others. Using mostly captured weapons, encountering severe Communist security measures with their lives forfeit if captured, the partisans carried on their campaign until the armistice of July 1953. With their province remaining in Communist control, the partisans had the alternatives of being evacuated to the south, joining the South Korean Army or attempting to blend into the countryside of their native area.[246]

A remarkable account of intelligence gathering is told by Arthur Boyd, who in 1951 was a twenty-two-year-old lieutenant in intelligence. As a result of President Truman's dissatisfaction with the quality of the reports he was receiving, he ordered the formation of a special intelligence unit outside the chain of command. With Boyd as a member, a small group of ten men from several military branches conducted a one-time but remarkable operation in January 1952. Posing as captives from a crashed B-29 and escorted by sixty-six Chinese Nationalists acting as their guards, the group moved near enemy lines beginning on the east coast for nearly a week. They were supplied with reports from in-place agents who claimed that Communist forces were growing in strength, well-equipped and preparing for a major offensive. The reports were transmitted in code to a periodically appearing plane, but after five days this unlikely venture was exposed by a Chinese security check point. Only three of the Americans managed to get to the west coast escape route; the fate of the Chinese Nationalists is unknown.[247]

Much of intelligence was derived from prisoner interrogation, although some intelligence officers doubted that ordinary enemy soldiers could know much about operations. While U.S. Marines were advancing to Chosin in November 1950, three captured Chinese soldiers claimed a detailed knowledge of Chinese plans to destroy the Marine division. A Marine officer recalled, "We doubted that ordinary private soldiers could be privy to such high level information," which led to the suspicion that the captured soldiers had been "plants," whose revelations were designed to mislead their opponents.[248] In fact, due to information they received as part of troop indoctrination, which included the democratic ethos of sharing and service for all, ordinary Chinese soldiers often did know of pending operations and, somewhat surprisingly, they were willing to reveal it.[249] Once battle lines became generally stable by mid–1951, the number of captured opponents declined drastically. Marine Martin Russ noted that in early 1953 "any man who captures a prisoner these days is promised a five-day R & R breather in Japan." The problem in his area was that the POWs never seemed to still be alive when intel people got to them.[250]

The South Korean Army had an intelligence branch as well as informants in North Korea, but as is the case in all large military organizations, in neither case were notable results forthcoming. When the South Korean Army was shattered at the beginning of the conflict its intelligence units were subsumed into American army and air force organizations.[251]

The other side also was most interested in intelligence findings. Communist supporters were present in the South Korean military command before the war, at least one reaching the general staff level. Particularly in the early months of the war, North Korean soldiers and South Korean Communist agents appeared all over the place. Although there are not public records about their activities, it can be assumed they knew a lot about their opponent's dispositions. Because of their different language and appearance, as well as a lack of technology, the Chinese apparently did not make a major intelligence effort. Confident in their military philosophy and cultural superiority, the Chinese concentrated on hammering at the enemy, while largely ignoring the mass of American radio transmissions. In any case, very few Chinese soldiers had radio receivers.[252]

A continuing difficulty with all American intelligence units was the shortage of Chinese linguists. Chinese-Americans could not be employed because of differences in dialects, while Nationalist Chinese were unfamiliar with Communist army terminology. Linguists were recruited from Chinese communities in Japan, Korea and Hong Kong as well as from Taiwan. With Russian pilots flying "Chinese" fighter jets in the north after November 1950, there also was a need to find Russian linguists.[253] Over time, intelligence operations did improve.[254]

Throughout the conflict the Army Security Agency continued to monitor enemy radio transmissions. It scored a notable success in the winter of 1951. Asked by the Eighth Army to confirm that the Chinese Tenth Army had arrived in Korea, ASA operatives picked up a North Korean transmission saying that farmers were complaining that soldiers from that army were stealing their rice.[255]

After the U.N. forces regained Seoul (for the last time) in March 1951, both the Army Security Agency and other intelligence outfits established stable bases in the capital where they succeeded in reliably tracking the order of battle (location and identification) of Chinese units. When the conflict settled down to static front lines, the other side improved its communications security methods, which required U.S. improvisation. Listening devices were embedded along the front. Low-level intercepts, originally operating from jeeps, proved to be so effective that the number of teams using this method increased from 15 in October 1952 to 22 by the end of the war.[256]

Air force intelligence also became more effective. Intercepted messages penetrated radio transmissions sent to Chinese planes, which provided a clear advantage to U.S. fighter planes. The CIA was able to create listening posts on both coasts of North Korea. In June 1951 it alerted the air force that a North Korean force was about to attack a partisan base on the west coast. The air force responded by destroying the enemy unit. Airborne personnel were equipped with escape kits as well, in some instances, including a reported $700,000 in gold bars for downed airmen "to use as bribes and payment in gold-conscious Korea," while the CIA struggled to provide escape and evasion facilities. To address this matter, the air force created its own small navy, the "grey boats," which had a substantial measure of success in recovering pilots. Due to increased internal Communist security, once the front lines became stable, the extraction of downed airmen became extremely difficult. Insertion of agents into the interior was virtually suspended, not only by the air force but also by the other organizations involved in the field. In his definitive study of the subject, Michael Haas has concluded that these operations were futile and ineffective, with no strategic impact on the war.[257]

None of the intelligence activity was satisfactory to James Van Fleet, who took command of the Eighth Army in April 1951. He saw intelligence deficiencies in just about everything — aerial photography, aerial visual reconnaissance, covert collection, ground reconnaissance and communications reconnaissance. After two years of fighting, he bemoaned, "Our intelligence operations in Korea have not approached the standards that we reached in the final year of the last war."[258]

In order to finally overcome duplication and lack of coordination, the National Security Agency pulled together various intelligence organizations when it was established in November 1952.[259] As a result of the Korean War, the CIA thrived, with a greatly increased budget, the bulk of which was devoted to covert operations, while by 1953 its employees increased by six times its founding numbers in 1946.[260] At the same time the Counterintelligence Corps (CIC) doubled in size. It is questionable if this growth was matched by a corresponding effectiveness.[261]

Psychological Warfare

As in all wars, both sides attempted to undermine the will of the other. There was a stark difference, however, in how the two sides dealt with psychological warfare in Korea. Having long anticipated an invasion of the south, the North Korean regime was fully prepared for this enterprise when it struck. As in other areas, the U.S. military and involved government agencies had completely closed down this activity at the end of the Second World War. There had been no post-war evaluation about this program, so when this activity was resumed in Korea it was a matter of starting from scratch.[262] Once fully developed, the United States program used psychological warfare to an unprecedented degree relative to the size of the war. As in the case of intelligence, an immediate question was who was in charge of this activity.[263] The army took control of tactical (frontline) psywar, while the Central Intelligence Agency, in its first venture into a war, got involved with a variety of things, including strategic (long-range) psywar appeals.[264] To deal with the conflicting bodies, in June 1951 President Truman established the Psychological Strategy Board to coordinate efforts, but as the board only had an advisory function, nothing was resolved in the ongoing bureaucratic tussle.[265] Two areas of major contention in the army's psywar campaign were the questions of on whom appeals should focus— ordinary soldiers, officers, etc.— and of how much intelligence should be supplied to the psywar practitioners.[266]

When the U.S. Army got geared up, it employed a full range of appeals to opposing forces, including radio broadcasts, loudspeakers, and leaflets dropped from planes and fired in artillery shells. Getting off to a fast start, masses of leaflets were air dropped, their message being that the Americans had arrived to save South Korea. As the U.N. forces eventually advanced, the message shifted to the inevitability of Communist defeat, with one leaflet exclaiming, "We are coming!" and "Seoul is free again." Particularly as the clash with the Chinese continued, U.S. planes showered their opponents with masses of leaflets urging surrender. The American approach clearly was one of "bury 'em" with the publications, but due to Chinese mass illiteracy and prohibitions against picking up the leaflets, U.S. Army field interrogations concluded that voice broadcasts, with the messages transmitted by Korean women, were more effective. One way or another, the appeals, combined with hunger, illness and frozen limbs, eventually produced results, to such an extent that the American military found itself dealing with a huge number of captured

North Korean captives, September 17, 1950. Courtesy Truman Library, 2007-452.

and surrendered Chinese and Korean soldiers. Many of those who crossed over said they were impressed with the signature of General MacArthur on a surrender pass that promised good treatment. On the opposite side of the pass was a replica of North Korean money. After April 1951 Matthew Ridgway's name replaced that of MacArthur and Chinese language was included. Since most North Korean and Chinese soldiers were illiterate, Ridgway urged that greater use be made of pictures. Prisoner interrogations indicated that many of those who surrendered initially concealed such passes in their clothing and body crevices. This appeal had its effects. In October 1951 at the fight for Heartbreak Hill, a dozen North Korean soldiers surrendered, some of them "carrying United Nations safe-conduct passes in their hands."[267]

Based on prisoner interrogations, an estimated 12 percent of those captured did so as a result of surrender appeals. The American psywar warriors soon sent out the word that surrendering opponents did not have to carry the surrender pass with them, which was dangerous for them to do. A study produced in February 1951 by a research team from Johns Hopkins University came up with the remarkable conclusion that from a financial point of view "the cost of a PsyWar capture to a conventional kill appears to have a probable ratio of 70:1 in favor of PsyWar."[268] Based on World War II experience, Martin Herz has observed, however, "The plain fact is that most prisoners have to be taken by the infantry."[269]

The Communist side attempted to counter this effort by imposing the death penalty for having a pass, spreading the story that the passes were infected with deadly germs, and threatening that the families of surrendering soldiers would face reprisals.[270] In his broad study of psywar Peter Watson has noted conflicting arguments about the effectiveness of this activity, especially regarding pamphlets, but concluded, "At any rate most armies want more of it, rather than less."[271]

A frequent theme in the American leaflet barrage was the claim that Koreans were just being used as puppets in the great game of world domination being pursued by the Chinese and the Russians: "Why die for China and Russia?" Those directed at Chinese soldiers asserted that they were being exploited by the Soviets. During the early period of the conflict when the North Koreans occupied almost all of the south, psychological war publications depicted the invaders as crude and brutal, manipulated by Soviet agents.[272]

The fear factor was also employed by American psywarfare. On one occasion dropped leaflets declared that the Chinese Communist leadership was prepared to have one in four Chinese killed, thus decreasing the homeland population to a manageable level.[273] Matthew Ridgway had a strong interest in psywar, passing along various suggestions, one of which was the employment of images to appeal not only to the many illiterate intended recipients, but also to bring home to them the carnage many of their comrades had experienced at the front and the massive U.S. Air Force bombings behind the lines. In a March 1951 message intended for Communist guerrillas operating in South Korea, they were informed, "The mouse has gnawed at the tiger's tail long enough." Allowing workers to flee and to disrupt production, leaflets were showered on northern industrial areas as a prelude to bombing.[274]

Flying along what airmen called "paper routes," a grand total of 2.5 billion leaflets were dropped behind the lines. By late 1951 American propaganda efforts expanded, resulting in increased Chinese desertions and surrenders. According to Shu Zhang, "These propaganda measures had a great effect on the Chinese troops.... Consequently, friction between formerly friendly units and disputes between officers and the troops increased.'"[275] In an April and May 1953 attempt to get possession of an advanced Russian jet fighter plane, a million and a half leaflets were dropped along the Yalu offering $100,000 to any pilot who would deliver one of the jets to Kimpo airport outside Seoul. There was no immediate response, but word of this offer spread among the Chinese military and beyond. According to Don Murray, this offer "proved astonishingly effective" with all MiGs being grounded for eight days. Shortly after the war ended a North Korean pilot did fly a MiG-15 there, claiming he had never heard of the financial reward for doing so.[276]

American psychological warfare efforts sometimes extended to military operations. Aware of the devastating effect of the American Inchon incursion, both General Peng and Chairman Mao anticipated a second landing and had stationed large forces along both coasts.[277] To encourage this concern, in March 1951, in conjunction with naval feints, U.S. psywar saw to it that "surrender leaflets were dropped in great quantities many miles behind the front lines, but only a short distance from the east coast beaches."[278]

At the same time that American psywar efforts were being expended in Korea, *Voice of America* radio broadcasts attempted to stir discontent in China. Its messages stressed Red China's subservience to Communist Russia, slights heaped on Mao not only by Stalin but by his successors, reluctant and inadequate Soviet support for China's war efforts and, repeatedly, how Chinese soldiers were merely cannon fodder for Moscow's "imperialist adventures."[279]

For its part, the Chinese government had been conducting a "hate America" campaign even before its forces intervened in Korea. Once it jumped into the conflict its appeals intensified, centering on the "Resist America and Aid Korea" campaign, which blanketed the country while people were urged to encourage "volunteers" for Korea and to donate cash and other valuables to help to buy fighter planes. The Chinese people were told of hard-won Chinese victories over cowardly U.S. soldiers, who were consumed with jazz music, wild dances, alcohol and pornographic pictures.[280]

The Communists conducted a much smaller-scale effort at psywar. At the beginning of the war the North Koreans conducted a powerful propaganda campaign to gain public support in the areas they occupied in the south, but this was offset by Communist violence and coercion. William Anderson experienced one novel North Korean effort: while they yelled abuse at their opponents, North Korean soldiers paraded a wagon with lanterns hanging down near the front line. Although Chinese musical instruments were primarily employed for troop direction, their use, particularly with South Korean troops, also had an unnerving impact on American servicemen. When capturing an allied position, bugles sounded what appeared to be Taps for the dead and reveille for the living; at other times Chinese buglers sounded off just to disturb the sleep of their opponents. The ChinComs also distributed leaflets, complete with photographs, with declarations of their "lenient policy" for POWs, promising battered American soldiers a safe incarceration and also appealing to African Americans to reject oppressive racial practices back home by switching over to the progressive, happy world of communism. The Chinese fired mortar rounds of leaflets, some of which included information about how to pronounce "I surrender" in Chinese and Korean as well as four "guarantees": survival in captivity, retention of personal belongings, protection against ill-treatment and provision of necessary medical care.[281]

Although there were a couple of instances when surrounded U.S. companies surrendered, there is no documented evidence of a single American soldier who willingly crossed over to the other side, but it is possible that such soldiers might be included in the "missing in action" category, which mounted to several thousand before the conflict ended.[282] James Brady recalls a Chinese effort to capture Marines: the reward for defection would be a ten-day furlough and 10,000 sen, which some of his fellow Marines found to be insultingly little in U.S. money.[283]

A notable technique that the Chinese employed was to light campfires and raise human clamor as deceptive measures at different points near the front. This was first used on a large scale on the night of December 1-2, 1950, as the U.S. Eighth Army was rolled backwards. Obviously to create a picture of overwhelming strength, that night the Chinese lighted thousands of fires near the front. U.S. air reconnaissance reported, "Last night it looked as though most of North Korea was on fire."[284]

American military authorities continued to be concerned about the impact of Red propaganda. While a Communist soldier faced execution for doing this, in the American ranks it was a court-martial offense to pick up one of the enemy's leaflets. When the *Chicago Tribune* printed one of them, sent home by a soldier to his family, the ever-vigilant FBI arrived to investigate where it had come from.[285] There were a few episodes of the families of American POWs being approached by unknown persons offering to send messages to their imprisoned kin. Parents of soldiers in Korea were urged to write to their congressman that they were opposed to sending "American boys to fight on foreign soil." Another Red objective was to raise humanitarian concerns about U.S. bombing of civilians and cities.[286]

A major Communist propaganda effort was made beginning in February 1952 to claim that Americans were practicing germ warfare in North Korea and Northeast China.[287] According to Mark Ryan, both Chinese military leaders in Korea and political heads in Beijing "truly believed" that this was happening. To support their claims, some friendly scientists were brought in who confirmed that this was the case, but an investigation by the International Red Cross was rejected by the Communists, who declared that organization was controlled by capitalist countries.[288] There was plenty of infectious disease in North Korea, but there is no substantial evidence that this was due to American action. The Communists, nevertheless, maintained their claims, backed by written and oral "confessions" by some U.S. Air Force POWs, that they had been involved in distributing the bugs. So persuasive were the Communist claims that they caused panic among some Chinese and North Korean soldiers. Admittedly the terrible flooding in North Korea in the summer of 1951 was an act of nature, but all incidents of hunger and disease there could be laid at the feet of the capitalist barbarians.[289]

The U.S. military, building on World War II Japanese research, had been studying biological warfare, and its air force had the capacity to drop germ containers in North Korea. During the previous war Japanese planes, in more than a few instances, had released anthrax germs in China, with slight result.[290] Despite a variety of circumstantial evidence that American planes did the same in Korea, there is no real proof that this took place. Even if it did happen, the effects were minor. Stephen Endicott and Edward Hagerman, two Canadian authors, examined the episode. They pointed to the conclusion of a Communist-selected "international commission" that declared the United States did this, but did not state who the commission's members were. Even their description of Dr. Joseph Needham of Cambridge University, supposedly a noted bio-chemist, is vague. Author of a massive history of Chinese science, Needham was the epitome of a fellow-traveler since the 1930s (and Cambridge was later revealed to be the nesting ground of a group of Soviet agents). Strangely, Endi-cott and Hagerman provide no evidence of casualties or long-term effects as a result of the attacks. They strongly believe that the U.S. Air Force knows more about the matter, but due to destruction of records, top-secret silence and still classified material, the full story is still under wraps. A great lover of China, Needham, who uncritically accepted the "evidence" presented to him, had to live with a barrage of criticism in England and elsewhere.[291]

In the view of the French writer Andre Fontaine, "The whole affair assumed the dimensions of an immense collective hallucination, carefully organized and exploited by cynical minds, mobilizing in the service of their improbable thesis the confessions extorted by torture from downed American pilots and the statements of naïve or obliging foreign observers."[292] Although the Soviet Union fully accepted and trumpeted the story of U.S. biological warfare at the time, in 1969, in a happier period of U.S.-Russians relations, its representatives confessed that it did not happen.[293] With his case in tatters, in 1979 the most Needham would allow was that "methods of biological warfare ... were attempted by the American side in the Korean war." He remained at Cambridge and in his old age and after the death of his wife he married his long-time Chinese mistress.[294]

A joint CIA/navy operation delivered Brigadier General Crawford Sams, the senior medical officer in the Far East Command, behind the lines in March 1951 to determine what diseases were affecting people in the Wonsan area. His conclusion was that the culprit was hemorrhagic smallpox, outbreaks of which had occurred elsewhere as well.[295]

The Communist side was presented with a bonanza for its propaganda campaign when it captured two high-ranking Marine airmen in July 1952. Colonel Frank Schwable, chief of staff of the First Marine Aircraft Wing, and Major Roy Bley, ordnance officer of the wing, flying in a Beechcraft along the front line on an "administration flight" (and to get in flight-time) lost their way, proceeded over enemy lines and were brought down by ground fire. Was it not irresponsible for these two important and experienced Marine officers to be flying along the combat front, with an obvious inability to find their way? It was not uncommon, however, for small American planes and helicopters to be flying all over the place, some with and some without authorized flight plans. After brutal treatment, the two officers "confessed" to being part of the germ warfare campaign, as did several other air force pilots.[296]

Anthony Farrar-Hockley remembers the coercive measures meted out to some of his British fellow POWs who refused to support germ warfare allegations. One effect of the Chinese and North Korean germ warfare campaign was to disguise their inability to deal with epidemics and at least partly counter the negative image that they were opposed to voluntary repatriation of POWs.[297]

In the propaganda contest both sides employed radio broadcasts and frontline loudspeakers to subvert their opponents, with the North Koreans making good use of the central radio studios in Seoul, left undisturbed by fleeing staffers at the beginning of war. PFC Victor Fox clearly remembered the nightly program of "Seoul City Sue": "This alluring voice spoke about the glories of Communism and of the intervention by the American imperialists. Suhr Anna, the broadcaster, also read the names of American POWs, their units and hometowns." Her performance was impressive: "What surprised many of us was how much she knew, not only the locations of other units, but where the 1st Cavalry Division was and where along the line its regiment's rifles were." She also included current popular songs: "Good Night Irene," "Mona Lisa." According to one report about her nightly broadcasts, which featured tirades against the American military, popular music and recorded statements by cooperative POWs, "Listening to Sue has been the most popular recreation" for frontline U.S. soldiers.[298]

As surmised by the Far Eastern Command, the broadcaster was Anna Wallace Suhr, an Arkansas-born Methodist missionary and teacher who, upon marriage to a Korean Marxist, became a convert to communism. When the tide turned, Suhr retreated with the North Koreans and with her husband conducted indoctrination efforts on POWs. She reportedly became head of all English-language periodicals and even was said to have been executed as a spy for South Korea in 1969. When a sole peacetime American defector later encountered her in Pyongyang, she quickly terminated the conversation.[299]

Pyongyang Radio celebrated imaginary victories over the U.S. Air Force,[300] while Chinese loudspeakers transmitted unpersuasive lectures on Marxism-Leninism mixed with popular American music, including "If I Knew You Were Coming I'd Have Baked a Cake" and "When the Moon Comes Over the Mountain." One GI recalled a loudspeaker transmission in which he heard "some gal in a sexy voice pleading with us to come over to their side, where she promised, 'We have beautiful girls and maids and you will never have to work again,'" while another remembered at Christmas 1952 a full range of Christmas carols sounded across the line, "to make us homesick, I presume."[301] More disturbing was at least one instance when Chinese propagandists read off the names of soldiers of an American infantry company.[302]

Another device the Chinese employed was to erect "peace mailboxes" between the lines which contained notes urging the Americans to quit fighting and go home.[303] British infantryman Tony Lovell, although he never saw them put there, remembered leaflets pinned on barbed wire entanglements, with images of fat cigar-smoking Americans lolling on a Miami beach.[304] Marine Martin Russ heard almost daily music and appeals being transmitted across the lines by loudspeakers. After a Christmastime message to the Americans saying that both sides leave Korea, Chinese broadcasters played the plaintive song "There Is No Place Like Home." As far as Russ was concerned, the propaganda effect was nil.[305] Wearying of a barrage of Communist music and talk, Sgt. Lou Horyza organized the firing of three tanks so that comparing azimuths led to the source of transmission. After a few shells were fired at that spot, "We could hear the needle scrape over the record and everything went dead. We never heard that music again."[306]

The Chinese sometimes broadcast more serious messages. In late December 1950 their loudspeakers declared that the Chinese military would shortly capture Seoul, which it briefly did. Chinese leaflets claimed in 1952 that its forces would again occupy Seoul, but this time they failed to do so.[307]

After an exhaustive study of the subject, Peter Watson has spelled out the varying assessments of the effectiveness of psywar, pointing out that one professional study done in Korea in 1953 concluded that "leaflet and radio broadcasts had minimal effect ... in altering enemy predispositions."[308]

American soldiers did not have to rely on Communist broadcasts for American popular music, as Armed Forces Radio in Japan supplied plenty of that. There were daily radio broadcasts directed at North Korea, and despite the scantiness of radios and severe penalties for listening to them, they apparently had a considerable audience.[309]

Since some Chinese soldiers picked up a bit of English there was a need to prevent them from mimicking American voices to lure American soldiers into fatal situations. To counter cries for "corpsman," Marines identified corpsmen by numbers or nicknames. Chinese soldiers sometimes shouted out threatening messages: "We're going to get you," "Marine, I'm going to get your paaarka." The effect of these shouts was slight.[310]

The U.S. Air Force employed slow moving planes, without lights and with their undercarriages painted black, to broadcast surrender messages to their opponents below using the services of a Korean woman with an attractive voice. One crewman recalled that bullets fired from below came after the plane has passed overhead. There was one alarming episode when a MiG fighter was identified as heading towards one of these planes, but the jet flew by without spotting the intruder.[311]

In an economic sabotage effort, the U.S. psywar unit in 1952 counterfeited North Korean paper currency and, through a maritime operation by air force boat crews, inserted it in the north. Counterfeiting the enemy's money was a common enough practice (the Germans did this in World War II), but the effect of this action in Korea apparently was slight, as there were no observable repercussions within the Communist regime.[312]

Before bombing raids on populated areas, warnings sometimes were issued by leaflets or broadcasts that this was about to occur. Following such attacks civilians were told to expect further bombings. An example of this was included in a broadcast by Radio Seoul: "Today the United Nations Air Force bombed fifty villages, towns and cities that were military targets. These were military targets along highways and railways. You may be next. Save your lives. Flee to the hills." Surely the death and destruction which followed such events had an effect in North Korea but strong internal security measures and expansion of anti-aircraft weapons apparently limited these efforts.[313]

There were other attempts to stimulate discontent among the civilian population in the north. In response to opposition by farmers to being forced to supply food to the "People's Army" as well as to Chinese soldiers' confiscating crops, Operation Farmer was mounted in the summer of 1951, dropping millions of leaflets in agricultural areas urging farmers to conceal some of their crop or to sell it on the black market. Although the U.N. incursion into North Korea the previous autumn had demonstrated that there were plenty of people there who were pleased to be rid of Communist control, state security now was very effective, which undoubtedly accounts for the lack of demonstrable opposition to the regime.[314]

Prisoners of War

The Korean conflict resulted in the capture of a large number of soldiers on both sides. They included approximately 7,245 Americans, more than 3,000 of whom died in captivity. Among U.N. military released at the end of the conflict, there were almost a thousand British soldiers and 243 Turks. About 75,000 South Koreans were captured and, on the other side, about 140,000 North Korean and Chinese, including 50,000 Korean civilians. The great bulk of captured (or surrendered) soldiers in the North Korean Army were taken, at its defeat, in the autumn of 1950.[315] Almost all of those who went into captivity had been in military service less than six months, including the large number of South Koreans who had been pressed into that force. Many of the well-trained and conditioned North Koreans did not give up but withdrew north; after December 1950 the number of new North Korean POWs plummeted.[316] Provision of housing and food for this large number of captured soldiers was a major undertaking. The daily food ration for them consisted of three hops of rice, two and a half hops of barley, one-sixth pound of fish and an allowance of 200 *won* per man for the purchase of such items of seaweed, fruit and vegetables from local farmers. The regular food provision surely was superior to what they were getting before they were captured. A contemporary study of the matter declared, "Many — perhaps most — of the PWs had come into U.N. custody undernourished and suffering from exposure." Reports of the International Red Cross concluded that the accommodation, medical care and food provided for them was adequate.[317] Visiting a U.S. POW camp in mid–1951, American journalist E. J. Kahn found the facilities much better than the refugee camp run by the South Korean government that he had seen. At the POW site he saw "a huge hospital with considerable equipment and facilities, including a dental clinic, and an eye, ear, nose and throat clinic.... Twenty-three American doctors were on duty when I dropped in."[318]

When the number of North Korean POWs rose to about 60,000 in the autumn of 1950 the allied military began a pilot rehabilitation project of about 500 prisoners under the direction of Monta Osborne, who had prior experience both in China and Japan. The program included the teaching of literacy, lectures and films on representative government, and group discussions. The project was disrupted by the massive Chinese intervention, but the attendees apparently now wanted to join the South Korean military.[319]

In the early stages of the conflict both South Korean and U.S. military units rounded up many persons who had been labeled as opponents and were thrust into POW camps. After a lengthy case-by-case examination many of these were deemed not to have supported the Communist invaders and were released. In June and July 1952 45,000 "civilian internees" were released, with another 16,000 following by the end of the year. The situation in the north was very different.[320]

Almost all the captured South Korean soldiers were incorporated into the "People's Army" as "liberated soldiers" and initially were put to work repairing war damage. Some were later incorporated in combat units. In the south the huge numbers of captured North Koreans were interned, which eventually led to severe problems. Seventy thousand enemy POWs, largely concentrated on the south coast island of Koje-do, despite great overcrowding received adequate treatment given their status. After interrogations determined that they had been forced into the ranks of the "People's Army," 40,000 South Korean soldiers were released.[321] Probably a majority of the Chinese soldiers who surrendered had been in the defeated Kuomintang army of Chiang Kai-shek and had been dragooned into the victorious Communist force.[322] Like others before him, it was the experience of South Korean Army general Paik Sun Yup that upon their capture Chinese soldiers' "docility knew no bounds. Prisoners even volunteered answers to questions our interrogators hadn't put to them."[323]

Beginning in 1951 there were conflicts between Communist supporters and their opponents, most of whom had formerly been in the Kuomintang. Communist agents, most of whom apparently had surrendered to gain access to the camps, managed to gain a strong measure of control in some of these camps and organized riots during 1952, at one point kidnapping the camp commander, all of this to the embarrassment of the U.S. military authorities. Communist supporters had created a system of underground tunnels.[324] Russell Williams recollected, "Safe from prying eyes of the guards, the prisoners had established their own system of Communist justice, including kangaroo courts.... They had to be gassed out of the tunnels and caverns they had dug." Stern measures effectively put an end to this agitation. That adequate care was provided for this mass of prisoners is seen in the very low death rate among them.[325]

The anti–Communist POWs were separated from the others. In the new camps Chinese linguists (some from Taiwan) were brought in. Anti-Communist and pro-democracy programs were provided in all of them, but some camp commanders, such as Col. William Robinette, went well beyond that. In his camp, again under the direction of Monta Osborne, the internees who had great success in tending vegetable gardens and staffing craft shops were provided with U.S. mail order catalogues being supplied for examples. Activities included classes in literacy, musical performances and theatrical productions. One result of such efforts was that when it came time for repatriation, about a third of them declined to return to China or North Korea. Under the terms of the armistice of July 1953, Communist representatives were allowed to urge more of them to return. This process continued until January 1954. Only 628 of the 22,604 who were interviewed decided to go back.[326]

According to one study, many of these POWs declared they were prepared to join the fight against Communist forces. Many of the Chinese prisoners refused repatriation to their homeland, while thousands of North Koreans "signed in blood a petition suggesting that the U.N. Command execute them rather than return them to Communist control."[327] To its intense embarrassment, the fact that many Chinese soldiers refused to be repatriated stripped away the claim of the Chinese government that its troops were volunteers for service in Korea. Contention about the issue of repatriation delayed the release of POWs for two long years.[328]

The treatment meted out to the American POWs was similar to that experienced by their World War II predecessors in Asia — little food, housing or medical facilities, with a high mortality rate, from their Japanese opponents. John Dille has argued that, with some exceptions, "the Communists treated most of our prisoners about as well as they treated their own soldiers. Should we have expected more?"[329] Chinese authorities declared that their soldiers also were experiencing malnutrition and disease. There was one important difference compared to Japanese treatment: the Chinese set out to indoctrinate their captors.[330]

Having been captured at the end of August 1950 by North Korean troops, Edward Gregory joined about 128 American POWs in a march north: "The wounded who could not keep up were shot. The Koreans urinated on their bodies."[331] At the beginning of the war the North Koreans carried out three mass killings of American prisoners. Donald Elliott remembers that when his squad was captured a North Korean soldier wanted to kill them but Chinese soldiers intervened: "The Chinese troops actually jerked his weapon away and booted the N.K. in the behind and sent him away from us."[332] A North Korean officer pointed a pistol at Billy Gaddy "right between my eyes" until a Chinese officer grabbed his arm and knocked the gun away. Gaddy was subjected to "tremendous abuse and anguish" at the hands of a North Korean officer as well as having to endure being mocked and threatened by civilians. Captured in late 1951, Richard Bassett was subjected to such virulent abuse by some Korean civilians that he required protection from his Chinese guards. He believed "they would have gladly killed us on the spot if given the chance." Billy Gaddy continued to have contrasting experiences. Because he was unable to eat the rice that was infested with bugs, a nurse gave him warm milk and an apple, but this caused him to vomit. Later a Chinese man (a soldier?) with a big knife "was about to cut my throat" when a wounded North Korean "stopped him with a crutch."[333]

Richard Bassett had a unique experience when captured by Chinese soldiers in October 1951: without being tied up, he was met with smiles and handshakes, to be followed by a statement of good treatment. After being marched to Pyongyang he had another such experience: twice he encountered Russian soldiers, to their mutual surprise. In an event not noted by anyone else, when Henry O'Kane of the Royal Ulster Rifles was captured by Chinese soldiers he was supplied with a safe-conduct pass. In an earlier episode, upon his capture in early November 1950 Bill Funchess was ordered to raise his hands, shortly to be confronted by a Chinese officer speaking perfect English, who proceeded to pull down one of his hands and shake it, declaring, "We are not mad at you. We are mad at Wall Street," a reference Funchess did not understand. When Funchess asked the officer what his nationality was the answer, after a pause, was North Korean, but "I knew he was lying."[334]

With the influx of prisoners and due to lack of facilities, the North Koreans, who demonstrated little interest in indoctrination, in October 1951 turned over almost all U.N. prisoners to the Chinese while retaining control of South Koreans. There was general agreement among POWs that, despite enduring privations, being under Chinese control was better than being under the North Koreans.[335] Before turning over prisoners, the North Koreans were prone to make examples of captured Americans. This was the experience of helicopter pilot John Thornton, who in March 1951 was moved through several villages where he was harangued by Communist spokesmen and assaulted by gathering crowds. Sometimes the North Koreans did interrogate American prisoners.[336] Lloyd Kreider was asked what his father's occupation was; when he replied carpenter his captors were pleased — the man was doing people's work — but an examination of his hands ended that charade. He noticed that many of his fellow POWs now claimed to be carpenters or farmers.[337] James Thompson recalled that some officers on the verge of being captured removed their insignia and other evidence of their rank. This also was done not to attract the attention of snipers, who were a constant threat in the combat area.[338]

When the tide turned against the North Koreans in mid–September 1950, internee Father Philip Crosbie noticed "from time to time disorderly little bands of North Korean soldiers went by, often without arms." Bits of news about the advance of U.N. troops brought hope to POWS and internees alike. Some of the guards also were affected by this development. A quartermaster threw open his supply room, whose principal store was warm winter caps. "There were enough for nearly all the POWs," noted Crosbie, "many of whom thus acquired their only warm article of attire." Their hopes were dashed by the arrival of Chinese soldiers beginning in October. The prisoners were subjected to another brutal trek, which Crosbie rightly described as a death march, to a more secure camp further north; more treks were to follow.[339] The half-dozen permanent camps were located near the Yalu, as far as possible from U.N. forces, which made escape nearly impossible; at best a few managed to evade recapture for a few days. William Funchess remembers many attempts at escape — all unsuccessful — and what followed: surrounding villages were alerted by telephone and students were given instructions that all family members were to join in the search. All the escapees were returned badly beaten and with their clothes in tatters.[340]

The best opportunity for escape was while being marched north. Edward Gregory took advantage of this opportunity but his freedom only lasted about a day when, spotted by a Korean farmer, he was caught, beaten until "I could hardly move," brought through a village, where "people spit on me, hit me with sticks, threw rocks and dung." He was returned to the prisoner train, where a North Korean officer declared, "If anyone else tried to escape, he would shoot ten men for every man who tried."[341] When one of the POWs asked why his camp did not have a fence around it, he was told, "We don't need barbed wire. Your faces are the barbed wire." Other camps had fences. Rewards for locating escapees were offered to local people and execution was imposed on those who offered any assistance to escapees. The Chinese officials imposed a varying range of retribution for attempting to abscond, sometimes imposing fatal punishment on whomever they saw as a leading man in the unit of the recaptured escapee.[342]

Most POWs had to endure about a three-week march to the north. When a medic attempted to use his first aid kit to help wounded soldiers, the kit was confiscated. Another time Chinese soldiers stripped American POWs of all medical supplies. Field jackets and personal items were taken. Lloyd Pate had a different experience: Chinese soldiers he encountered allowed an American medic to patch up the wounded in the group in which he was captured, while Korean mule drivers used their whips on his column as the POWs were marched north. The Chinese obviously were intent on taking prisoners, which would explain why they allowed barely ambulatory POWs to keep going.[343] With a shattered ankle, William Funchess dragged himself along, guarded by as single Chinese soldier. Hobbling along far behind the main prisoner column, Funchess was confronted with a mountain he could not climb, whereupon his guard gave him his rifle and loaded him on his back.[344]

Not surprisingly, the largest haul of Americans prisoners took place during the massive Chinese attack in November 1950, when 3,000 soldiers in the IX and X Corps were captured. For most POWs their captivity was to last for two and a half years. Although truce negotiations had begun in the summer of 1951 no agreement emerged for two years, the sticking point being the repatriation of prisoners. Citing the Geneva Convention on how to deal with prisoners, the Communist side insisted that all North Korean and Chinese prisoners be returned, while the United Nations representatives were adamant that the prisoners be allowed to decide what they were going to do.[345] As the dominant influence on the U.N. side, the American team, with bitter memories of the 1945 forced repatriation of many of their POWS into the vengeful hands of the Soviet Russians, demanded choice. Recalling the procedure followed at the end of the previous war, President Harry S. Truman was firm in his position that this was not to be done this time. Held hostage in this extended wrangle were the Americans and their allies in North Korea prison camps, while the same condition existed for U.N. prisoners.[346]

As has been seen, from the point of capture, the U.N. POWs experienced long and brutal marches north. The Chinese eventually established eight permanent camps along the Yalu, far from the front lines, which was a major factor in preventing any Americans from escaping from them.[347]

More than 3,000 U.S. POWs died in the first nine months of captivity; these estimates need to be seen in the context of the 8,000 missing in action total.[348] Spencer Tucker estimates that 99 percent of those who died did so in the first year of captivity.[349] William Funchess has a vivid memory of the fatalities at that time: "I saw the piles of bodies. They were stacked like cordwood. The stacks were three to four feet high and often 30 or 40 yards long." Punishment for infractions could be severe. One POW was put in a shower in the middle of winter and kept there until he began to freeze. The guards "waited too long to take him out, because he lost both feet to frostbite and gangrene."[350]

In January 1951 Chinese administrators consolidated four camps into one of 3,500 prisoners at Pyoktong. Two doctors had to deal with mounting medical problems. One of these, Sidney Esensten, recalled that initially, "We didn't have any medicine, food, heat or shelter" to deal with disease and illness— beriberi, pellagra, pneumonia, dysentery, and hysteria, to name a few. The lack of drugs made aspirin "worth more than gold." The resulting soaring death rate was largely due to vitamin deficiency and inadequate food, with the youngest POWs dying first. Improvisation was the order of the day: surgical instruments were forged out of the metal arches of combat boots, wire was used to treat disjointed wrists, ripped-up undershirts served as bandages. Adding to the staggering death toll were the brutal physical punishments imposed by guards, a common one being to tie hands high around the back then hoist the body off the ground. In the face of these horrific conditions, Chinese efforts at indoctrination seemed ludicrous: the POW response to these efforts, Esensten recalled, was, "You really don't want us to stay alive. Look how many men are dying."[351]

A chaplain who stands out in the memory of those who were in the Pyoktong camp was Father Emil Kapaun, who was credited with saving "hundreds of lives—dozens on battle fields, hundreds in the camps by stealing food, making pots to boil water, picking lice out of armpits" of diseased inmates (Bill Funchess recalled the lice could become so thick there that they would bleed a man to death in three days). He arrived in Korea with the First Cavalry Division in July 1950 and was captured in November. All the while he preached hope and forgiveness. Kapaun died in captivity in November 1951.[352]

The Chinese separated their captives on the basis of rank and race. Having thus divided the POWs into different categories and removed the discipline of rank for enlisted men, they set to work to gain their consent if not indoctrinate them.[353] Larry Zellers, who observed the pattern of Chinese manipulation, declared that it was unfair to compare the conduct of professional officers with that of young, immature draftees.[354]

James Thompson recalled that in his camp white non-commissioned officers insisted that black NCOs be housed with them. Thompson assumed that the white sergeants wanted "to keep an eye on us." He said that their Chinese captors often sought to stir up racial conflict among the POWs. For example, a few blacks would be called into a room, then platters of food would be brought in from the outside; remarks made by whites about blacks and vice versa were passed along in distorted form. Their efforts were fruitless. In Thompson's view, "The Chinese were artists at blending fact and fiction to their own advantage. However, one thing they kept misreading was the American spirit. Given all the ills America has, we, as a people become one family when put upon by an outside common foe."[355]

The total of African American POWs can be estimated at about 1,000, and the Communist staff made it a point to stress the injustices faced by this group in America. Jerry Morgan, for one, was not impressed by this appeal: at a "group session" he commented, "Hobos and bums eating out of garbage cans back in the States live better than these Chinese." Through greater group cohesion and more difficult life experiences, blacks had a survival rate that exceeded that of whites. In his camp, James Thompson said, blacks agreed not to pick up cigarette butts discarded by guards, who, he said, respected the blacks for their self-control. Many of them adopted a casual attitude, mixed in with lively talk and gales of laughter, which were disconcerting to their guards.[356] Drawing on a background of religion in rural black churches, they also formed choirs. There also was a little-known "Golden Cross" organization among blacks, which was designed to bolster patriotism and morale.[357]

Turkish prisoners were also singled out by their Chinese captors. Appeals were made to Turks to join forces with the other people of oppressed minorities in the world, but with negligible effect. A major limitation was the lack of Turkish interpreters. Rejecting all blandishments and disobeying camp regulations, John Thornton declared that the Turks "were engaged in a war of their own and their goal was simple. If they were to be in captivity, it would be on *their* terms to the fullest extent possible."[358] They not only retained unit discipline but they vigorously scavenged any plant life, no matter how small, out of which they brewed a "weed tea," containing traces of vital vitamins and minerals. Their example was followed by others. As a result of all these factors, the Turks had the best survival rate on any group.[359]

Other POWs followed the Turkish example in weed consumption, with dramatic results. In Gene Lam's camp everyone had severe beriberi, until weed eating quickly cured the disease.[360] The Turks also knew that garlic could deal with tape worms, as Donald Slagle found out: "I traded my boots to a Turk for two balls of garlic and ate it all. That's what got rid of my worms and helped to save my life. I pulled out some of the worms with my hands. Some were six to eight inches long and one quarter inch in diameter." In addition, the Turks freely provided their unique knowledge of massage, which had excellent effect, as James Thompson recalled.[361]

British POWs also had a better survival rate than did Americans. The apparent reason for this was the strong allegiance and cohesion provided by their identity with their regiment, in which discipline was combined with a commitment to all of its members. At least some British POWs were shocked by the lack of comradeship, not to say discipline, among U.S. prisoners. When some American enlisted men refused to carry litters of disabled soldiers, a British sergeant major exploded: "I've always hated you God-damned Yanks but I never knew why until now. You won't even carry your own wounded."[362]

American soldiers were under orders that upon capture they were to reveal only name, rank and serial number. How unrealistic a mandate this was became clear to Nick Tosques in his first interrogation. Having repeated the three basic statements, Tosques saw that they would not be enough: "But you can say that for only so long. You see some of the other guys getting hit in the back or the kidneys with a rifle butt, and hit hard, and you start thinking about what else you can say without really telling them anything." He remembered "a lot of interrogation sessions, but I don't think anybody actually told them very much."[363]

Donald Elliott recalls Jim O'Boyle, who after being captured by Chinese soldiers in May 1951 after three days was sent across American lines ("keep going"), whereupon O'Boyle was given a rifle and sent to the front, then was recaptured. He died in a POW camp in February 1952.[364]

Relying on a dubious U.S. Army report after the war, David Rees has declared that among U.S. POWs there was a "collapse of morale," but provides no substantial evidence for this sweeping claim. The Chinese divided the POWs on the basis of the willingness of the captors to give at least nominal interest in the indoctrination that was forced on them. Thus, there were a small number (perhaps 5–10 percent) of "progressives" (who gave at least lip service to the Communist line), a large majority who remained indifferent or neutral and a small group of "reactionaries" (perhaps 10 percent), who overtly rejected the Chinese attempt to force their ideology on their prisoners.[365]

Among those who were in the "progressive" category, apparently the great majority just played along with the Chinese attempts to win them over to communism. This paid important dividends: better food slipped in, release from demanding labor and the promise of early release — the last happening to at least one group in 1951. The "progressives" were obvious by their better weight and health.[366] Some of them argued that their pretense made it better for the POWs, but this element often faced physical attack by some other POWs.[367] The "progressive" Claude Batchelor, who later went to China, is credited with getting medicine from the Chinese for sick POWs.[368] One POW recalled in an initial lecture being harangued by "a half dozen brainwashed POWs who made odd-sounding speeches, using all the same words the Communists used."[369] The POWs were broken into small "discussion" sessions, often presided over by Chinese mentors who spoke perfect English, some of them being graduates of American universities.[370] When their Chinese captors eventually (in November 1951) made it clear to some of the "progressives" that they could not anticipate early release, the reaction was that the Chinese had "not carried out their part of the bargain." At this point, a few of them attempted to reverse course, telling their fellow POWs that they had seen the light, were no longer deceived by the ChinComs, etc.[371] These efforts almost always failed. When the release of sick and wounded prisoners took place (the Little Switch) in April 1953, it was a source of anger in more than one camp when perfectly healthy "progressives" was released while severely wounded were not.[372] At least a few POWs feigned illness to get released.[373]

There also was another category called "rats," a small number who informed to the Chinese. The Chinese sometimes tried to give the impression that this practice was widespread. One POW recalled being called to camp headquarters for no apparent reason, which suggested to his fellow inmates that he was passing along some kind of information. Due to extreme hostility by some other POWs, including beatings, the "rat" element was housed separately in at least one camp.[374] There, POW Wayne Simpson put those in this category as low as 1 percent.[375] With one possible exception, none of the "progressives" were "rats." Donald Legay remembers that those who cooperated with their captors were called "number one boys," who got "extra privileges like not having to do any work," and that after the Chinese abandoned compulsory attendance at lectures "some of the fellows kept on going though — some of the number one boys."[376] Anthony Farrar-Hockley recalled that after he joined with three others in his officer compound in careful and secretive preparation of an escape attempt, they were arrested on the eve of the operation. Was there an informer or had the guards observed the preparations?[377]

The final group of POWs was the "reactionaries" (sometimes called "tigers" by their fellow POWs), who resisted any cooperation with their captors. This hardy group was about 5 percent. To deal with these opponents the Chinese usually separated them from the rest of the prisoners.[378] While a prisoner a Marine corporal talked about escaping; the words were passed on by an informer, with the result that the Marine spent ten days in "the Hole" without food.[379] A notable example of a "reactionary" was Ranger Sgt. Marvin Watson, whose plane was shot down in March 1951 while on a covert operation. Watson's determined opposition to the camp authorities extended to organizing a demonstration against the pending arrival of a British communist speaker. As a result of his obstreperous behavior, Watson was the very last POW released under the terms of the armistice in July 1953. Lloyd Pate records instances in the march north where POWs nudged guards over cliffs and American truck drivers assured maximum damage to their vehicles. Once in camp some of the hard cases made efforts to obstruct the prison regimen. Moving along a road, members of Pate's platoon, for at least a time, implanted nails in the ground resulting in repeated punctures of truck tires. More importantly, Pate's coterie of "reactionaries" urged other POWs not to cooperative with their captors, applying physical force in some cases.[380]

There was another small number of POWs who took advantage of their situations to steal food from their fellows, strip the dying of clothing and boots, or sell food intended for starving inmates. Due largely to the craving of some for marijuana and tobacco, Richard Bassett recalled having to keep close watch on personal items, even clothes left out to dry. These relatively rare actions later formed the basis of the many charges made about the conduct of some of the POWs made by other POWs upon their release.[381] After the full exchange of prisoners in 1953 only eleven (of fourteen charged) of the most notorious of these offenders were convicted and given long prison sentences, such as at Fort Leavenworth. As he had promised himself and the offender, Lloyd Pate provided testimony at a court martial that convicted an individual of manslaughter and collaboration, for which he received life imprisonment.[382] At least in some camps a sad situation arose among those prisoners who gambled away their food and tobacco rations, with the winners eagerly checking mess halls to get their extra meals, skimpy as they were. The resulting lack of food among gambling addicts increased the death toll.[383]

Hunger, illness and death were the realities of the mass of POWs during the time of North Korean control. Stripped of first aid kits and any kind of medicine, one of the first effects of vitamin deprivation was night blindness.[384] Philip Crosbie remembered the deplorable lack of medical care: "Those 'hospitals' were hovels where sick prisoners shed the last remnants of their morale. Half-naked, lice-ridden, blanket-less, the starving skeletons lay on the floor awaiting death. Dysentery patients staggered out, while they could still walk, to latrines in the arctic cold."[385] The camp commander, known as "The Tiger," claimed that all the health problems could be addressed by fresh air and exercise. From a rostrum, he led daily exercises before the POWs who were almost all clad merely in the remains of the summer uniforms they had been wearing at the time of their capture. "Those early morning parades in the November cold," Larry Zellers recalled, "were death sentences for many."[386] There were cases where Chinese guards showed consideration for their captives. James DeLong recalls that Epsom salts, provided by Chinese guards in his camp, cured dysentery, while William Funchess says the guards suggested the successful remedy for diarrhea was eating charcoal.[387]

Food was the principal weapon employed by the Chinese, but they also employed other methods.[388] For propaganda purposes the Chinese occasionally would parade some healthy (and cooperative) prisoners for the edification of Communist and friendly journalists.[389] One of these was Monica Felton, a very left-wing English activist, who, on her second visit to Korea, gave a lecture in at least one of the camps and offered to deliver mail. Her anti–American diatribes (along with those of Hewlitt Johnson, the "Red Dean" of Canterbury Cathedral) were available for prisoner reading.[390] Among others who addressed the POWs was *Daily Worker* correspondent Michael Shapiro, a British communist woman named Quinn, and an Australian communist man. After visiting North Korea in March 1952, London solicitor Jack Gaster asserted that POWs received more meat and fats "than anyone in Britain receives from a ration book."[391] Richard Bassett recalls seeing a middle-aged white woman (Monica Felton?) being rapidly escorted through a prison compound while British soldiers hurled abuse at her. The adamantly pro-communist journalist Australian Wilfred Burchett visited POW camps in Chinese army uniform and described them as like "holiday resorts in Switzerland," saying claims about ill-treatment were "all lies." Along with Alan Winnington of the London *Daily Worker*, he is credited with urging, indeed pressuring, the captives to sign confessions, helping them to prepare such statements, and threatening those who did not cooperate. In his interview with captured general William Dean, Burchett revealed his allegiance, referring to the Communist forces as "we" and "our side." Photographs of a fit Dean, living in isolation, Burchett claimed, had the result that "the propaganda line about massacres and ill-treatment of US prisoners was torn to tatters."[392]

In his last autobiography, he briefly acknowledges that he talked with two air force men who claimed they had taken part in spreading germs, but that is all. Rather, he claimed he was helpful to American journalists covering the extended armistice negotiations. He went on to further journalistic ventures in Vietnam, then retired to Bulgaria.[393]

A small number of POWs, almost entirely due to pressure and desire to survive, participated in overt propaganda efforts — writing testimonies, signing a peace appeal to the United Nations, participating in a "Central Peace Committee" and recording radio broadcasts.[394] The statement provided by Frank Noel, a captured Associated Press photographer, extolled the food, facilities, services and medical care to such an extent that, if true, would have tempted non–POWs to migrate to the camps.[395] With the assistance of communist journalists and the consent of the North Korean government (but without the knowledge of the U.S. military), a couple of his Associated Press colleagues sent Noel a camera at the end of 1952 and he began transmitting via radiotelegraph pictures of POWs with their names and home addresses. The AP journalists involved thought it was a "great scoop" for their organization, but when combined with his totally unbalanced statement about POW conditions and his Communist-censored photographs, Noel had assisted the Communist line in the matter of American POWs. Some of his happy POW photographs appeared in a communist publication. When Noel was released he quickly declared that his actions had been coerced.[396]

Eventually — in 1952 — the Chinese administration allowed POWs to participate in sports, which most POWs welcomed. Despite the Chinese forbidding such activity and the total lack of materials, POWs organized classes in a variety of subjects, including mathematics, science and languages; some of them staged theatrical productions.[397] The Chinese in 1952 went so far as to organize an "Inter-Camp POW Olympics" which was given appropriate coverage in the Communist press.[398] Based on articles apparently written in captivity by a few POWs, after the war Peking's New World Press produced a volume of glowing recollections of POW experiences — smiling Chinese soldiers greeting captured Americans, good food and medical care, full recreational facilities.[399] Dallas Mossman remembers occasional softball games and ping-pong matches.[400]

At one point the administrators of the camp in which Bill Funchess was resident decided to stage a peace march. Inmates, now in new blue fatigues, were provided with a can of beef for every three of them — to be collected after the demonstration. With hidden cameras to record the event, banners and pennants were provided. The POWs spoiled this effort by dragging the banners on the ground, distorting their uniforms and slumping and staggering along, in response to which the Chinese guards, "mad as hornets," removed the cans of beef. No further attempt to stage a similar event was made in this camp.[401]

Those Americans who were captured in November 1950 in North Korea remained in captivity for two and a half years. One of these was soldier James DeLong, who recalls that, rather than being cooped up in one camp, his group of POWs often were moved from place to place, covering an estimated distance of two thousand miles. The repeated long marches undoubtedly served to show the North Korean population how successful the Peoples' Army was. DeLong's contingent was a work group, hauling supplies of all sorts, including bags of rice, which allowed for irregular acquisition of a bit more food. In addition, his group was subjected to the usual Communist indoctrination, but each was provided with a small Christmas present in 1950 — two cigarettes. About two years later (as an armistice loomed) a sugar and tobacco ration was added.[402] Dallas Mossman was also a long-term prisoner, having been captured in early 1951. Because he was badly wounded, his Chinese captors provided him with a fifteen-year-old boy to help him on his trek. An unusual feature of his captivity was flamenco music played by Juan Gusman on a guitar bought by their Chinese guards. He also recalls that twenty POWs were killed when their camp was bombed by American planes. It was a long time before his camp was marked by some form of red and white roof signs.[403]

A form of solace was provided with the discovery by Turkish prisoners that marijuana grew wild in Korea. Access to the bush was provided by frequent sorties to collect wood for fires.[404] Robert MacLean was adamant in claiming the beneficial use of the drug — it helped stimulate the appetite of some who were refusing to eat and it washed away Chinese efforts at brainwashing. Wilfred Ruff also saw the positive effects of marijuana use: "Let me tell you, that helped keep us alive." Some Chinese guards were bewildered by the behavior of some of the users of the "weed" but, according to one source, never discovered from where the effects derived. Harry Spiller says that in three camps as many as 30 percent of the prisoners used the drug and that Chinese controllers "made unsuccessful attempts to stop the use of the drug."[405] This was in keeping with the Communist effort to stamp out opium addiction in China when they took over the country in 1949. It was Richard Bassett's experience that addiction to marijuana and tobacco resulted in constant minor theft among prisoners, while Jim Crosbie recalled that the drug use created a sense of relief and relaxation to the point that "you'd never know we were in a POW camp." The Chinese opposition to drug use was ruefully recalled by James Thompson. One Chinese instructor declared that China had earlier been consumed in self-defeat by the use of drugs and dope, and that would happened to America: "First drugs will rip through your universities and colleges. It will destroy minds of bright students.... Then, drugs and dope will reach down into secondary schools. When that happens ... and it will ... your America will experience a revolution. Kids will rise up against authority." Many years later, observing the toll taken by drug addiction, Thompson remembered this prediction and joined in a drug education program in Detroit.[406]

Of the 7,245 American POWs, 2,806 died in captivity, about 38 percent of the total. In the widely anticipated period leading up to the exchange of prisoners, the Chinese made belated efforts to "fatten up" the POWs in an attempt to cover up their harsh treatment of them.[407] As a practical health requirement, they demanded that all POWs boil water before drinking it.[408]

When negotiations seem to be heading to agreement, the food improved and new clothing and blankets were issued; when the negotiations were broken off or stalemated, the food declined and the uniforms and blankets were withdrawn.[409] Probably due to the fact that James DeLong's POW group did a lot of marching and heavy labor, their shredded footwear was replaced with Chinese sneakers.[410]

U.S. Air Force flyers were given escape kits to evade capture, but 263 of them were apprehended.[411] The Chinese gave special attention to these, culminating in a series of signed confessions that the air crews had participated in germ warfare in North Korea. Because these statements obviously were coerced, no one on the American side gave them any weight. The whole "germ warfare" hoax was an apparent effort of the Communists to shift attention from the hunger and disease suffered by many North Korean civilians, as well as to divert attention from the idea that prisoners be allowed to choose if they wanted repatriation.[412] After the 1953 armistice, fifteen American airmen convicted of intruding into Chinese air space remained in prison until 1955.[413]

A unique form of diversion for POWs located near "MiG Alley" in the northeast corner of North Korea was to watch the air combat between American and Chinese planes.[414] Donald Legay remembered this experience: "The Commies kept telling us how many Sabres they were shooting down, but they never told us their MiG losses. One day we saw a MiG hit the dirt just a little ways away. The pilot went down with it and we cheered like hell. The guards were mad, but they didn't do anything."[415] Nick Tosques recalls another reaction from the guards: "The guards would come running up, waving their rifles and yelling at us not to cheer or they'd shoot us."[416]

Strangely, no effort was made by the air force to in any way contact the POWs until the day before the truce came into effect, when some U.S. planes came over flapping their wings, which did demonstrate that the air force knew where the camps were located.[417] Did the air force consider even dropping a small supply of vitally needed drugs for the dying prisoners? As one of them said, even if a plane had wagged its wings, the POWs would have got a boost from that. With all of its flights along the Yalu, the air force must have had a good idea where most of the camps were located, although American planes, obviously believing they were attacking Chinese installations, occasionally strafed POW camps; in one episode twenty POWs were killed. While recovering from wounds, Billy Gaddy recalled, "When the Americans bombed the area, I fought for my life in a mountainside foxhole without any food or water."[418]

In the air force's 700-plus page history of its involvement in the war, there is not a word about the plight of the several thousand POWs whose camps were regularly overflown by U.S. planes.[419] But the air force did know they were there: John Thornton recalled that when the armistice terms were finally

Five UN POWs released by Chinese, February 10, 1951. Left to right: Private First Class Robert B. Duncan, Private First Class Joseph A. Collins, Corporal Lawrence Buckland, Lieutenant Angus MacDonald, and 1st Lieutenant George E. Dowrie. Courtesy Truman Library 207-473.

agreed to in July 1953, a B-29 flew over his camp, dropping leaflets announcing the event.[420]

The POWs did receive occasional attention from the Far East Command's Liaison Command. When a report in August 1951 suggested that Gen. William Dean was being held with an undetermined number of other prisoners at a POW camp about forty miles northeast of Pyongyang, a rescue plan was developed, with new, bigger H-19 helicopters. A reconnaissance B-26 was shot down over the site, however, after which Dean was quickly moved to an unknown location and the operation was canceled. A sabotage operation, whose secondary mission was to locate a POW camp, was put into operation in January 1952. This also met with failure, with all sixteen of the agents being either killed or captured.[421] Did this, or any other U.S. organization, consider doing something to help the POWs? There was an unusual episode recorded by William Funchess which indicates that some effort was made — an unsuccessful effort at assassination of the hated camp commander, General Deng, by a lone gunman dressed in white firing from a nearby hill.[422]

Chinese prison officials claimed that the almost total lack of medical supplies was due to U.S. air interdiction, but all of the POW camps were lined up close to the Yalu, almost in sight of safe Manchuria.[423] What was occasionally provided were strange medical practices, such as sewing a chicken gizzard or liver in an infected limb, and the removal of a testicle of a dying POW.[424] The Communists refused the International Red Cross (which they viewed as a capitalist organization) the opportunity to inspect the camps and obstructed its attempts to send in vitally-needed drugs.[425] Philip Deane, an English journalist internee, saw masses of loaded trucks pouring across the Yalu and considered how much a case of desperately needed medicine would have helped the dying POWS, but Billy Gaddy was fortunate in receiving a massive dose of penicillin, captured from American supplies, which saved his leg from being amputated.[426]

Chinese officials expressed surprise that American soldiers had not been subjected to psychological conditioning to deal with what they might encounter in enemy hands. Despite this, the crude, forced efforts of the Chinese at indoctrination were almost wholly ineffective, despite the resources and personnel the Chinese devoted to this project. Apparently the principal obstacle to this effort was the firmly-held set of shared popular values of American soldiers, beyond class, ethnicity or race; obviously, they believed in the promise if not the current fulfillment of the American future, rather than the claims of Asian zealots about "pie in the sky" communism. This situation prevailed despite the fact that the average POW was only 21 years of age, with most of the young group being recent draftees. William L. White has commented of this group: "In no sense were they yet soldiers."[427]

All POWs initially were required to attend long lectures on communist theory and history, with several of them being conducted by Anna Suh, formerly a Christian missionary who became well known as "Sue City Sue" of Pyongyang radio fame. The lecturers were followed by group "discussions" often led by POW monitors and requiring detailed note taking, with inmate notebooks being reviewed by their captors.[428] Soldier Donald Barton recalls the experience: "In the camps we were subjected to political indoctrination on the beauties of life in the Soviet Union. We usually agreed the Russians had it made. Agreement meant our rations weren't cut."[429] According to Nick Tosques, at least in some of study sessions in their huts, little attention was paid to the finer points of communism: "We'd put one guy on watch and then we'd talk about anything *but* communism. What kind of car did you drive? Do you have any girlfriends?"[430] While being watched by his Chinese group tutor, John Thornton recalled being called upon to comment on Karl Marx's *The Decay of Capitalism*, whereupon he recited "Casey at the Bat," much to the confusion and ultimate anger of his tutor.[431] POWs also were urged to write articles denouncing American capitalist excesses, while a small group of them were forced to make broadcasts, with about 250 of the recordings being transmitted by Radio Pyongyang and Radio Peking.[432]

By the spring of 1951 Chinese officials in charge of this program obviously assumed their efforts were having some effect, as a group of apparent "progressives" were released near American lines, which they crossed on May 24. Chinese general Du Ping claimed that there were several releases of small number of POWs; he recalls one release, "on the Has," of some POWs, but does not say when this happened, although it was probably at the end of 1950 or very early in 1951.[433] On the May occasion, of the 134 released there were forty-one Americans, five British, three Australians and eighty-three South Korean soldiers. Ping was told that those about to be released observed "a sharp contrast between the Volunteer's lenient treatment and the Americans and ROKs crimes." After a "special dinner and a send-off party," the releasees said "they would never again be cannon fodder for Wall Street's big shots and for Syngman Rhee after their return."[434]

At length, the Chinese, concluding that civilian prisoners were interfering with indoctrination efforts, barred them from attending the lectures or even talking with the military prisoners. The authorities had difficulty getting GIs to attend, requiring guards to round up prisoners.[435] Wadie Roundtree recalls that the Chinese gave up their indoctrination efforts in the spring of 1952, while Lloyd Pate remembers that in the following August the Chinese gave up on mass indoctrination, concentrating their efforts on the "progressives."[436]

What brought about this change, in part, was a refusal, in March 1952, of a compound of four hundred sergeants to participate in the program. Donald Barton believes the change came about when POWs "began to recover some of their physical strength and gathered courage to argue with the Chinese."[437] The Chinese administration then declared that the program would be voluntary, with obvious benefits for those who continued, some out of interest in the subjects, others out of self-interest and others to deal with prison boredom.[438] In one camp "progressives" were provided with a "private clubhouse" for their deliberations; in another camp known informers were kept out of reach of their fellows by having them gather in the library which was the only building with a twenty-four-hour guard.[439]

After the Chinese had effectively given up on forced indoctrination, they focused on harsh control. Camp infractions led to courts-martial with the verdict invariably being "guilty," followed by extended terms of hard labor.[440]

The whole threat of indoctrination worried at least one U.S. agency. In February 1952 the State Department commented on the possible subversive effect this group might have upon their return to America. With the exchange of lists of prisoners in December 1951, the Communist captors, obviously concerned about further large-scale deaths of POWs, improved the food and care of its prisoners.[441] When the truce was announced in Richard Bassett's camp it was met with general jubilation,[442] while in William Funchess's one a different scenario was played out: the Chinese, for the first and only time, played some jazz music through the loudspeaker system; the announcement itself was met by no overt response by the prisoners, much to the obvious surprise of a gathering of Communist journalists and photographers. Funchess recalled, "We did not want to give the Chinese any satisfaction at all."[443]

This was in contrast to the announcement of the death of Stalin in April which was met by cheers by the bulk of POWs, much to the anger of their Chinese guardians. There was a different response from some of the "progressives," one of whom burst into tears when he heard the news, while a group of them in one camp sent a letter of condolence to Moscow.[444]

When a full exchange of prisoners began in August 1953 of the 4,439 Americans survivors, only 21 (in addition to one Briton and 367 Koreans), most of whom were informers to the Chinese, chose not to return. This tiny number formed the basis of extended journalistic treatment, which led to self-righteous assertions about extensive collaborations by many POWs. From there, the process turned to partisan, outlandish and insulting claims about the lack of moral fiber, etc., among the soldiers who served in Korea.[445] Without any evidence, one "historian" claimed that 20 percent of them had been seriously influenced by Red propaganda.[446]

As provided by the terms of the July 1953 armistice, POWs who declined to accept repatriation had an opportunity to consider the matter during a ninety-day period in the "Neutral Zone." Agents from both sides appealed to those involved to return home. The Communists only had twenty-three Americans who refused repatriation and during that period, as before, they offered this group a variety of inducements to stay on their side. The Chinese spokesmen informed them that many of the "progressives" who were in the process of returning to the United States would help pave the way for a revolution already taking shape. After a five-year period of study in China, the twenty-three would be ready to become leaders in this movement.[447] The Communist-controlled World Peace Conference in 1952 had produced an account by "progressives" of American POW experiences. In 1955 three of these edited a book, *Thinking Soldiers*, in which they justified their decision. Two of the twenty-three decided they had had enough of Lenin, Stalin and Mao and decided to return to the United States. The others did go to China, studied and married there, then trickled back to the United States over a period of several years, where they lived quietly and certainly not as Communist revolutionaries.[448]

The Communists held back a hard core of oppositionists for several weeks after other POWs had been released. James Thompson said he was one (and the only black) of thirty-three in this group.[449] Another "reactionary," William Funchess, who earlier had heatedly rejected the Chinese claim that American soldiers had been responsible for the killing of Communist civilians and their families at Anak, had been threatened with being charged as a war criminal and had been subjected to enticements by the American "turncoats," was held to the very last day: September 6.[450] Another group was not released at all.

Although for years the Chinese and Russian governments denied this, a small number (probably about 20–30) of air force prisoners with knowledge of advanced U.S. planes were transported to the Soviet Union. After the collapse of communism, in 1993 a joint U.S.-Russian commission concluded this had taken place.[451]

Upon their release the ex–POWs generally were greeted with open arms by American officers, although Richard Bassett recalled that an officer did not return his salute, which Bassett took to mean that the POWs were viewed with suspicion by at least some people. Some returnees were offered sumptuous meals—steaks, ice cream, anything they wanted—wholly inappropriate for half-starved men. Nick Tosques recalled that his stomach had shrunk so much he could only get down a couple of spoonfuls of food.[452] John Thornton initially just settled for ice cream and a cigar, but did notice the healthy, well-fed appearance of the Chinese and North Koreans heading the other way.[453] Wilfred Ruff found that even coffee and doughnuts sickened him.[454] Others recalled that they were given simple meals they could tolerate.[455] What soon followed was a series of psychology tests.

While being shipped back to the United States, apparently most were segregated from other soldiers as well as by race.[456] Wilfred Ruff, however, recalled his group of POWs were mixed in with other returning soldiers, who could not understand their weakened condition: "They laughed at us a lot. There was talk. As weak as we were, we got into fights with them." Ruff dismissed these antagonists as "punchy young kids who hadn't seen any fighting."[457]

Returning to the States with some ex–POWs, Arthur Smith was told that there were men among them who had helped the enemy. When he asked what they were going to do to them, he was told, "Nothing. They'll have to live with it."[458] Dallas Mossman had a completely different experience of how collaborators were dealt with. In his ship this element was put in protective custody to prevent them from being thrown overboard. On Richard Bassett's ship there was an informal kangaroo court dealing with informers, resulting in several beatings, requiring the intervention of the military police. In one instance an offender later was tracked down and beaten.[459]

All of the released POWs were subjected to what appeared to be ludicrous interrogations by members of the Counter-Intelligence Corps, psychologists and others like them.[460] Eugene Inman recalls these people were fully employed "picking our brains" on the return voyage. A few ex–POWS were detained due to medical and mental problems, but upon arrival the mass of them were provided with good food, new uniforms and appropriate decorations, and sent on leave. Some of them recall that they were told not to talk to civilians about their POW experiences. Richard Bassett recalls signing a statement that he would not disclose "military information" about his time as a POW, which could be interpreted to mean just about anything.[461] For some ex–POWs these stipulations had the effect of internalizing their prison experiences. Combined with the lack of prompt counseling, this situation led for many to long-term mental problems.

Recalling the desire of journalists to hear "atrocity" accounts, John Dille said that the few returnees he talked to declared that they had not been mistreated.[462] Based on interviews, 500 of the ex–POWs made complaints about some of their fellow internees, but almost all of these were about selfish and malicious behavior, not collaboration with their captors.[463] After a lengthy process, 82 of them were recommended for court martial by the army; fourteen were brought to trial, with eleven convictions. Despite harsh original sentences for some enlisted men, upon review all of them were reduced and all were released in a decade.[464] Although few of their members had been POWs, none of the other services pursued legal action against their members. Like other veterans, the former prisoners could avail of treatment at Veterans Administration facilities, but there were no specific programs for them.

Two years after the POWs' return the army put out a flawed report that claimed "large numbers" of the ex–POWs had been collaborators.[465] There were lingering suspicions about some of them, and they were covertly watched by the CIC and the FBI for years afterwards, but none of them were found to be communist sympathizers, undercover Reds or anything like that. Richard Basset, for one, was affronted: "It was terrible. We were all under suspicion." Others experienced the same thing. Herbert Brownell, who was attorney general at the time, later said, "FBI chief J. Edgar Hoover mounted a vast surveillance campaign on returned POWs, fearing 'Manchurian Candidates'" (indoctrinated undercover agents for the Reds). Communist moles and plots had to be found elsewhere; over time, some of these turned out to be in the FBI and the Central Intelligence Agency.[466]

After interrogating the ex–POWs, and despite dubious and misleading claims put out by the army, little more than a handful were found guilty of anything. Lewis Carlson's conclusion: "Only 3/10 of one percent of the surviving POWs were convicted of a collaborative or treasonous offense."[467] The most succinct rebuttal of the claims about soft POWs, etc., is provided by H.H. Wubben in an article in the *American Quarterly*, but as few people were familiar with such scholarly work, these claims continued to be tossed around for many years in such places as barroom gatherings. The whole episode was a matter of blaming the victim. A similar pattern was followed by the army in Vietnam twenty years later.[468]

A little noted aspect concerning POWs was the 75,000 South Korean prisoners, of whom only 11,559 were returned. The Communist negotiators claimed that almost all of the other 65,000 had been "re-educated" and "released at the front"— that is, incorporated into the North Korean Army — while others had died in captivity.[469] The great majority of the captured South Koreans, termed "liberated warriors," were put to work in construction projects of various sorts.[470] Charges have been made, however, that many of these were simply kept as prisoners after the war and were scattered around "the remotest corners of North Korea." Similarly, the one-third of the Chinese POWs who elected to return to mainland China, for allowing themselves to be captured, were subjected to occupational disabilities and, particularly during the hysterics of the "Great Cultural Revolution," extended interrogations.[471]

Back Home

The outbreak of the Korean War and the widescale intervention of American forces was greeted initially with public dismay in the United States. In an unfortunate phrase, President Truman termed this development a police action, but as the conflict unfolded it was seen as a desperate rear-guard operation to stop the North Korean invasion. Public opinion and political commentators were strongly in favor of this intervention, and the success in holding the Pusan Perimeter followed by the sensational Inchon operation were viewed by the public with relief and satisfaction. The invasion of North Korea also appeared to the general public as another successful venture and, as in Korea itself, was seen as a prelude to success and the end of a conflict that had lasted only five months. According to a Gallup poll, 68 percent of respondents favored going all the way into North Korea.[472]

In an effort to maintain a nonpartisan posture about the war in the November 1950 congressional elections, President Truman did not campaign nor did he urge voters to elect Democratic candidates who uniformly supported the war effort. On the other hand, Truman's October trip to Wake Island to confer with Douglas MacArthur was viewed by many Republicans, as well as by MacArthur, as an effort to boost Truman's public standing, which would be of benefit to embattled Democratic candidates. Some Republican leaders declared that the Thomas Dewey–led fiasco of two years before had too soft a tone; now there was a need for a brass-knuckle campaign. A widely used Republican poster declared the election was about "Communism, Corruption and Korea." As was the case in almost all off-year elections, the opposition party did well, but this time there were very substantial Republican gains. It should be remembered, however, that based on their 1948 successes the Democrats continued to control Congress, but that situation marked the end of the social and economic goals of Truman's "Fair Deal" program, which included medical coverage for all Americans.

With television just spreading, the war was extensively reported in newspapers and on radio news, with over three hundred journalists from various countries arriving on the scene. William Lawrence of the *New York Times* had an interesting experience at the beginning of the Korean conflict. Reporting on a Democratic primary (effectively all-white) for U.S. senator in South Carolina, in which the two principal candidates competed with each other as champions of racial segregation, he shortly found himself in Tokyo where he viewed wounded U.S. soldiers, black and white, coming off hospital planes. No segregation there. Lawrence commented on the scene: "Here they were united in the bond of sacrifice, suffering and fighting in a battle so that some yellow men could rule themselves. It was a far cry from the ranting of Johnston and Thurmond on the theme that only white men were fit to rule and that Negroes must always play a subordinate role to white master."[473]

In Korea, at first there were only self-administered restrictions on what the journalists reported. MacArthur, forgetting the tight control he imposed during the late Pacific war, declared that censorship was "abhorrent" in a free society. Soon a variety of pressures were brought to bear on reporters who appeared too critical of the operations of the military high command. Two journalists were temporarily stripped of their press accreditation on charges of giving aid and comfort to the enemy. When Chinese intervention turned the conflict upside down, however, strict press censorship was imposed in January 1951. These restrictions excluded not only some reports of military operations, but also writing that could injure the morale of U.N. forces, or embarrass the United States, its allies or neutral countries. Press censorship was imposed by Tokyo's intelligence organization whose head, Charles Willoughby, often objected to what he saw as "inaccurate, biased and petulant" reportage. After MacArthur and Willoughby left the scene, censorship was moved to the public relations staff and restrictions applied only to matters of "security," but there were widely varying definitions of what constituted security.

There were times when reporters' relationships with soldiers could be mutually raw and disdainful.[474] Very late in the conflict, Richard Holmsten together with two other soldiers were dragooned into being interviewed by a bright young thing from the *New York Times* seeking to hear the views of those in the enlisted reserve. She got a earful on a variety of subjects, centering on army ineptitude — issuing summer clothing in December, RHIP (rank has its privileges), etc. — which did not suit her intended purpose of hearing of the high morale and determined opposition to communism that she sought. After being misdirected, she defecated in an officer's tent and huffed off to seek more amenable sources.[475] Much more seriously, one restriction obviously remained: as in World War II, no photographs of dead Americans were to appear in the press.

While U.N. forces were rapidly closing towards the Yalu in the autumn of 1950, many people saw the end of the conflict in sight. This was to the advantage of the Truman administration and, conversely, undermined the hardly veiled charges of Republican opponents about being soft on communism. The thunderous Chinese intervention and the rapid retreat of the American army, however, quickly created a climate of fear at home. A more rapid change from the anticipation of victory to the reality of a disastrous retreat is hard to imagine. Further reports of defeat poured in. One hair-raising account, among several, of brutal Chinese treatment of wounded Americans caught up in the retreat from the Changjin (Chosin) Reservoir was related by one of the survivors: the "Chinese threw about ten or more into a truck, some naked, some still alive, threw blankets and gasoline over them and set them afire."[476] Richard Johnston reported in the *New York Times* (Dec. 3, 1950) on the flight from Pyongyang, with the headline reading, "Roads from Front Recall the Bulge; Confusion, Tragedy and Cold Mark Retreat in Korea, as in the Ardennes."[477] In the dark days of December 1950 Truman declared a national emergency, which appeared to give him power to control military production, but when a steel workers' strike arose his action in seizing control of the steel industry was declared to be unconstitutional by the Supreme Court. Military disaster found an echo across the Atlantic with "very great" concern about the situation being reported in the British press.[478]

The extent of public alarm about the turnabout in Korea was voiced by Hanson Baldwin, the noted military journalist of the *New York Times*, who wrote in the December 1 edition this alarming statement: "The United States faces today the greatest danger in our history." Basing his conclusions on thousands of miles of just-completed travel through northern Asia, he declared, "Military, economic and political destruction of Western civilization and of our American way of life are definite possibilities if the danger from the East is not met boldly, imaginatively and with united effort." As a result of the information he gathered in his travels, he commented, "Americans in the Orient who were cognizant of the carefully planned strategy of the Chinese Reds" and the close military backing of the Soviet Union "have been amazed in recent weeks not only by the mistaken estimates in Tokyo but by the wishful thinking and unrealistic patter of some of the discussions in Washington and at Lake Success" (then the location of the United Nations organization). Those directly involved in the conflict, he declared, saw things differently: "To our troops in Korea fighting in some of the most terrible country in the world against the overwhelming manpower of the Orient the United States seemed to be living in a kind of 'never-never-land.'" He attributed the disaster in North Korea to the action of Douglas MacArthur, who "altering prior plans" drove close to the Manchurian frontier instead of stopping at the Sinaju-Songjin line "along which it had been expected we would hold our advance." The result, he said, was that "today we are involved in precisely the type of war which we can never win, a land struggle on the Asiatic continent in a theatre where no decision is possible against the hordes of Asia."

Baldwin was a prophet: the sad truth is that the United States would continue to butt its head against the Great Wall of Asia; Western civilization was for the West, while Asia was for the Asians, as the Japanese claimed in the previous war.

MacArthur's role in the Korean debacle drew justification from an unusual quarter. Henry Van Dusen, president of the Union Theological Seminary, wrote a letter that was prominently displayed in the *New York Times* (Dec. 12, 1950) in which he argued that, although "MacArthur and his staff were guilty of a grave error in judgment which brought the Chinese Communist hordes upon us," the failure was primarily a political one. There had been the assumption, principally fostered by Owen Latimore and others of his ilk in the State Department, that "Chinese Communism was basically different from Soviet Communism." His conclusion: "If blame must be placed, let us lodge it where it belongs—in the first place, upon these professed 'experts' who misread and misreported the character of Chinese communism ... then upon the leaders of Government who accepted their advice ... but most of all upon ourselves, who surrendered to the illusions of wishful thinking, and now take refuge in the easy device of scape goating."

With the rapid retreat of American forces alarm bells rang loudly at home. After the initial Chinese assault against the Eighth Army at the end of November and early December, that army rapidly retreated to the 38th parallel, outrunning the Chinese troops for ten days. To the east the Marine Division had conducted a fighting withdrawal which drew the X Corps back to the relative safety of the coastal plain and Hungnam by December 10. At this point the U.N. forces had 300,000 soldiers, complete air and naval supremacy and mountains of equipment and other supplies along its front. Worse defeats, however, were real possibilities or were anticipated. It was in this context that President Truman on December 15 made an alarming and unnerving national address in which he declared, "Our homes, our nation, all the things we believe in are in great danger." He declared a "national emergency," the ramifications of which were unclear. Truman's speech did nothing to rally support for the war effort, but did send a shiver of fear through the country.[479] His defeated presidential rival, Governor Thomas E. Dewey, followed suit: "For the first time since the very early days of our nation we face the genuine possibility of an attack upon our homeland by a foreign enemy."[480]

Congress had reinstated the draft in June, but now former Secretary of War Robert Patterson advocated the immediate draft of all eighteen-year-old males for two years of military service, with no deferments for college students and the elimination of "fantastic standards" for inductees. "There was only one chance of avoiding a war of world dimensions," he proclaimed, and that lay in greatly strengthening the country's military power as well as abandoning the practice of excusing and rationalizing the sinister purposes of communist China and Russia. Employing academically correct language, Patterson's proposal was endorsed by the Association of American Universities.[481]

In its first year the Korean War resulted in a tripling of the size of the army (from 593,000 to more than 1.5 million), with major increases in numbers in the other services. Now the numbers games began — who was to go to war and who was not. These matters were addressed by local draft boards, in which political influence played a role. With the outbreak of the conflict a recommendation of the draft advisory board allowed deferments for "superior" college students, with further exemption "if their training and capabilities were of use elsewhere in the defense program" (which could mean just about any job). That effectively pushed many young men beyond the draft age. The convoluted draft system gave deferment to any college student who did anything more than face expulsion for academic failure. A controversial intelligence test kept many students in college.[482] Others exempted were many farmers and, for some reason, fathers. By January 1953 1.4 million fathers had been deferred. Thirteen thousand students a month were able to turn temporary deferments into permanent exemptions by becoming fathers until this loophole was closed in August 1953, a few weeks after the conflict ended.[483]

The threat of the draft motivated many young men to join the air force or the navy. For example, there was a huge surge of enlistments in the relatively safe air force.[484] Thus, the effect of the government policy was war for the working class and others like them or, in the case of the enlisted reserve, young men being yanked out of jobs and college to serve in the colors. Despite this situation, its clear inequities did not rouse significant public opposition.[485] If you could get a college-related deferment, then you probably would not be called up until the shooting was over.

The implementation of troop rotation for those serving in Korea surely helped to divert attention from this situation. Another factor was that many of those who were drafted were sent to Europe to strengthen the United States' commitment to NATO. By 1952, the U.S. military totaled 3.7 million; so many people were being drafted that the army could not handle all of them and draft calls were reduced in early 1951. All told, 75 percent of the draft-age cohort served in the military, while two-thirds of the others were 4-F, lacking in necessary mental and physical qualities, while a smaller percentage with student deferments avoided military service by going to graduate school.[486]

Oscar Ewing, Federal Security Administrator, proposed that high schools incorporate military training in their curricula. A logical next step would be to extend this program to primary schools, like the Nazis and Communists did. Two members of the draft board in Wolf Point, Montana, gained a moment of fame when they declared they would no longer participate in the draft process "until the atomic bomb was used in Korea."[487] Strangely enough, unlike what happened during the Vietnam conflict, there was almost a complete lack of popular opposition to the draft or to U.S. involvement in Korea. There were small anti-war demonstrations in San Francisco and Chicago in 1951 and 1952.[488]

With a largely stalemated battlefront and long, drawn-out truce negotiations, Chinese Communist leaders anticipated that a growing public warweariness would lead to a demand for the United States to get out of Korea. Its policy of protracted war, it believed, was having this effect on the American people. As early as June 1951 Marshal Peng saw the emergence of a major "peace movement" in the United States, but this did not achieve widespread support.[489] One of the reasons it did not was most likely due to the massive number of deferments from military service. Another reason might be that, with the American military buildup in western Europe, not as many servicemen were sent to Korea and the war didn't last long; for many of them their time in Korea could be as short as one year, with those in combat leaving after nine months.[490] In one instance, political influence allowed an army draftee to be stationed in Japan rather than in Korea, his reward being an ear infection that lasted a lifetime.[491] James Brady recalls that one Marine, through political influence, left his troop ship at Japan.[492]

Swiftly responding to the grim mentality sweeping the country, a half dozen senators proposed that their chamber establish an "Un-American" investigative committee, which, of course, would compete with the House body in the hunt for subversives. Reds under the bed must have been frightened, but the proposal went no further.[493]

Adding fuel to the fire was Truman's apparently blustering suggestion that atomic weapons might be employed in Korea. This was one of the reasons that British prime minister Clement Atlee made a hurried visit to Washington, although this was not decisive.[494] To bring pressure on the Chinese, atomic bombs were loaded on B-29 bombers in Guam, for movement to Okinawa, where, if need be, they could fly to targets in Korea. In the fall of 1951 four simulated bomber flights (without the bombs), Operation Hudson Harbor, were conducted. The air force concluded that with few concentrations of enemy the employment of atomic bombs was operationally unsound.[495]

In any case, the Truman administration was determined to use atomic weapons only in the most extreme circumstances, such as the possibility of American forces being totally overwhelmed or driven out of Korea. In the Philippines, which had a tiny contingent in the U.N. effort in Korea and was dealing with a violent communist movement itself, President Elpidio Quirino warned, "Mankind is facing its most desperate hour"; moreover, "Any chance spark that passes the vigilance of the world's most responsible leaders may ignite the explosion that can blow us to dust." In a little observed note of reassurance, on December 4 a flight of U.S. Air Force jet planes "roared over Formosa ... cheering Chinese Nationalists depressed over the Korean situation."[496] Given the Korean hatred engendered by the just-ended Japanese occupation of their country, it would seem preposterous that the Japanese government saw the need to announce that it would not allow any young men to volunteer to serve in the U.N. effort in Korea.

As the impact of Korea hit home, quickly advocates of major efforts for civil defense shouted their message. Some House members advocated giving the president sweeping powers in this matter, including the creation of the Federal Civil Defense Administration and greatly increased federal money for state programs. Another effort at reassurance or alarm can be seen in the photograph appearing in many newspapers under the heading "Atom Bomb Jets Now Shown in Production," of jet bomber production at the Boeing plant at Wichita, Kansas. There was a flood of newspaper accounts of how city and state government officials were responding, with most of them centering on planning for major bombing attacks and evacuations. New York City was seeking 500,000 civil defense volunteers, with a statewide defense alert following. Similar manifestations took place nationwide. One alarming report declared that if the deluge came large cities would not allow the evacuation of persons involved in vital military production.[497]

Prominent clergymen entered the fray. Henry Knox Sherrill pondered the use of the atomic bomb. The presiding bishop of the Episcopal Church and now president of the newly-formed National Council of Churches of Christ, Sherrill declared that he opposed using nuclear weapons in "holy" or preventive war, but that they could be used in response to an atomic attack on this country, a position in accord with the conclusions of "a group of Protestant theologians." Jesuit Edmund Walsh, vice president of Georgetown University, argued that using the atomic bomb would be morally justified if the country was on the verge of being attacked.[498] Rising to the occasion, the leaders of the four largest veterans' organizations urged President Truman to grant General MacArthur "full authority" to use any means to protect U.S. troops in Korea, charging that many GIs had died because of the "imposed limitations which have prevented them from fighting on equal terms with the Communist aggressors."[499]

One way that the American public could support the war effort was by donating blood, which was in increasingly short supply in Korea. An advertising campaign soon followed. According to Steven Casey, there was a massive response to this need. He further noted, "It also helped to sell the war." Despite partisan charges to the contrary, the overall death rate was far below that of previous wars. This, military spokesmen asserted, was "almost entirely due to plasma and whole blood." Forward medical facilities (MASH units) also were a factor in this achievement.[500]

It was in the midst of this period of widespread public alarm as Chinese forces drove to the line with South Korea that thirteen Asian and Middle Eastern governments, not involved in the war, proposed ending the conflict along the 38th parallel, the point of origin. This effort was led by India, with its prime minister Pandit Nehru advocating not only negotiations to stop the fighting but also an attempt to deal with the matter of Formosa, noting that any resolution of these issues would not "have any particular value unless China was associated with it." Both President Truman and the visiting British prime minister supported the idea of negotiations.[501] To give this effort any hope of success the U.N. General Assembly invited representatives of Communist China to attend. After a leisurely ten-day trip to New York, Wu

Hsiu-chuan, the head of the delegation, declared that a necessary precondition to any settlement was the removal of foreign troops from both Korea and Formosa. For his part, Syngman Rhee declared that he would never accept any continuing Communist control in North Korea and mistakenly believed that the U.N. forces had created an "impregnable" defense line above Seoul.[502]

So ended this unrealistic attempt to end the fighting. When the victorious U.S. forces pursued the beaten North Korean military across the 38th parallel, Red China warned that it would intervene and it did, at its own time and place. This delayed entry led American intelligence to assume that this meant the "Chincoms" would not do this (oblivious to Sun Tzu's doctrine that two key factors in military operations are deception and surprise). Now that the U.S. and South Korean forces were being driven back, they wanted to call off the chase. Just as the Americans could not resist plunging north, now the Chinese could not, and would not, fail to attempt to build on their on their achievement and drive south. The opportunity to further defeat and humiliate the world's leading imperialist nation was too great to resist.

Hanson Baldwin returned to the Korean situation in an article on December 6, declaring, "The dangerous alternatives of another Munich or an Oriental Dunkerque loomed yesterday as the Korean crisis darkened." He repeated his advice that if the Chinese could not be stopped, Red bases in Manchuria should be bombed, but he rejected the use of atomic bombs. No longer subjected to press censorship, three journalists returning from Korea painted the darkest possible picture. Writing and lecturing beginning in January 1951 both Hal Boyle and Don Whitehead judged that the Eighth Army faced further defeat, while Jim Lucas believed that army would be forced out of Korea in six weeks.[503] The Far East Command kept a tight rein on the press in its theatre, reportedly expelling a dozen journalists during the first year of the war. When the editor of the *Stars and Stripes* allowed the reproduction of a photograph of General William Dean in North Korean captivity, MacArthur had him removed. As was the case in World War II, no photographs of dead American soldiers were published. MacArthur was, however, quick to claim success, sometimes prematurely and inaccurately, an example being the capture of Seoul in September. When the U.N. effort deteriorated, formal press censorship was imposed on December 20, 1950, to be followed up on March 16, 1951, by news clearance not only by the Eighth Army but also by the Far East Command.[504] Edwin Hoyt claims that this propensity "drove a wedge between the news reporters and the military."[505]

How to turn back the Red Menace in Korea? There was the advice of Hanson Baldwin: the bombing of the "privileged sanctuary" of Manchuria if only to slow down Communist reinforcements, combined with a naval blockade of the China coast. This course of action was being actively promoted by Douglas MacArthur, obviously keen to blot out the stain of an astounding military defeat. MacArthur's gloomy prognostications about the future course of the war if his advice was not heeded were soon to be contradicted by the remarkable recovery of the Eighth Army under the leadership of Matthew Ridgway, which, when combined with the mass of soldiers and Marines withdrawn from the Hungnam enclave of the northeast coast, beginning in early 1951 successfully pushed the Communist forces back to and above the 38th parallel. But with mounting casualties and a need for more troops, draft requirements doubled (from 40,000 to 80,000 a month) between the autumn and the end of 1950, with the total of those drafted or about to be "called to the colors" totaling 450,000 since the beginning of the war.[506]

The Truman administration had decided against a wider war and when MacArthur insistently advocated attacks on China, Harry Truman removed him in April 1951. MacArthur's removal came at the end of a series of clearly insubordinate acts by the general. There were administration officials who had urged this step earlier, but David Halberstam surely is right when he declares that MacArthur possessed such prestige these people were "more afraid of him than they wanted to admit." This, he says, "was always the great secret of the Korean War."[507] Harry Truman, however, was not afraid of him. The great majority of journalists in the Far East agreed with Truman's decision,[508] but that was not the apparent response in the United States.

What followed MacArthur's removal can best be described as an alarming but brief episode of public hysteria or mass suggestion. Quickly flying back to this country, after an absence of fifteen years, the five-star general was greeted by massive, cheering crowds. Speaking before a joint session of Congress, MacArthur employed his rhetorical ability in providing his perspective on the Korean conflict. This was received with even more public approbation. It is arguable that had the Korean episode ended with the unification of Korea, that is, before the Chinese intervention, MacArthur would have been elected president in 1952. The extended Senate hearings that followed his oration, however, showed the unanimous opposition of the Joint Chiefs of Staff to his proposals. A nationwide speaking tour (during which he still wore his uniform) began the process of tempering public support, and by early 1952 he was reduced to keeping to his free accommodation in the Waldorf Astoria tower block, where one of his neighbors was Herbert Hoover. Perhaps they reminisced about MacArthur's action against the "Bonus marchers" in 1932. (At that time, MacArthur insisted that staffer Dwight Eisenhower be in uniform when Doug sailed out to confront the veterans, who he said were "animated by the essence of revolution.")[509] He became a supporter of Robert A. Taft for the presidential nomination and as the keynote speaker at the 1952 Republican convention presented an anticlimactic address: although he included barbs against big government, etc., most people had heard the gist of his message several times already. His efforts did nothing to prevent the nomination of his old subordinate D.D. Eisenhower.[510]

So what was all the public excitement about and why did it so rapidly subside? Many people grasped the opportunity to honor the famous old general and to shout cries of patriotic emotion, but that was all. Most Americans, when they thought about it, were not prepared to support a wider war. For many it was enough to blame Harry Truman for the whole thing, and even after preliminary negotiations for a cease-fire began in the summer of 1951 to bemoan the bitter taste of the last dregs of this war. At least for the first two years of the conflict, U.S. public opinion supported the war effort. For its 1951 selection of the "man of the year," *Time* magazine (January 1, 1951) chose the "American fighting man."

Now gradually fading away, as he claimed to anticipate, MacArthur's judgment became increasingly questionable. At a chance meeting, he told Henry Cabot Lodge in 1953 that Syngman Rhee would shortly be overthrown. But this condition probably was not something new: during his 1951–1952 speaking tour he made increasingly serious charges against the Truman administration's Korean policy.[511] The retired five-star general was invited to the Eisenhower White House — once. His *Reminiscences* lacked any insight or broader view of his life and times: it was the world according to MacArthur.

The bumpy course of the war, including the firing of MacArthur, turned public opinion against the Truman administration. This was beneficial to the Republicans, who once again sought to regain control of the presidency after an absence of twenty years. Mindful of their surprising and devastating defeat in 1948, they had to proceed carefully. While criticizing the conduct of the war, as well as attacking on issues such as political corruption, inflation, communist subversion and whatever else they could think of, they did not generally embrace MacArthur's proposals for a wider war. Beyond doubt, however, the MacArthur controversy was seen as evidence of disarray within the government about what to do about Korea. After a few outraged cries for the impeachment of Harry Truman for getting rid of MacArthur, the Republican congressional leadership decided it was best to center its acrimony on Secretary of State Dean Acheson, and on the eve of his departure for a major European security conference put forward a resolution demanding his removal. Truman ignored this effort.[512]

Given his conservative politics and prickly personality, it is unlikely that Senator Robert A. Taft could have led his party to success in the looming presidential election. A unifying figure, indeed an ideal candidate, was found in the person of Dwight Eisenhower, World War II "hero" and current commander of the North Atlantic Treaty Organization. Hugely experienced in military matters and long experienced in bureaucratic infighting in the army, yet seen as a man above party politics, the publicly affable Ike had not been part of the backbiting partisanship of Washington and bore no responsibility for the misfortunes of the Korean conflict. In regard to Korea, all he had to do was amplify public discontent about the course of the conflict. He topped this off late in the campaign with a purely grandstanding declaration that if elected,

"I will go to Korea." He had already concluded that the war needed to be ended as it stood, so his short "inspection" tour of Korea (for seventy-two hours) was a public relations exercise at its emptiest.

Taking a dim view of Eisenhower's announcement, which he saw as "pure show biz," Omar Bradley, noting that Eisenhower already was fully informed about the Korean situation, later declared that Ike could achieve nothing by going to Korea, nor did he. Given the prevailing political climate in the country, even without this gesture Eisenhower's election in 1952 seemed almost preordained.[513]

The Chinese government anticipated that Eisenhower would likely intensify U.S. involvement to force closure to the conflict. Aware of the fact that he had commanded the largest amphibious action ever at Normandy in 1944, Mao and company were concerned that a repeat of this enterprise was likely, centering on the west coast leading to Pyongyang. Major defense activity took place along that coast, but Eisenhower pursued other means to force a truce, employing vague threats of nuclear bombardment, including the use of an atomic cannon, which was tested in the Nevada desert in May 1953, and later deployed in Korea, but never fired there.[514]

Obviously getting caught up in the apparent spirit of the time, during his short-lived employment on the staff of the Senate Permanent Investigations Committee, chaired by Senator Joseph McCarthy, young Robert Kennedy conducted his sole investigation that dealt with relations with some of the United States' allies. Based on his investigation, conducted during the spring of 1953, Kennedy concluded that "fourteen owners of eighty-two ships flying flags of U.S. allies were trading with Communist China." He wrongly concluded that British-owned vessels were transporting Chinese troops. At first, McCarthy publicly deplored this activity by the nation's allies, but, under pressure from the new Eisenhower administration, specifically Vice President Richard Nixon, he let the matter drop.[515]

Second only to "Irene, Goodnight," the only other popular song to emerge from the Korean War period was, appropriately, "Dear John," produced just after the truce of 1953 (not the Hank Williams song with a different message of 1951) which was clearly set in the Korean episode. Hollywood did not have time to crank out heroic movies about the conflict when things went bad in Korea. There were a couple of low-budget films—*Steel Helmet* and *Fixed Bayonets* (both 1951) and *Retreat, Hell* (1953)—but any others set in Korea came after the war ended. In a quickly forgotten 1954 production, *Prisoner of War*, B-movie actor Ronald Reagan played the part of an army doctor who parachuted into a POW camp in North Korea to see what was happening there. *M*A*S*H* (1970) was a film that portrayed emergency field surgery as an occasion for fun and sex. In all of these films the Korean people were almost nonexistent or, at best, extras for crowd scenes.[516] *The Manchurian Candidate*, released in 1962, was a thriller that related how diabolical Commies had succeeded in brainwashing a few American POWs with long-term disastrous effects, which reinforced in the popular mind the belief that this kind of thing had taken place. It hadn't, but for many people, what they see in the movies or on television they take to be at least close to the true state of affairs.[517]

As part of the armistice agreement finally signed in July 1953 came the release of prisoners of war. Here was another opportunity for the critics of the war to weigh in. In the process, the army was perfectly willing to deflect public disappointment about its outcome by blaming the soldiers, including the POWs, for the result. This was in keeping with a general desire of fearmongers and other super-patriots to discredit the war and its warriors. This perception affected many military men who served there; their honorable, demanding service was now seen by many of them as having been futile and even disreputable.[518]

Although the Defense Department rejected this assertion, Major William Mayer, a psychiatrist, claimed that one-third of POWs had been affected by Communist indoctrination. In what had to be viewed as an official capacity, Mayer spread this message in a nationwide speaking tour as well as in tape recordings of his speeches. His efforts were to eventually find reward with a military patronage appointment in the Reagan administration. Among those who knew him, he was credited with being an effective public speaker, but also as being unstable, unreliable, deceitful, manipulative, publicity-hungry and more. In a book published in 1959, Mayer was joined by journalist Eugene Kinkead with the same assertions, who made the suggestion that POWs under enemy interrogation should simply remain silent.[519]

While they were carrying forth their message, national figures such as Lewis Hershey, head of Selective Service, J. Edgar Hoover, fake-combat veteran and alcoholic Joseph R. McCarthy and others declared that American young men had become soft, self-absorbed, unpatriotic and more. President Eisenhower commented on "the sad record of Americans in Korea." But he said people should show forgiveness to those affected, which lent support to the claims that many prisoners had gone wrong. In his history of the U.S. Army published in 1967, Russell Weighley agrees with this position, without providing any specifics, declaring that some American POWs "behaved badly"; he explained that this was the case among young newly captured soldiers, but argued that the situation was substantially rectified by the addition of mature, combat-experienced captives.[520] The whole controversy rambled on within the context of charges and sometimes evidence of communist penetration of the U.S. government — at least in the recent past.

Having first peddled its charges, the army now claimed it was carrying out a major study of the experiences of the POWs, but what emerged in its 1955 report were confused and ambivalent statements about the matter. Two years later the social scientist Albert Biderman, after exhaustive research in military records, totally refuted Mayer's accusations. Notwithstanding these studious findings of the academician, the mighty blasts of the platform patriots and media "exposés" took root in the minds of many Americans, reinforced by the likes of all-round military critic David Hackworth, who as late as 1989 claimed that during the war many American POWs ratted on and stole the food of their fellow inmates or allowed themselves to be used for propaganda purposes. He asserted that 43 percent of them collaborated in some manner, basing this claim on an obscure army report.[521]

Raw partisan politics overlaid the narrative of the Korean War and its aftermath. The long, drawn-out truce negotiations along with limited combat in a stalemated battlefield greatly reduced public interest in what was happening in Korea, but a reading of the daily press shows that the conflict received significant continuing coverage. With a few exceptions, returning veterans of that war were not greeted with victory parades and the like, and were spared the patriotic effusions of barroom orators at the local Legion post. Yet Curtis Morrow recalled that when his troopship arrived in San Francisco in mid–1952 the soldiers were greeted with an outpouring of public acclaim. When he returned to his hometown he was hailed as a war hero.[522] Richard Holmsten was on a 3,000-man troopship arriving at Seattle after the armistice: there were "small craft speeding by, people waving, shouting. On the pier the band played again, 'Stars and Stripes Forever,' 'When Johnny Comes Marching Home.'"[523]

The most exceptional return trip from Korea took place in April 1953 when a troopship with 2,600 soldiers aboard set sail on a 10,000-mile, 26-day voyage, first stopping in Colombia to release Colombian soldiers, with another brief stop at the Panama Canal (which featured a major brawl with the navy's shore patrol, with an SP station wagon being pushed off the dock), another at Puerto Rico for offloading soldiers from there, and culminating with arrival at New York to be greeted by a fire boat shooting water on high and blaring fog horns. During a brief period of guarantee the soldiers were provided with an all-star show of Broadway performers, presided over by Ed Sullivan, followed by a cross–Manhattan truck convoy to a reception with the mayor.[524] The ship in which Allen Wilkinson returned was given a lively reception in San Francisco, but in a cross-country jaunt Wilkinson found many people who shared his negative views about the whole war.[525] Although often not greeted as war heroes, there were several other veterans who recalled that they were warmly received when they returned and not just by their families and neighbors.

Most Korean veterans came back individually, and, due to the rotation system, at different times, not in units, and surely most were just happy to be home and left it at that. By law, they were war veterans, with the benefits that went with that status, although the educational provision in the Korean War Bill of Rights was about 75 percent of that provided for World War II veterans.[526]

The fact that not many Korea veterans took advantage of the educational benefits, contrary to Paul Edwards, is not evidence that they had a negative view of their military service. Unlike those who served in the "Big One," a majority of those who served in Korea only were there for a year, so their military service was a relatively minor rather than a major disruption of their lives. Few of them joined existing veterans organizations, but that was also true of those who served in World War II and, later, in Vietnam.[527] Max Hastings overstates the case when he declares, "Many United Nations veterans came home from Korea to discover that their experience was of no interest whatsoever to their fellow countrymen."[528] This may be true of his fellow Britons, but only a handful of them were in Korea; 95 percent of non–Koreans who served in Korea were Americans. A couple of anecdotes by American returnees do not make the case for his assertion. It would be extremely unlikely that a returned soldier did not receive regard and respect from his family, friends and neighbors. As well, there are numerous examples that soldiers returning from Korea did receive appreciative welcomes. John Thornton, ex–POW, certainly received a lively reception when he returned to his home in Philadelphia, complete with motorcade and police escort.[529] It was also the case that most combat veterans, including POWs, as in other wars, did not want to talk about their experiences— at least frequently and at length.

There is no evidence that the servicemen were greeted with the hostility or abuse with which some soldiers returning from Vietnam had to contend. Moreover, the claim that the Vietnam veterans sometimes were spat upon is a myth, largely perpetrated by draft-dodgers who drew upon themselves the cloak of ideological opponents of what was transpiring in Vietnam, as well as opposition to other aspects of American life.[530] It took half a century before the Korean War received public recognition in the form of a Korean War memorial in the capital of the United States of America.

The varying public perception of the Korean affair found a variety of expressions, but rarely was the matter dealt with as in the experience of Charles Brown. Hitchhiking across the country with an army buddy, he encountered a highway patrolman who wanted to know what they were doing. When informed that they were soldiers returning from Korea, the patrolman responded, "Oh, that police action!" to be met with the reply, "Yes, for a police action there are a lot of dead cops." Hugely offended (and probably guilty-minded), the cop issued an order: "Get out of my state!"[531]

The ending of the fighting in Korea brought a new concern to U.S. military leaders: not only was there the continued communist demand for Formosa (was the Seventh Fleet going to remain permanently on patrol?), but there was the anticipation that the Chinese would greatly increase their support for the communist-led campaign in adjoining Vietnam. Korea was a dead end as far as communist expansion was concerned, but Eisenhower believed that communist victory in Vietnam probably would lead to communist control of the rest of Indochina and southeast Asia as well. U.S. military aid to the French forces there had been expanded since the beginning of the Korean War, but was now further increased. The Chinese followed suit, with expanded political support, weapons and training facilities in southern China, but did not intervene directly. In 1953 and 1954 the position of the French and their Vietnamese allies declined drastically, leading to the crisis at the isolated fortress of Diem Bien Phu. The call of the French military for at least U.S. Air Force involvement to save the day was not responded to (although some disguised CIA planes did fly in supplies). Even as Eisenhower pondered the matter, he was told that the congressional Democratic leadership, recalling Republican abuse heaped on their party for similar action in Korea, opposed the venture. He also concluded that any direct American participation would likely meet with similar response by the Chinese. Just the next year, however, being able to utilize its naval power, the United States got directly involved in preventing the Chinese Communists from seizing a couple of islands directly on its coast, an action which was repeated in 1958–1959. Communist occupation of these small coastal bits in itself was of no strategic importance, but the Republican administration, after all that had gone before, could not be seen as being weak on communism. The aftermath of the Korean conflict had long legs.[532]

CHAPTER FOUR

Peninsula War, International Consequences

China Confronts America

Whatever else happened in Korea, the American and South Korean military did frustrate the ultimate ambition of Mao Zedong. According to Chang and Halliday, Mao was not content merely to drive the Americans out of North Korea but wanted them out of the whole country. As the conflict wore on Mao obviously raised his bet, with large increases in troops and new equipment. When Peng Dehuai proposed stopping at the 38th parallel, Mao said no. With the U.S. Air Force pounding the towns and infrastructure in the north to bits, Kim Il Sung in early 1952 urged a stop to the conflict, but Mao again was opposed. When truce negotiations began in June 1951 the fact that they were extended over two years was largely due to Chinese intransigence, principally over the issue of repatriation (with many Chinese and Koreans opposed to returning to Communist lands), but also due to their belief that protracted warfare would wear down U.S. commitment.[1] In a plea to Stalin in December 1952 for more military equipment as well as arms-producing factories, Mao offered to subsidize the North Korean government for three years.[2]

Mao's long-term goal apparently was to get atomic weapons, and in this he ultimately succeeded. Newly inaugurated President Dwight Eisenhower suggested, on February 2, 1953, that the United States might use atomic weapons to force an ending to the fighting in Korea (and in May field-tested an atomic cannon at Los Alamos).[3] Mao responded by asking Stalin for nuclear weapon capacity; the short message was, give me the Bomb, so that you will not be drawn into a nuclear war with America. Stalin did not want to give the Chinese the Bomb and undoubtedly with this mind decided to end the war in Korea, which precluded the transfer of nuclear capacity to Peking. This decision, which immediately preceded Stalin's death in early March 1953, was carried forward by the new Russian leaders, who informed their Chinese allies of this decision on March 21. China continued its effort to get Russian cooperation in its A-bomb quest, which required close relations with the Soviet Union and huge exports of foodstuffs to such a degree that China experienced periodic famines. Once China later got the Bomb, however, differences with the Soviet Union soon grew to open hostility.[4]

The conflict was presented by the Chinese as essentially ideological, but surely there were also deep-rooted ethnic and cultural factors involved. Dean Acheson's aspiration, if not expectation, of a break in Sino-Russian relations had eventually come to pass, but not before a bloody Sino-American confrontation.[5]

In his study published in 1963, Tang Tsou has argued that, even without the Korean war, Red China and the United States were bound to come into conflict. This was, Tsou declared, due to "the ideological component in Peking's foreign policy and the quest for greatness which had always been deeply imbedded in Chinese history and culture, and which was reactivated by a revived sense of power and unity after a century of humiliation and defeat." Moreover, Tsuo believed, "The revolutionary and national interests of an awakened China under Communist leadership clashed sharply with the American policy of containment and with American efforts to bolster non-Communist regimes in Asia." The brawl in Korea greatly magnified this collision: it "precipitated this emergent international configuration and added to the equation of power new political and emotional factors which otherwise would not have existed." The American interposition in Formosa and the United States move across the 38th parallel were enough to lead to a head-on clash in wintry North Korea, which, to say the least, "basically altered Sino-American relations."[6]

In his pursuit of total victory the cost in lives and resources experienced by Communist China seemed to be of little importance to Chairman Mao and his supporters, but by any objective measurement it was substantial.[7] Mao recognized that the Chinese action in Korea had been costly. In 1952 he declared, "Last year what we spent on the war to resist U.S. aggression and aid Korea more or less equaled our expenditures for national construction."[8]

Even before its involvement in Korea had ended the Chinese communist regime began supporting the communist-led uprising against French control of Vietnam. This began when the first units of the People's Liberation Army arrived on the Vietnamese border in early 1949, and was followed by Beijing's diplomatic recognition of the Democratic Republic of Vietnam in January 1950. Throughout 1952, while armistice negotiations dragged on, the Truman administration and its military leaders anticipated that the Chinese would greatly increase their support for their communist allies in Vietnam, even to the point of direct intervention. The ending of the fighting in Korea in July 1953 allowed the Chinese to do just that. To meet this challenge the United

States hugely expanded its financial and military support for the faltering French forces there, while it contemplated joint action with Britain, France and Australia, including warning China to stay out. There were general discussions about bombing Chinese cities if the Chinese came in, but these were tempered by the reality of a huge expansion in Chinese air power. Furthermore, although China was supporting the growing Viet Minh revolt in Vietnam (Bradley estimated that there were 10,000 Chinese military providing assistance), it had no need to directly intervene. Additionally, if the British military had conducted bombing against Chinese cities, its valuable colony Hong Kong could have seen swiftly seized by the Chinese.[9]

Meanwhile, the Chinese expedition in Korea had plenty of problems. Demonstrating a lack of concern by the Chinese leadership, clothing and footwear were totally inadequate for winter conditions, the result being wholesale disability from frostbite among Chinese infantry.[10] There were the recurring matters of supply shortages of all sorts, the constant interdiction of supply routes by the U.S. Air Force and the need for massive reinforcement of soldiers.[11] Many of the weapons supplied by the Russians were old and worn.[12] As the war went on, Soviet aid was reluctantly provided, and had to be paid for — in the form of badly-needed agricultural exports. A lot of the Chinese ammunition was defective. Morale declined: large-scale Chinese surrenders began in 1952.[13] There were frequent episodes of deserters marauding along the Yalu border.[14] Despite these problems, by that year the Chinese built up a military force of 1.2 million troops, together with a growing air force, which it could not tactically deploy initially due to the inability to provide aviation fuel or trained pilots. Efforts to build air bases in North Korea in 1951 were abandoned when the Chinese realized these were becoming prime targets of American bombers.[15] As well, there were chronic problems with relations with Korean civilians.[16] To meet the demands of North Korean leader Kim Il Sung that Communist forces regain the 38th parallel and to strengthen the Communist position in pending negotiations, Peng Dehuai made plans to launch a new massive offensive that, after delay and indecision, was precluded by the armistice of July 1953.[17] The huge costs and meager results of its Korean intervention brought about evidence of Chinese domestic discontent, which became an increasing source of concern to the Communist leadership.[18]

Cease Fire

In anticipation of the cease fire of July 27, 1953, Chinese frontline soldiers, obviously stimulated by propaganda personnel, made enthusiastic preparations. When the day, or rather, the night, arrived, some Chinese soldiers, dancing and singing, waved lighted candles, flashlights, banners and posters, the basic message being that they were celebrating the conclusion of a difficult but successful campaign.[19] For them the threat of death or mutilation had ended. Search lights from both sides lit up the night, which soldier Norman String found to be a strange experience after fighting in dark nights for months.[20] On one contested hill a Chinese loudspeaker invited the troops opposite to join in singing "My Old Kentucky Home." There were several Communist invitations to "come over and talk as brothers." A few American soldiers responded, only to face courts martial for "fraternizing with the enemy."[21]

Marine Martin Russ remembers the evening of the cease fire: "At 10 P.M. the hills were illuminated by the light of many flares; white star clusters, red flares, yellow flares and other pyrotechnics signifying the end of the thirty-seven month battle that nobody won and which both sides lost." The setting was certainly evocative:

> A beautiful full moon hung low in the sky like a Chinese lantern. Men appeared along the trench, some of them had shed their helmets and field jackets. The first sound we heard was a shrill group of voices, calling from the Chinese positions behind the cemetery on Chongum-ni. The Chinese were singing. A hundred yards or so down the trench someone began shouting the Marine Corps hymn at the top of his lungs. Others joined in.

Then the finale: "The men from outpost Ava began to straggle back, carrying heavy loads. Later in the night a group of Chinese strolled over to the base of Ava and left candy and handkerchiefs as gifts. The men that were still on Ava stared, nothing more."[22] The same threat to them also had ended.

A nineteen-year-old South Korean soldier was at the front to see the end. H.K. Shinn recalled the event:

> Suddenly artillery duels stopped and the entire region became deadly silent. It felt eerie not knowing what to do next. The following day we saw hundreds, perhaps thousands, of Chinese soldiers emerging from the underground tunnels on the hillside opposite our positions. I could not imagine that for so long we had been facing such a frightfully large number of enemy soldiers just a few hundred yards away.[23]

The scene that greeted Marine Robert Hall the morning after the beginning of cease fire provided a vivid memory: "At earliest light the troops came up out of the ground to look. At first we stood in the trenches. Then some climbed up to the forward edges, then to the tops of the bunkers, for a better look. It was unheard of—standing in the open in daylight. An incredible feeling.... Just the simple, natural act of standing erect in the sunshine." The soldiers in Paul Leyva's company would not believe that at last the fighting had ended until "a trailer truck showed up filled with hundreds of cases of beer." In a similar situation a soldier was digging a bunker on top of a hill when Major John Eisenhower climbed up the slope to tell him the armistice had gone into effect and cases of beer were in the valley below. The soldier told Eisenhower he did not drink and was not interested in carrying up the cases for the other members of his squad who had been lying around while he dug the bunker.[24]

Artilleryman Richard Holmsten also was on hand for the event: "Peace had come to Korea. Ironically, our army estimated that the Chinese had lost 72,000 men during the month of July, more than 25,000 of those killed in action." He looked at the result: "What a waste. Peace talks and death, hand in hand, as if one was impossible without the other. And how many of our boys had died? We didn't know or weren't told. But now it was over. Both sides could weep for their dead."[25]

Maxwell Taylor had a different kind of experience of that happening. Flying down to section of the front early the next morning, he saw that "the Communist troops were already out in force, standing on their battered hilltops, waving flags and banners bearing Communist slogans and shouting songs of defiance and victory." He believed the demonstrations he witnessed were designed to impress "the world that they were the victors and we the anguished — a reminder that for them the conflict had not ended with the shooting. Our men watched this propaganda display in silence, merely glad that the ordeal of battle was over."[26]

American POWs in North Korea were informed of this development. When Richard Bassett's company got the good news it was met there was general jubilation. A different scenario was played out in James DeLong's camp: 600 POWs were marched out to a soccer field where the news of the armistice was met with total silence, which puzzled their Chinese captors. The POWs had anticipated that the truce was near, but they did not want to give their guardians the satisfaction of seeing their American guests celebrating the event.[27]

Strategies and Outcomes

The People's Republic of Korea, the Communist government of Kim Il Sung, had a simple strategy for uniting Korea: blitzkrieg — a massive attack to achieve a quick victory. Supplied, trained and directed by professional Russian army soldiers, North Korea launched a sudden, strongly-organized and well-armed invasion of the south in the ready expectation that it could sweep down three hundred miles to the end of the peninsula in about three weeks. It believed not only that the government of Syngman Rhee was in a weak condition, but that its invasion would meet with considerable popular support. It took Joseph V. Stalin a long time to approve of this venture, but the clear expectation was that the South Korean Army, poorly trained and lacking in heavy weapons, could be overwhelmed within that time frame. The quick capture of Seoul (3 days) re-endorsed that belief. Many North Korean leaders believed that the capture of Seoul combined with anticipated Communist-led rebellions in the rest of the country would effectively ending substantial opposition. Erratic efforts by shattered ROK units seemed to do little more than slow down what was seen as a victory march, but that resistance did have the partial effect of slowing down and somewhat disrupting the timetable of the invaders.

All of this was based on the proposition that the U.S. military would not intervene, and even if it did, it would be a matter of too little, too late. Given the conflicting signals that the U.S. government gave about its intentions concerning Korea, the powerful fear and opposition to communism in America would clearly indicate that the Truman administration would not and could not take this expansion of communist control in Asia lying down, and it did not. From a domestic political perspective, "Who lost China?" was still echoing in the lungs of Republican orators, to which "Who Lost Korea?" could not be added. The poorly trained and disciplined mass of 200,000 U.S. soldiers next door in Japan could be quickly thrown into the conflict, and they were. In addition, there were the powerful U.S. Navy and Air Force standing by; they generally were prepared for this eventuality, or quickly reached combat level.

By the end of July 1950 the defensive enclave in the southeast corner of Korea — the Pusan Perimeter — had been formed and was powerfully reinforced by the American military with its ready access to American facilities next door in Japan. Pitched battles raged around the perimeter, but the North Korean Army battered itself to bits trying to break in. Kim Il Sung and company obviously had no other strategy.

This is clearly seen with the U.S. amphibious invasion at Inchon in September. Why didn't the North Koreans take more effective measures to prepare for what was widely seen as a pending U.S. operation? The probable answer is that they did not possess the forces and weaponry to deal with both. The "People's Army" did put up a spirited but short-lived effort in Seoul, but its subsequent tumultuous flight out of the south demonstrates how fragile its occupation actually was. Only a remnant managed to flee north of the 38th parallel, but this turned out to be a hardy force. As well, some of its units never left the north and were expanded by rigorous forced recruitment. But above all, it was a run for the mountains, with one strong assembly point being just above the line in the central mountain area that became known as the Iron Triangle. For the rest, they fled north to and above the Yalu, where they were reequipped and reorganized by the Chinese army. Their renewed effectiveness can be seen by their successful reintroduction into the conflict, which coincided with the Chinese intervention. Until the end of the conflict North Korean units generally were capable fighting organizations.

The initial Korean Communist strategy, however, proved to be disastrous. It heaped death and destruction on the whole country, managing only to preserve a communist regime in the north and this was entirely due to the Chinese communist military. The continuing massive American air bombardment of the north drove the communist leadership to despair. Both the Chinese leadership and Stalin were aware of North Korean wavering, but neither wanted to end the conflict just yet. Obviously, it was of little concern to them that the massive destruction of the war was fought in someone else's country. As far as Stalin was concerned, the Koreans had suffered nothing, except for casualties. Kim Il Sung and his colleagues were trapped. After the war, with the Soviet Union providing the bulk of the resources for North Korean reconstruction, the Chinese leadership plotted the overthrow of Kim. In response, Kim ordered the remaining Chinese forces to leave in 1957, with their withdrawal to be completed by the next year. At the same time North Korean hagiography greatly reduced acknowledgement of the force that had saved its regime from extinction.[28]

The South Korean strategy for dealing with a northern invasion proved to be ludicrously inadequate. Lacking tanks, planes and heavy artillery, it was faced with devising a defense plan that had to incorporate the capital city of Seoul very near the poised enemy. With massive desertions and disorganized leadership, it stumbled south. Some of its efforts did slow down North Korean advances, but, by accounts, these efforts alone would not have prevented a total Communist victory. With training and reequipping by the U.S. Army, South Korean divisions had a mixed record within the Pusan Perimeter, but they did fight, and they provided the personnel the United States did not have there, particularly in the early days.

After the allied break-out of the perimeter, South Korean forces, chasing the retreating North Koreans, raced up the east coast, sweeping through Wonsan while the American invasion force was still bobbing in boats. Along the coastal plain and facing light opposition, it reached almost to the Soviet border in November. Its turnabout, however, was equally rapid. With the Chinese intervention and North Korean soldiers coming down from the hills, the South Korean units were withdrawn by U.S. Navy evacuations. The massive Chinese assaults, whose soldiers were greatly feared by the South Koreans, made their units unstable and prone to precipitous retreat. By the end of the war, when supplied with heavy weapons and extended combat experience, the army of the Republic of Korea could at least hold its own in facing its northern countrymen. There would have been no Republic of Korea or its army, however, without American intervention.

The stubborn determination of Syngman Rhee to hold political power well into old age retarded the development of stable representative government. Having devoted a lifetime to Korean independence, he probably could not conceive of the idea that anyone else should be in charge, a common belief of authoritarian rulers everywhere. After a series of rigged elections, he was finally forced to resign in 1960. After a short period of civilian wrangling, the military seized control and held effective power for two decades. On the other hand, this period of dictatorship also saw the massive flowering of Korean industry. By its own standards, the Republic of Korea has since achieved a functioning and effective system of representative government.

Later, the South Korean government, then a military dictatorship, sent an infantry division to back up the American effort in Vietnam, thus becoming the only other country to provide substantial support for that war. In doing so, the Korean soldiers earned a reputation for brutality. Not surprisingly, there was no Nationalist Chinese participation. Why give Red China a further opportunity to support the North Vietnamese/Viet Cong movement?[29]

United States

Given its somnolent condition, the U.S. Army in Japan did what it could once the decision to intervene had been made. Beginning on July 4, small combat teams were flown in prevent a total Communist occupation. Battered, bleeding and dead, they paid the price for the faulty, disastrous assumptions of the U.S. Army in Japan, from its supreme commander on down. But they did buy time and the defensive ring of the Pusan Perimeter was the result. The Inchon incursion and the capture of Seoul, which Lisle Rose characterized as the last clear U.S. military victory for forty years, broke the back of the North Koreans, but, obviously playing one more card, Douglas MacArthur launched an east coast amphibious repetition, which was delayed in implementation and inept in strategy, dividing the U.S. forces and culminating in disaster.[30]

Driving north across the parallel, quickly capturing the northern capital of Pyongyang, the U.S. Eighth Army under General Walton Walker, and on the east coast the X Corps, seemed unstoppable. As in the bitter winter of late 1944 in western Europe, the Quartermaster Corps failed to provide winter clothing and other supplies for many of the troops in the mountains of North Korea. Supply bottlenecks, frigid weather and a large measure of the belief that the war was about over were factors in what happened next, but the traumatic entry of the Chinese Communist forces was by far the decisive event in the rout and hectic retreat of the American/South Korean units.

The question remains: could the American forces have been better prepared for this onslaught? The short answer is probably no. MacArthur was pursuing a strategy of rapid advance to the Yalu to quickly at least occupy central and western parts of the north; thus rear area defensive preparation was not adequately considered. There was an obdurate and mindless state of denial about the likelihood of the Chinese coming in. Surely another factor was the irrepressible development of the victory disease. The Eighth Army had no ability in or even disposition to anticipate defensive warfare. In any case, the allied forces, baffled and overwhelmed, turned and retreated for two hundred miles, all in three weeks. If it had made basic efforts to prepare for defensive warfare it would not have collapsed. If the X Corps had been part of the Eighth Army's command it could have provided the necessary support; instead it went off on a race to the Yalu along the west coast. For all that, the Eighth did outrun the opposition in a humiliating flight in which the Chinese had neither the expectation nor logistics to keep up the chase. From there on, having employed their only effective tactic — a large-scale surprise attack — the Chinese turned to massive direct assaults, but they were countered by superior American armaments.

Renewed and invigorated by new equipment and troop replacements plus the inspired leadership of Matthew Ridgway, the Eighth Army cushioned the subsequent massive blows of its Chinese adversaries and drove them north, beyond the 38th parallel, which was a powerful achievement and, given the U.S. government's decision not to reinforce its military commitment in Korea, more than enough for one war.

The most important consequence of the Korean episode is that it demonstrated, firstly, to the United States the need for a great expansion of its military capability and, secondly, that these expanded resources were not going to be poured into the deadlocked and increasingly fruitless conflict there. In a decision reached in mid-1951, the focus was to be on western Europe, where the most vital national interests were at stake. This condition was well stated by historian Walter Millis in 1956:

> The overriding thought was not the specific outcome in Korea but whether or not the Russians were about to march.... What was wanted was military strength — every and any kind of military strength — and it was wanted immediately. In the winter of 1950–51 Congress quadrupled military appropriations.... The North Atlantic Treaty Organization, which until then had been mainly a political and diplomatic alliance, was abruptly converted to a straight-out military system.[31]

Korea therefore produced a clear wake-up call, something that Comrade Stalin certainly had not intended when he initiated the Korean enterprise.

People's Republic of China

Based on charges of communist sympathies and the partisan uproar about the Communist victory in China, the hounding-out from the State Department of several experts on Chinese affairs surely had the effect of underestimating the new government there and resulted in a reliance on recollections of ineffective Chinese military operations in the recently concluded Asian war. No one in the American high command took seriously Chinese threats to intervene if the Americans drove to the Yalu. There did not seem be undue concern even if the Chinese did come in. MacArthur believed that massive U.S. Air Force bombing along that border had sealed off the battlefield, but a mass of Chinese soldiers were already in Korea, and even after interdiction the Chinese, at great cost, managed to keep open the Yalu route.

Making excellent use of concealment, camouflage and deception, on November 25 the Chinese sprang the trap, sending the Americans and allies

U.S. soldiers greet Truce announcement, July 1953. Courtesy National Archives, Signal Corps photograph no. 306-PS-53-11547 [PRS].

spinning south. This mighty achievement could not be consolidated because of the Chinese inability, due to massive casualties, troop exhaustion and a weak supply system, to sweep their opponents to destruction. These weaknesses were not overcome in subsequent encounters. The Chinese lacked the industrial capacity to do so, and the addition of some Russian tanks and fighter planes did not alter this situation. For the U.S. Army, however, one surprise was enough. What followed was a series of massive Chinese offensives, designed to use the great Chinese superiority in manpower, which met the countervailing U.S. advantage in weaponry.

One factor in the conflict that is often overlooked is the concern of the Chinese (and the North Koreans) that their opponents would use the American and British naval power to effect another behind-the-lines amphibian assault. It deployed an estimated quarter of a million troops in anticipation of such an action.[32] As has been seen, James Van Fleet, who succeeded Mathew Ridgway as Eighth Army commander, unsuccessfully urged this end-run.

If the Chinese leaders hoped that the bloody, small-scale slugging match that encompassed the last two years of the conflict would work to their advantage, they were to be disappointed. At great financial and material cost (with the massive deaths of their soldiers apparently of little concern), Communist China had driven the Americans out of North Korea (and revived the Communist regime there) but failed in its attempts to further defeat U.S. forces. This was apparent with the failure of the Chinese "fifth" offensive in the spring of 1951. Recognizing that Chinese manpower could not defeat U.S. firepower, the Chinese build a massive underground, in-depth defensive network, which Bevin Alexander declares "stunned" the American leadership with the rapidity of its construction. The deeply entrenched fortifications were able to contain massive U.S. air and artillery bombardment during the period from August to November 1951.

The only alternative for the United States, as noted by Chairman Mao, was for the Americans to launch another amphibious operation, for which the other side was prepared and which would entail significant costs without any guarantee of success. Thus, effective stalemate resulted. At this stage, according to Adam Ulam, the Chinese leaders "were eager for peace in Korea," while becoming increasingly angry about the failure of the Soviet Union to provide economic and technological assistance. Chang and Halliday present a different picture. Although Stalin had decided to end the war on February 28 and his successors transmitted that decision on March 23, the Chinese wanted to continue the fight and reluctantly agreed only in May, with the Soviets providing the sweetener of large-scale economic and technological aid (minus the A bomb).[33] An indication of the beginning of the division with Soviet Russia could be seen in the short (six minutes) speech of aging Joe Stalin at the October 1952 party congress in which he praised some western European communist parties but said not a word about Red China and its travails in Korea. The Sino-American clash in Korea resulted in a bitter U.S. stance concerning that regime, but this eventually became a triangle of animosity, exasperated by the Vietnam eruption.

The negotiations for ending the fighting, begun in July 1951, stretched over two years. What emerged as the principal bone of contention was the issue of the release of prisoners, with the Communist side insisting that all POWs be shipped back to their place of origin while the U.N. held that the prisoners be allowed to decide if they wanted repatriation. The determination by both the Truman and incoming Eisenhower administrations to uphold the principle of choice had the ugly effect of keeping American POWs in continuing captivity for almost two additional years. Another factor was an obvious Chinese desire to keep the process from unraveling, apparently in the expectation that, with the growing desire in the United States to end the conflict, the Americans would eventually tire of this game and make concessions. Surely, there was some Oriental cultural perspective involved in the meandering path followed by the Chinese negotiators. This situation even began to irritate old Joe Stalin at some point in late 1951. When he ascertained that the Chinese and North Korean leaders had no clear idea of what they hoped to achieve through the negotiations, he proceeded to "give them a lecture on the differences among 'conventional diplomatic norms' regarding cease-fires, truces, armistices and peace agreements."[34]

When, at length, the fighting ended in July 1953, Chairman Mao turned his attention to the Great Leap Forward, then the Proletarian Cultural Revolution, quashing any of his colleagues, including Peng Dehuai, who did not agree with what he saw as the antiquated military philosophy of the Great Helmsman, and a mighty reckoning with the "Marxist deviants" of Communist Russia. The chairman retained what has been called his "military romanticism" about great masses of men overwhelming modern capitalist armaments. The propaganda line of the Chinese in the aftermath of the Korean War was that it was a great victory over American (white) imperialist outreach. At the same time, particularly during the inquisitional Cultural Revolution, the loyalty and behavior of returned POWS came under attack. No mention was made that most Chinese POWs did not want to return to the People's Republic.[35]

Republic of China (Formosa Annex)

The Korean War saved the remnant of the Nationalist government of Chiang Kai-shek on the island refuge of Formosa. Without the war and the resulting imposition of the U.S. Navy into the Formosa Straits there is little doubt that the Chinese Communists would have sooner rather than later successfully invaded and extinguished this last outpost of a defeated regime. Although Truman's action in inserting the navy off Formosa was a leading if not the decisive factor in precipitating the bloody clash of the Americans and Chinese in Korea, it did result in the United States maintaining a protective shield for Chiang and company, until the "unleashing of Chiang" in early 1953. This was followed by a mutual defense treaty that substantially deepened U.S. involvement; in the late 1950s the U.S. Navy provided full support to the Nationalist forces at the barely-offshore islands of Quemoy and Matsou when confronted with Communist bombardment.

Over time and employing classic capitalist methods, Formosa emerged as a viable and then flourishing economy. It also gradually developed the rudiments of representative government. American protection, however, led the United States to the internationally embarrassing need to continue to block Red China's admission to the United Nations and other international organizations. In the early 1960s John Kennedy, recognizing the unviable position of the United States in this matter yet taking into account continued hostility in the United States, was prepared to fend off, on a year to year basis, the growing support for the admission of Communist China. It took the long-time outspoken opponent of communism, Richard Nixon, in a ploy to play off the split between the Soviet Union and Red China, in 1973 to give diplomatic recognition to the Red Colossus of Asia. What followed was the opening of trade with the United States, which continues to be massively imbalanced in favor of the Chinese.

The total cost — financially, militarily and politically — of backing the wrong horse in China, before 1949 and after, was very great, but given the political culture of the United States of that time seems nearly inevitable.

USSR

Comrade Stalin and associates hoped to derive benefit from a Communist takeover of South Korea and seemed surprised when the United States intervened, which surely is a commentary on the Communist perception of the United States, circa 1950. Based on the Atlantic treaty of the previous year, America was committed to increasing its military presence in western Europe, which required increased military expenditures and troop commitment. The Korean War only drove these commitments and costs to higher levels. The Russians had equipped and trained the North Korean Army and then had to watch as it was shattered. The Chinese Communist government had already decided to intervene in Korea, but still sought Soviet promises of material help, the most important of which was provision of air cover. Stalin held back on this for months and when the Russian did provide MiG jet fighter planes (and pilots) in 1951, they were used to fend off American bomber attacks in the far north. At no point did the Chinese have fighters for tactical use. The few tanks the Russians supplied had little impact on Chinese operations.

If the Russians anticipated that their support for the North Korean invasion and subsequent American involvement would substantially tie down American military capacity, they were mistaken. Stimulated by the Korean crisis, American leadership continued building up the North Atlantic military alliance. As well, the firmly held belief that Stalin and the Kremlin were behind the Korean outbreak reinforced American hostility to the Soviet Union. The material cost of Russian support for the Communist venture in Korea was real and growing, but had at length no corresponding political benefits. Stalin's emerging impatience about the war became clear when, confronted with a new Chinese request in late 1951 for expanded military assistance and the deadlocked truce negotiations, he informed his Chinese visitors that a truce agreement should not attempt to bring about a general peace settlement.[36] Although he reportedly had then decided to end the conflict, his timely death provided his successors with the opportunity, with reluctant Chinese consent, to end the hostilities and clear the way for a relationship with the United States that was not permanently tottering on the verge of war.

Japan

As was the case in American-occupied Germany, Japan responded to defeat by a rapid accommodation to the new situation, and, as in Western Germany, American soldiers quickly formed a most favorable opinion of the people of Nippon. Thus, there was the political scenario of the transformation of enemies into allies. In the Korean War the availability of American bases, supply facilities and adequate port facilities were great advantages. Japan also provided a mass of minesweeper vessels to clear the port of Wonsan and then Chinnampo, the port of Pyongyang, as well as thirty-four ships for the Inchon invasion. Charts and studies of Korea left over from the days of Japanese occupation also were most useful. Although MacArthur's staff considered the matter at the beginning of the war, due to determined Korean opposition, no Japanese military were direct participations in the conflict, despite occasional Communist claims.

Robert Murphy, ending his diplomatic career serving as ambassador to Japan, declared in his memoirs: "Japanese shipping and railway experts worked in Korea with their well-trained crews under American and United Nations commands. This was top secret." He claimed that "thousands of Japanese" were involved. Top secret indeed; there are few references to this civilian involvement as both the Defense and State departments stopped any press mention of Japanese involvement.[37] Syngman Rhee was totally opposed to bringing Japanese technicians of any sort into the country and several times ordered the arrest of any Japanese found there. As a result, Japanese workers were housed on U.S. bases and given military transport to their work sites.[38] John Dille recalls that, due to Japanese policy during their occupation of Korea, the "natives" were prevented from developing a variety of skills.[39] Because Koreans had not been allowed to operate the heavy cranes in the Pusan port, Japanese port operators were returned to their previous positions. A large number of Japanese ships and stevedores were employed in transporting the X Corps to the North Korean east coast in late September 1950.[40]

While many Americans decried the sanctuary that Manchuria provided for the Communist forces, two ROK divisions were trained in Japan on U.S. military bases. By the Americans not attacking Manchurian bases, Japan was spared Communist counter-actions of one sort or another. The wonder of the five-day minimum R and R pass from the grim, battered countryside in Korea to the clean, hospitable, bright lights of Japan greatly cemented GI Joe's opinion of Japan. Equally important was the great stimulus the war provided for Japanese services and manufacturing.[41] Following the American-engineered Japanese peace treaty of 1951 a military agreement provided for the continuing presence of American military bases, which, greatly reduced in size, remain there more than sixty years after the war with Japan.[42] The American involvement in Korea provided protection and assurance for the Japanese people, almost totally disarmed after their defeat, and deflected the Chinese desire to avenge the brutal Japanese treatment to which they were subjected in that conflict.

Britain

The only other state to have a substantial involvement in the United Nations' effort in Korea was the United Kingdom of Great Britain and Northern Ireland, Britain for short. The Communist take-over of China in 1949 presented Britain with a clear need to adapt to the new situation. There was long history of British interference in China, with Mao Zedung now committed to ending foreign domination of the country. With its colony of Hong Kong on the Chinese coast, Britain was clearly exposed. An 1898 treaty granting Britain possession of it for ninety-nine years could easily have been rejected by the Communist government as one of several forced impositions on the old China, and China could have marched in at any time. That Britain promptly extended diplomatic recognition of the Communist regime can be seen in that light. Given Britain's dire economic condition, there was an important need to maintain, and, if possible, increase its exports to China.

When the North Koreans invaded the south beginning in June 1950, Britain followed the lead of the United States in condemning that action. Furthermore, it provided limited naval and land forces to stem this aggression. As has been seen, other than the United States, it was the only country to do so in any substantial manner. It supported the vague U.N. resolution to carry the war into North Korea. On top of increased military spending for NATO, the Korean War was an additional financial burden for a cash-strapped Britain. To many people the death and disabling of British soldiers only seemed to be a postscript to a long history of British sorties, incursions, invasions and wars all over Africa, Asia and the Middle East. Given the pressing needs at home (with some forms of rationing still in place) and the cost of rearmament in Europe, Korea was not a popular enterprise. There were a few demonstrations against British involvement and British communists urged mothers and wives of POWs to attend meetings and belong to the National Assembly of Women. Women who showed any willingness in this regard promptly received mail from POWs.[43] Another British consideration was the rumbling of an uprising (Chinese-led) in Malaya. Someone was making a profit from the remnants of empire, but it was not the British taxpayer.

The U.K. government, however, did not always simply conform to American policy. Like the other European allies, it did not support the U.S. government's action in putting the U.S. Navy in the Formosa Straits to prevent a Communist invasion of the final refuge of the defeated Nationalists. In December 1950 and in the wake of the Chinese intervention, the British government, along with other European ones, was alarmed by President Truman's statement, muddled though it was, that the United States did not rule out the use of atomic bombs in Korea. At the time Prime Minister Clement Atlee quickly came to Washington to secure agreement that that weapon would not be used without prior consultation.[44]

As the U.N. forces drove deeply into North Korea beginning in October 1950 and then approached the Yalu, to ward off Chinese intervention Britain became a strong advocate of allowing a buffer zone to the approaches of that international boundary. This proposal was not accepted by the United States, and the Chinese, as promised, swept in and things followed from there, with British units demonstrating remarkable ability in rear-guard operations.

With the ending of the Korean conflict the United States devoted greater resources to the tottering French position in Vietnam. Despite the vigorous efforts by the Eisenhower administration, led by John Foster Dulles, the British declined to get involved. In the view of its Asian Commonwealth members and Asia in general, what was happening in Vietnam was a dirty colonial struggle, and U.S. efforts to change that would not succeed. As well, British forces were now engaged in dealing with a communist-led uprising in Malaya. Winston Churchill, newly restored to office, while mourning the growing disintegration of empire, succinctly stated his position: if the British people were willing to let India go they certainly would not fight for French Indochina.[45]

Since the Korean War and beyond Vietnam, the Anglo-American relationship generally has been well founded, but there were some substantial difficulties over time. Beginning with flight of two officials to the Soviet Union in 1951 there were series of incidents that revealed systematic failures in British intelligence organizations. The United States condemned the fantastic 1956 Anglo-French-Israeli caper directed at Gamal Abdul Nasser and Arab nationalism. For its part, Britain did not support the long American intervention in Vietnam and was actively involved in diplomatic efforts to achieve compromise in Indochina. Despite strong internal opposition, Britain joined in the contentious American campaign against Saddam Hussein in Iraq, but this part of the Middle East had long been a major area of British control or influence, with British air bases and army posts remaining in the oil-rich Gulf Emirates along the lower rim of the Arabian peninsula (not mention Brunei, another oil-rich sultanate, this in Borneo), an aspect of the subject rarely mentioned in media accounts. The small remaining British contingent, located in Basra in southern Iraq, was withdrawn in late 2009, following charges of torture and sexual abuse by British personnel.[46] The long arm of Arab terrorism reached home with the London bombings in the summer of 2006, resulting in British participation in the campaign against the Taliban in Afghanistan; as in Iraq, the Brits had been there before, such as in their activities in the Khyber Pass, and expeditions (one of them fatal) to Kabul in the nineteenth century.

With Hong Kong being an important source of international currency and technology, the Chinese government allowed the 1898 treaty provisions to spin out to the end. On the eve of the end of it all, on the last day of June 1997, the British government staged an exceptional public relations act, flying out a bevy of important public figures to mark the termination of the British presence. The message: we are not ashamed in any way about having been there; rather, we are proud of what has been achieved—the opening up of China, introduction of European ideas and structures, etc. It was on the basis of this kind of self-confidence, selective memory and more that an empire was built.

France and Vietnam

Although it supported the U.S. decision to plunge into the Korean conflict, France only had a minor direct involvement in the war. It sent an elite battalion of 1,400 soldiers that became noteworthy, as did that of the Turks, for its bayonet charges.[47] The small part it took in Korea was due to its full commitment to the defeat of the Vietnamese communist movement, as well as to the rearmament cost of the obligations of the North Atlantic Treaty of 1949. American aid to the effort of the French in Vietnam predated the Korean War, but this support was greatly increased almost immediately once the Korean conflict began, with U.S. support rising to provide about 85 percent of the financial cost. Just as the United States backed the French and their Vietnamese allies, so Communist China provided increasing support for the Vietnamese communists. The Vietnam affair, therefore, in a major respect, was a continuation of the Korean clash, with the U.S. military taking the plunge into that conflict only a dozen years later.

From the beginning, the French campaign seemed unlikely to succeed. Reporting from Saigon in late November 1950, Hanson Baldwin saw a looming "major crisis." He declared that Saigon "is more or less a French-held 'island' in a Vietminh sea," while in the Red River delta in the north, "French-Vietnamese ability to beat off the attacks will depend to some extent upon the availability of United States aid." He noted that while U.S. military materiel was arriving "in large quantities," Communist China provided Viet Minh training centers just above the Vietnam border.[48] One of those who perceived this dire situation was young congressman John F. Kennedy, who spent several days in Saigon in 1951. As he later declared, as long as communist forces fought behind the banner of nationalism they were bound to prevail. He was not in the least an enthusiastic supporter of the Korean venture. Earlier, in August 1950, he had declared, "It is idle now to discuss whether we should have gone into Korea. We are in and according to the President, we are in to stay." He was concerned that American participation in the peninsula would deprive the U.S. military of the ability to respond to challenges elsewhere, particularly in Europe. The following November, speaking off the record, he reportedly told a seminar at Harvard that he did not know of any good reason why the United States was involved in the Korean conflict; he quickly disavowed that report. As part of his 1951 seven-week tour, accompanied by brother Bobby and sister Pat, he intended to go to Korea, but ill health prevented him from doing so; as a result we do not have his immediate perceptions of that conflict.[49]

In 1952 the U.S. government opposed a pending agreement about Vietnam. When the Korean War ended in July 1953, the United States continued to fully support the French campaign in Indochina. In his inaugural speech, Dwight Eisenhower declared that French soldiers in Vietnam were fighting for freedom and democracy just as the British were doing in Malaya.[50] French writer and journalist Joseph Kassel, a member of Académie française, in 1966 told this writer of his experiences in Vietnam: "We killed them by the truckload and it didn't do any good. The same thing will happen to you."[51] In the wake of military failure, the French were soon forced to give up their involvement in Vietnam, proceeding to an equally failed effort to hold on to Algeria.

Unlike the measured achievement of the United States in Korea, the U.S direct involvement in Vietnam gave that conflict very long legs indeed, but the end of it all was failure.

Having poured increasing resources and dispatched a variety of advisors into Vietnam, the U.S. military and government were strongly critical of the French effort there. The French had refused to grant effective self-government to Vietnam and had rejected U.S. offers to train a Vietnamese army; now they had backed into defending a misplaced fortress at Dien Bien Phu. Seeking to avert a defeat of what it viewed as the "free world," the new Eisenhower administration, spearheaded by the restless John Foster Dulles, unsuccessfully sought to draw Britain, Australia and New Zealand into the conflict, with, of course, an expanded American presence. Despite the best efforts of Dulles, the 1954 Geneva agreement partitioned Vietnam. With the French now out, the Americans stepped in, confident that they possessed the competence and resources to deal with the continuing communist threat, not just to Vietnam, but to Indochina and southeastern Asia. This, then, is the direct if extended link between the U.S. involvement in Korea and Vietnam.[52]

Turkey

The Republic of Turkey, now a NATO ally, was second (with Britain) in responding to the United Nations' call for military opposition to the North Korean invasion; it was also second in the number of soldiers provided. There was a long history of Turkish antipathy to Russians, which was ethnic, political and religious. It sent a remarkable brigade of three infantry battalions and one of artillery, comprising 5,000 troops, which arrived in Korea on October 17, 1950. During the course of the war more than 15,000 Turks served in Korea. It suffered 721 killed in action, 2,111 wounded and 168 missing (most of whom were POWs), constituting losses second only to Britain among the substantial participants. Some Turkish units continued as occupation troops in Korea until 1966.[53]

After a short period of orientation and training, the brigade, rushed into combat, was badly chewed up when it was thrust into blocking effort to stem the Chinese breakthrough of November 1950. From November 20 to November 30 it was subjected to massive Chinese attacks, with a resulting loss of 15 percent of its soldiers and a remarkable loss of 70 percent of its equipment. At this time its problems were greatly exacerbated by disorganization, communications breakdowns and language barriers with U.S. Second Division headquarters.[54] After this initial setback, it was soon to even the score.

It was during November that U.S. Army sergeant Anthony Herbert became attached to a company in the Turkish Brigade. He found that although these soldiers were surrounded, "they couldn't have been happier. They were having a picnic. Every way they looked, it was the front. They could fire in any direction and kill Chinese." Herbert was amazed to find that every other unit in the Eighth Army was heading south "while the Turks were moving north looking for Chinese — and the Chinese were trying desperately to avoid them." Even when the Turks did retreat, "they would swing north and attack at every opportunity." When Chinese soldiers closed in on a retreating column of Americans, "the Turks rose as one man, with fixed bayonets, and met the charge head on about twenty yards out from the column flanks, steel clashing against steel, screams of pain and terror intermingling. But not a word from the Turks." The Chinese were routed, leaving behind their dead and wounded: "These wounded the Turks finished off. They gave no quarter, and they asked for none."[55]

During the Chinese offensive of January 1951 the brigade successfully stopped a Chinese attack estimated at three times its size. To some observers this action was early evidence that the Chinese "hordes" could be met and matched. For this exploit the brigade was awarded a Distinguished Unit Citation by President Truman. There was almost universal praise for the Turkish troops. After one of its bloody engagements Rene Culforth came upon a hillside of Chinese bodies—"Turks' Ridge"—where the Turks had mounted one of their noted bayonet charges, this time at one o'clock in the morning (reversing the usual Chinese pattern): "There were 800 bodies on the ridge, and nearly every one of them died that way. The bodies were scattered all over the ridge top and the first side of its southern slope." The company commander told Culforth he had passed the word around to his soldiers that the Chinese troops up on the ridge were the ones that "cut us up so badly at Kun-ri where we were surrounded and fought out through miles of ambushes." As a result of this claim, the Turkish officer declared, "My men went up the slope as if they were running a race."[56] Serving in an artillery unit, Richard Holmsten felt best when Turkish infantry soldiers were in front of him. He also observed what seemed to be one of their customs in war: "They would form a circle around the Chinese (prisoners) and bat them around inside the circle until they couldn't stand. Then they would drag them away."[57]

Turkish POWs also were impressive. They maintained high levels of discipline and mutual help, and because of their unique language were not harangued by their Chinese captors about the glories of communism, etc. Not one of the 229 Turkish POWs died in captivity. In addition, they discovered that marijuana grew wildly all around. The "weed," whose effect was rejected by the Chinese, became a source of solace and enjoyment for many POWs.[58]

The raw aggressiveness of Turkish soldiers became legendary. Cutforth passes on the story that Turkish soldiers were "supposedly to have complained bitterly in one battle that the artillery fire put in to soften the enemy position before their charge had been so heavy that there had not been enough active Chinese left on the hilltop to put up an interesting fight."[59] Claims made by Turkish patrols of the number of enemy killed seemed inflated, so they began dragging bodies back to make their case. American occupation troops in Korea in the mid-1950s heard of episodes of Turkish heroics—for example, a unit of surrounded Turkish soldiers with their long knives and bayonets slicing up heaps of attacking Chinese. Their proficiency with the bayonet caused General Ridgway to all order all infantry companies entering battle to have bayonets attached to their rifles.[60]

In addition to all that, according to Culforth, "The Turks were popular with everybody — and that includes that not very often included element, the South Korean people. Turkish camp fires always had their rabble of refugee children around them, sharing the soldiers' food."[61] In the years to follow Turkey, ever ready to fight any Russian encroachment, has remained a stalwart partner with the United States in world affairs.

The drawn-out conclusion to the fighting and negotiations, however, did create public frustration as well as lessening of attention to the conflict. The frustration led to the Republican Party barely regaining control of Congress in 1952. The man who dragged that party to this result was General Dwight D. Eisenhower, its presidential candidate, who declared that, if elected, he would employ deeds, not words, to end the conflict. In a memorable speech, after laying the responsibility for the deaths of 20,000 American soldiers on the multiple failings of the Truman administration, he declared, if elected, "I will go to Korea," which resonated with many voters: perhaps Ike could figure out what had gone wrong there. Bevin Alexander rightly calls Eisenhower's declaration "absurd," while Harry Truman characterized it as "a piece of demagoguery," but it obviously was good politics.[62] In fact, smiling Ike spent three days looking around and posing for photographs, but neither then nor later could he find anything wrong with troop dispositions, etc. Upon his return, for the only time, he listened to Douglas MacArthur's assessment of the situation, including his proposal to encircle the northern Korean border with nuclear waste.[63] This was the man who declined to defend his great patron George C. Marshall from outrageous accusations shouted by the belligerent alcoholic but widely reported Joseph McCarthy.

When he became president Eisenhower engaged in some "sound and fury signifying nothing"—gestures—"unleashing Chiang" to contemplate a return to the mainland, giving more money to expand the size of the South Korean military, which generated the Republican sound bite, "Let Asians fight Asians." In his inaugural address he referred to French soldiers in Vietnam as among those who were fighting for freedom in the world (with much more about Vietnam to follow in his administration and after). He later indicated that he accepted the idea that many American POWs had not resisted Communist indoctrination.

Beyond political grandstanding, he is due some credit for the armistice that arrived six months into his term of office. His threats of dire consequences—if the stalemate continued he was willing to bomb Chinese bases in Manchuria, and he made guarded mention of nuclear weapons being employed — probably had some effect, but, in any case, the whole negotiating process was dragging to a conclusion. The Chinese leadership surely must have been concerned about what measures he would take. With a prototype appearing in the January 1953 inaugural parade, an atomic cannon was test fired in Nevada in May 1953. Would tactical atomic weapons be brought to Korea? Here was a famous and victorious general, who, with a strong mandate behind him, could do just about whatever he wanted. Eisenhower remained convinced that his nuclear bombast was effective. Historian Gordon Chang casts doubt on this judgment, declaring that Beijing might never had received his confidential warning, knew from the beginning that the United States had atomic bombs and, perhaps underestimating the impact of atomic attacks, did not seem to be unduly concerned about the threat of their use. In fact, it was widely known that Eisenhower was threatening to use nuclear weapons to force an end to the conflict.[64] In their biography of Mao, according to Jung Chang and Jon Halliday, Eisenhower's bluster was "music to Mao's ears." Mao could use this threat to extract the technology to build an atomic bomb from his Soviet allies, something that Mao had long been after and which the Soviets were completely reluctant to supply.[65] There were other factors that were decisive. There was the decision of Stalin on February 28, the day before his fatal strike, to end the war, which was promptly ratified by his successors two weeks later. Kim Il Sung was delighted to end the continuing destruction of his statelet, but not Mao, who wanted to drag on the struggle. Now deprived of Soviet support,

Mao had to acquiesce, but the end of the war meant no A-bomb for China at that time.[66]

The matter of using atomic bombs in Korea had first come to public notice when Harry Truman in the dark days at the beginning of December 1950 included it in possible American responses to the crisis created by the Chinese intervention. When some top government officials proposed such an action, George Marshall, secretary of defense, was dismissive of the idea — what was left to bomb? Dean Rusk later declared that the U.S. Air Force had bombed "everything that moved, every brick standing on top of another brick." The rugged topography of the northern part of the peninsula greatly reduced the potential impact of the weapon. But at that time MacArthur requested the right to use nuclear weapons if necessary and drew up a list of targets to be hit with thirty-four A-bombs; Mathew Ridgway, his successor, renewed that request, and in turn, Mark Clark proposed this employment.[67] The U.S. Army already fired an atomic cannon, but with its short range and massive carriage, it was outmoded by the time it was deployed. The new Eisenhower administration had on hand a tactical nuclear bomb, a weapon of limited explosive area, which President Eisenhower in February 1953 suggested could be used at a specific site in North Korea. A study of the planning board of the National Security Council the following April presented a generally negative report about the use of nuclear weapons in Korea.[68]

Both Stalin and Mao affected that they were not cowed by the threat of American A-bombs. In January 1953 a committee of Soviet intelligence analysts informed Stalin that "the U.S. military leaders are not convinced of the practicality of using the atomic bomb in Korea. They are afraid that, if the use of atomic weapons does not ensure the real preponderance of the United States, a final blow will be dealt to U.S. prestige."[69] While the Soviets now also had at least some primitive atomic bombs, Stalin was apprehensive about what measures the new Eisenhower administration would take.

Mao was dismissive of the impact of atomic bombing. As far as he was concerned, America, even with its nuclear capacity, was a "paper tiger." Should the United States employ this ultimate weapon on China, it would mean little due to the reality of China's huge population: "As long as the green mountains are there, one need not worry about firewood."[70] He later told Nikita Khrushchev that if the United States launched an atomic attack on China the Communist regime would abandon its coastal cities and withdraw deep into the interior, just like it had done earlier in its contest with Chiang Kai-shek.[71]

With the new Soviet leadership declaring its desire to reduce international tensions and urging the Chinese to end the conflict (including informing Beijing that the germ warfare claims were false and embarrassing to the Soviets),[72] the ultimate breakthrough in the negotiations came when the Communist side finally conceded, through an involved formula, that released prisoners of war could freely choose whether or not to return to their place of origin.[73] As feared by the Reds, many declined to return to the lands of "People's" governments: of the 20,000 Chinese POWs 14,000 declined repatriation to China and were shipped to Formosa, while 36,000 of the 112,000 North Koreans refused to return to the north. What was missing from the agreement was the fate of the estimated 60,000 South Korean prisoners, who were not released.[74]

Conclusion:
The Measure of It All

At the outbreak of the war, the message barked out by Syngman Rhee to Douglas MacArthur was prescient: "Had your country been a little more concerned about us we would not have come to this! We warned you many times. Now you must save Korea!"[1] Although there were other factors, it is apparent that initial American complacency, overconfidence and lack of understanding of Asia and Asians, not to mention xenophobia and partisan rivalry at home, were the decisive factors in bringing about the early state of affairs in Korea. As in the case of North Korea's assault, it was only in their beginning surprise attack that the Chinese scored their sweeping success; the Japanese had achieved similar results at Pearl Harbor and in the Philippines. Once the U.S. and South Korean forces established conventional warfare, they were successful in grinding away at their Chinese and North Korean opponents. Right from the beginning of the Chinese intervention, however, Dean Acheson foresaw how the conflict would unfold when he predicted, "The Chinese could not be defeated in Korea; they could always put in more forces than the United States."[2] Not only did the Chinese have a huge numerical superiority, but as the war progressed, with Russian aid, they improved their artillery and supply capacity.

The riposte to the famous declaration of Douglas MacArthur, "There is no substitute for victory," is that in a limited war there will be limited results and the alternative to limited war is unlimited war.

By any measure the Korean War was a nasty affair, first and foremost for the Korean people, of whom about three million were killed, one-tenth of the population. Along with this were huge numbers of refugees driven hither and yon who had to confront the massive destruction to their infrastructure and dwellings. It is a great tribute to that indomitable people that in the south there was not only total reconstruction but the creation of a modern, developed and thriving community. The all-consuming but overconfident ambition of the Communist dictatorship in the north resulted, not to understate the matter, in death, destruction and shame, but, of course, that was of little consequence to the originators of this catastrophe.

Once it took the plunge, Communist China made an increasing commitment to the war, both in manpower and in resources. The cold indifference with which Chairman Mao and his comrades threw masses of their countrymen to their deaths in a quest for victory is monumental. The Chinese Communists poured 450,000 soldiers into Korea at the beginning of its involvement in November 1950 and then doubled that to 950,000 five months later. Badly clothed and fed and poorly armed throughout the conflict, the Chinese died in heaps until even the likes of Mao, Stalin and Kim Il Sung were forced to recognize that mass assaults could not defeat the firepower and technology of the Americans. Chinese forces in Korea reached a peak of 1.45 million men in December 1952. Together with 600,000 civilian laborers, Chinese participation reached the grand total of 3.1 million.

With tardy but substantial Russian help, the Chinese did develop an air force by the end of 1953 that totaled three thousand planes, almost all fighters, making that force the third largest in the world. It began its air war defending the Yalu facilities and the surrounding area — so-called MiG Alley. At no point did it use its planes to attack U.N. land forces or bases. This was due to its failed effort to establish viable air bases in North Korea combined with the eventual withdrawal (in the spring of 1953) of Soviet pilots, which marked the end of the Chinese air effort. The financial cost of the Korean venture to Red China was extraordinary, representing about forty percent of its government expenditures.

The cost of the war to the United Nations participants was considerable but not colossal; including South Korean military involvement, there was a total of about 474,000 killed, wounded and missing in action. Of the 5,700,000 servicemen in the U.S. armed forces in 1950–1953, 54,000 American servicemen died in Korea (34,000 of them from combat causes), 103,000 were wounded and 8,176 were missing in action. Those who were in the military anywhere during the Korean War period (and through 1955) were recipients of the Korean-era GI bill of rights, which while not as generous as the World War II act did provide adequate money for education, training and services. More than a million servicemen were in (and out of) Korea. The U.S. financial cost of the war was great, but this blended into the expanded military expenditure that was a major consequence of that war.

The American military achieved a creditable level of effectiveness, as after a learning period did the South Korean military. Although its record was spotty and at times inadequate, the U.S. Army did provide enough resources in supplies, food, logistical support and weaponry to keep the war effort within reasonable bounds. A notable development was the great improvement in military medical care and facilities. For the million American servicemen who were there, the Korean experience was an abrupt introduction to the realities of Asian warfare and Asian culture. The troop rotation program greatly reduced the pain, not to say the dislocation of lives, of the survivors of that experience.

Among the failures in the operations of the American military in that period was its intelligence sector. It failed to anticipate the North Korean invasion as well as the Chinese intervention. On a lesser scale, it had no knowledge of the surreptitious mining of the eastern ports of Wonsan and Hungnam when MacArthur's X Corps launched its planned landings at Wonsan.

What must stand as the most serious blunder of the U.S. government was its action of sealing off Nationalist China at the beginning of the Korean conflict. Using its effective navy to do so, it prevented the new Communist regime from completing its seizure of control of all Chinese territory. In doing this the United States reached outside the place where the conflict originated. The Chinese Communist response was to use its effective resource — a mass peasant army — in adjacent Korea. Related to that was the U.S. decision in late 1950 to occupy all of North Korea in the face of adamant Chinese declarations that it would not allow foreign control of its frontier area, with fateful consequences. Granted there was enormous domestic pressure to go all the way to the Yalu, but, in retrospect, it would have been much wiser to conclude the Korean enterprise with the already achieved goal of rescuing South Korea and defeating aggression.

The presence of a million American servicemen in war-torn Korea over a three-year period had both negative and positive aspects. Their presence led to inflation, expanded prostitution and more, but these were offset by continuing economic support and freedom from communism. Moreover, whatever the Americans were doing there, their ultimate purpose was to bring a free, democratic nation in being. Despite a continuing commitment to defend that country, the great mass of U.S. troops were gone with the ending of the war.

Although the bodies of all available American fatalities were returned for burial in the United States, there seemed to be a strange official reluctance to indicate where they died. After a lengthy debate, the place of death on government-provided tombstones was simply given as "Korea." Was this part of an effort to diminish the public recollection of the Korean conflict in order to make the emerging Vietnam venture into a new, unique occurrence? That seems to be the obvious conclusion to draw from this matter. It took almost fifty years before a Korean War memorial was erected in the nation's capital. When some Korean veterans wanted the names of all the fatalities of that war engraved on the structure, as was done with the previously erected Vietnam memorial, a strange objection, which carried the day, was that it would make these dead Americans look like victims. Engraving all the names could only draw further attention, as did the Vietnam memorial, to public apprehension about the carnage of war experienced by young American men, and obviously raise questions about why these violent events happened.

There would have been no Korean War if the United States had had a ready military structure in June 1950. After the enormous expenditure of Word War II, resulting in a massive national debt, the reductions in military spending by the Truman administration and the Congress were responsible for this condition. The need for a substantial buildup of U.S. forces strongly recommended by a top-level study issued in March 1950 (and accepted by Truman the following September) came too late to affect the status of the American military when confronted by the North Korean invasion of the south. It is obvious that the Soviet and North Korean leadership had a clear understanding of the U.S. military condition in Japan. They assumed that the United States would not intervene in Korea or, if it did, such action would come too late to prevent what the North Koreans believed would be a rapid seizure of the south.

The ragged improvisation that constituted the initial U.S. military response was due to the incredible lack of planning by the Far Eastern Command of Douglas MacArthur and his motley command staff. It was a rerun of the situation in the Philippines in 1941–1942. In both places the forces under MacArthur had five years to plan for the looming likelihood of attack and in both cases the response was shambolic. The response of MacArthur to the humiliating defeat in North Korea in late 1950 of the arrogant and ill-conceived attempt to end the conflict with the total occupation of the north was to demand an expansion of the war to China.

The powerful Chinese intervention together with MacArthur's removal from command in April 1951 stirred up domestic controversy and marked the beginning of the decline of public support for the war effort, which now became a raw partisan issue. As a result of greatly expanded U.S. involvement in western Europe through the NATO commitment and the success of U.N. forces directed by Mathew Ridgway in driving Communist opponents up to and somewhat above the 38th parallel where the conflict had begun, the Truman administration decided to go no further. Aggression had been defeated and to carry the war forward when confronted with the wall of a massive Chinese soldiery, whose weapons and logistics were improving, would result in greatly increased casualties and financial cost.

Then along came Dwight D. Eisenhower, who again came to prominence as the nominal leader of the NATO alliance, the very force which required a huge increase in military involvement in western Europe and a corresponding move to begin to limit U.S. involvement in Korea. As the Republican presidential nominee in 1952 Eisenhower was critical of various aspects of U.S. policy in Korea; never supporting MacArthur's call for a wider war, but famously declaring that if elected he would go to Korea — the idea being that he would find out what was going wrong over there. Although he was fully informed about the situation, he was now obliged to go. He briefly did, looked around, and when he became president changed nothing about the immediate position there.

Smiling Ike obviously was determined to ride the hobbyhorse of a stronger opposition to Asian communism than arguably had been the case of the Truman administration. He claimed that deeds, not words, would suffice to bring the conflict to an end, but what he used was words. As has been seen, in his inaugural address Eisenhower asserted that French forces in Vietnam were fighting for freedom. He increased U.S. aid to the French effort, which proceeded to the debacle of Dien Bien Phu the next year. In the spring of 1953 Eisenhower announced that the United States would no longer act as a barrier to hostilities in the Formosa Straits, the so-called action of "unleashing Chiang," the remnant of the Chinese Nationalists on Taiwan whose continuing existence had been dependent on the blockade provided by the U.S. Navy at the beginning of the Korean conflict. This was followed by a military alliance with the Chiang gang, resulting in the navy intervening in 1954 and 1958 to prevent Communist seizure of two islands on the immediate coast of China. Eisenhower was convinced that his saber rattling brought about the cease-fire in Korea, rather than that being due to the decision of the new Soviet leadership to end the continuing financial and political drain of the war. When the prisoners of war were released in the summer of 1953 he bought into the charge that the conduct of many American POWs had somehow been less than honorable, but he said that people should be forgiving on this matter. Thus, Eisenhower and his new-found Republican allies bear responsibility for perpetuating a negative perspective about the whole American role in Korea. It suited his party and him to take this position, but it created a sour recollection of the conflict that both had supported until partisan advantage could be taken of subsequent developments.

One of the undoubted positive developments that emerged from the Korean experience was the effective ending of racial discrimination in the U.S. armed forces, which, despite a long and in many ways violent process, opened the door to achieving the same in civilian life of the country.

The end of the fighting in Korea came as an almost dull dead end. The first year of the war was filled with large territorial changes combined with major battles; this was followed by two years of military stalemate before the truce terms were finally agreed upon, based on the great principle of freedom of choice for those being released from captivity. In the aftermath of the conflict there were many people, both military and political, pumped up by recollections of total triumph in World War II, who expressed their disappointment and sometimes disgust about the limited results of the war. What followed beginning a dozen years later in Vietnam, however, resulted in an infinitely worse outcome, both in human and financial cost as well as in world opinion. There are those who argued as does Paul Edwards that the United States "lost disgracefully in Korea" and that "the people of America were strangely willing to accept the idea that Korea was a major defeat."[3] Korea was no defeat; Vietnam was.

In both cases the United States intervened in a civil war. Among the differences with which the United States had to contend in Vietnam were a much more widely based and unconventional conflict and open borders. It was similar to Korea in that white and black Americans, with Asian allies, were fighting Asians. The massive bombing of North Vietnam was no more decisive than what the air force did in North Korea. When Lyndon Johnson was contemplating pouring troops into South Vietnam in 1965, heeding air force claims, he first turned to bombing North Vietnam to force the northern regime to desist from supporting the southern rebellion. Largely on the basis of this reasoning, the Vietnam tragedy accelerated. When, eventually, after seven years, the full cost of that venture was tallied up, the Korean conflict began to look a lot better.[4]

After the Korean conflict ended an agency of the U.S. Army produced a report on the lessons learned there, but little apparently was learned in the sense that these revelations could be applied elsewhere. Among those historians who compared the two conflicts was Bernard Brodie, who concluded that the leaders of the United States "overlooked or ignored" the lessons of limited warfare that could have been drawn from the Korean experience.[5] One lesson that could be learned from that conflict is that massive aerial bombing far behind the lines did not effectively deter the opposition, but the air force rejected that finding, just as it did a similar conclusion made about the same matter after World War II. Another lesson, still unheeded: do not fight Asian masses on their mainland.

In the aftermath of the war, due entirely to domestic political influence (no one wanted to be soft on communism), the United States continued to protect Taiwan, refused to recognize the Beijing government, and successfully fought to keep Red China out of the United Nations. Three wrong policies do not make a right one. A half century after the war, the U.S. military maintains a force of more than 30,000 soldiers and several air bases in South Korea.

On the other hand, American intervention in both Formosa and South Korea eventually (despite dire predictions) provided the basis in security for a remarkable economic blossoming and effective representative government in both places in the decades ahead, while North Korea descended into an impoverished, fossilized, Stalinist state that has been experimenting with nuclear weapons and ballistic missiles. Red China, with its communist party still in political control, has become a beehive of capitalist enterprise. Mao Zedong would not have been pleased; his mausoleum in Tiananmen Square was closed to the public the two times this writer recently was there.

The direct involvement of the United Nations in the conflict enhanced its stature and importance; it was, in many ways, a rough coming-of-age experience for the world body, but in its name aggression was defeated. The approval and nominal support provided by the U.N. connection gave the American action at least the veneer of an international enterprise, but it was the United States, in conjunction with the South Koreans, that directed and fought the war. There was to be no repetition of U.N. intervention on that scale. In Vietnam, the United States essentially was on its own. Another effect of the Korean episode was a sense of insecurity in both the United States and the USSR, which resulted in hugely increased military expenditures. The temperature in the Cold War was elevated, with Red China becoming the principal adversary, which calls to mind the query of the Chinese engineer I encountered in Beijing: "Who won that war?"

There are many appropriate, indeed profound, observations about war (all the way back to the *Iliad*), but this one will suffice:

> In the presence of the violent reality of war, consciousness takes the place of imagination.
>
> — Wallace Stevens

Despite the searing experience of a war that encompassed all of their land and the continuing disruptive ambitions of the erratic and criminal North Korean regime, most of the resilient, indomitable people of that turbulent peninsula continue on the road to making their country, once again, the land of the morning calm, and a prosperous one.

The United States, in war and peace, and at very considerable human and financial cost, can rightly claim a constructive role in making this happen.

Reference Notes

Chapter One

1. Robert Heinl, *Victory at High Tide*, 29.
2. James Palais, "Search for Korean Uniqueness," *Harvard Journal of Asiatic Studies* 55, no. 2: 409–425.
3. Milton Rosen, *Rabbi in Korea*, 46.
4. Gregory Henderson, *Vortex*, 137; Michael Sandusky, *America's Parallel*, 81–85, 97–98, 177; Keyes Beech, *Tokyo and Points East*, 123–124.
5. Lewis Purifoy, *Harry Truman's China Policy*, 128–129.
6. Tsou, *America's Failure in China*, 527, 529, 560.
7. Lowe, *Origins of Korean War*, 179.
8. 1947 Joint Chiefs—Purifoy, 191; 1948 and 1949 National Security Council statements—Joseph Goulden, *Korea: The Untold Story*, 28–30.
9. Purifoy, 192; Goulden, 31; Spencer Tucker, *Encyclopedia*, 775.
10. Bok, *Impact of U.S. Forces in Korea*, 28; Henderson, "Korea 1950," in Cotton and Neary, eds., *Korean War in History*, 178.
11. Purifoy, 195.
12. James Matray, "Hodge," in Sandler, *KW Encyclopedia*, 134–135; Adwin Wigfall Green, *Epic of Korea*, 53–55.
13. Henderson, "Korea 1950," 176–177.
14. Cumings, *Place in Sun*, 211–224.
15. Sandusky, 289–292, 306.
16. Beech, *Tokyo*, 138. While in Greece this writer was told that Greeks, with their tendency for political argumentation, were "the Irish of the Mediterranean."
17. Henderson, *Vortex*, 170–173, 347–350.
18. Beech, 133–134.
19. Portway, *Morning Calm*, 46; Bong-young Choy, *Korea*, 291.
20. McCune and Gray, *Korea Today*, 245.
21. Yu Song-Chol in Kim Chullbaum, ed., *Truth About Korean War*, 147–148; Cumings, *Place in Sun*, 228–235.
22. John Ranelagh, *CIA Rise and Decline*, 181.
23. Andrei Lankov, *Stalin to Kim Il Sung*, 26–27, 32–33.
24. McCune, *Korea: Land of Broken Calm*, 102; McClure and Gray, 146–151.
25. Carl Berger, *Korean Knot*, 90; State Dept. —Goulden, 544.
26. J. Wilz, "Encountering Korea: American perceptions and policies to June 25 1950," in Williams, *Revolutionary War*, 51.
27. Faber, "Soviets and Korean War," in Sandler, *KW Encyclopedia*, 320–322; Kargi et al., 329.
28. Khrushchev, in Wilkinson, 61–62.
29. 72,000 Soviet personnel—Lester Brune, "Soviets and Korean War," in Lester Brune, *Korean War*, 213–214; Richard Bassett, *Wind Blew Cold*, 39.
30. Lester Brune, 198; Millett, 42; Alan J. Levine, *Stalin's Last War*, 39.
31. Bok, 35.
32. Xiaobing Li, *Modern Chinese Army*, 322n9.
33. Vladislav Zubok and Constantine Pleshakov, *Inside the Kremlin's Cold War*, 54–55; Youngho Kim, "Border Clashes," in Tucker, 86.
34. Levine, 38.
35. Zubok and Pleshakov, 55.
36. Goncharov, Sergei Lewis and Litai Wue, *Uncertain Partners*, 144–145.
37. Millett, *Korean War*, 216.
38. Schnabel, *Policy and Direction*, 30.
39. Stueck, *Road to Confrontation*, 169.
40. Acheson's March and May 1950 statements—John Wilz, "Korea and the United

States, 1945–1950," in Sandler, *KW Encyclopedia*, 177.

41. J. Wilz, "Encountering Korea," in Williams, *Revolutionary War*, 52–53; Berger, 91.

42. Stueck, *Road to Confrontation*, 154–155.

43. MacArthur—Stueck, 244–245.

44. Wilz, "Encountering Korea," 54.

45. Terrence Gough, *U.S. Army Mobilization and Logistics*, 24; Julian Thompson, *Lifeblood of War*, 106, 358 ref. 4.

46. John Singlaub, *Hazardous Duty*, 163; lost plan — Ron Miller interview.

47. Willoughby–Goulden, 40.

48. John Gunther, *Riddle of MacArthur*, 166–169.

49. Goulden, 53, 75.

50. Russell Buhite, *MacArthur*, 129; James Schnabel and Robert Watson, *History of Joint Chiefs*, 308, 333.

51. W.D. Reeve, *Republic of Korea*, 32; Glyn Jones in Knox, 295.

52. Bruce Cummings, *Korea's Place in the Sun*, 216–217.

53. Eckert et al., *Korea Old and New*, 348–349.

54. Millett, *Korean War*, 202–203.

55. Portway, 47, 50.

56. Yim, *Forty Year Fight*, 303.

57. Cumings, *Place in Sun*, 350–351.

58. Jinwung Kim, "Koch'ang Incident," in James Matray, *Historical Dictionary of the Korean War*, 230.

59. Steven Lee, *Korean War*, 97.

60. Weintraub, *MacArthur's War*, 22.

61. Lankov, 60.

62. Jin Hung Kim, "Pak Hon-Yong," in Matray, *Historical Dictionary*, 370.

63. Millett, *Korean War*, 166–174; "Ordeal of General Dean," in Quentin Reynolds and James Grashow, *With Fire and Sword*, 369–370; John J. Muccio in Lisle Rose, *Cold War to Main Street*, 193.

64. Kevin Mahoney, *Formidable Enemies*, 45.

65. Weintraub, 22; Anthony Farrar-Hockley, *British Part*, v. 1, 40–41.

66. Goulden, 42.

67. Ibid, 40.

68. Yim, 305–306.

69. Schnabel, *Policy and Direction*, 36–37, 39; O.H.P. King, *Paper Tiger*, 128.

70. Millett, *Korean War*, 202, 246–251, 256.

71. KMAG — Goulden, 34.

72. William J. Sebald, *With MacArthur*, 182–183.

73. James Schnabel, 36, 39–40.

74. Schafer, "Republic of (South) Korea Army," in Sandler, *Korean War Encyclopedia*, 294.

75. Millett, *Their War for Korea*, 256.

76. Stueck, *Confrontation*, 157, 166, 169.

77. Stressed — Millett, *Their War for Korea*, 257; Korean officer — Millett, 83.

78. Goncharov, Lewis and Wue, 150, 154–155.

79. Jack Cardoza, "Canada in Korean War," in Sandler, *KW Encyclopedia*, 61.

80. T.R. Fehrenbach, *This Kind of War*, 114, 118.

81. Marguerite Higgins, *War in Korea*, 88; James M. Minnich, *People's Army*, 60; *Army Almanac*, 615.

82. A-bombs, Air Force assumption — Max Hastings, *The Korean War*, 268; John Spanier, "Truman versus MacArthur: Achilles Rebound," in Alan Guttmann, ed., *Korea and Theory of Limited War*, 106–107.

83. Schnabel, *Policy and Direction*, 56.

84. James Doolittle, *I Can Never Be So Lucky Again*, 438–443.

85. Schnabel, 58–59.

86. Julian Thompson, *Lifeblood*, 107.

87. Michaelis, "This We Learned."

88. Haas, *Devil's Shadow*, 6.

89. 6 C-54 planes—Goulden, 112; Lyle Rishell, *Black Platoon*, 16.

90. Carl Eigabrodt, "Opposing Forces," in Sandler, *KW Encyclopedia*, 258–260.

91. 1948 plan — Gough, 24; Ron Miller interview.

92. Wilson Heefner, *Patton's Bulldog*, 151.

93. Fehrenbach, 172.

94. Hastings, *Korean War*, 52; see also 78–81, 87.

95. Ridgway, *Soldier*, 191; D. Clayton James, *Refighting Last War*, 138.

96. J. Lawton Collins, *Lightning Joe*, 348–349; Joint Chiefs to Japan/Korea? Jan.–Feb. 1950 — Schnabel and Watson, *History of Joint Chiefs*, v. 3, part 1. During World War II in Seventh Army morning reports, only 2 of 11,000 declared that morale was less than excellent (Keith Bonn, *When Odds Were Even*, 117–118).

97. Collins—James, 138; Kim Chum-kon, *Korean War*, 697; Michael Schaller, *American Occupation of Japan*.

98. Thomas E. Hanson, *Combat Ready?* 109–116.

99. Stanley Sandler, *The Korean War: An Encyclopedia*, 318.

100. William Manchester, *American Caesar*, 548.

101. Schnabel and Watson, *History Joint Chiefs*, 49–53.

102. King, *Paper Tiger*, 127–128.

103. Sebald, 184–185.

104. Millett, *Their War*, 165, 45.

105. Rishell, 25.

106. Lankov, 60; Vietnam — Michael Herr, *Dispatches*, 100–101.

107. Edwin P. Hoyt, *On to Yalu*, 14.

108. Rishell, 45.
109. Weintraub, 12–13.
110. Hanson, 109–116.
111. Heefner, 150–161.
112. Hastings, *Korean War*, 98, 87.
113. David Rees, ed., *Korean War*, 31; Michael P. Hickey, *Korean War*, 47–48.
114. William F. Dean, *General Dean's Story*, 29, 52–86.
115. Ibid.
116. Ridgway, *Korean War*, 26, 13–15.
117. "Sorely unprepared"— Singlaub, *Hazardous Duty*, 254.
118. John J. Muccio— Oral History Interview, Truman Library; Schnabel, *Policy and Direction*, 374–376.
119. Beech, *Tokyo*, 145–146.
120. Charles Bussey, *Firefight at Yechon*, 43.
121. Weintraub, 12, 284–285.
122. Ike with troops— Stephen Ambrose, *Eisenhower*, 294, 358; Ambrose, *Supreme Commander*, 321, 347, 536–537.
123. James, 43.
124. Sebald, 195.
125. Manchester, 538, 558.
126. Thomas Boettcher, *First Call*, 235.
127. Weintraub, 127.
128. Bradley, *A General's Life*, 523.
129. John Ohl, "Courtney Whitney," in Sandler, *KW Encyclopedia*, 353–354.
130. Whitney, *MacArthur: His Rendezvous with History*, 1956.
131. Dale Wilson, "Recipe for Failure," *Journal of Military History*, July 1992.
132. Appleman, *South to Naktong*, 490; Halberstam, *Coldest Winter*, 531, 160, 516–518, 531–532, 546–548, 552.
133. Shelby Stanton, *Tenth Legion*, 12–16, 28, 42, 52, 100, 104–105.
134. Clayton Laurie, "Willoughby," in Tucker, 739–740.
135. Weintraub, 211.
136. Robert Eichelberger, *Our Jungle Road to Tokyo*, in Harold DeWeerd, "Lessons," 599.
137. H. DeWeerd, "Lesson of Korean War," *Yale Review* (Summer 1951), 593–603.
138. Norman Graebner, CIA report, "Current Capabilities of North Korean Regime," in James Matray, *Historical Dictionary*, 107–108.
139. Esposito, "CIA," in Sandler, *Korean War Encyclopedia*, 66.
140. McGowen, "Military Intelligence," in Tucker, 446–447.
141. John Haynes, Harvey Klehr and Alexander Vassiliev, *Spies: Rise and Fall of KGB in America*, 401–402.
142. James Van Fleet, in Arthur Boyd, *Operation Broken Reed*, 258.
143. Christopher Andrew, *President's Eyes Only*, 185–187.

144. Haas, 12–13; William Breuer, *Shadow Warriors*, 20–21.
145. John Dille, *Substitute*, 39–45; see also 50–51.
146. Donald Nichols, *How Many Times*, 123.
147. Rene Catchpole, *Korean War*, 309–320.
148. Singlaub, 183.
149. Ibid., 165–168.
150. Ibid.
151. Esposito, "CIA," in Sandler, *KW Encyclopedia*, 66.
152. Tucker, 104.
153. McGowen, in Tucker, 446.
154. Graebner, "Current Capabilities," in Matray, ed., *Historical Dictionary*, 107–108; false alarms— King, *Paper Tiger*, 127–128.
155. Hastings, *Korean War*, 83.
156. DeWeerd, "Lessons," 595.
157. Chen Jian, "In Name of Revolution," 104.
158. Zubok and Pleshakov, 54–64.
159. 50 days— Gye-dong Kim, "Who Initiated," 37.
160. Three tanks— Appleman, *South to Naktong*, 231–233.
161. Muccio interview.
162. Stueck, *Confrontation*, 153.
163. H.W. Brands, "Connally," in Matray, 127.
164. Maxwell Taylor, *Uncertain Trumpet*, 13–14.
165. Paul Pierpaoli, *Truman and Korea*, 17–19; Taylor, 12–14.
166. James, *Refighting Last War*, 207.
167. Ibid, 137–138.
168. Geoffrey Perret, *Eisenhower*, 424–425.
169. Bok, 29; Louise Perret, *War to be Won*, 195–196.
170. Dulles, not necessary— U.S. State Department, *Foreign Relations of the United States: Korea*, v. 7, 108 (henceforth "*U.S. For. Rels.: Korea*"); proposed Pacific pact— Lloyd Gardner, *Approaching Vietnam*, 96.
171. Berger, 99.
172. Farrar-Hockley, v. 1, 40–41.
173. Rotation — Stueck, *Confrontation*, 165.
174. CIA report — *U.S. For. Rels.: Korea* 7, 7, 115–119.
175. Muccio, June 23 communication; ibid., 121; Goulden, 275–276.
176. Wilz, "Encountering Korea," 57–58.
177. Cumings, *Korea's Place in the Sun*, 262–264.
178. Lester Brune, "U.N and Korean War," in Brune, *Handbook*, 85–88.
179. Peter Faber, "Soviet Union and Korea," in Sandler, *KW Encyclopedia*, 321–322; Zubok and Pleshakov, 54–55, 62–64.
180. Evgueni Bajanov, "Origins of Korean War," www.alternativeinsight.com/Korean War.

181. John Haynes and Harvey Klehr, *Venona: Decoding Soviet Espionage in America*, 10 –11.

182. John L. Gaddis, *We Now Know*, 98 –100.

183. Stalin's strong interest in super-weapons, including long-range missiles— Gaddis, 237.

184. Weintraub, 190; Brune, "UN and Korea," in Brune, 90.

185. Jeffrey Grey, *Commonwealth Armies and Korea War*; Canada — David Bercuson, *Blood in the Hills*; Australia — Robert O'Neill, *Australia in Korean War*.

186. No helmets— Charles and Eugene Jones, *Face of War*, 156.

187. MacArthur, Truman, Acheson and Rusk on the French in Vietnam — *U.S. For. Rels.: Korea*, v. 7, 957–958, 961.

188. Slowly arriving, British hurry: Callum MacDonald, *Britain and Korean War*, 22; Schnabel and Watson, *History Joint Chiefs*, 161–173.

189. Weintraub, 238; A.K. Starbuck, "Turkish Brigade," *Military History*, Dec. 1997; see ch. 4, refs. 54, 55.

190. Weintraub, 190.

191. Joint Chiefs— *U.S. For. Rels.: Korea*, v. 7, 997–1000.

192. *New York Times*, 22 Nov. 1950.

193. Turkish disaster — Appleman, *Disaster in Korea*, 269, 376–378.

194. Hastings, *Korean War*, 89; Callum MacDonald, *Korea: The War Before Vietnam*, 21.

195. Farrar-Hockley, v. 1, 332, 334, 336, 136, 138.

196. MacDonald, *Britain and Korean War*, 21–22.

197. Schnabel and Watson, 173; William Worden, "Britain's Gallantry Is Not Dead," *Saturday Evening Post*, Feb. 17, 1951.

198. 3% Commonwealth forces— Schnabel and Watson, 174; British 14,000 — Anthony Farrar-Hockley in Sandler, *KW Encyclopedia*, 55.

199. Jeffry Gray, "Archibald Cassels," in Matray, *Historical Dictionary*, 74.

200. "Military courtesy"— Portway, 72.

201. Stanley Karnow, *Vietnam*, 177; Hanson Baldwin, *New York Times*, Nov. 22, 1950.

202. Kennan — *U.S. For. Rels.: Korea*, v. 7, 624.

203. Ibid., 957–958, 961, 1327, 1480, 1621–1622.

204. Schnabel and Watson, 174; Boettcher, 279; James Matray, 480–481.

205. William Stueck, "March to the Yalu," in Cumings, ed., *Child of Conflict*, 207–209, 217, 237; Steuck, *Road to Confrontation*, 231–233; Joint Chiefs— Russell Weigley, *History of the U.S. Army*, 514; 10 days— Schnabel and Watson, 308; G-4 — Schnabel, *Policy and Direction*, 228; G-3 — Schnabel, 230.

206. Richard Peters and Xiaobing Li, *Voices*

from the Korean War, 112; Ibid., 236; Knox and Coppel, *The Korean War*, 211.

207. Rene Cutforth, *Korean Reporter*, 13.

208. Jean Larteguy, *Face of War*, 148.

209. Ely J. Kahn, *Peculiar War*, 8.

210. Cutforth, 15 –16, 63.

211. Brady, *Coldest War*, 123 –124.

212. James Dill, "Winter of the Yalu," 37.

213. Zubok and Pleshakov, 55; Bill Shinn, *Forgotten War*, 101.

214. King, *Paper Tiger*, 128 –130 (planes), 130 (ammo), 163 –164 (bug-out).

215. Jiyul Kim, Review.

216. Millett, *Their War*, 45.

217. King, 140 –141.

218. Ibid.

219. Farrar-Hockley, v. 1, 42–43.

220. Choy, *Korea*, 292.

221. John Tarpey, "Korea: Twenty-five Years Later," *U.S. Naval Institute Proceedings* 104 (August 1978): 56; torpedo boats— Charles Cole, *Korea Remembered*, 39.

222. Riley and Schramm, *Reds Take a City*, vi; B. Shinn, *Forgotten War*, 66, 72–74.

223. Korean Institute of Military History, *Korean War*, v. 1, 113 –114; Jinwung Kim, "Pak Hon-yong," in Matray, *Historical Dictionary*, 369–370.

224. "Muccio the Modest," *Newsweek*, Nov. 13, 1950.

225. Appleman, *South to Naktong*, 231–233.

226. William Funchess, *Korea P.O.W.*, 4, 10.

227. Charles Hanley, "60 Years Later, Korea Vets Return," Associated Press, June 13, 2010.

228. John W. Downey, Francis C. Downey interviews.

229. Edwards, ed., *Korean War*, 66–69; Walter Bradford interview.

230. Farrar-Hockley, v. 1, 42–43, 119–120; William Dean in Knox, *Oral History*, 13.

231. MacArthur to Joint Chiefs, July 9, 1950 — *U.S. For. Rels.: Korea*, 336.

232. MacArthur to Joint Chiefs, July 7 — Appleman, *South to Naktong*, 118.

233. Edwards, ed., *Korean War*, 49.

234. Millett, "Casualties," in Tucker, 100; Elizabeth Schafer, "Rotation," in Tucker, 574–575.

235. James Huston, "Logistics," in Sandler, *KW Encyclopedia*, 199.

236. General Reserve — Goulden, 134–136.

237. David Zabecki, "U.S. Army," in Tucker, 691.

238. Robert Arvin, "U.S. Reserve Forces," in Tucker, 710–711.

239. Joe Dunn, in Tucker, 193.

240. Edwards, ed., *Korean War*, 46, 40; percentage — Portway, 75.

241. Knox, *Oral History*, 17–18, 15, 12.

242. Henderson, "Korea, 1950," in Cotton and Neary, eds., *Korean War in History*, 181.

243. Dean Hess, *Battle Hymn*, 106.

244. Hess, "Eyewitness to Early Days," HistoryNet.com, 3.

245. Tomedi, 3.

246. Harold Noble, *Embassy at War*, 107.

247. Melvin House in Hanley, "60 Years Later."

248. Richard Mack, *Memoir*, 15–16, 18.

249. Five thugs — Philip Day in Knox, 9.

250. Jessup in Millett, 176.

251. Korgie in Knox, 33.

252. Mack, 20–24.

253. George Forty, *War in Korea*, 28–33, 37.

254. Goulden, 146.

255. Ibid., 139–141.

256. Henderson, "Korea, 1950," 181.

257. Warner, "Early Days Korea," 1–2, 6.

258. Ibid.

259. Raymond Lech, *Broken Soldiers*, 11–15.

260. *U.S. For. Rels.: Korea*, 337, 344.

261. *USA Today*, April 13, 2007; Charles Hanley, Martha Mendoza and Sang-hun Choe, *Bridge at No Gun Ri*.

262. "Another Korean War Massacre Report Surfaces," *Pacific Stars and Stripes*, Oct. 7, 1999; "Ex-GIs Say No Gun Ri Orders Came from Higher HQ," *CNN.com*, Nov. 21, 2000; *Seattle Times*, Aug. 4, 2008.

263. Robert Bateman, *No Gun Ri: A Military History of the Korean War Incident*; Dept. of Army, Inspector General, "Report of the No Gun Ri Review," 2001.

264. Hanley et al., *No Gun Ri*.

265. Inspector General report.

266. Hanley and Jae-soon Chang, "Thousands killed by U.S.'s Korean ally," Associated Press, May 19, 2008; related AP report, July 5, 2008; examples of executions — Denis Warner, "Early Days Korea," 6.

267. Muccio — *U.S. For. Rels.: Korea*, 1579–1587.

268. Weintraub, 199; Taejon — Li and Peters, 67–68.

269. Farrar-Hockley, v. 1, 205, v. 2, 415.

270. Warner, "Early Days Korea," 7.

271. Farrar-Hockley, v. 1, 132.

272. *Khrushchev Remembers*, 146–147.

273. Riley and Schramm, 5, 89.

274. Chum-kon Kim, *Korean War*, 393–395.

275. Rosen, *Rabbi in Korea*, 35.

276. John Toland, *In Mortal Combat*, 125–126; Goulden, 130–131.

277. Toland, 125.

278. Kang, *Home Was the Land*, 106–111.

279. Chum-kon Kim, *Korean War*, 401.

280. Esposito, "South Korea Occupation," Tucker, 604–606; Riley and Schramm, 7f, 103–110.

281. Steven Lee, 141–142.

282. Chum-kon Kim, *Korean War*, 398–400.

283. Esposito, in Tucker, 604.

284. Choy, *Korea*, 291.

285. Chum-kon Kim, 395–396.

286. Toland, 125.

287. William Daugherty, "Communist Patterns of Propaganda," 838–840.

288. Li and Peters, 207.

289. Knox, 364.

290. Ju Young-bok in Millett, 45.

291. Daugherty, "Communist Patterns," 840.

292. Ibid., 830–831.

293. 200,000 — Chum-kon Kim, 390–391; Toland, 124–126.

294. Lee Young Ho in Li and Peters, 187–190.

295. Hastings, 89–93; Henderson, *Vortex*, 197; Mahoney, 8–10.

296. Andrew Nahm and James Hoare, *Dictionary Republic of Korea*, 119.

297. Kahn, 31–33.

298. Rolf Jacoby, "USIE," in William Daugherty, ed., *Psychological Warfare Casebook*, 225–227.

299. North Koreans, 58,000 casualties — Hastings, *Korean War*, 82; Mahoney, 10.

300. Robert Service, *Stalin*, 534.

301. Insook Park, "Cho Pyong-ok," in Tucker, 143–144.

302. Robert Oliver, *Rhee*, 312–313.

303. W.D. Reeve, *Republic of Korea*, 36–37.

304. Kang, 119–120.

305. Robert Oliver, *Verdict in Korea*, 103–109, 193.

306. R. Bruce Wareing, *Korean War Educator* <http://www.koreanwar-educator.org/memoirs/wareing_bruce/index.htm>.

307. Riley and Schramm, 52–53.

308. Esposito, in Tucker, 606.

309. Henderson, *Vortex*, 169.

Chapter Two

1. Nichols, *How Many Times Can I Die*, 127–128.

2. Max Hastings, *Korean War*, 82.

3. Sun Yup Paik, *From Pusan to Panmunjom*, 33.

4. Korean Institute of Military History, *The Korean War*, v. 1, 569–570.

5. Ibid., 114.

6. Boris Spiroff, *Korea: Frozen Hell on Earth*, 58–59; James Cameron, *Point of Departure*, 132–133.

7. Korean Institute, v. 1, 569–570.

8. Joseph L. Collins, *War in Peacetime*, 196–197.

9. Toland, *Mortal Combat*, 381.

10. Rod Paschall, *Witness Korea*, 76.

11. Farrar-Hockley, *British Part*, v. 1, 335–336.

12. Harold Shelley, *Korean War Educator* <http://www.koreanwar-educator.org/memoirs/selley/index.htm>.

13. Roy Appleman, *Ridgway Duels for Korea*, 97–138.

14. *New York Times*, December 6, 8, 12, 18, and 19, 1950.

15. Yong-ho Ch'oe in Matray, *Historical Dictionary*, 531; see also Rene Cutforth, *Korean Reporter*, 98–121; John Denson, "Bitter Week End in Seoul," *Colliers*, Jan. 27, 1951.

16. H.W. Baldwin, "Tense Lands in China's Shadow," *New York Times Magazine*, Dec. 24, 1950.

17. Walter Hermes, *Truce Tent and Fighting Front*, 63–65, 208–214.

18. Melvin Voorhees, *Korean Tales*, 144–145; Paul Braim, *Will to Win*, 272, 275–277; Van Fleet's views—Hermes, 211–212.

19. Alexander George, *Chinese Communist Army*, 32–36, 154–189.

20. Schnabel, *Policy and Direction*, 40; ROKs —Weintraub, *MacArthur's War*, 78; Farrar-Hockley, *British Part*, v. 2, 420.

21. Wright, in Schnabel, *Policy and Direction*, 167; Scherer in Paschall, *Witness*, 42.

22. Robert Smith, *MacArthur in Korea*, 76–77.

23. Korean Institute, v. 1, 517.

24. Weintraub, 247; Ely J. Kahn, *Peculiar War*, 116–117.

25. Rishell, *Black Platoon*, 58.

26. John G. Westover, ed., *Combat Support*; Brady, *Coldest War*, 56–57, 117.

27. Westover, ed., *Combat Support*, 242, 25, 42.

28. Martin Russ, *Breakout*, 107, 190; Hamel, *Chosin*, 338, 377–378.

29. Weintraub, 114, 121–122, '39, 71–72; Kahn, *Peculiar War*, 116–117; Eliot Cohen and John Gooch, "Aggregate Failure," 183; Millett, *Their War for Korea*, 173; Appleman, *South to Naktong*, 667; John W. Downey interview.

30. B.H. Liddell Hart, *Strategy*, 232–235, 339–342; Marguerite Higgins, *War in Korea*, 157–166.

31. Joseph Collins, *War in Peacetime*, 296.

32. Carol Lee, "White Horse Hill," in Tucker, 737–738; Stephens, *Old Ugly Hill*, 130–131.

33. McAleer, *Out of Savannah*, 321; James W. Elkins, *Korean War Educator* <http://www.koreanwar-educator.org/memoirs/elkins_james/index.htm>.

34. Chris Sarno, *Korean War Educator* <http://www.koreanwar-educator.org/memoirs/sarno/index.htm>; see also James Elkins in ibid.

35. Sarin and Dvoretsky, *Alien Wars*, 65; Frank, *Long Way Round*, 104, 147, 172–173.

36. *New York Times*, Dec. 17, 18, 19, 1950; Frank, 104, 147, 172–173.

37. Pease, *Psywar*, 138.

38. William Daugherty, "Communist Patterns of Propaganda"; Sue — Knox, *Oral History*, 315.

39. Farrar-Hockley, v. 1, 261.

40. Appleman, *Escaping Trap*, 271, 273.

41. Halberstam, *Coldest Winter*, 27.

42. Korean Institute, v. 1, 778, 814, 859.

43. Anak-Spiller, *American POWs in Korea*, 43–44.

44. Paik, *Pusan to Panmunjom*, 246.

45. Hastings, *Korean War*, 242; Cameron, *Point of Departure*, 132–133.

46. Richard Allen, *Korea's Syngman Rhee*.

47. Appleman, *Disaster*, 427–431; Schnabel and Watson, *History Joint Chiefs*, 334; Dae-sook Suh, *Kim Il Sung*; Tania Branigan, "North Korea holds 200,000 political prisoners, says Amnesty," London *Guardian*, May 4, 2011.

48. Catchpole, *Korean War*, 309–317; Appleman, *South to Naktong*, 721–728.

49. Truman —*U.S. For. Rels.: Korea*, v. 7, 960.

50. Paul Edwards, *Acknowledge a War*, 72.

51. Phillip Deane, *Captive in Korea*, 10; Thompson, *Cry Korea*, 44.

52. Cameron, *Point of Departure*, 109–110, 100–102.

53. Louis G. Buttell, *Korean War Educator* <http://www.koreanwar-educator.org/memoirs/buttell_louis/index.htm>.

54. Hanley, et al., *No Gun Ri*, 70–71.

55. Knox, *Oral History*, 27.

56. Joseph Goulden, *Korea*, 146.

57. Beech, *Tokyo and Points East*, 137.

58. Hastings, *Korean War*, 248.

59. Toland, 337.

60. William L. White, *Captives of Korea*, 46.

61. David Skaggs, "KATUSA Experiment."

62. Cardinal—*Oral History*, 409; Anderson, Bolt, and Brummer —<http://www.koreanwar-educator.org>; Lonsford —Arthur W. Wilson, *Korean Vignettes*, 39; Allen Wilkinson, *Up Front Korea*, 362.

63. Justice —A.W. Wilson, *Korean Vignettes*, 45; McGrath —A.W. Wilson, 25; Chatham —A.W. Wilson, 245; James Neely, *Korean War Educator* <http://www.koreanwar-educator.org/memoirs/neely_james/index.htm>.

64. Paul Noll, <http://www.paulnoll.com>.

65. James Huston, *Guns and Butter*, 339–342.

66. Appleman, *South to Naktong*, 110.

67. William Anderson, *Korean War Educator* <http://www.koreanwar-educator.org/memoirs/anderson_william/index.htm>.

68. Eggs— James Christiansen, *Korean War Educator* <http://www.koreanwar-educator.org/memoirs/christiansen_jim/index.htm>.

69. Goulden, 32–41.

70. Paik, *Pusan to Panmunjom*, 7, 20, 33, 53–

54, 64, 115–117, 125–126, 120; see also Lee Chan Shik, in Peters and Li, 168.

71. Ibid.
72. Kirsh — A.W. Wilson, 75. Peters and Li, 130.
73. Paik, 91.
74. Ibid., 120.
75. James Neely, "Story of Bull Run," <http://www.koreanwar-educator.org>.
76. Harris, "My Typewriter War," *Greybeards*, Nov.-Dec. 2009.
77. Buttell, <http://www.koreanwar-educator.org/memoirs/buttell_louis/index.htm>.
78. Ridgway, *Korean War*, 93.
79. Noel Monks, *Eyewitness*, 318.
80. Appleman, *Ridgway Duels*, 94, 298.
81. Van Fleet — Dille, 26–32.
82. Robert Doyle, *A Prisoner's Duty*, 171–175.
83. McAllister — A.W. Wilson, 209.
84. Barton —ibid.
85. Funchess, *Korea P.O.W.*, 20.
86. Gregory — A. Wilson, 27; Pate, *Reactionary!* 40, 45–49, 51.
87. Albert Styles, *Korean War Educator* <http://www.koreanwar-educator.org/memoirs/styles_albert/index.htm>; Eldon Stanley, *Korean War Educator* <http://www.koreanwar-educator.org/memoirs/stanley_ike/index.htm>.
88. Michael Njus, *Korean War Educator* <http://www.koreanwar-educator.org/memoirs/njus/index.htm>.
89. William Sports, *Korean War Educator* <http://www.koreanwar-educator.org/memoirs/sports_william/index.htm>.
90. William Dillon, *Korean War Educator* <http://www.koreanwar-educator.org/memoirs/dillon_william/index.htm>.
91. Kahn, *Peculiar War*, 106–107, 111–115.
92. Haas, *In Devil's Shadow*, 151, 122–123.
93. Westover, ed., *Combat Support*, 65–66; cable crew —ibid., 234.
94. Huston, *Guns and Butter*, 287–288.
95. Ibid., 350–351.
96. Phillip Knightley, *First Casualty*, 372.
97. Charles Brown, *Korean War Educator* <http://www.koreanwar-educator.org/memoirs/brown_charles/index.htm>; Tucker, *Encyclopedia*, 366–370.
98. Brady, *Coldest War*, 19.
99. Rishell, 61; Paul Edwards, ed., *Korean War*, 132.
100. Martin Russ, *Last Parallel*, 165.
101. Alfred Gale, *Korean War Educator* <http://www.koreanwar-educator.org/memoirs/gale_alfred/index.htm>.
102. Knox, *Oral History*, 95; Wilkinson, 132.
103. William Anderson, *Korean War Educator* <http://www.koreanwar-educator.org/memoirs/anderson_william/index.htm>.
104. Robinson — A.W. Wilson, 255; see also capture of North Korean women — Billy Clark, ibid.
105. James Elkins, *Korean War Educator* <http://www.koreanwar-educator.org/memoirs/elkins_james/index.htm>.
106. Brady, *Coldest War*, "Blue boys" 56–57.
107. Aiple — A.W. Wilson, 351.
108. Peter Rendina, *Korean War Educator* <http://www.koreanwar-educator.org/memoirs/rendina_pete/index.htm>.
109. Funchess, *Korea POW*, 31, 130.
110. Paschall, 151–152; Hastings, 306–313; Monks, 326, 329.
111. William H. Vatcher, *Panmunjom*, 131.
112. Wright in Knox, 293; Saluzzi in Knox, 297; Doyle, 173–175.
113. Dannenmaier, 159.
114. Homer Hill, <http://www.koreanwar-educator.org>.
115. Leonard Martin, *Korean War Educator* <http://www.koreanwar-educator.org/memoirs/martin_leonard/index.htm>.
116. Larteguy, *Face of War*, 145–146.
117. Ahn Junghyo, "Double Exposure of War," in West, Levine and Hiltz, eds., *America's Wars in Asia*, 163–164; Brady, 176–179, 201.
118. Richard Bohart, *Korean War Educator* <http://www.koreanwar-educator.org/memoirs/bohart_richard/index.htm>.
119. Albert Zentko in A.W. Wilson.
120. Leguire, *Graybeards*, March-April 2011.
121. Barry Jones in A.W. Wilson, 189.
122. Capt. Sam Holliday, *Korean War Educator* <http://www.koreanwar-educator.org/memoirs/holliday_sam/index.htm>.
123. Knox, 44; see also 656, 657, 673; Herman Nelson in Peters and Li, 73.
124. Curtis Morrow, *What's a Commie*, 15–16, 19.
125. Joseph Siren account.
126. Mary Kathleen Wilson interview.
127. Herman Brummer, *Korean War Educator* <http://www.koreanwar-educator.org/memoirs/brummer_ross/index.htm>.
128. Jeffers, "Korean War Orphans, KWVA," in *Forgotten War Remembered*.
129. Stephens, *Old Ugly Hill*, 164, 166; Brady, 133–134.
130. Eldon Stanley, *Korean War Educator* <http://www.koreanwar-educator.org/memoirs/stanley_ike/index.htm>.
131. George Gatliff, *Korean War Educator* <http://www.koreanwar-educator.org/memoirs/gatliff_george/index.htm>.
132. Ralph Abell, in Russ, *Breakout*, 382.
133. Bales in Eric Hammel, *Chosin*, 398.
134. Michael Caine, *What's It All About?*, 77.
135. Allen Scott, *Korean War Educator* <http:

//www.koreanwar-educator.org/memoirs/scott
_allen/index.htm>.

136. Hopkins, in Russ, *Breakout*, 420.
137. William Anderson, *Korean War Educator* <http://www.koreanwar-educator.org/memoirs/anderson_william/index.htm>.
138. Paul Noll, <http://www.paulnoll.com>.
139. Frank, *Long Way Round*, 162.
140. Hess, *Battle Hymn*, 86, 106–110, 145, 221–223, 237–238; George Drake letter, "Is Colonel Hess a Korean War fraud or hero?" in *ROK Drop*, June 23, 2010.
141. Paul Edwards, *Combat Operations*, 117–118, 129–130.
142. Appleman, *East of Chosin*, 280–283, 273–274.
143. Ibid., 285–286.
144. Frank, 92, 165.
145. Dille, *Substitute for Victory*, 135–136, 143–145.
146. Public Affairs— Voorhees, *Korean Tales*, 149, 197–199; Frank, 111; Dille, 130.
147. Dille, 143, 145.
148. Menninger in Knox, 44.
149. Ibid., 657.
150. Victor Fox in Knox, 673.
151. Herbert, *Soldier*, 42.
152. Kahn, *Peculiar War*, 174.
153. Deerfield, "A Walk Down a Road Near Pusan," *Greybeards*, Jan.-Feb. 2009.
154. Frank, 69.
155. Caine, *What's It All About?*, 65.
156. Kahn, 178–179.
157. Ibid, 174–175, 38.
158. Lafferty, "Personal Reflections," *Greybeards*, March-April 2009.
159. Dallas Mossman, *Korean War Educator* <http://www.koreanwar-educator.org/memoirs/mossman_dallas/index.htm>.
160. James Elkins, *Korean War Educator* <http://www.koreanwar-educator.org/memoirs/elkins_james/index.htm>.
161. Noble, *Embassy at War*, 201.
162. Fox, in Knox, 371–372.
163. Brian in Knox, 392, 375–376.
164. Seoul — Li and Peters, *Voices*, 82.
165. Lee in Russ, *Breakout*, 350; evacuation —*New York Times*, Dec. 5, 1950.
166. Cutforth, *Korean Reporter*, 189–190.
167. Voorhees, *Korean Tales*, 187.
168. Cutforth, 64–65.
169. ROK majority as of June 1952 — Sandler, 199.
170. Katherine Moon, *Sex Among Allies*, 1–97; Thomas Greland interview.
171. Elizabeth Kim, *Ten Thousand Sorrows*, 7–10, 29–30; see also Kang, *Home Was the Land of the Morning Calm*.
172. During war — Dave Koegel and Leonard Korgie in Knox and Coppel, 268, 275–276; 2009

estimate — Coalition Against Trafficking in Women; Donald MacIntyre, "Base Instincts," *Time*, Aug. 5, 2002; Choe Sang-hun, "Ex-prostitutes say South Korea enabled sex trade near bases," *New York Times*, Jan. 8, 2009.
173. Caine, 67, 81.
174. Samuel L.A. Marshall, *Bringing Up the Rear*, 220–221.
175. Russ, *Last Parallel*, 204–205.
176. Brady, 112–113.
177. John Genrich, *Korean War Educator* <http://www.koreanwar-educator.org/memoirs/genrich_jon/index.htm>.
178. Herbert, *Making of a Soldier*, 36.
179. E. Kim, 16.
180. 57 released —*New York Times*, Nov. 25, 1950; apologized, shot —*New York Times*, Dec. 12, 1950.
181. Dallas Mossman, *Korean War Educator* <http://www.koreanwar-educator.org/memoirs/mossman_dallas/index.htm>.
182. Appleman, *Ridgway Duels for Korea*, 192, 194.
183. Robert Rigg, "Chinese Army Indoctrination," in Daugherty, ed., *Psychological Warfare Casebook*, 482–485; Happy Valley — Lewis Carlson, *Remembered Prisoners*, 270n18.
184. Doyle, *Voices from Captivity*,172.
185. Appleman, *Ridgway Duels*, 192, 289, 366, 368, 401, 500, 529–530; Anthony Farrar-Hockley, *Edge of Sword*, 124–125, 261–262.
186. Westover, ed., *Combat Support*, 57; G.I.s retrieved — Knox, 437; did not fire — Charles Moore, "Marines rescue 300 shot-up GIs from Chosin ice," *Stars and Stripes*, Jan. 1951.
187. Russell Gugeler, *Combat Actions in Korea*, 77.
188. White, *Captives of Korea*, 127.
189. Robert Rigg, *Red China's Fighting Hordes*, 124, 131–133.
190. Hammel, *Chosin*, 205–210.
191. Russ, *Breakout*, 384–385.
192. Ibid., 372, 382; Young — Hammel, 398.
193. Stewart — Russ, *Breakout*, 390.
194. James Bolt, *Korean War Educator* <http://www.koreanwar-educator.org/memoirs/bolt_james>.
195. Richard Bohart, *Korean War Educator* <http://www.koreanwar-educator.org/memoirs/bohart_richard/index.htm>.
196. Goulden, 341.
197. Hammel, 347.
198. Hammel, 375.
199. Appleman, *East of Chosin*, 289–290, 281–282.
200. Pease, *Psywar*, 123.
201. McAleer, *Out of Savannah*, 94.
202. Wood in A.W. Wilson, 349; W.B. Woodruff, Jr., in Knox and Coppel, 204.
203. Farrar-Hockley, *Edge of the Sword*, 67.

204. Millett, *Their War for Korea*, 116.

205. Russ, *Breakout*, 192, 219–220.

206. Knox, *Korean Oral History*, 644.

207. Albert Styles, *Korean War Educator* <http://www.koreanwar-educator.org/memoirs/styles_albert/index.htm>.

208. Thank you— *New York Times*, Dec. 11, 1950.

209. Herbert, *Soldier*, 52.

210. Herbert, *Making of a Soldier*, 1.

211. Czuboka, "Chinese kill about 68 African-Americans," KWVA, *Greybeards*, March-April 2009.

212. MacArthur— Appleman, *Ridgway Duels*, 291.

213. A.W. Wilson, 279.

214. James DeLong, *Korean War Educator* <http://www.koreanwar-educator.org/memoirs/delong_james/index.htm>.

215. Michael Njus, *Korean War Educator* <http://www.koreanwar-educator.org/memoirs/njus/index.htm>; Brady, 33, 39–40.

216. Army Peter Cummings in A.W. Wilson, 297.

217. Ted Heckelman, *Korean War Educator* <http://www.koreanwar-educator.org/memoirs/heckelman_ted/index.htm>.

218. Caine, *What's It All About?*, 81.

219. Bevin Alexander, *War We Lost*, 300–301.

220. Marshall, *Pork Chop Hill*, 21.

221. Edwards, *Acknowledge a War*, 62.

222. Political officers— Toland, 454.

223. James DeLong, *Korean War Educator* <http://www.koreanwar-educator.org/memoirs/delong_james/index.htm>; O.P. Smith, <http://www.koreanwar-educator.org>; John Genrich, *Korean War Educator* <http://www.koreanwar-educator.org/memoirs/genrich_jon/index.htm>; Kenneth Kendall, *Korean War Educator* <http://www.koreanwar-educator.org/memoirs/kendall_kenneth/index.htm>; O.P. Smith— Russ, *Breakout*, 264.

224. James Elkins, *Korean War Educator* <http://www.koreanwar-educator.org/memoirs/elkins_james/index.htm>.

225. Brady, 140.

226. William Anderson, *Korean War Educator* <http://www.koreanwar-educator.org/memoirs/anderson_william/index.htm>.

227. Li, *History of Chinese Army*, 91; Kevin Mahoney, *Formidable Enemies*, 36–37; L. Peisakhin and P. Pinto, "Army as Forge of Political Loyalty," 3–4; George, *Chinese Communist Army*, 195.

228. Chullbaum Kim, *The Truth about the Korean War*, 204.

229. Paschall, *Witness Korea*, 172–176, Hastings, *Korean War*, 286–304.

230. Li and Peters, *Voices*, 232.

231. Clarance Adams, *American Dream*, 56–57, 103–104.

232. Edwards, *Acknowledge a War*, 33–36.

233. Knightley, 384–385.

234. Russ, *Last Parallel*, 320.

235. Dr. Harold Secor, *Korean War Educator* <http://www.koreanwar-educator.org/memoirs/secor_harold/index.htm>.

236. Andrei Lankov, *Stalin to Kim Il Sung*.

237. Allen Whiting, *China Crosses the Yalu*, 43.

238. Ibid., 44, 105.

239. Ibid., 43.

240. Ibid., 105, 43–45.

241. Goncharov, Lewis and Wue, *Uncertain Partners*, 145.

242. Paik, 57, 84.

243. Party cards abandoned— Gordon Paige, *Korean People's Democratic Republic*, 87.

244. Alan Levine, *Stalin's Last War*, 100; Leckie, *Conflict*, 147; Robert Simmons, *Strained Alliance*, 163.

245. Ibid., 179.

246. Goncharov et al., 189.

247. Whiting, 124–125.

248. Goncharov et al., 201; Lankov, 61.

249. Kim and Peng— Joe Dunn, "Kim," in Tucker, 315.

250. Suh, *Kim Il Sung*.

251. John Gittings, *Chinese Army*, 131; Wang Xuedong in Li and Peters, 124, 119.

252. Millett, *Their War*, 135.

253. Kim denounces— Dunn, in Tucker, 315.

254. U.S. bombing— Clint Mundinger, "O'Donnell," in Tucker, 495.

255. Sarin and Dvoretsky, 76–77, 79–86, 65.

256. Zubok and Pleshakov (*Inside Kremlin*, 155) state that the decision was made by the new leadership immediately after Stalin's death.

257. Within days of Stalin's death Zhou Enlai requested Soviet assistance in speeding up negotiations and concluding an armistice (ibid.).

258. Steven Avella, "Kim," in Sandler, *KW Encyclopedia*, 163.

259. Chinese left in 1958— Hua Quingzhao, "CPVA," in Matray, *Historical Dictionary*, 92.

260. Avella, in Sandler, 163–164; Don Oberdorfer, *Two Koreas*, 393–396.

261. Ibid., 20–22; Elizabeth Schafer, "North Korea," in Sandler, *KW Encyclopedia*, 253.

262. Dunn, in Tucker, 316–317.

263. Famine— Oberdorfer, 397–399; nuclear— Brune, 326, Lankov, 75.

264. Schafer, in Sandler, 252.

265. Lankov, 67–68; Tania Branigan, "North Korea holds 200,000 political prisoners, says Amnesty," *Guardian*, May 4, 2011; "South Korea foils murder attempt on defector-activist," *Irish Times*, Sept. 17, 2011.

266. Thailand— Republic of Korea, Ministry

of National Defense, *History of UN Forces in Korean War*, v. 1, 498–595.

267. Starbuck, "Turkish Brigade;" Appleman, *Disaster*, 269, 376–378.

268. Republic of Korea, *History*, v. 1, 678–679; Marshall in Carlson, 271, ref. 27.

269. Republic of Korea, *History*, v. 1, 677.

270. Hastings, 278–279; Jeffry Grey, *Commonwealth Armies*, 85; Ondrish, "Korea: My Story," *Graybeards*, March/April 2007.

271. Tony Lovell in Adrian Walker, *Barren Place*, 85.

272. Killing Koreans—*New York Times*, Dec. 17–19, 1950; U.S. Navy chaplain Glyn Jones, in Knox, 295.

273. Monks, 316.

274. Rum swapped—Holmstead, *Ready to Fire*, 55; gin/stoves—Monks, 319.

275. Tony Lovell in Adrian Walker, *Barren Place*, 85.

276. Gerald Kingsland, *Quest for Glory*, 137.

277. Ibid.

278. Grey in Walker, *Barren Place*, 73.

279. Fowley in Walker, 67; Maud in Walker, 106–107, 120.

280. Grey, in Walker, 76.

281. Walding in Walker, 98.

282. Fun—Maud, in Walker, 106; honorable—Alan Causer in Walker, 142.

283. Atlee—Lloyd Gardner, *Approaching Vietnam*, 105; Atlee talking with Hugh Dalton—MacDonald, *Britain and Korean War*, 45.

284. Morris McGregor, *Integration of Armed Forces*, 428–430.

285. Weintraub, 80–81, 88.

286. Edwards, ed., *Korean War*, 50.

287. Lester Brune, *Korean War Handbook*, 246.

288. 98 percent—McGregor, 428.

289. Singlaub, *Hazardous Duty*, 161–163, 169–170.

290. Marshall, *River and Gauntlet*, 34, 286, 290, 295, 301; Higgins, *War in Korea*, facing 129, 89–90.

291. Buckley, *American Patriots*, 357–359.

292. Bussey, *Firefight at Yechon*, 89.

293. Morrow, 8–9, 77, 35, also 25–27; Bowers et al., *Black Soldier, White Army*.

294. Marshall, *Bringing Up the Rear*, 182, 184–185, 208.

295. High school draft—Elizabeth Mitchell Gerry interview.

296. "White negroes"—Max Hastings, *Armageddon*, 497.

297. Morrow, 41.

298. Eric Goldman, *Crucial Decade and After: America, 1945–1960*, 184–185; Stephens, *Old Ugly Hill*, 15.

299. Thurgood Marshall, *Report on Korea:*

The Shameful Story of the Courts Martial of Negro GIs (New York: NAACP, 1951).

300. Bowers et al., *Black Soldiers, White Army*, 185–189.

301. Appleman, *South to Naktong*, 485–486; McAuliffe in Goldman, 185; Collins, *Lightning Joe*, 356; see also 354–358.

302. McGregor, *Integration*, 433, 438–439.

303. Steven Casey, *Selling Korean War*, 321.

304. Bowers et al., 184–185, 188, 257.

305. Rishell, 47, 50, 55–58, 60, 81.

306. Brady, 99, 79; Daley recollection—*Graybeards*, Sept.–Dec. 2007; Koegel in Knox and Coppel, 268.

307. Bowers et al., 203–204.

308. Li et al., *Mao's Generals*, 83–84, 256 ref. 21.

309. Bowers et al., xiii.

310. Westover, ed., *Combat Support*, 221.

311. Cutforth, *Korean Reporter*, 109–110.

312. Hastings, *Korean War*, 298; see also Morrow, 69.

313. Carlson, *Remembered Prisoners*, 93.

314. Ibid., 314.

315. Bowers et al., 222.

316. Carlson, 207–211, 217–219.

317. Morrow, 34, 44–45, 85; see also 26–27; King—Luke Macauley, "Passing from Memory," 66.

318. Morrow, 111.

319. McGregor, 439; 12 percent—Appleman, *Ridgway Duels*, 572.

320. Ibid., 434.

321. Rosters—McWilliams, *Hallowed Ground*, 149.

322. Li and Peters, 137.

323. Pete Rendina, *Korean War Educator* <http://www.koreanwar-educator.org/memoirs/rendina_pete/index.htm>.

324. Otto Junkermann in A.W. Wilson, 313.

325. McWilliams, 149; Herbert, *Making of a Soldier*, 93–94, 112.

326. Herbert, *Making of a Soldier*, 93.

327. Bob Ondrish, "Korea: My Story—1950–1951," *Graybeards*, March/April 2007.

328. Jack Wright in Knox and Coppel, 19–20.

329. Li and Peters, 175; Edward Gregory, Jr., in Knox, *Oral History*, 373; Jimmy Marks, ibid., 625.

330. Morrow, 36.

331. Toland, 459, also 454. See also Tucker, *Korean War Encyclopedia*, 11–14, 692.

332. Edwards, ed., *Korean War*, 50.

333. Puerto Ricans—McWilliams, 150.

334. Voorhees, 186.

335. Millett, *Their War for Korea*, 176–177; Asian—Roy Shiraga in A.W. Wilson, 119.

336. Herb Wong, *Korean War Educator* <http://www.koreanwar-educator.org/memoirs/wong_herb/index.htm>.

337. Frank, 61–62.

338. Marshall, *Bring Up the Rear*; loads — referred to in his book *The Soldier's Load*, 204–205; fatigue/fear —ibid., 205–206.

339. Leftovers— Appleman, *South to Naktong*, 115; Harry Summers, *Almanac*, 52, 163–164.

340. Paschall, 144; Westover, ed., *Combat Support*, 162–169; Edwards, ed., *Korean War*, 80, 89.

341. Complaint — Smith, *MacArthur in Korea*, 204.

342. John Graham, *Korean War Educator* <http://www.koreanwar-educator.org/memoirs/graham_john/index.htm>.

343. Army Roy Wilson in A.W. Wilson, 311.

344. Morrow, 36, 44; Wilkinson, 363.

345. Kondysar, *Greybeards*, Sept.-Oct. 2007.

346. Huston, *Guns and Butter*, 195–196. More on food — Edwards, ed., *Korean War*, 80–82, 87.

347. Tootsie Rolls— Michael Pezzella, *Korean War Educator* <http://www.koreanwar-educator.org/memoirs/pezzella_mike/index.htm>; Appleman, *South to Naktong*, 745; truckload — George McMaster, *Korean War Educator* <http://www.koreanwar-educator.org/memoirs/mcmaster_george/index.htm>; disguise — Edward Szymciak, *Korean War Educator* <http://www.koreanwar-educator.org/memoirs/szymciak/index.htm>.

348. Wright in Knox, 108; Rishell, 61–62, 66.

349. Brady, 111; Welsh interview.

350. Herbert, *Making of a Soldier*, 29; Appleman, *Ridgway Duels*, 165.

351. Wilkinson, 252; Hong Xuezhi, *Mao's Generals*, 116; more on water — Edwards, ed., *Korean War*, 88–94, 99–100; melted snow — Raymond Davis in Knox, 575.

352. John Graham, *Korean War Educator* <http://www.koreanwar-educator.org/memoirs/graham_john/index.htm>.

353. Wilkinson, 253; Barr — in Tomedi, *No Bugles, No Drums*, 77.

354. Charles Brown, *Korean War Educator* <http://www.koreanwar-educator.org/memoirs/brown_charles/index.htm>.

355. William Anderson, *Korean War Educator* <http://www.koreanwar-educator.org/memoirs/anderson_william/index.htm>.

356. Charlie Carmin, *Korean War Educator* <http://www.koreanwar-educator.org/memoirs/carmin/index.htm>.

357. Charles Brown, *Korean War Educator* <http://www.koreanwar-educator.org/memoirs/brown_charles/index.htm>.

358. Wilkinson, 272.

359. William Dillon, *Korean War Educator* <http://www.koreanwar-educator.org/memoirs/dillon_william/index.htm>.

360. Caine, 73.

361. Fowley in Adrian Walker, ed., *Barren Place*, 67.

362. Wilkinson, 139.

363. Kingslad, *Quest for Glory*, 137.

364. Volney Warner, *Korean War Educator* <http://www.koreanwar-educator.org/memoirs/warner_volney/index.htm>; captured American tank — Charles Payne in Knox, 94.

365. Paschall, 147–148.

366. Ibid., 132.

367. Dill, "Winter of Yalu," 48.

368. Paul Noll <http://www.paulnoll.com>.

369. Lippert in Li and Peters, 132.

370. Stephens, 72; Sullivan, *Toy Soldiers*, 94, 96.

371. Bauser, *Greybeards*, March-April 2011.

372. Socks— Edwards, ed., *Korean War*, 93; Brady, 132.

373. Charles Brown, *Korean War Educator* <http://www.koreanwar-educator.org/memoirs/brown_charles/index.htm>.

374. William Dillon, *Korean War Educator* <http://www.koreanwar-educator.org/memoirs/dillon_william/index.htm>; Frank Muetzel in Knox, 204–205.

375. Clark and Rasch in A.W. Wilson, 148.

376. John Everts, in A.W. Wilson, 321; Dill, "Winter of Yalu," 39; Volney Warner, *Korean War Educator* <http://www.koreanwar-educator.org/memoirs/warner_volney/index.htm>.

377. Glenn Schroeder, *Korean War Educator* <http://www.koreanwar-educator.org/memoirs/schroeder/index.htm>; Dallas Mossman, *Korean War Educator* <http://www.koreanwar-educator.org/memoirs/mossman_dallas/index.htm>.

378. Dill, 39.

379. Tucker, *Encyclopedia*, 574–575.

380. Cohen and Gooch, "Aggregate Failure," 173; B. Alexander, *War We Lost*, 396–398.

381. Martin Russ, *Last Parallel*, 117.

382. Eric Bergerud, *Touched with Fire* (Guadalcanal, etc.), 440.

383. David Esposito, "Rotation System," in Sandler, *KW Encyclopedia*, 310; McWilliams, 146.

384. Singlaub, 187–188.

385. Herbert, *Making of a Soldier*, 199.

386. William M. Donnelly, "Best Army ... in the Circumstances," 818; Stephens, 168.

387. Murdo MacLennan, *Korean War Educator* <http://www.koreanwar-educator.org/memoirs/maclennan_murdo/index.htm>.

388. Jing Li, "People's Liberation Volunteer Army," in Sandler, *KW Encyclopedia*, 266; William Whitson, *Chinese High Command*, 97.

389. Summers, *Almanac*, 228.

390. Appleman, *Ridgway Duels*, 165, 405.

391. Lewis Sorley, "Reserve Forces," in Williams, *Revolutionary War*, 116–117; Woodruff,

in Knox and Coppel, 151; see also Donald Chase, ibid., 193, Doug Koch, ibid., 206; Wilkinson, 169.

392. McAleer, 380; Martin Van Creveld, *Command in War*; Peter Watson, *War of the Mind*, 232.

393. Donnelly, "Best Army," 818, 202–221.

394. Goulden, 135; Vinson —"2 Years' Service for all Youths," *U.S. News and World Report*, Oct. 27, 1950; see also "Losses in Korean War Show Why the Army Needs Draft to Get Men," *U.S. News and World Report*, October 20, 1950.

395. William Anderson, *Korean War Educator* <http://www.koreanwar-educator.org/memoirs/anderson_william/index.htm>.

396. Donnelly, 829, 825–826; Baldwin in H.W. Blakeley, "Esprit de What?: Our Army and Morale," *Quartermaster Review*, Nov.-Dec. 1954, p. 10 (reprint from *The Reporter*); combat pay — Edwards, ed., *Korean War*, 83.

397. James Brady, *Scariest Place*, 108.

398. Herbert, *Soldier*, 49.

399. Ibid., 48–49.

400. Donnelly, 830, 841–842, 837, 845–846.

401. Stephens, 106.

402. Brady, 143.

403. William Sports, *Korean War Educator* <http://www.koreanwar-educator.org/memoirs/sports_william/index.htm>.

404. Brady, 143

405. Pete Rendina, *Korean War Educator* <http://www.koreanwar-educator.org/memoirs/rendina_pete/index.htm>.

406. Brady, 97–99.

407. Arthur Smith, *Korean War Educator* <http://www.koreanwar-educator.org/memoirs/smith_arthur/index.htm>.

408. Morton Wood, *Korean War Educator* <http://www.koreanwar-educator.org/memoirs/wood_morton_pete/index.htm>.

409. Kenneth Kendall, *Korean War Educator* <http://www.koreanwar-educator.org/memoirs/kendall_kenneth/index.htm>.

410. Brady, 89.

411. Bruce Wareing, *Korean War Educator* <http://www.koreanwar-educator.org/memoirs/wareing_bruce/index.htm>.

412. Charles Brown, *Korean War Educator* <http://www.koreanwar-educator.org/memoirs/brown_charles/index.htm>.

413. Jon Genrich, *Korean War Educator* <http://www.koreanwar-educator.org/memoirs/kendall_kenneth/index.htm>.

414. Arthur Wilson, *Korean War Educator* <http://www.koreanwar-educator.org/memoirs/smith_arthur/index.htm>.

415. Eldon Stanley, *Korean War Educator* <http://www.koreanwar-educator.org/memoirs/stanley_ike/index.htm>.

416. James DeLong, *Korean War Educator* <http://www.koreanwar-educator.org/memoirs/delong_james/index.htm>; Emory Walker, *Korean War Educator* <http://www.koreanwar-educator.org/memoirs/walker_emory/index.htm>.

417. Shot himself in foot — Floyd Akins in Knox, 95; Marine Paul Welsh, interview.

418. Hammel, 338, 356–357.

419. Zong—Tomedi, 99; deep foxhole — Beech, *Tokyo*, 148; Chatham in A.W. Wilson, 245.

420. Michaelis, "This We Learned in Korea," *Colliers*, Aug. 18, 1951.

421. Biebel in A.W. Wilson, 169.

422. Frank Torres, ibid.

423. William Dillon, *Korean War Educator* <http://www.koreanwar-educator.org/memoirs/dillon_william/index.htm>.

424. John Graham, *Korean War Educator* <http://www.koreanwar-educator.org/memoirs/graham_john/index.htm>.

425. Harold Reinhart, *Korean War Educator* <http://www.koreanwar-educator.org/memoirs/reinhart_harold/index.htm>.

426. Soldiers— Roy Oxenrider and Robert Ayala in A.W. Wilson.

427. Furlough — Stephens, 73.

428. Brady, 229.

429. John A. Sullivan, *Toy Soldiers*, 101.

430. Stephens, 115.

431. Donnelly, 844, 847.

432. Ibid., 836–837.

433. Stephens, 81.

434. Morrow, 6; condom — Dave Koegel in Knox, 473.

435. Richard Bohart, *Korean War Educator* <http://www.koreanwar-educator.org/memoirs/bohart_richard/index.htm>.

436. Dill, 46; Brady, 29, 45.

437. Appleman, *South to Naktong*, 485.

438. Russ, *Last Parallel*, 43.

439. Stephens, 63.

440. Turnstall, *I Fought in Korea*, 106–107.

441. Russ, *Last Parallel*, 41; Morrow, 78; Cutforth, 31, 56–57; case — Stephens, 66, 158.

442. Sullivan, *Toy Soldiers*, 99.

443. Brady, 142; Schlatter Family Site, "The Liquor Officer" <http://www.schlatter.org/liquor>.

444. Liquor distribution — Emory Walker, *Korean War Educator* <http://www.koreanwar-educator.org/memoirs/walker_emory/index.htm>; Knox and Coppel, *Korean War: Uncertain Victory*, 24; Walter Bradford interview.

445. Martin Markley, *Korean War Educator* <http://www.koreanwar-educator.org/memoirs/markley_martin/index.htm>.

446. Applejack — Allen Scott, *Korean War Educator* <http://www.koreanwar-educator.org/memoirs/scott_allen/index.htm>; Dean Servais, *Korean War Educator* <http://www.koreanwar-educator.org/memoirs/servais_dean/

index.htm>; Cornley — Robert Dvorchak, *Korea: A.P. History*, 142.

447. Days plus — B. Alexander, *War We Lost*, 396–398.

448. Eighth Army paid — Voorhees, 70.

449. "I & I" — Tucker, 563.

450. Prostitution — Edwards, ed., *Korean War*, 156–157; Francis Downey interview; VD from Japan — Appleman, *Ridgway Duels*, 421–422.

451. William Anderson, *Korean War Educator* <http://www.koreanwar-educator.org/memoirs/anderson_william/index.htm>.

452. Carton — Albert Giaguinto, *Korean War Educator* <http://www.koreanwar-educator.org/memoirs/giaquinto_albert/index.htm>.

453. Peter Rendina, *Korean War Educator* <http://www.koreanwar-educator.org/memoirs/rendina_pete/index.htm>.

454. Frank McGill, *Korean War Educator* <http://www.koreanwar-educator.org/memoirs/mcgill_frank/index.htm>.

455. Caine, 76; officers' club — Ibid.

456. Kenneth Kendall, *Korean War Educator* <http://www.koreanwar-educator.org/memoirs/kendall_kenneth/index.htm>.

457. John Kane, *Korean War Educator* <http://www.koreanwar-educator.org/memoirs/kane_john/index.htm>.

458. Russ, *Last Parallel*, 123–128.

459. Frank, 93.

460. Caine, 75–76.

461. Rear echelon to front line: 4 to 1 ratio — Ron Miller interview.

462. Jim Christiansen, *Korean War Educator* <http://www.koreanwar-educator.org/memoirs/christiansen_jim/index.htm>.

463. Carlo D'Este, *Eisenhower*, 484, 590–591; ignored — Brueur, *Feuding Allies*, 251.

464. Herbert, *Soldier*, 277; no lice — Brady, 132.

465. Appleman, *South to Naktong*, 485; Summers, *Almanac*, 232, 173, 177.

466. Pease, 164; see also 163; Brady, 63.

467. Pease, 164.

468. Eric Ambler, *Here Lies: An Autobiography*, 198, 200, 212–213.

469. *G.C. Marshall Papers*, v. 3, 464, 489, 523.

470. Perret, *War to Be Won*, 517.

471. Norman Zehr, "Medics, Combat," in Tucker, 428–429.

472. Kamperschroer in A.W. Wilson, 11.

473. Jack McCallum, "Military Medicine," ibid., 447–451.

474. Silver, ibid., 217.

475. Albert Cowdrey, "Medical Service," in Sandler, *KW Encyclopedia*, 220–224.

476. Jack McCallum, "Military Medicine," in Tucker, 428–429; hemorrhagic — Cowdrey, in Sandler, 222.

477. Harold Secor, *Korean War Educator* <http://www.koreanwar-educator.org/memoirs/secor_harold/index.htm>; Jack Jaunal, *Korean War Educator* <http://www.koreanwar-educator.org/memoirs/jaunal_jack/index.htm>; British soldier Alfie Fowler in Walker, *Barren Place*, 65.

478. Taps — Marshall, "Our Army."

479. Bevin Alexander, *Korea: The First War We Lost*, 146.

480. Griffith, *Chinese Army*, 132, 141–142; Farrar-Hockley, *British Part*, v. 1, 332.

481. Marshall, *Bringing Up the Rear*, 201–203.

482. Ted Heckelman, *Korean War Educator* <http://www.koreanwar-educator.org/memoirs/heckelman_ted/index.htm>.

483. Howling — Russ, *Breakout*, 133.

484. Stephens, 69, 117.

485. Marshall, "Our Army"; yelled back — Beech, *Tokyo*, 193.

486. *New York Times*, Dec. 31, 1950.

487. Russ, *Last Parallel*, 63; Pease, *Psywar*, 163.

488. Stephens, 87.

489. Chris Sarno, *Korean War Educator* <http://www.koreanwar-educator.org/memoirs/sarno/index.htm>.

490. Tom Farrell, "Forgotten War," *History Ireland*, Sept./Oct. 2010.

491. Christopher DeRosa, *Political Indoctrination in U.S. Army*, 93–95.

492. Appleman, *Ridgway Duels*, 21, 157–158; Ridgway, *Korean War*, 264–265; Paik, *Pusan to Panmunjom*, 130.

493. Appleman, *Ridgway Duels*, 186–187, 351–352.

494. DeRosa, 102, 104, 118–120.

495. Luke Macauley, "American Servicemen's letters: Korea, 1950–1954," in *Greybeards*, Sept.-Oct. 2007, p. 67; Brian McGinn, "Quiet heroes of a forgotten war," Irish American Cultural Institute, *Ducas*, Nov. 2001; "Irish heroes of Korean War," *Western People* (Ireland), July 2005.

Chapter Three

1. Terrence Gough, *U.S. Army Mobilization and Logistics*, 62–63, 72, 76–77.

2. Weigley, *U.S. Army*, 511.

3. James Spellman in Paschall, *Witness Korea*, 4, 51.

4. Weintraub, *MacArthur's War*, 225.

5. Appleman, *Ridgway Duels*, 294.

6. Spellman in Paschall, 52, 54.

7. Spellman in Westover, ed., *Combat Support*, 187–188.

8. Appleman, *Disaster in Korea*, 37.

9. Weintraub, 225.

10. Cardinal in Weintraub, 279; Fox, in Knox, 658.1.

11. Norman Allen in Knox, 658.

12. Westover, ed., *Combat Support*, 150.

13. Clark Rasch in A.W. Wilson, 145.

14. Weintraub, 225.

15. Ray Vallowe, "Chosin Reservoir: Chapter Eight," <http://www.koreanwar-educator.org/topics/chosin/vallowe_research/vallowe_chapter_08.htm>.

16. Brady, 112.

17. Edwards, ed., *Korean War*, 79–80.

18. Charles Brown, *Korean War Educator* <http://www.koreanwar-educator.org/memoirs/brown_charles/index.htm>.

19. Ibid., 638, 664.

20. Brady, 53–55, 65, 87.

21. Ibid., 117; Russ, 231–232; McAleer, *Out of Savannah*, 181–182.

22. Tucker, "Armored Vests," in Tucker, 49–50.

23. Keyes Beech, "These Soldiers have Charmed Lives," *Saturday Evening Post* 225, no. 11 (1952).

24. Weintraub, 95–96.

25. Schnabel, *Policy and Direction*, 215, 259, 300–303.

26. Alexander George, *Chinese Communist Army*, 147; Hastings, 172; booby trapped — Francis Killeen in Knox, 530.

27. Griffith, *Chinese Army*, 131.

28. Nie Rongzhen, "Beijing's Decision," in *Mao's Generals*, 54–55.

29. Hong Xuezhi, "Combat and Logistics;" Millett, *Their War*, 134.

30. Arthur Wilson, *Korean War Educator* <http://www.koreanwar-educator.org/memoirs/smith_arthur/index.htm>.

31. Cutforth, *Korean Reporter*, 21, 63–64, 85, 89.

32. Ely J. Kahn, *Peculiar War*, 170; stolen jeep — Muetzel, in Knox, 208.

33. John W. Downey interview.

34. White, *Captives of Korea*, 51.

35. Charles Bielecki in Li and Peters, 128; Gough, *Mobilization*, 11.

36. Appleman, *Ridgway Duels*, 297–298, 352, 186–187.

37. Li, *Modern Chinese Army*, 100.

38. Fei Zhang (Patrick Reiter translator), "Initial Communist Logistics," *Quartermaster Bulletin*, Autumn 2004.

39. Soviet trucks, munitions— Shu Guang Zhang, *Deterrence and Strategic Culture*, 111, 130.

40. Charles Shrader, *Communist Logistics in Korean War*, 116–118; Li, Millett and Yu, eds., *Mao's Generals Remember Korea*, 55, 123.

41. Halberstam, *Coldest Winter*, 519–529; Eighth U.S. Army, "Characteristics of Chinese Communist Forces," Nov. 20, 1950, RG 319, box 1131; Marshall, "Our Army," 24.

42. Appleman, *South to Naktong*, 719; Russ, *Breakout*, 225; Walter Kretchik, *U.S. Army Doctrine*, 164–166.

43. Caine, *What's It All About?* 78–79.

44. Appleman, *East of Chosin*, 87; Pease, *Psywar*, 129–130; white coveralls— Bielecki, in Li and Peters, 146; North Korean sandbags— Muetzel, in Knox, 155; Americans— Payne, in Knox, 94.

45. Marshall, *Infantry Operations*, 93.

46. William Harrington, "Mortars," in Tucker, 460.

47. Leyva in Tomdei, 238; James Elkins, *Korean War Educator* <http://www.koreanwar-educator.org/memoirs/elkins_james/index.htm>; Jones in A.W. Wilson, 189; John Kane, *Korean War Educator* <http://www.koreanwar-educator.org/memoirs/kane_john/index.htm>.

48. Wilkinson, *Up Front Korea*, 252–253, 169.

49. Appleman, *Ridgway Duels*, 308, 447; Eighth U.S. Army, "Chinese Communist Combat Doctrine," 17 Dec. 1950, RG 319, box 1327; Pease, 129–130.

50. Mahoney, *Formidable Enemies*, 78–79.

51. Louis Buttell, *Korean War Educator* <http://www.koreanwar-educator.org/memoirs/buttell_louis/index.htm>.

52. Paul Gallagher interview.

53. Wilkinson, 156.

54. Appleman, *Disaster*, 88, 108, 163, 171, 180, 319.

55. Herbert, *Soldier*, 44; Goulden, *Korea*, 292.

56. Houston, 360; Nichols, *How Many*, 138–139.

57. Shrader, 94–98, 101.

58. Rigg, *Hordes*, 185–186.

59. Nichols, 140–141.

60. William Anderson, *Korean War Educator* <http://www.koreanwar-educator.org/memoirs/anderson_william/index.htm>.

61. Burchett, *Rebel Journalist*, 367–368.

62. Appleman, *Ridgway Duels*, 102.

63. Mahoney, 75.

64. Wilkinson, 289.

65. Appleman, *Escaping the Trap*, 351–352; Wang Xuedong, in Peters and Li, 119.

66. Charlie Carmin, *Korean War Educator* <http://www.koreanwar-educator.org/memoirs/carmin/index.htm>.

67. Russ, *Breakout*, 209–210.

68. George Rasula in A.W. Wilson.

69. Edwards, ed., *Korean War*, 69.

70. Marshall, *Infantry Operations*, 4, 61; Marshall, *Bringing Up Rear*, 191.

71. Russ, *Breakout*, 203.

72. Pease, 155–156, 130, 136.

73. Marshall, *Bringing Up Rear*, 190; Appleman, *Ridgway Duels*, 185, 327–328.

74. Rishell, *Black Platoon*, 158–159; John Sullivan, *Toy Soldiers*, 56, 59.

75. Appleman, *Disaster*, 178, 186.

76. McAtee in A.W. Wilson, 307.

77. Bridges below water — James Neely, *KW Ed.*

78. Robert Leckie, *Helmet for My Pillow*, 91–92; Eric Bergerud, *Touched by Fire*, 388, 400–401.

79. Pease, 131–136; Haas, *Devil's Shadow*, 103.

80. Appleman, *Disaster*, 356; Catchpole, *Korean War*, 252–253.

81. Volney Warner, *Korean War Educator* <http://www.koreanwar-educator.org/memoirs/warner_volney/index.htm>.

82. Mahoney, 86.

83. Manchester, *American Caesar*, 614.

84. Marshall, "Our Army," 26; Heefner, *Patton's Bulldog*, 309; Toland, *Mortal Combat*, 373.

85. Appleman, *Disaster*, 414–418, 341–342; James, *New York Times*, Dec. 5, 1950.

86. Hickey, *Korean War*, 142–146, 150, 163, 166–167; MacDonald, *War Before Vietnam*, 216–217; Catchpole, *Korean War*, 84.

87. Hastingsm *Korean War*, 165–166, 175.

88. Turnstall, *I Fought in Korea*, 44, 55–56, 77.

89. Halberstam, 501.

90. Bi Yu, "What China Learned," *Mao's Generals*, 17; Hastings, *Korean War*, 173–174.

91. Marshall, *Bringing Up Rear*, 190–191.

92. Ridgway, *Soldier*, 205–207; Ridgway, *Korean War*, 88.

93. Mausers— Russ, *Breakout*, 223.

94. M-1— Arthur Wilson, *Korean War Educator* <http://www.koreanwar-educator.org/memoirs/smith_arthur/index.htm>; Fox, in Knox and Coppel, 260.

95. Haas, 109–110.

96. M-2 carbine — W.B. Woodruff, Jr., in Knox and Coppel, 33.

97. Few rifles— Appleman, *Disaster*, 177–178.

98. Bob Ondrish, "Korea: My Story," *Greybeards*, March-April 2007; Eighth U.S. Army, "Notes on Chinese Tactics," Dec. 17, 1950, RG 319, box 1133; dud grenades-Peters and Li, 108, 128.

99. McWilliams, *Hallowed Ground*, 180.

100. One in five — Hoyt, *Day Chinese Attacked*, 92; Li and Peters, 108.

101. Poor shooters— Richard Bohart, *Korean War Educator* <http://www.koreanwar-educator.org/memoirs/bohart_richard/index.htm>; hand to hand — Fred Lawson in A.W. Wilson, 191.

102. Bussey, *Firefight*, 192–193.

103. Kondysar; *Greybeards*, Sept.-Oct. 2007; Brady, *Coldest War*, 62.

104. Cutforth, 176–177.

105. Knox, 282.

106. McAleer, 250.

107. Ibid., 376.

108. Booby traps— John Jarvis in A.W. Wilson, 347.

109. Harrington, in Tucker, 460.

110. Appleman, *Ridgway Duels*, 492.

111. Mason in A.W. Wilson, 185.

112. Edwards, ed., *Korean War*, 89, 105; Carlson, 160.

113. Bunker in Tucker, 472–473.

114. Elizabeth Schafer, "Golden Rain," in Sandler, *KW Encyclopedia*, 227.

115. Carl Brunson interview.

116. Schafer, in Sandler, 227–228; Ransone in Knox, 552.

117. Arthur Wilson, editor, *Korean Vignettes*, 147, 117; Knox, *Oral History*, 552.

118. Tucker, "Bazooka vs. Tank," in Sandler, *KW Encyclopedia*, 48–49; Tucker, "Bazooka," in Tucker, 67–68.

119. Bluff— Simmons, *Strained Alliance*, 143–145; Charles Cole, *Korea Remembered*, 119; Malcolm Muir, Jr., "United States Navy," in Tucker, 705; Blockade —ibid.; Edward Marolda, "Navy, US," in Sandler, *KW Encyclopedia*, 244; battleships— Muir, "Naval Gunfire Support," in Tucker, 478.

120. Hungnam — Richard Hallion, "Naval Air Operations," in Sandler, *KW Encyclopedia*, 233.

121. Muir, "United States Navy," in Tucker, 707; Wonsan — Cole, 120.

122. David Hallsworth memoir, Imperial War Museum, Cat. No. 10702.

123. Mine sweepers— Cole, 108–109; Muir, in Tucker, 706–707; corpse — Cole, 191; blockade — Malcolm Cagle and Frank Manson, *Sea War*, 354, 356–357; Wonsan — Corky Johnson, *Korean War Educator* <http://www.koreanwar-educator.org/memoirs/johnson_corky/index.htm.

124. Other naval forces— Marolda, in Sandler, *KW Encyclopedia*, 241; planes lost —ibid.; casualties— Muir, in Tucker, 707–708.

125. Richard Hallion, "Naval Operations," in Williams, *Revolutionary War*, 233.

126. Huston, "Logistics, U.S.," in Sandler, *KW Encyclopedia*, 197.

127. John Bell, "Partridge," in Tucker, 514.

128. Taegu refueling— Appleman, *Ridgway Duels*, 415; attacked troops— Louis Buttell, *Korean War Educator* http://www.koreanwar-educator.org/memoirs/buttell_jack/index.htm; Jack Burkett, *Korean War Educator* http://www.koreanwar-educator.org/memoirs/burkett_jack/index.htm; William Anderson, *Korean War Educator* <http://www.koreanwar-educator.org/memoirs/anderson_william/index.htm>.

129. Panels-Volney Warner, *Korean War Ed-*

ucator <http://www.koreanwar-educator.org/memoirs/warner_volney/index.htm>.

130. Spiked — Conrad Crane, *American Airpower*, 81.

131. Hastings, *Korean War*, 253, 267–268.

132. Smudge pots— Guy Bordelon, in Knox and Coppel, 248; flack traps— Carl Brunson interview; Millett, *Their War*, 72.

133. Road sentries— Hastings, *Korean War*, 257.

134. AA — Brune, *Handbook*, 214; intelligence coordination — Daniel Kuehl, "Refighting the Last War," 109.

135. 2000 AA guns— Robert Jackson, *Air War Over Korea*, 144.

136. Jake Huffaker, *Korean War Educator* <http://www.koreanwar-educator.org/memoirs/huffaker_jake/index.htm>.

137. Steel bars— Jack Jaunal, *Korean War Educator* <http://www.koreanwar-educator.org/memoirs/jaunal_jack/index.htm>.

138. Kuehl, 88.

139. Brian Cull and Dennis Newton, *With Yanks in Korea*, 327–328; Earl Swinhart, "Mikoyan — Gurevich MiG-15," Aviation History Museum, pp. 1–5; Thomas Cardwell, "U.S. Air Force," in Sandler, *KW Encyclopedia*, 13.

140. John Haynes and Harvey Klehr, *Venona: Decoding Soviet Espionage in America*, 10–11.

141. Night fighter — Jackson, *Air War*, 151.

142. Brune, *Handbook*, 214.

143. Xiaoming Zhang, *Red Wings over the Yalu*, 173, 77, 87, 141, 188.

144. Steven Agoratus, "Aircraft," in Sandler, *KW Encyclopedia*, 8; Kuehl, 91.

145. Millett, *Their War*, 141–142; Oleg Sarin and Lev Dvoretsky, *Alien Wars*, 71–74, 76–78.

146. Panic — Swinhart, 1.

147. Shocked — Hallion, in Williams, *Revolutionary War*, 133.

148. Meteor — Agoratus, in Sandler.

149. Robert Futrell, *U.S. Air Force in Korea*, 286, 647–651, 704–707.

150. 75 percent — Mark Franchetti article, "Russia Fought Secret Air Battle."

151. Russian pilots: anon., "Yevgeni Pepelyayev: A Red Predator over 'MiG Alley,'" pp. 13 <rt66.com/-korteng/Small Arms/RussianPilots.htm>. "Russian Aces Over Korea," Acepilots.com, pp. 10 <acepilots.com/Russian/rus_aces.html>; Brune, *Handbook*, 214–216.

152. Chinese pilots, North Korean AA — Millett, *Their War*, 141–142.

153. North Korean Air Force proposal — ibid., 62.

154. Chosin survival — Hastings, *Korean War*, 158–159.

155. Appleman, *Ridgway Duels*, 403–404.

156. Numbers— Brune, *Handbook*, 215; Millett, *Their War*, 139.

157. Soviet claims— Millett, *Their War*, 61, 143.

158. B-29s lost— Kuehl, 107.

159. Crane, 85–88.

160. Lemay —ibid., 90, 69.

161. Chaff— Kuehl, 103–104; other tactics— ibid., 109–110.

162. Night fighter — Crane, 91.

163. X. Zhang, *Red Wings*, 111–112; Futrell, 286–287, 301–307, 312, 404, 406–408, 416–418, 424–425.

164. Xiaoming Zhang, "Air Combat for People's Republic," 273, 277.

165. Callum MacDonald, "Battle of Namsi," in Matray, *Historical Dictionary*, 40–41; Crane, 69, 87, 161–162; Billy Mossman, "Ebb and Flow," 378.

166. Jackson, *Air War*, 85, 88, 95, 122–124, 159; Carl Brunson interview; B. Mossman, 379; mounting concern about expanded Chinese air capacity: Bradley, Rusk, Ridgway and others— *U.S. For. Rels.: Korea*, v. 7, part 1, 355–359, 385–386, 1290–1291. In May 1952 Bradley declared there were 412 Chinese jets on fields within 50 miles of the Yalu, on the north side — *U.S. For. Rels., 1952–1954*, part 1, 89.

167. McGowen, "Chinese Air Force," in Tucker, 122.

168. Futrell, 670.

169. X. Zhang, *Red Wings*, 183–184, 191–192.

170. Kuehl, 97–98, 101–102; Sarin and Dvoretsky, 74.

171. Soviet aid — Brune, *Handbook*, 214.

172. "Token"—ibid., 98, 101, 105, 108.

173. Jackson, *Air War*, 148–149.

174. Kimpo fighters— David Peppin and Jack Wright, in Knox, 268–269; in the north — Appleman, *Disaster*, 356, 360.

175. Kim — X. Zhang, *Red Wings*, 188–189.

176. Sometimes the planes were known as "Sewing Machine Charlies" and even "Washing Machine Charlies"

177. Futrell, 308–310; Agoratus, "Aviation," in Sandler, *KW Encyclopedia*, 8.

178. Elizabeth Shafer, "Kimpo Airfield," ibid., 165; Jackson, 95–97, 133; Futrell, 308, 312.

179. Robert Drew letter, *Greybeards*, Sept.-Oct. 2008; Navy — Cagle and Mason, 476–478; Jake Huffner, *Korean War Educator* <http://www.koreanwar-educator.org/memoirs/huffner_jake/index.htm>.

180. Bordelon: Bell, in Tucker, 514–515.

181. Paschall, 124–126; Futrell, 308–311.

182. Shoestring — Crane, 90, 75; Brenner — William Head, "Vandenberg," in Tucker, 725.

183. Brunson interview.

184. Ineffective, flak traps— John Halliday, "Air Operations," in Williams, *Revolutionary War*, 136–137.

185. In Dec. 1951 Bradley said there were two

such Chinese air attacks; *U.S. For. Rels: Korea*, v. 7, part 1, 1290; strangulation — Julian Thompson, *Lifeblood of War*, 130–131.

186. Crane, 165–166; Brune, 215; two–three minutes — Youngho Kim, "Hot Pursuit," in Tucker, 264.

187. Brunson interview.

188. Almost daily incursions — Halliday, in Williams, *Revolutionary War*, 154–155.

189. F-86 copter — ibid., 159.

190. Stalin — X. Zhang, *Red Wings*, 188.

191. Oct. 8, 1950 — Eric Osborne, "Soviet Airfield Incident," in Tucker, 608; Antung — Appleman, *South to Naktong*, 486–487.

192. Thomas Cardwell, "Air Force, U.S.," in Sandler, *KW Encyclopedia*, 15, 233; Zhou — X. Zhang, "Air Combat," in Ryan et al., 277.

193. Goaded — Hallion, in Williams, *Revolutionary War*, 133; Soviet pilots — Millett, *Their War*, 139, 143.

194. Hallion, 143; anti-shipping missile — Citizendium, "Signals intelligence" <encitizen dium.org/wiki?File: DirectionalSpectra.png>.

195. Robert Bunker, "Nuclear Warfare," in Tucker, 492–494.

196. Hastings, *Korean War*, 317–318.

197. Equipped — X. Zhang, *Red Wings*, 197.

198. Hallion, in Williams, *Revolutionary War*, 138–140; Cagle and Manson, 460–468.

199. Sup'ung (Suiho) bombings — William Head, "Sup'ung (Suiho) and the Korean Electrical Power Campaign," in Tucker, 623–624; X. Zhang, *Red Wings over the Yalu*, 187–189; Crane, 118–119, 121–123, 130–131; Jackson, 141–143; attack base — Carl Brunson interview.

200. Halliday, in Williams, *Revolutionary War*, 158.

201. Peter Faber, "Power Plants," in Sandler, *KW Encyclopedia*, 268–269; Kuehl, 103.

202. Irrigation system — Air University Quarterly Staff, "The Attack on the Irrigation Dams in North Korea," *Air University Quarterly Review* 4 (1953): 40–61.

203. Cagle and Manson, *Sea War*, 458.

204. Rotation — Millett, *Their War*, 143; Carter Malkasian, *Korean War*, 83.

205. Expenditures — Yu Bin, "What China Learned," Ryan et al., 13; X. Zhang, *Red Wings*, 186–198.

206. Dissent — Shu Zhang, *Mao's Romanticism*, 223.

207. Kim — end conflict — X. Zhang, *Red Wings*, 197.

208. X. Zhang, *Red Wings*, 196.

209. Crane, 177–178, 80, 179.

210. Looking ahead — "The Korean War Speaks to the Indo-Chinese War," *Air University Quarterly Review*, Spring 1954, 44–62.

211. Lloyd Gardner, *Approaching Vietnam*, 174–175.

212. Rusk — Warren Cohen, *Dean Rusk*, 240, 272; Shrader, *Communist Logistics*, 144–145, 181–182.

213. Chae-Jin Lee, *China and Korea*, 35–36.

214. Laeteguy, *Face of War*, 152–153.

215. Halliday, in Williams, *Revolutionary War*, 158–170.

216. Li, *Modern Chinese Army*, 108–109.

217. Kuehl, 110–111; see also Walter Boyne, "Aerial Combat," in Tucker, 8.

218. Haas, 104–111.

219. Edwards, *Combat Operations*, 166–167.

220. Korean Liaison Office — William Breuer, *Shadow Warrior*, 20–21.

221. Haas, 12–13.

222. Ridgway — Matthew Aid, *Secret Sentry*, 31–32.

223. David Foy, "Willoughby," in Sandler, *KW Encyclopedia*, 354–357; James, *Refighting*, 70.

224. Aid, *Secret Sentry*, 23, 25.

225. John P. Finnegan, *Military Intelligence*, 114–115.

226. Aid, 26–28; Wonsan — Schnabel, *Policy and Direction*, 208–209, 216–218.

227. Aid, 29–31; David Hatch, "Korean War Sigint," 4–10; Rankin cable — Griffith, *Chinese Army*, 350–351 reference notes.

228. Ridgway on MacArthur — Aid, 32.

229. Toft — Goulden, 462–475.

230. Andrew Tully, *CIA*, 190–193.

231. David Esposito, "CIA," in Sandler, *KW Encyclopedia*, 66–67.

232. Chinese linguists — White, *Captives of Korea*, 113–114.

233. Aid, 33–35, 39; Appleman, *Disaster*, 465.

234. Finnegan, *Military Intelligence*, 117.

235. John Ranelagh, *CIA Rise and Decline*, 223, 217; Tully, *CIA*, 185–188, 30.

236. Haas, 202–205; Ben Malcolm, *White Tigers*, 129.

237. Andrew, *President's Eyes*, 193–194.

238. Edwards, *Combat Operations*, 168, 165, 158.

239. Ed Evanhoe, *Dark Moon*, 158–159.

240. Hatch, "Sigint," <webharvast.gov/peth 04/20041023122008/http://www.nasa.gov/publications/publ1000.

241. Dille, *Substitute for Victory*, 39–45.

242. Haas, 78–79; Nichols account — *How Many Times*, 123.

243. Catchpole, *Korean War*, 309–320f.

244. Haas, 33–34, 50, 62, 66, 68.

245. Breuer, *Shadow Warriors*, 159–160.

246. Malcolm, *White Tigers*, 35, 110, 118–129, 205–206, 190–103; partisan numbers — Finnegan, 118.

247. Boyd, *Operation Broken Reed*, 25–29, 132–143.

248. Russ, *Breakout*, 79–80.

249. Hatch, "Sigint," 8–9.
250. Russ, *Last Parallel*, 117.
251. Rees, 138.
252. White, 113–114.
253. Finnegan, 18–119.
254. Hatch, "Sigint," 11.
255. Ibid., 11–13.
256. Haas, 19–22, 59–61.
257. Ibid., 102, 196–197, 202–208; CIA involvement — Goulden, 468–469; Ranelagh, 217.
258. Hatch, 13–14; Van Fleet — Finnegan, 115.
259. Hatch, 25–26.
260. CIA — Esposito, in Sandler, *KW Encyclopedia*, 67.
261. CIC — Finnegan, 115.
262. Murray Dyer, *Weapon on the Wall; Rethinking Psychological Warfare*, 770, 113–116.
263. Clayton Laaurie, "Psywar," in Tucker, 535–538.
264. Army— ibid., 203; CIA —ibid., 129.
265. Board —ibid., 133–136.
266. Targets and goals—ibid., 41; intel— ibid., 203–206.
267. American Association for Public Opinion, "Psychological Warfare in Korea," *Public Opinion Quarterly* 15, no. 1 (April 1951); Pease, 81–82.
268. Gugeler, *Combat Actions*, 220, 70; Haas, 102, also 73, 96–97.
269. Herz, "Combat Leaflet: Weapon of Persuasion," in Daugherty, ed., *Psychological Warfare Casebook*, 561–566.
270. W.E.D., "Credibility in Leaflet and Poster Illustrations," ibid., 751–753.
271. Watson, *War of the Mind*, 430–431.
272. Pease, 41–46.
273. *New York Times*, Dec. 24, 1950.
274. Appleman, *Ridgway Duels for Korea*, 404; Pease, 40, 47, 83–85.
275. Shu Zhang, *Mao's Romanticism*, 214; desertions, ibid., 211.
276. U.S.A. Korean War Commemoration, "Fact Sheet: Psywar," <korea50.army.mil/history/factsheets/psychowar.shtml>; MiG Pilot— Millett, *Their War*, 57–62; [Murray, "Operation American Dollar," *Saturday Evening Post*, May 8, 1954.
277. Shu Zhang, "PLA's Offensives," 110.
278. W.E.D., "Evaluation of Combat Propaganda," in Daugherty, ed., *Psychological Warfare Casebook*, 689.
279. David Mayers, *Cracking the Monolith*, 115–116.
280. James Gao, "Myth of Heroic Soldier," 192–194.
281. William Anderson, *Korean War Educator* <http://www.koreanwar-educator.org/memoirs/anderson_william/index.htm>.Weintraub, 278.
282. Herbert A. Friedman, "Communist North Korean War Leaflets," 50 pp., psywarrior.com/NKoreaH.html; Pease, 13–138, 162, 182; Catchpole, 213.
283. Brady, *Coldest War*, 229.
284. W.E.D., "Old Technique Employed in a Modern Setting," in Daugherty, ed., *Psychological Warfare Casebook*, 643–644.
285. Pease, 136, 123, 88–85.
286. Letters— King, *Paper Tiger*, 22.
287. Pease, 139–143; Shu Zhang, *Mao's Romanticism*, 181–183.
288. Mark Ryan in Chen Jian, "Chinese Policy and Korean War," in Brune, 200.
289. Crane, 143–150.
290. Japanese — Jonathan Fenby, *Chiang Kai-shek*, 353; David Caute, *Fellow-Travelers*, 72–73, 185–194, 228, 245, 258.
291. Stephen Endicott and Edward Hagerman, *U.S. and Biological Warfare*, 106, 154, 161–165, 189–190; biography of Joseph Needham — Simon Winchester, *Man Who Loved China*, 203–216.
292. Fontaine — Larteguy, *Face of War*, 159.
293. Russian disavowal — Endicott and Hagerman — 248–249n; Mary Rolicka, "Forgotten Episode of the 'Forgotten War,'" *Military Medicine* 160 (1995): 97.
294. Needham 1979 statement — Toland, 585.
295. Haas, 170.
296. Millett, *Their War*, 250–251. Toland (551–552) says their plane was shot down by fighter planes.
297. Farrar-Hockley, *Edge*, 236–237; Elizabeth Schafer, "Bacteriological Warfare" in Sandler, *KW Encyclopedia*, 47.
298. Fox, in Knox, 315; "Answer to Sue," *Newsweek*, Sept. 4, 1950, 49.
299. "Anna Wallace Suhr," *Biographical Outline*, 8 pp. <mauiholm.org/ohanna/aws.html; Friedman "Communist War Leaflets," p.3; "Anna Wallace Suhr,"*Wikipedia*, 2 pp, en.wikipedia.org/wiki/Seoul City Sue"; *Newsweek*, Sept. 4, 1950, 49.
300. Charles Jenkins, *Reluctant Communist*, 115–116.
301. Pease, 130; girls— Li and Peters, 152; carols—ibid., 131.
302. Names— McWilliams, 244–245.
303. Dille, 110.
304. Adrian Walker, *Barren Place*, 83.
305. Russ, *Last Parallel*, 61–62, 84, 105, 116.
306. Lou Horyza," *Greybeards*, March-April 2011.
307. Seoul — Stephens, *Old Ugly Hill*, 87.
308. Watson, 430, 530n14.
309. American broadcasts— A.A. P.O.R, "Psywar," 73–74.
310. Shouts— McAleer, 102, 164.
311. John W. Downey interview.

312. Haas, 113.

313. Edwards, *Combat Operations*, 148.

314. Adrei Lankov, *Formation of North Korea*, 108–109, 153; Edwards, *Combat Operations*, 121.

315. Lewis Carlson says 7140 (*Remembered Prisoners*, 111, 280n4). U.N. POWs released — "U.N. Involvement," in *Korean War Educator*, p.4, Koreanwar-educator.org/memoirs/ htm.

316. Recruited — White, 42–43; civilian internees — Sunghun Cho, "Civilian Internee Issue," in Tucker, 150; Mahoney, 18.

317. Diet — Appleman, *Ridgway Duels*, 3; undernourished — William Bradbury et al., *Mass Behavior in Battle and Captivity*, 235; International Red Cross — White, 33–34, 38, 58–59, 80–81, 98–99, 119, 135–136.

318. Kahn, 178–179.

319. White, 35–37.

320. Edwards, *Combat Operations*, 149.

321. Bradbury et al., *Mass Behavior in Battle and Captivity*, 296–297.

322. Most Kuomintang — Toland, 463.

323. Paik, *Pusan to Panmunjom*, 91.

324. Agent surrendered — Woodruff, in Knox and Coppel, 194; riots — Sunghun Cho, "Pongam-do Prisoner-of-War Uprising," in Tucker, 524.

325. Russell Williams, "LST, Navy Work Horse," in A. Wilson, 61.

326. Robinette, Osborne — White, 111–116.

327. Edwards, *Acknowledge a War*, 89–90; Zhao Zuorui, "Organizing the Riots on Koje," in Li and Peters, 243–258; Catchpole, 207–210; interviewed — James Stokesbury, *Short History*, 250–251.

328. Chae-Jin Lee, 48.

329. Dille, 116.

330. Hastings, *Korean War*, 288.

331. Edward Gregory, "Death March," in A. Wilson, 27.

332. Donald Elliott, in Spiller, 7.

333. Billy Gaddy, in Spiller, 78; Bassett, *Wind Blew Cold*, 37.

334. Ibid., 21–22, 39; Henry O'Kane, in Knox and Coppel, 176; Funchess, in Spiller, 45.

335. Carlson, 88, 122–123; Beech, *Tokyo*, 231.

336. Carlson, 51, 81; John Thornton, *Believed to Be Alive*, 113–115.

337. Lloyd Kreider, in Tomedi, 54–55.

338. James Thompson, *True Colors*, 15.

339. Philip Crosbie, *Three Cold Winters*, 126, 138–163.

340. Funchess, 93–95.

341. Edward Gregory,"Death March," in A.W. Wilson, 27.

342. Nick Tosques, "Living with the Enemy," in Tomedi, 229; Robert Doyle, *Prisoner's Duty*, 179; Lloyd Pate — in Robert Doyle, *Voices from Captivity*, 186–187, 223; punishment — Carlson, 174–175.

343. Medic Lawrence Donovan, in Knox and Coppel, 336; Pate, *Reactionary!*, 28, 38.

344. Funchess, 21, 23, 34.

345. Hastings, *Korean War*, 305–306.

346. Harry S. Truman, *Memoirs*, v. 2, 460.

347. Eight camps — Edwards, ed., *Korean War*, 164.

348. Death rate — Funchess, 61.

349. Tucker, 58; Bin Yum, *Mao's Generals*, 61.

350. Funchess, 61; shower — Knox and Coppel, 336.

351. Sidney Esensten recollection, *Greybeards*, Sept.–Dec. 2007.

352. Kapaun —*Greybeards*, March-April 2011.

353. Wadie Rountree, in Li and Peters, 226; White 84; John Thornton, 177–179.

354. Larry Zellers, *In Enemy Hands*, 161, xv.

355. James Thompson, *True Colors*, 80, 124, 51.

356. Jerry Morgan, in Carlson, 143–144, 191–193; Thompson, *True Colors*, 124.

357. Golden Cross— White, 263n.

358. John Thornton, 173–176, 245–247.

359. White, 86, 93–95.

360. Gene Lam, in Carlson, 112.

361. Donald Slagle, in Spiller, 107; James Thompson, 22.

362. White, 96, 52.

363. Tosques, in Tomedi.

364. Elliott in Spiller, 7.

365. Rees, *Korea: The Limited War*, 344–345; POW Lloyd Pate estimated that 5 percent were "progressives," 5 percent were "reactionaries," and 5–10 percent were Rats (informers of one sort or another), which left about 80 percent in the middle (Carlson, 200).

366. White, 126, 128, 134, 141–143.

367. Betters for others— Knox and Coppel, 343.

368. Claude Bachelor, in Carlson, 207.

369. Brainwashed— ibid., 341.

370. Perfect English —ibid., 343.

371. Lech, *Broken Soldiers*, 154.

372. John Thornton, 248–249.

373. James Thompson, *True Colors*, 131; Bassett, 72.

374. Edwards, ed., *Korean War*, 164.

375. Wayman Simpson, in Carlson, 200.

376. Dille, *Substitute for Victory*, 124.

377. Anthony Farrar-Hockley, *Edge of the Sword*, 252–253.

378. Tigers— Doyle, *Prisoner's Duty*, 183–184.

379. Ten days— John Graham, "Escape from Manpojin," in A. Wilson, 281.

380. Evanhoe, 62; Pate, *Reactionary!*, 38–40, 92–97.

381. Bassett, 54; Deane, *Captive in Korea*, 149.

382. 11 of 14 convicted — Carlson, 270; White, 126; Lech, 74–77, 79–80, 265, 272; Pate on James Gallagher, 58–60, 73–74, 87–88, 94–96, 146–150.

383. Zellers, 387.

384. White, 47.

385. Crosbie, 166–167.

386. Zellers, 160.

387. James DeLong, *Korean War Educator* http://www.koreanwar-educator.org/memoirs/delong_james/index.htm; Funchess, *Korea P.O.W.*, 60.

388. Carlson, 123–124.

389. Catchpole, 217–219.

390. Felton — White, 126; Pate, *Reactionary!*, 65–66.

391. Quinn — Dallas Mossman, *Korean War Educator* <http://www.koreanwar-educator.org/memoirs/mossman_dallas/index.htm>; Shapiro and Gaster — Rees, 341–342.

392. Bassett, 66; Caute, 292, 300–301; London *Times*, March 9, May 11, and Dec. 22, 1951,; Jack Giffort, "POW Question," in Sandler, *KW Encyclopedia*, 275; Elizabeth Schafer, "Western Press," in Sandler, *KW Encyclopedia*, 271; "Burchett," Wikipedia,<en.wikipedia.org/Wiki/Wilfred Burchett>.

393. Burchett, 107–108, 384–391, 414–415; Caute, 276–277, 301–302.

394. Carlson, 227.

395. George Forty, *War in Korea*, 147–149.

396. John Faber, "Great News Photos," *New York Times*, Aug. 10, 1953; Dvorchak, *Korea*, 127, 242–243.

397. Li and Peters, 227–228.

398. Carlson, 142.

399. A. Condron, R.Goren, L. Sullivan, *Thinking Soldiers by the Men Who Fought in Korea*, 160–161; treatment — ibid., 3, 75, 141–144, 148–149, 153.

400. Dallas Mossman, *Korean War Educator* <http://www.koreanwar-educator.org/memoirs/mossman_dallas/index.htm>.

401. Funchess, 79–80.

402. James DeLong, *Korean War Educator* <http://www.koreanwar-educator.org/memoirs/delong_james/index.htm>.

403. Dallas Mossman, *Korean War Educator* <http://www.koreanwar-educator.org/memoirs/mossman_dallas/index.htm>.

404. Hastings, *Korean War*, 293; Carlson, 27, 129, 182–183.

405. Robert MacLean, in Carlson, 27; Wilfred Ruff, in Spiller, *American POWs*, 94, 159.

406. Bassett, 54; Crosbie, in Carlson, 129; James Thompson, 76–78.

407. Roundtree, in Li and Peters, 228.

408. Carlson, 127.

409. Tosques in Tomedi, 233.

410. James DeLong, *Korean War Educator* <http://www.koreanwar-educator.org/memoirs/delong_james/index.htm>.

411. Catchpole, 220–221; Carlson, 182–183.

412. Ibid., 134, 182, 220n6; Roundtree, in Li and Peters, 229.

413. 15 airmen — Albert Biderman, *March to Calumny*, 77, 191; see also Edwards, *Acknowledge a War*, 69–70.

414. Dille, 124.

415. Ruff in Spiller, 159; Donald Legay, in Dille, 124.

416. Tomedi, 232.

417. No contact — Biderman, 184.

418. Strafed — Ruff, in Spiller, 161; White, 57–58, 144–145; Gaddy, in Spiller, 79.

419. Futrell, *U.S. Air Force in Korea*.

420. JohnThornton, 249.

421. Evanhoe, 118–122, 157.

422. Funchess, 108–109.

423. Lech, 73, 62.

424. James DeLong, *Korean War Educator* http://www.koreanwar-educator.org/memoirs/delong_james/index.htm; Bassett, 66.

425. Obstructed — White, 97, 121–122.

426. Deane, 150.

427. White, 84.

428. Lech, 92–95, 101–102, 118–119.

429. Donald Barton, "POW Camp Indoctrination," in A.W. Wilson, 208.

430. Tosques, in Tomedi, 231.

431. John Thornton, 209.

432. Broadcasts— Lech, 17.

433. Charles Quiring, in Spiller, 148–149; Lech, 86; "flop"— Biderman, 75; resources— Biderman, 72–73.

434. Du Ping, "Political Mobilization and Control," in Li, Millett and Yu, *Mao's Generals*, 85. Another early albeit small release — Funchess, *Korea P.O.W.*, 35–36.

435. Zellers, 168–169.

436. Roundtree — Li and Peters, 230; Carlson, 202.

437. Barton, in A.W. Wilson, 283.

438. Lech, 150–152.

439. Library — Zellers, 161.

440. Barton, in A.W. Wilson, 283.

441. State Dept.— Edwards, ed., *Korean War*, 164, 167; improved food and care — Li and Peters, 228.

442. Bassett, 75.

443. Jazz — Li and Peters, 231; Funchess, *Korea P.O.W.*, 130.

444. Stalin — Slagle, in Spiller, 109; Lech, 153.

445. Catchpole, 207–226.

446. 20 percent — Lech, 193–194.

447. Ibid., 192–196.

448. *Shall Brothers Be* (1952), Andrew Condron, Richard Corden, Larance Sullivan, *Thinking Soldiers*, in Robert Doyle, *Voices from Captivity*, 207.

449. James Thompson, 138–140.

450. Funchess, *Korea P.O.W.*, 13, 103, 104, 133–134.

451. Spiller, 73–74; Associated Press report, Sept. 27, 1993; Tim Tzouliadis, *The Forsaken*; Associated Press report, June 20, 2008; Lech, 279–292.

452. Bassett, 89–90; Tosques, in Tomedi, 223.

453. John Thornton, 257–258.

454. Ruff, in Spiller, 158.

455. Simple meals— White, 254.

456. Edwards, ed., *Korean War*, 166–168.

457. Ruff, in Spiller, 159.

458. Arthur Smith, *Korean War Educator* <http://www.koreanwar-educator.org/memoirs/smith_arthur/index.htm>.

459. Dallas Mossman, *Korean War Educator* http://www.koreanwar-educator.org/memoirs/mossman_dallas/index.htm; Bassett, 83.

460. Carlson, 219–228.

461. Eugene Inman, in Spiller, 91; don't talk —ibid., 230; Bassett, 94.

462. Not mistreated — Dille, 124.

463. Biderman, 205.

464. Trials—ibid., 270n18, 280n101; sentences— Lech, 264–276.

465. 1955 Army report — Richard Severo and Lewis Milford, *Wages of War*, 323–324.

466. Bassett, 90; others— James Dick, Akira Chikami, and Valder John, in Carlson, 222, 47, 104; FBI surveillance — Jung Chang and John Halliday, *Mao*, 377n.

467. Carlson, 18, 270n11, 47–48, 104–105, 221–222, 270n18.

468. H.H. Wubben, "American Prisoners of War in Korea," 3–19.

469. Chang and Halliday, 377–378; Allen, *Korea's Syngman Rhee*, 154.

470. Sunghun Cho, "Communist POW administration," in Tucker, 529.

471. Zellers, 169.

472. Casey, *Selling the Korean War*, 971.

473. David Lawrence, "Journey into War," *New York Times Magazine*, Aug. 6, 1950, in Lloyd Gardner, ed., *Korean War*, 94–100.

474. Edwin Emery, *The Press and America*, 532–536.

475. Richard Holmsten, *Ready to Fire*, 107–113.

476. *New York Times*, Dec. 1, 1950.

477. Richard Johnston, *New York Times*, Dec. 3, 1950.

478. British —*New York Times*, Nov. 29, 1950.

479. Truman — Purifoy, *Truman's China Policy*, 234, 265–266.

480. Dewey —ibid., 234.

481. George Flynn, *The Draft*, 128; Joe P. Dunn, "Draft," in Tucker, 193.

482. Flynn; "2 Years Service for All Youths?"

U.S. News and World Report, 27 Oct. 1950, 24–25.

483. Harold Martin, "Why Ike Had to Draft Fathers," *Saturday Evening Post*, Sept. 1953.

484. Larry Benson, "USAF's Korean War Recruiting Rush," *Aero History* 25, no. 2 (1978): 61–73.

485. R.W. Coakley et al., "Anti-war sentiment in Korean war," in Sandler, *KW Encyclopedia*, 20–23.

486. Flynn, *Draft*, 126, 116, 143.

487. *New York Times*, Dec. 1, 8, 19, 20, and 1, 1950.

488. Edwards, *Acknowledge a War*, 109.

489. Peng, Mao on protracted war — Shu Guang Zhang, *Deterrence*, 128–129.

490. Edwards, *Acknowledge a War*, 142.

491. Mitchell family interview.

492. Brady, *Coldest War*, 73.

493. *New York Times*, Dec. 3, 1950.

494. *New York Times*, Dec. 5, 1950; Edward Keefer, "Truman and Atomic Diplomacy in Korea," in Brune, 299–302.

495. Robert Hunter, "Hudson Harbor," in Tucker, 493.

496. Crane, *American Airpower*, 71.

497. *New York Times*, Dec. 16, 22, and 23, 1950.

498. Sherrill and Walsh —*New York Times*, Nov. 25, 1950.

499. *New York Times*, Dec. 8, 25, 1950.

500. Casey, 322–323.

501. Schafer, "Nehru," in Tucker, 480; *New York Times*, Dec. 7, 1950.

502. *New York Times*, Nov. 25, 1950; Dec. 5, 7, 9, 10, 14, 17 and 20, 1950.

503. Peter Braestrup, *Battle Lines*, 55–56.

504. Dean photographs— Toland, 498–499; Braestrup, 53–56.

505. Hoyt, *America's Wars*, 469–470.

506. *New York Times*, Dec. 29, 1950.

507. Halberstam, 331.

508. Most journalists— Cutforth, 179.

509. "Bonus marchers"— Piers Brendon, *Dark Valley*, 92–93.

510. MacArthur afterward — Halberstam, *The Fifties*, 203–204.

511. Among the charges he made against the Truman Administration was that, in the hope for armistice, it was prepared to give Formosa to the Communists and allow Red China to take China's seat in the UN (Manchester, 682).

512. *New York Times*, Dec. 12, 16, 1950.

513. Bradley — McCullough, *Truman*, 912; Bradley, *A General's Life*, 656.

514. Shu Guang Zhang, *Deterrence*, 131–134; "M65 Atomic Cannon," Wikipedia <http://en.wikipedia.org/wiki/M65_Atomic_Cannon>.

515. James Hilty, *Robert Kennedy*, 79.

516. Films— West, Levine and Hiltz, *America's Wars in Asia*, 268–269.

517. Carlson, 2–3.
518. Severo and Milford, *Wages of War*, 317–344.
519. Mayer and Kinkead — Christopher DeRosa, *Political Indoctrination in U.S. Army*, 127–128.
520. Lisle Rose, *Cold War to Main Street*, 317–320; Carlson, 4–7, 16–20; Weigley, *U.S. Army*, 521.
521. David Hackworth, *About Face*, 360–361, ref. 837.
522. Morrow, *What's a Commie*, 84, 86.
523. Holmsten, 200.
524. Tony Kondysar and Richard Rosa," *Greybeards*, Sept.-Oct. 2007,
525. Wilkinson, *Up Front Korea*, 369–370.
526. Sandler, *KW Encyclopedia*, 347.
527. Edwards, *Acknowledge a War*, 32.
528. Hastings, *Korean War*, 330–331.
529. John Thornton, 261–262.
530. Jerry Lembcke, *Spitting Image: Myth, Memory and Legacy of Vietnam*
531. Charles Brown, *Korean War Educator* <http://www.koreanwar-educator.org/memoirs/brown charles /index.htm>.
532. Shu Guang Zhang, *Deterrence*, 155–159, 162; 1958–1959, offshore islands— Thomas Bingay interview.

Chapter Four

1. Chang and Halliday, 365, 367–369, 373–374.
2. Shu Guang Zhang, *Deterrence and Strategic Culture*, 129.
3. Brain VanDeMark, *Into the Quagmire*, 77; atomic cannon: "M65 280mm Atomic Cannon" <http://theatomicannon.com/history>.
4. Chang and Halliday, 374–375, 377, 381–417.
5. Rosemary Foot, *Wrong War*, 46–47.
6. Tsou, *America's Failure in China**, 1941–950, 587–589.
7. Farrar-Hockley, *British Part*, v. 2, 15, 29.
8. Ross Terrill, *Mao*, 209.
9. Chang and Halliday, *Mao*, 356–357; William Duiker, *Ho Chi Minh*, 415–421, 436–438, 449–454; *U.S. For. Rels., 1952–1954*, v. 7, part 1, 9–22, 55–68, 113–114, 128–132, 187–192.
10. Li and Peters, *Voices*, 263; Appleman, *Disaster in Korea*, 465.
11. S. Zhang, *Mao's Romanticism*, 165; interdiction — Hong Xuezhi, "CPVF's Combat and Logistics," in Li, Millett and Yu, eds., *Mao's Generals*, 123.
12. Xu Xianggian, "Purchase of Arms from Mosow," in *Mao's Generals*, 146.
13. Reluctant aid —ibid., 143–146; ammunition — Li and Peters, 108.
14. Xuezhi, in Li, Millett and Yu, 99; S. Zhang, *Mao's Romanticism*, 211–24.
15. See chapter 3 of this volume, subsection "On the Sea and in the Air."
16. S. Zhang, *Mao's Romanticism*, 86–87, 206–210.
17. Kim and Peng, ibid., 156–158.
18. Ibid., 223.
19. Cagle and Manson, *Sea War*, 488–489.
20. Norman Spring, *Korean War Educator* <http://www.koreanwar-educator.org/memoirs/spring_norman/index.htm>.
21. Come over — Jake Huffaker, ibid.
22. Russ, *Last Parallel*, 320.
23. H.K. Shinn, *Remembering Korea*, 161.
24. Robert Hall, in Knox and Coppel, 505; Leyva, in Tomedi, 240.
25. Holmsten, *Ready to Fire*, 197.
26. Maxwell Taylor, *Swords and Plowshares*, 147–148.
27. Bassett, *Wind Blew Cold*, 75; John DeLong, *Korean War Educator* <http://www.koreanwar-educator.org/memoirs/delong_John/index.htm>.
28. Chang and Halliday, 367–369, 402, 570, 377.
29. South Korean participation: 10 battalions, 40,000 troops— Stanley Karnow, *Vietnam*, 437, 656, 663.
30. Rose, *Roots of Tragedy*, 223.
31. Millis, *Arms and Men: A Study of American Military History*, 330. On Korea and NATO development — William Stueck, "The Korean War, NATO and Rearmament," in Williams, *Revolutionary War*, 171–184.
32. S. Zhang, *Romanticism*, 150, 225–226, 233.
33. Bevin Alexander, *Future of Warfare*, 155–157; Ulam, *Stalin*, 733; Chang and Halliday, 375.
34. S. Zhang, *Romanticism*, 245.
35. Ibid., 154–155; Pingchao Zhu, "Korean War at Dinner Table," in West, Levine and Hiltz, eds., *America's Wars in Asia*, 187–190.
36. S. Zhang, *Romanticism*, 245; Chang and Halliday, 374.
37. Robert Murphy, *Diplomat Among Warriors*, 347–347.
38. Nam G. Kim, *From Enemies to Allies*, 65–67.
39. Dille, *Substitute*, 27.
40. James Auer, *Postwar Rearmament of Japanese Maritime Forces*, 66.
41. Reinhard Drifte, "Japan's involvement in the Korean War," 120–134; training ROKs— S. Zhang, *Romanticism*, 146.
42. U.S. occupation — Dille, 216–219.
43. Opposition — George Forty, *War in Korea*, 153–154.
44. Formosa — Thomas Christensen, *Useful Adversaries*, 130–13, 135; Atlee — Hastings, *Korean War*, 180–184; A-bomb —ibid., 188.

45. Gardner, *Approaching Vietnam*, 23, 226, 262, 242–243, 276–277, 159, 245.

46. London *Times*, Jan. 2, 2010.

47. Schafer, "French Battalion," in Sandler, *KW Encyclopedia*, 114–116.

48. Hanson Baldwin, *New York Times*, Nov. 22, 1950.

49. Kennedy — Michael O'Brien, *John F. Kennedy*, 232, 234–237, 394.

50. Alonzo Hamby, *Beyond the New Deal*, 430.

51. Kassel interview, April 1966.

52. Gardner, *Approaching Vietnam*, 139, 218–230, 119–120, 130.

53. Musret Ozelcuk, "Turkish Brigade in Korean War," *International Review of Military History* 46 (1980): 253–272.

54. William Worden, "Terrible Hours of the Turks," *Saturday Evening Post* 223 (320) (1951), 28–29, 68; Eighth U.S. Army, command report, "Activities of Turkish Brigade," Dec. 22, 1950, RG 319, box 1133.

55. Herbert, *Soldier*, 45–47; Herbert, *Making of a Soldier*, 14–18.

56. Cutforth, *Korean Reporter*, 164–165.

57. Holmsten, 99; see also 95, 150, 168.

58. Carlson, *Remembered Prisoners*, 8, 141–142, 271n27; "weed" — ibid., 27, 129; Hastings, *Korean War*, 293.

59. Cutforth, 165.

60. Schafer, "Turkish Brigade," in Sandler, *KW Encyclopedia*, 338–340; Francis Downey interview.

61. Cutforth, 165–166.

62. Weintraub, *MacArthur's War*, 30.

63. B. Alexander, *War We Lost*, 469; Robert Donovan, *Nemesis: Truman and Johnson in the Coils of War in Asia*, 180.

64. Toland, *Mortal Combat*, 548, 550–551.

65. Gordon Chang, *Friends and Enemies*, 88–89.

66. Chang and Halliday, *Mao*, 374–375.

67. Ibid., 368, 374, 377; Rusk quoted in Lloyd Gardner, review of T.V. production *Korea: The Unknown War*, 1178.

68. MacArthur request — Robert Bunker, "Nuclear Warfare," in Tucker, 493; cannon — Hastings, *Korean War*, 318–319.

69. National Security Council report — Steven Lee, *Korean War*, 149.

70. Zubok and Pleshakov, *Inside Kremlin*, 76.

71. Ibid., 219.

72. John Gaddis, *We Now Know*, 104; Chang and Halliday, 376–377.

73. Ibid., 377; Farrar-Hockley, v. 2, 415, 420.

74. Chang and Halliday, 377–378; casualties: *World Book, 1979*, 324.

Conclusion

1. Weintraub, *MacArthur's War*, 30.

2. James Schnabel and Thomas Watson, *History of Joint Chiefs of Staff*, v. 3, part 1, 341.

3. Edwards, *Acknowledge a War*, 17, 31, 145.

4. Donovan, 63–65.

5. Brodie, *War and Politics*, 106–107.

Bibliography

Interviews

Beech, William
Bingay, Thomas
Bradford, Walter. U.S. Army Center of Military History
Brunson, Carl
Craig, Mark
Dillard, Douglas
Donnelly, William. U.S. Army Center of Military History
Downey, Francis C.
Downey, John W.
Gerry, Elizabeth Mitchell
Greland, Thomas and Margaret
McClure, Frank A.
Miller, Ron. 8th Army Historian, Seoul Korea
Oh, Hyunju
Polk, Richard
Ro, Kyungchan
Siren, Joseph B
Stoy, Monika
Welsh, Paul
Wilson, Mary Kathleen

Government Sources

Eighth U.S. Army, Record Groups 319, 461, 601. U.S. National Archives.
Harry S. Truman Presidential Library, Independence, MS.
U.S. State Department. *Foreign Relations of the United States, 1950: Korea and China.* Volume 7, part 1. Washington, D.C.: U.S. Government Printing Office, 1976.

_____. *Foreign Relations of the United States, 1952–1954: East Asia and the Pacific.* Volume 12, part 1. Washington, D.C.: U.S. Government Printing Office, 1984.

Books and Periodicals

Adams, Clarance. *An American Dream: The Life of an African American Soldier and POW Who Spent Twelve Years in Communist China.* Amherst: University of Massachusetts Press, 2007.
Ahn, Junghyo. "A Double Exposure of the War." In West, Levine and Hiltz, eds., *American's Wars in Asia,* 161–171. Armonk, NY: M.E. Sharpe, 1997.
Aid, Matthew. *The Secret Sentry: The Untold History of the National Security Agency.* New York: Bloomsbury Press, 2009.
Air University Quarterly Review Staff. "The Attack on Electric Power in North Korea." *Air University Quarterly Review* 6, no. 2 (1953): 13–20.
_____. "The Attack on the Irrigation Dams in North Korea." *Air University Quarterly Review* 6, no. 4 (1953): 40–61.
_____. "The Korean War Speaks to the Indo-Chinese War." *Air University Quarterly Review,* Spring 1954, 44–62.
Alexander, Bevin. *The Future of Warfare.* New York: W.W. Norton, 1995.
_____. *Korea: The First War We Lost.* New York: Hippocrene Books, 1986.
Alexander, Joseph. "Fleet Operations in Mo-

bile Warfare: September 1950–June 1951." In Edward Marolda, ed., *U.S. Navy in the Korean War*, 175–237. Annapolis, MD: Naval Institute Press, 2000.

American Association for Public Opinion Research. "Psychological Warfare in Korea." *Public Opinion Quarterly* 15, no. 1 (Spring 1951): 65–75.

Andrew, Christopher. *For the President's Eyes Only: Secret Intelligence and the American Presidency from Washington to Bush*. New York: Harper Perennial, 1995.

Appleman, Roy. *Disaster in Korea: The Chinese Confront MacArthur*. College Station: Texas A&M University Press, 1989.

_____. *East of Chosin: Entrapment and Breakout in Korea, 1950*. College Station: Texas A&M University Press, 1987.

_____. *Escaping the Trap: The US Army X Corps in Northeast Korea, 1950*. College Station: Texas A&M University Press, 1990.

_____. *Ridgway Duels for Korea*. College Station: Texas A & M University Press, 1990.

_____. *South to the Naktong, North to the Yalu: The United States Army in the Korean War*. Washington, D.C.: Center of Military History, U.S. Army, 1992.

Armstrong, Charles. "The Cultural Cold War in Korea, 1945–1950." *Journal of Asian Studies* 62, no. 1 (Feb. 2003): 71–99.

Babb, J.G.D. "China, People's Republic: Navy." In Spencer Tucker, ed., *Encyclopedia of Korean War*, 126–128. New York: Checkmark Books, 2002.

Bajanov, Evgueni. "The Korean War: An Interpretation from the Soviet Archives." In *The Korean War: An Assessment of the Historical Record*, conference, Georgetown University, 1995.

Baldwin, Frank, ed. *Without Parallel: The American–Korean Relationship Since 1945*. New York: Pantheon Press, 1973.

Barclay, C.N. "Lessons of the Korean Campaign." *Brassey's Annual, 1954*, v. 10, B82, 122–133.

Bassett, Richard. *And the Wind Blew Cold: The Story of an American POW in North Korea*. Kent, OH: Kent State University Press, 2002.

Bercuson, David. *Blood in the Hills: The Canadian Army in the Korean War*. Toronto: University of Toronto Press, 1999.

Berger, Carl. *The Korea Knot: A Military-Po-litical History*. Philadelphia: University of Pennsylvania, 1964.

Biderman, Albert. *March to Calumny: The Story of American POWs in the Korean War*. New York: Macmillan, 1963.

Bin, Yu. "What China Learned from Its 'Forgotten War' in Korea." In Xiaobing Li, Allan Millett, and Bin Yu, eds., *Mao's Generals Remember Korea*, pp. 9–29. Lawrence: University of Kansas Press, 2001

Blair, Clay. *The Forgotten War: America in Korea, 1950–1953*. New York: Times Books, 1987.

Boettcher, Thomas. *First Call: The Making of the Modern U.S. Military, 1945–1953*. Boston: Little, Brown, 1992.

Bok, Lee Suk. *The Impact of US Forces in Korea*. Washington, D.C.: National Defense University Press, 1987.

Bonn, Keith. *When the Odds Were Even: The Vosges Mountain Campaign, October 1944–January 1945*. Novato, CA: Presidio, 1994.

Boose, Donald. "Perspectives on the Korean War." *Parameters*, Summer 2002.

Bowers, William, et al. *Black Soldier, White Army: The 24th Infantry Regiment in Korea*. Washington, D.C.: U.S. Army Center of Military History, 1996.

Bradbury, William, Samuel Meyers, and Albert Biderman. *Mass Behavior in Battle and Captivity: The Communist Soldier in the Korean War*. Chicago: University of Chicago Press, 1968.

Bradley, Omar, with Clay Blair. *A General's Life: An Autobiography by General of the Army Omar N. Bradley*. New York: Simon and Schuster, 1983.

Brady, James. *The Coldest War: A Memoir of Korea*. New York: Orion, 1990.

Braestrup, Peter. *Battle Lines: Report of the Twentieth Century Fund Task Force on the Military and the Media*. New York: Priority Press, 1985.

Braim, Paul. *The Will to Win: The Life of General James A. Van Fleet*. Annapolis, MD: Naval Institute Press, 2001.

Breuer, William. *Shadow Warriors: The Cover War in Korea*. New York: John Wiley, 1996.

Brodie, Bernard. *War and Politics*. New York: Macmillan, 1973.

Brown, Wallace. *The Endless Hours: My Two and a Half Years as a Prisoner of the Chinese Communists*. New York: W.W. Norton, 1961.

Brune, Lester, ed. *The Korean War: Handbook*

of Literature and Research. Westport, CT: Greenwood Press, 1996.

Burchett, Wilfred. *Memoirs of a Rebel Journalist: The Autobiography of Wilfred Burchett*. Sydney: University of New South Wales Press, 2005.

Bussey, Charles. *Firefight at Yechon: Courage and Racism in the Korean War*. Washington, D.C.: Brassey's, 1991.

Cagle, Malcolm, and Frank Manson. *The Sea War in Korea*. Annapolis, MD: U.S. Naval Institute, 1957.

Caridi, Ronald. *The Korean War and American Politics: The Republican Party as a Case Study*. Philadelphia: University of Pennsylvania Press, 1969.

Carlson, Lewis. *Remembered Prisoners of a Forgotten War: An Oral History of Korean War POWs*. New York: St. Martin's, 2002.

Casey, Steven. *Selling the Korean War: Propaganda, Politics and Public Opinion in the United States, 1950–1953*. New York: Oxford University Press, 2008.

Catchpole, Brian. *The Korean War: 1950–53*. New York: Carroll and Graf, 2000.

Caute, David. *The Fellow-Travelers: A Postscript to the Enlightenment*. New York: Macmillan, 1973.

Chang, Gordon. *Friends and Enemies: The United States, China and the Soviet Union, 1948–1972*. Stanford, CA: Stanford University Press, 1990.

Chang, Jung, and John Halliday. *Mao: The Unknown Story*. New York: Alfred A. Knopf, 2005.

Chen, Jian. *China's Road to the Korean War: The Making of the Sino-American Confrontation*. New York: Columbia University Press, 1994.

_____. "In the Name of Revolution: China's Road to the Korean War Revisited," in William Stueck, ed., *The Korean War in World History*, 93–125. Lexington: University Press of Kentucky, 2004.

Cho, Sunghum. "Civilian Internee Issue." In Spencer Tucker, ed., *Encyclopedia of the Korean War*, 150–151. New York: Checkmark Books, 2002.

Christensen, Thomas. *Useful Adversaries: Grand Strategy, Domestic Mobilization and the Sino-American Conflict, 1947–1958*. Princeton, NJ: Princeton University Press, 1996.

Cohen, Eliot, and John Gooch. "Aggregate Failure: The Defeat of the American Eighth Army in Korea, November–December 1950." In *Military Misfortunes: The Anatomy of Failure in War*, pp. 165–194. New York: Free Press, 1990.

Collins, Joseph L. *War in Peacetime: The History and Lessons of Korea*. Boston: Houghton Mifflin, 1969.

Condron, Andrew, Richard Corden, and Larance Sullivan, eds. *Thinking Soldiers, by the Men Who Fought in Korea*. Peking: New World Press, 1955.

Cottrell, Alvin, and James Dougherty. "The Lessons of Korea: War and the Power of Man." In Allen Guttmann, ed., *Korea and the Theory of Limited War*, pp. 79–92. Boston: D.C. Heath, 1967.

Crane, Conrad. "Raiding the Beggar's Pantry: The Search for Air Strategy in the Korean War." *Journal of Military History* 63, no. 4 (Oct. 1999): 885–920.

Crane, Conrad. *American Airpower Strategy in Korea, 1950–1953*. Lawrence: University Press of Kansas, 2000.

Crosbie, Philip. *Three Cold Winters*. Dublin: Brown and Nolan, 1955.

Cumings, Bruce. Introduction. In B. Cumings, ed., *Child of Conflict: The Korean–American Relationship, 1943–1953*, pp. 3–56. Seattle: University of Washington Press, 1983.

_____. *Korea's Place in the Sun: A Modern History*. New York: W.W. Norton, 2005.

_____, Ed. *Child of Conflict: The Korean–American Relationship, 1943–1953*. Seattle: University of Washington Press, 1983.

Cutforth, Rene. *Korean Reporter*. London: Alan Wingate, 1952.

Daugherty, William. "Communist Patterns of Propaganda and Control in South Korea — 1950." In Daugherty, *Psychological Warfare Casebook*, 828–844. Baltimore: Johns Hopkins University Press, 1958.

Daugherty, William, ed. *Psychological Warfare Casebook*. Baltimore: Johns Hopkins University Press, 1958.

Dean, William F. *General Dean's Story*. New York: Viking Press, 1954.

Deane, Philip. *I Was a Captive in Korea*. New York: W.W. Norton, 1953.

DeRosa, Christopher. *Political Indoctrination in the U.S. Army from World War II to the Vietnam War*. Lincoln: University of Nebraska Press, 2006.

DeWeerd, Harold. "Lessons of the Korean War." *Yale Review* 40 (Summer 1951): 592–603.

Dill, James. "Winter of the Yalu." *American Heritage* 34 (1982): 33–48.

Dille, John. *Substitute for Victory*. Garden City, NY: Doubleday, 1954.

Donnelly, William M. "The Best Army that Can Be Put in the Field in the Circumstances." *Journal of Military History* 71 (July 2007): 809–847.

Drifte, Reinhard. "Japan's Involvement in the Korean War." In J. Cotton and I. Neary, eds., *The Korean War in World History*, 120–134. Atlantic Heights, NJ: Humanities Press, 1989.

Du, Ping. "Political Mobilization and Control." In Xiaobing Li, *et. al., Mao's Generals*, pp. 61–105. Lawrence: University Press of Kansas, 2001

Eckert, Carter, Ki-baik Lee, Young Ick Lew, and Michael Robinson. *Korea, Old and New: A History*. Cambridge, MA: Ilchokak for Korea Institute, Harvard University, 1990.

Edwards, Paul. *To Acknowledge a War: The Korean War in American Memory*. Westport, CT: Greenwood Press, 2000.

_____. *Combat Operations of the Korean War*. Jefferson, NC: McFarland, 2010.

Edwards, Paul, ed. *The A to Z of the Korean War*. Lanham, MD: Scarecrow Press, 2005.

_____. *The Korean War: An Annotated Bibliography*. Westport, CT: Greenwood, 1990.

Endicott, Stephen, and Edward Hagerman. *The United States and Biological Warfare: Secrets from the Early Cold War and Korea*. Bloomington: Indiana University Press, 1998.

Evanhoe, Ed. *Dark Moon: Eighth Army Special Operations in Korean War*. Annapolis, MD: Naval Institute Press, 1995.

Fairbanks, John K. *The United States and China*. New York: Viking Press, 1958.

Fairbanks, John K., and Edwin Reischauer. *China: Tradition and Transformation*. Boston: Houghton Mifflin, 1978.

Farrar-Hockley, Anthony. *The British Part in the Korean War*. Vol. 1: *A Distant Obligation*. London: HMSO, 1990.

_____. *The British Part in the Korean War*. Vol. 2: *An Honorable Discharge*. London: HMSO, 1995.

_____. *The Edge of the Sword*. London: Alan Sutton, 1993.

Fehrenbach, T.R. *The Fight for Korea: From the War of 1850 to the Pueblo Incident*. New York: Grosset and Dunlap, 1969.

_____. *This Kind of War: The Classic Korean War History*. Washington, D.C.: Brassey's, 1994.

Feis, Herbert. *The China Tangle: The American Effort in China from Pearl Harbor to the Marshall Mission*. New York: Atheneum, 1967.

Felton, Monica. *That's Why I Went*. London: Lawrence and Wishart, 1953.

_____. "Korea! How to Bring the Boys Home." 7 pages. London: Britain–China Friendship Association,1952.

_____. "What I Saw in Korea." 12 pages. London: Britain-China Friendship Association, 1951.

Field, James A. *History of United States Naval Operations: Korea*. Washington, D.C.: U.S. Government Printing Office, 1962.

Finkelstein, David. *From Abandonment to Salvation: Washington's Taiwan Dilemma, 1949–1950*. Fairfax, VA: George Mason University Press, 1993.

Finnegan, John P. *Military Intelligence*. Washington, D.C.: U.S. Army Center of Military History, 1998.

Foot, Rosemary. *The Wrong War: American Policy and the Dimensions of the Korean Conflict, 1950–1953*. Ithaca, NY: Cornell University Press, 1985.

Forty, George. *War in Korea*. Shepperton, Surrey, UK: Ian Allan, 1982.

Franchetti, Mark. "Russia Fought Secret Air Battle with US During Korean War." *Sunday Times*, London, July 9, 2000.

Frank, Pat. *The Long Way Round*. Philadelphia: J.B. Lippincott, 1953.

Funchess, William. *Korea P.O.W.: A Thousand Days of Torment, November 4, 1950–September 6, 1953*. Clemson: South Carolina Military Museum, 202.

Futrell, Robert. *The United States Air Force in Korea, 1950–1953*. Washington, D.C.: Office of Air Force History, 1983.

Gaddis, John L. *We Now Know: Rethinking Cold War History*. New York: Oxford University Press, 1997.

Gao, James. "Myth of the Heroic Soldier and Images of the Enemy." In Philip West, Steven Levine, and Jackie Hiltz, eds., *America's Wars in Asia*, 192–202. Armonk, NY: M.E Sharpe, 1997.

Gardner, Lloyd. *Approaching Vietnam: From World War II to Dienbienphu*. New York: W.W. Norton, 1988.

Gardner, Lloyd. Review of T.V. program *Korea: The Unknown War. Journal of American History*, Dec. 1991, pp. 1176–1178.

George, Alexander. *The Chinese Communist Army in Action: The Korean War and Its Aftermath*. New York: Columbia University Press, 1967.

Godwin, Paul. "Change and Continuity in Chinese Military Doctrine, 1949–1999." In Mark Ryan, David Finkelstein, and Michael McDevitt, eds., *Chinese Warfighting*, 23–55. Armonk, NY: M.E. Sharpe, 2003.

Goncharov, Sergei, John W. Lewis, and Litai Wue. *Uncertain Partners: Stalin, Mao and the Korean War*. Stanford, CA: Stanford University Press, 1993.

Goulden, Joseph. *Korea: The Untold Story of the War*. New York: Time Books, 1982.

Graebner, Norman. "1950–1951 Central Intelligence Reports." In James Matray, *Korean War Dictionary*, 107–112. Westport, CT: Green Wood Press, 1991.

Grasso, June. *Truman's Two-China Policy, 1948–1950*. Armonk, New York: M.E. Sharpe, 1987.

Green, Adwin Wigfall. *The Epic of Korea*. Washington, D.C.: Public Affairs Press, 1950.

Grey, Jeffry. *The Commonwealth Armies and the Korean War*. Manchester, UK: Manchester University Press, 1988.

Griffith, Samuel. *The Chinese People's Liberation Army*. New York: McGraw-Hill, 1967.

Gugeler, Russell. *Combat Actions in Korea*. Washington, D.C.: U.S. Army Center of Military History, 1987.

Haas, Michael. *In the Devil's Shadow: UN Special Operations during the Korean War*. Annapolis, MD: Naval Institute Press, 2000.

Halberstam, David. *The Coldest Winter: America and the Korean War*. New York: Hyperion, 2007.

Halliday, Jon. "Air Operations in Korea: The Soviet Side of the Story." In William J. Williams, ed., *A Revolutionary War: Korea and the Transformation of the Postwar World*, 149–170. Armonk, NY: M.E. Sharpe, 1998.

Hammel, Eric. *Chosin: Heroic Ordeal of the Korean War*. Novato, CA: Presidio, 1990.

Hanley, Charles. "60 Years Later, Korea Veterans Return to Remember 'Forgotten War.'" Associated Press, June 13, 2010.

Hanley, Charles, Sang-Hun Choe, and Martha Mendoza. *The Bridge at No Gun Ri: A Hidden Nightmare from the Korean War*. New York: Henry Holt, 2001.

Hanson, Thomas E. *Combat Ready?: The Eighth U.S. Army on the Eve of the Korean War*. College Station: Texas A&M University Press, 2010.

Hart, B.H. Liddell. *Strategy*. New York: Frederick A. Praeger, 1954.

Hastings, Max. *The Korean War*. New York: Touchtone, 1987.

Hatch, David, with Robert Benson. "The Korean War: The SIGINT Background." National Security Agency. Central Security Service. <http://www.nsa.gov/about/cryptologic_heritage/center_crypt_history/publications/koreanwar_sigint_bkg.shtml>.

Heinl, Robert. *Victory at High Tide: The Inchon-Seoul Campaign*. Philadelphia: J.L. Lippincott, 1968.

Henderson, Gregory. "Korea, 1950." In J. Cotton and I. Neary, eds., *The Korean War in History*, pp. 175–182. Atlantic Highlands, NJ: Humanities Press, 1989.

_____. *Korea: The Politics of the Vortex*. Cambridge, MA: Harvard University Press, 1968.

Herbert, Anthony. *The Making of a Soldier*. New York: Hippocrene Books, 1982.

_____. *Soldier*. New York: Holt, Rinehart and Winston, 1973.

Hermes, Walter. *Truce Tent and Fighting Front*. Washington, D.C.: U.S. Army, 1966.

Hess, Dean. *Battle Hymn*. New York: McGraw-Hill, 1956.

Hickey, Michael P. *The Korean War: The West Confronts Communism*. Woodstock, NY: Overlook Press, 2000.

Higgins, Marguerite. *War in Korea: The Report of a Woman Combat Correspondent*. Garden City, NY: Doubleday, 1951.

Higgins, Trumbull. *Korea and the Fall of MacArthur*. New York: Oxford University Press, 1960.

Holmsten, Richard. *Ready to Fire: Memoir of an American Artilleryman in the Korean War*. Jefferson, NC: McFarland, 2003.

Hong, Xuezhi. "The CPVF's Combat and Logistics." In J. Cotton and I. Neary, eds., *The Korean War in History*, pp. 106–138. Highlands, NJ: Humanities Press International, 1989.

Hoyt, Edwin P. *On to the Yalu.* New York: Military Heritage Press, 1984.

Hunt, Michael. "Beijing and the Korean War Crisis, June 1950–June 1951." *Political Science Quarterly* 107, no. 3 (Autumn 1992): 453–478.

Huston, James. *Guns and Butter, Powder and Rice: U.S. Army Logistics in the Korean War.* Selingrove, PA: Susquehanna University Press, 1989.

Jackson, Robert. *Air War Over Korea.* London: Ian Allan, 1973.

James, D. Clayton, with Anne Sharp Wells. *Refighting the Last War: Command and Crisis in Korea, 1950–1953.* New York: Free Press, 1993.

Jervis, Robert. "The Impact of the Korean War on the Cold War." *Journal of Conflict Resolution* 24 (Dec. 1980): 563–592.

Kahn, E.J. *The China Hands: American Foreign Service Officers and What Befell Them.* New York: Viking, 1975.

Kahn, Ely J. *The Peculiar War: Impressions of a Reporter in Korea.* New York: Random House, 1951.

Kang, K. Connie. *Home Was the Land of Morning Calm.* Reading, MA: Addison Wesley, 1995.

Karig, Walter, Malcolm Cagle, and Frank Manson. *Battle Report: The War in Korea.* New York: Rinehart, 1952.

Kaufman, Burton. *The Korean Conflict.* Westport, CT: Greenwood Press, 1999.

Keefer, Edward. "Truman, and Eisenhower: Strategic Options for Atomic War and Diplomacy in Korea." In Lester Brune, *Korean War Handbook,* pp. 285–305. Westport, CT: Greenwood Press, 1996

Kennedy, Edgar. *Mission to Korea.* London: Derek Verschoyle, 1952.

Kim, C.I. Eugene. "The Impact of U.S. Military Presence on the Republic of Korea." In J.C. Dixon, ed., *The American Military and the Far East,* proceedings of the U.S. Air Force Military History Symposium, 1980, pp. 220–230. Colorado Springs, CO: U.S. Air Force History Symposium, 1980 .

Kim, Chullbaum, ed. *The Truth About the Korean War: Testimony 40 Years Later.* Seoul, Korea: Eulyoo, 1991.

Kim, Chum-kon. *The Korean War.* Seoul: Kwangmyong, 1973.

Kim, Elizabeth. *Ten Thousand Sorrows: The Extraordinary Journey of a Korean War Orphan.* New York: Doubleday, 2000.

Kim, Gye-Dong. "Who Initiated the Korean War?" In J. Cotton and I. Neary, eds., *The Korean War in World History,* pp. 33–46. Atlantic Heights, NJ: Humanities Press, 1989.

Kim, Jiyul. Review of *The Korean War: Volume One,* by the Korean Institute of Military History. *Joint Forces Quarterly,* Spring/Summer 2001, 117–119.

Kim, Nam G. *From Enemies to Allies: The Impact of the Korean War on U.S.–Japan Relations.* San Francisco: International Scholars Press, 1997.

King, O.H.P. *Tail of the Paper Tiger.* Caldwell, ID: Caxton Printers, 1962.

Korea Herald, <http://koreaherald.com>.

Korean Institute of Military History. *The Korean War.* Vol. 1. Lincoln: University of Nebraska Press, 2000.

Korean War Educator. <http://www.korean-war-educator.org>.

Korean War Veterans Association. *The Forgotten War … Remembered.* Paducah, KY: Turner, 1993.

_____. *Gray Beards.* <kwva.org/gray/beards>.

Kretchik, Walter. *U.S. Army Doctrine: From the American Revolution to the War on Terror.* Lawrence: University Press of Kansas, 2011.

Kuehl, Daniel. "Refighting the Last War: Electronic Warfare and the U.S. Air Force B-29 Operations in the Korean War, 1950–1953." *Journal of Military History* 56, no. 1 (Jan. 1992): 87–112.

Lankov, Andrei. *From Stalin to Kim Il Sung: The Formation of North Korea, 1945–1960.* New Brunswick, NJ: Rutgers University Press, 2002.

Larteguy, Jean. *The Face of War: Reflections on Men and Combat.* Indianapolis, IN: Bobbs-Merrill, 1976.

Lech, Raymond. *Broken Soldiers.* Urbana: University of Illinois Press, 2000.

Leckie, Robert. *Conflict: The History of the Korean War, 1950–53.* New York: G.P. Putnam's Sons, 1962.

Lee, Chae-Jin. *China and Korea: Dynamic Relations.* Stanford, CA: Hoover Institute, 1996.

Lee, Steven. *The Korean War.* New York: Longman, 2001.

Levine, Alan J. *Stalin's Last War: Korea and the Approach to World War III.* Jefferson, NC: McFarland, 2005.

Li, Xiaobing. *A History of the Modern Chinese Army.* Lexington: University Press of Kentucky, 2007.

Li, Xiaobing, and Richard Peters, eds. *Voices from the Korean War: Personal Stories of American, Korean and Chinese Soldiers.* Lexington: University Press of Kentucky, 2004.

Lowe, Peter. *The Origins of the Korean War.* London: Longman, 1986.

Macauley, Luke. "Passing from Memory: An Analysis of American Servicemen's Letters, Korea, 150–1953." *Greybeards,* July-August 2007.

MacDonald, Callum. *Korea: The War Before Vietnam.* New York: Free Press, 1987.

MacGregor, Morris. *Integration of the Armed Forces, 1940–1965.* Washington, D.C.: Center of Military History, 1981.

Mack, Richard. *Memoir of a Cold War Soldier.* Kent, OH: Kent State University Press, 2001.

Mahoney, Kevin. *Formidable Enemies: The North Korean and Chinese Soldier in the Korean War.* San Rafael, CA: Presidio, 2001.

Manchester, William. *American Caesar: Douglas MacArthur, 1880–1964.* Boston: Little, Brown, 1978.

Marolda, Edward. "Invasion Patrol: The Seventh Fleet in Chinese Waters." U.S. Navy Historical Center, Collegium on Contemporary History, Seminar 3, 2003. Annapolis, MD: Naval Historical Center, 2003.

Marolda, Edward, ed. *U.S. Navy in the Korean War.* Annapolis, MD: Naval Institute Press, 2000.

Marshall, Samuel. "Our Army in Korea — the Best Yet." *Harpers* 203, no. 1215 (March 1951): 27.

Marshall, Samuel L.A. *Bringing Up the Rear: A Memoir.* San Rafael, CA: Presidio, 1970.

_____. *Commentary on Operations and Weapons Usage in Korea: Winter of 1950–51.* Chevy Chase, MD: Operations Research Office, Johns Hopkins University, 1951.

_____. *The River and the Gauntlet: Defeat of the Eighth Army by the Chinese Forces, November 1950, in the Battle of the Chongchon River, Korea.* New York: Time, 1953.

_____. *The Last Parallel: A Marine's War Journal.* New York: Rinehart, 1957.

Matray, James. *The Reluctant Crusade: American Foreign Policy in Korea, 1941–1950.* Honolulu: University of Hawaii Press, 1985.

_____. "Revisiting Korea: Exposing Myths of the Forgotten War." Korean War Teachers Conference, Abilene, KS: Eisenhower Presidential Library, 9 February 2001.

Matray, James, ed. *Historical Dictionary of the Korean War.* Westport, CT: Greenwood, 1991.

Mayers, David A. *Cracking the Monolith: U.S. Policy Against the Sino-Soviet Alliance, 1949–1955.* Baton Rouge: Louisiana State University Press, 1986.

Mayers, David. *Dissenting Voices in America's Rise to Power.* New York: Cambridge University Press, 2007.

McAleer, James. *Out of Savannah: Dog Company, USMCR.* Savannah, GA: James Edward McAleer, Jr., 2003.

McCune, George, and Arthur Grey. *Korea Today.* Cambridge, MA: Harvard University Press, 1950.

McFarland, Keith. *The Korean War: An Annotated Bibliography.* New York: Garland, 1986.

McGovern, James. *To the Yalu: From the Chinese Invasion of Korea to MacArthur's Dismissal.* New York: William Morrow, 1972.

McGowen, Stanley. "China, People's Republic: Air Force." In Spencer Tucker, ed., *Encyclopedia Korean War,* pp. 122–124. New York: Checkmark Books, 2002.

Meade, E. Grant. *American Military Government in Korea.* New York: King's Crown Press, 1951.

Merrill, John. "Internal Warfare in Korea, 1948–1950: The Local Setting of the Korean War." In Bruce Cumings, ed., *Child of Conflict: The Korean–American Relationship, 1943–1950,* pp. 133–162. Seattle: University of Washington Press, 1983.

Michaelis, John. "This We Learned in Korea." *Colliers,* August 18, 1951, pp. 13–15, 38–43.

Milkowski, Stanis. "To the Yalu and Back." *Joint Forces Quarterly,* Spring/Summer 2001, pp. 38–46.

Millett, Allan. "Historiography of the Korean War." In Spencer Tucker, ed., *Encyclopedia of the Korean War,* 248–257. New York: Checkmark Books, 2002.

_____. "A Reader's Guide to the Korean War." *Journal of Military History,* July 1997, pp. 119–126.

_____. *Their War for Korea: American, Asian and European Combatants, 1945–1953*. Washington, D.C.: Brassey's, 2002.

Millett, Allan, ed. *Mao's Generals Remember Korea*. Lawrence: University Press of Kansas, 2001.

Milliken, Jennifer. *The Social Construction of the Korean War: Conflict and Its Possibilities*. Manchester, UK: Manchester University Press, 2001.

Minnich, James M. *The North Korean People's Army: Origins and Current Tactics*. Annapolis, MD: Naval Institute Press, 2005.

Monks, Noel. *Eyewitness*. London: Fredrick Muller, 1955.

Moon, Katherine. *Sex Among Allies: Military Prostitution in U.S.–Korean Relations*. New York: Columbia University Press, 1999.

Morrow, Curtis. *What's a Commie Ever Done to Black People?: A Korean War Memoir of Fighting in the U.S. Army's Last All Negro Unit*. Jefferson, NC: McFarland, 1997.

Mossman, Billy. "Ebb and Flow: November 1950–July 1951." In Center of Military History, *United States Army in the Korean War*, pp. 551. Washington, D.C.: U.S. Army Center of Military History, 1990.

Muccio, John J. Oral History Interview. Truman Presidential Library.

Nalty, Bernard. *Strength for the Fight: A History of Black Americans in the Military*. New York: Free Press, 1986.

Neustadt, Richard. *Presidential Power: The Politics of Leadership*. New York: Mentor, 1964.

Nie, Rongzhen. "Beijing's Decision to Intervene." In Allan Millett, ed., *Mao's Generals*, pp. 38–60. Lawrence: University Press of Kansas, 2001.

Noble, Harold. *Embassy at War*. Seattle: University of Washington Press, 1975.

Noll, Paul. "Stories about Paul Noll in Korean War." <http://paulnoll.com/Korea/Story>.

O'Neill, Mark. "Soviet Involvement in the Korean War: A View from the Soviet-Era Archives." *OAH Magazine of History* 14, no. 3 (Spring 2000).

O'Shaughnessy, John P. *The Chinese Intervention in Korea: An Analysis of Warning*. Master's thesis. Washington, D.C.: Defense Intelligence College, 1985.

Oh, Bonnie. "Review Article: The Korean War, No Longer Forgotten." *Journal of Asian Studies* 57, no. 1 (Feb. 1998): 156–160.

Pace, Frank, Jr. Secretary of U.S. Army, 1950–1953. Oral History Interview. Truman Presidential Library.

Paige, Glenn. *The Korean Decision: June 24–30, 1950*. New York: Free Press, 1968.

_____. *The Korean People's Democratic Republic*. Stanford, CA: Hoover Institute, 1966.

Paik, Sun Yup. *From Pusan to Panmunjom*. Washington, D.C.: Brassey's, 1992.

Palais, James. "A Search for Korean Uniqueness." *Harvard Journal of Asiatic Studies* 55, no. 2 (Dec. 1995): 409–425.

Pease, Stephen. *Psywar: Psychological Warfare in Korea, 1950–1953*. Harrisburg, PA: Stackpole Books, 1992.

Pelz, Stephen. "U.S. Decisions on Korean Policy, 1943–1950." In Bruce Cumings, ed., *The Korean–American Relationship, 1943–1950*, pp. 93–132. Seattle: University of Washington, 1983.

Peng, Dehuai. "My Story of the Korean War." In Xiaobing Li, Allan Millett, and Bin Yu, eds., *Mao's Generals*, pp. 30–37. Lawrence: University Press of Kansas, 2001.

Pierpaoli, Paul. *Truman and Korea: The Political Culture of the Early Cold War*. Columbia: University of Missouri Press, 1999.

Portway, Donald. *Korea: Land of Morning Calm*. London: George Harrap, 1953.

Pratt, Sherman. *Decisive Battles of the Korean War: An Infantry Company's Commander's View of the War's Most Critical Engagements*. New York: Vantage Press, 2000.

Province, Charles M. "General Walton H. Walker: Forgotten Hero of the Forgotten War." General Walton Walker Society, 2004. Create Space International Platform com., 2008.

Purifoy, Lewis. *Harry Truman's China Policy: McCarthyism and the Diplomacy of Hysteria, 1947–1951*. New York: Franklin Watts, 1976.

Rees, David. *Korea: The Limited War*. Baltimore, MD: Penguin Books, 1970.

Rees, David, ed. *The Korean War: History and Tactics*. London: Orbis, 1984.

Regan Geoffrey, *Snafu*. New York: Avon, 1993.

Ridgway, Matthew. *The Korean War*. Garden City, NY: Doubleday, 1967.

_____. *Soldier: The Memoirs of Matthew B. Ridgway*. New York: Harper and Brother, 1956.

Rigg, Robert. *Red China's Fighting Hordes*.

Harrisburg, PA: Military Service Publishing, 1951.

Riley, John, and Wilbur Schramm, eds. *The Reds Take a City: The Communist Occupation of Seoul*. New Brunswick, NJ: Rutgers University Press, 1951.

Rishell, Lyle. *With a Black Platoon in Combat: A Year in Korea*. College Station: Texas A&M University Press, 1993.

Roe, Patrick. *The Dragon Strikes: China and the Korean War, June–December 1950*. Novato, CA: Presidio, 2000.

ROK Drop; Korea North to South, newsletter.

Rose, Lisle. *The Cold War Comes to Main Street: America in 1950*. Lawrence: University Press of Kansas, 1999.

_____. *Roots of Tragedy: The United States and the Struggle for Asia, 1945–1953*. Westport, CT: Greenwood Press, 1976.

Rosen, Milton. *An American Rabbi in Korea: A Chaplain's Journey in the Forgotten War*. Tuscaloosa: University of Alabama Press, 2004.

Russ, Martin. *Breakout: The Chosin Reservoir Campaign, Korea 1950*. New York: Fromm International, 1999.

_____. *The Last Parallel: A Marine's War Journal*. New York: Rinehart, 1957.

Ryan, Mark, David Finkelstein, and Michael McDevitt, eds. *Chinese Warfighting: The PLA Experience Since 1949*. Armonk, NY: M.E. Sharpe, 2003.

Sandler, Stanley. *The Korean War: An Encyclopedia*. New York: Garland, 1995.

_____. *The Korean War: No Victors, No Vanquished*. Lexington: University Press of Kentucky, 1999.

_____. "The First Casualty ... Germ Warfare, Brainwashing and Other Myths of the Korean War." *Times Literary Supplement*, 16 June 2000.

Sarin, Oleg, and Lev Dvoretsky. *Alien Wars: The Soviet Union's Aggressions Against the World, 1919 to 1989*. Novato, CA: Presidio, 1996.

Sawyer, Robert. *Military Advisors in Korea: KMAG in Peace and War*. Washington, D.C.: U.S. Army Center of Military History, 1988.

Schaller, Michael. *The American Occupation of Japan: The Origins of the Cold War in Asia*. New York: Oxford University Press, 1985.

Schnabel, James. "Joints Chiefs of Staff and the Relief of General Douglas MacArthur." In Stanley Sandler, ed., *The Korean War: An Encyclopedia*, 152–156. New York: Garland, 1995.

_____. *Policy and Direction: The First Year*. Washington, D.C.: U.S. Army, Office of the Chief of Military History, 1972.

Schurmann, Franz, and Orville Schell. *Communist China*. New York: Vintage Books, 1967.

Sebald, William J. *With MacArthur in Japan: A Personal History of the Occupation*. New York: W.W. Norton, 1965.

Severo, Richard, and Lewis Milford. *The Wages of War: When America's Soldiers Came Home — from Valley Forge to Vietnam*. New York, Touchtone Books/Simon and Schuster, 1990.

Sheldon, Walt. *Hell or High Water: MacArthur's Landing at Inchon*. New York: Macmillan, 1968.

Shin, H.K. *Remembering Korea 1950: A Boy Soldier's Story*. Reno: University of Nevada Press, 2001.

Shinn, Bill. *The Forgotten War Remembered: Korea: 1950–1953*. Elizabeth, NJ: Holly International, 1996.

Shrader, Charles. *Communist Logistics in the Korean War*. Westport, CT: Greenwood Press, 1998.

Simmons, Robert. "The Communist Side." In F. Heller, ed., *The Korean War: A Twenty-five Year Perspective*, pp. 157–204. Lawrence: Regents Press of Kansas, 1977.

_____. *The Strained Alliance: Peking, Pyongyang, Moscow and the Politics of the Korean Civil War*. New York: Free Press, 1975.

Singlaub, John. *Hazardous Duty: An American Soldier in the Twentieth Century*. New York: Summit Books, 1991.

Skaggs, David. "The KATUSA Experiment: The Integration of Korean Nationals into the U.S. Army, 1950–1865." *Military Affairs* 38, no. 2 (April 1974): 53–58.

Sloan, Bill. *The Darkest Summer: Pusan and Inchon 1950*. New York: Simon and Schuster, 2009.

Smith, Robert. *MacArthur in Korea: The Naked Emperor*. New York: Simon and Schuster, 1982.

Spanier, John. *The Truman–MacArthur Controversy and the Korean War*. Cambridge, MA: Belknap Press, 1959.

Spanier, John W. "Truman versus MacArthur:

Achilles Rebound." In A. Guttmann, ed., *Korea and the Theory of Limited War*, pp. 106–116. Boston: D.C. Heath, 1967.

Spence, Jonathan. *The Search for Modern China*. New York: W.W. Norton, 1990.

Spiller, Harry, ed. *American POWs in Korea: Sixteen Personal Accounts*. Jefferson, NC: McFarland, 1998.

Spurr, Russell. *Enter the Dragon: China's Undeclared War Against the U.S. in Korea, 1950–51*. New York: Owl Book/Henry Holt, 1989.

Stanton, Shelby. *America's Tenth Legion: X Corps in Korea, 1950*. Novato, CA: Presidio, 1989.

Stephens, Rudolph. *Old Ugly Hill: A G.I.'s Fourteen Months in the Korean Trenches*. Jefferson, NC: McFarland, 1995.

Stokesbury, James. *A Short History of the Korean War*. New York: William Morrow, 1988.

Stone, Isidore. *Hidden History of the Korean War*. New York: Monthly Review Press, 1952.

Stueck, William. "The March to the Yalu: The Perspective from Washington." In Bruce Cumings, ed., *The Korean–American Relationship, 1943–1953*, pp. 195–238. Seattle: University of Washington, 1983.

Suh, Dae-Sook. *Kim Il Sung: The North Korean Leader*. New York: Columbia University Press, 1988.

Sullivan, John A. *Toy Soldiers: Memoir of a Combat Platoon Leader in Korea*. Jefferson, NC: McFarland, 1991.

Summers, Harry. *Korean War Almanac*. New York: Facts on File, 1990.

_____. "Through American Eyes: Combat Experiences and Memories of Korea and Vietnam." In Philip West, Steven Levine, and Jackie Hiltz, eds., *America's Wars in Asia*, pp. 172–182. Armonk, NY: M.E. Sharpe, 1997.

Thompson, James. *True Colors: 1004 Days as a Prisoner of War*. Port Washington, NY: Ashley, 1989.

Thompson, Julian. *The Lifeblood of War: Logistics in Armed Conflict*. London: Brassey's, 1991.

Thornton, John. *Believed to Be Alive*. Middlebury, VT: Paul Ericksson, 1981.

Thornton, Richard. *Odd Man Out: Truman, Stalin, Mao and the Origins of the Korean War*. Washington, D.C.: Brassey's, 2000.

Toland, John. *In Mortal Combat: Korea, 1950–1953*. New York: Quill, William Morrow, 1991.

Tsou, Tang. *America's Failure in China, 1941–1950*. Chicago: University of Chicago Press, 1963.

Tucker, Spencer. *Encyclopedia of the Korean War*. New York: Checkmark Books, 2002.

Tully, Andrew. *CIA: The Inside Story*. New York: William Morrow, 1962.

Van Creveld, Martin. *Command in War*. Harvard, MA: Harvard University Press, 1985.

_____. *Fighting Power: German and U.S. Army Performance, 1939–1945*. Westport, CT: Greenwood Press, 1982.

Vatcher, William H. *Panmunjom: The Story of the Korean Military Armistice Negotiations*. Westport, CT: Greenwood, 1973.

Voorhees, Melvin. *Korean Tales*. New York: Simon and Schuster, 1952.

Wagner, Edward. *Korea, Old and New: A History*. Seoul: Ilchokak, 1990.

Walker, Adrian, ed. *A Barren Place: National Servicemen in Korea, 1950–1953*. London: Leo Cooper, 1994.

Weatherby, Kathryn. "The Soviet Role in the Korean War." In William Stueck, ed., *The Korean War in World History*, pp. 61–92. Lexington: University Press of Kentucky, 2004.

Weigley, Russell. *The American Way of War: A History of United States Military Strategy and Policy*. Bloomington: Indiana University Press, 1977.

_____. *History of the United States Army*. New York: Macmillan, 1967.

Weintraub, Stanley. *MacArthur's War: Korea and the Undoing of an American Hero*. New York: Free Press, 2000.

West, Philip. "Interpreting the Korean War." *American Historical Review* 94, no. 1 (Feb. 1989): 80–96.

West, Philip, and Suh Ji-moon, eds. *Remembering the "Forgotten War" Through Literature and Art*. Armonk, NY: M.E. Sharpe, 2001.

Westover, John G., ed. *Combat Support in Korea*. Washington, D.C.: U.S. Army Center of Military History, 1987.

White, William L. *The Captives of Korea*. New York: Scribners, 1957.

Whiting, Allen. *China Crosses the Yalu: The Decision to Enter the Korean War*. Stanford, CA: Stanford University Press, 1960.

Wilkinson, Allen. *Up Front Korea*. New York: Vantage Press, 1968.

Williams, William J., ed. *A Revolutionary War: Korea and the Transformation of the Postwar World*, 149–170. Chicago: Imprint Publications, 1993.

Wilson, Arthur W., ed., and Norman Strickbine, photographer. *Korean Vignettes: Faces of War*. Portland, OR: Artwork Publications, 1996.

Wilson, Dale E. "Recipe for Failure: Major General Edward M. Almond and Preparation of the U.S. 92nd Infantry Division for Combat in World War II." *Journal of Military History* 56 (July 1992): 473–488.

Wilz, John. "Korea and the United States, 1945–1950." In Stanley Sandler, ed., *The Korean War: An Encyclopedia*, pp. 172–179. New York: Garland, 1995.

_____. "The Korean War and American Society." and "Comments." In Francis Heller, ed., *The Korean War; A 25-Year Perspective*. Lawrence: Regents Press of Kansas, 1977

Winchester, Simon. *Korea: A Walk Through the Land of Miracles*. New York: Harper Perennial, 1988.

Wubben, H.H. "American Prisoners of War in Korea: A Second Look at the 'Something New in History' Theme." *American Quarterly* 22, no. 1 (Spring 1970): 3–19.

Yim, Louise. *My Forty Year Fight for Korea*. New York: A.A. Wyn, 1951.

Yu, Bin. "What China Learned from Its 'Forgotten War' in Korea." In Mark Ryan, et al., *Chinese Warfighting*, pp. 123–142. Armonk, NY: M.E. Sharpe, 2003.

Zellers, Larry. *In Enemy Hands: A Prisoner in North Korea*. Lexington: University Press of Kentucky, 1991.

Zhai, Qiang. *The Dragon, the Lion and the Eagle: Chinese/British/American Relations, 1949–1958*. Kent, OH: Kent State University Press, 1994.

Zhang, Fei. "Initial Communist Chinese Logistics in the Korean War." Translated by Patrick Reiter. *Quartermaster Professional Bulletin*, Autumn 2004.

Zhang, Shu Guang. *Deterrence and Strategic Culture: Chinese–American Confrontations, 1949–1958*. Ithaca, NY: Cornell University Press, 1992.

_____. *Mao's Military Romanticism: China and the Korean War, 1950–1953*. Lawrence: University Press of Kansas, 1995.

Zhang, Shu. "Command, Control and the PLA's Offensive Campaigns in Korea, 1950–1951." In Mark Ryan et al., *Chinese Warfighting*, pp. 91–122. Armonk, NY: M.E. Sharpe, 2003.

Zhang, Xiaoming. "Air Combat for the People's Republic." In Ryan *et. al., Chinese Warfighting*, 270–300. Armonk, NY: M.E. Sharpe, 2003.

_____. *Red Wings Over the Yalu: China, the Soviet Union and the Air War in Korea*. College Station: Texas A&M University Press, 2002.

Zhisui, Li. *The Private Life of Chairman Mao*. New York: Random House, 1994.

Zhu, Pingchao. "The Korean War at the Dinner Table." In West, Levine and Hiltz, eds., *America's Wars in Asia*, 183–191. Armonk, NY: M.E. Sharpe. 1997.

Zubok, Vladislav, and Constantine Pleshakov. *Inside the Kremlin's Cold War*. Cambridge, MA: Harvard University Press, 1996.

Index